Fraught Balance

Shayna M. Silverstein

FRAUGHT BALANCE

The Embodied Politics
of *Dabke* Dance Music in Syria

Wesleyan University Press   Middletown, Connecticut

Wesleyan University Press
Middletown CT 06459
www.wesleyan.edu/wespress
Text and photographs unless otherwise noted
© 2024 Shayna M. Silverstein

Manufactured in the United States of America
Designed by Mindy Basinger Hill
Typeset in Minion Pro

The publisher gratefully acknowledges support from
the AMS 75 PAYS Fund of the American Musicological Society,
supported in part by the National Endowment for the Humanities
and the Andrew W. Mellon Foundation.

Library of Congress Cataloging-in-Publication Data

Names: Silverstein, Shayna M., 1978– author.

Title: Fraught balance : the embodied politics of dabke dance music
in Syria / Shayna M. Silverstein.

Description: Middletown, Connecticut : Wesleyan University Press,
2024. | Series: Music/culture | Includes bibliographical references
and index. | Summary: "Fraught Balance positions one of Syria's beloved
performance traditions, dabke, at the center of the country's political
contestations and social tensions. Dabke's embodied politics
of performance both sustains social life and solidifies bonds,
while also reproducing divisions" — Provided by publisher.

Identifiers: LCCN 2023047034 (print) | LCCN 2023047035 (ebook) |
ISBN 9780819501028 (cloth) | ISBN 9780819501035 (trade paperback) |
ISBN 9780819501042 (ebook)

Subjects: LCSH: Folk dancing—Syria. | Folk dancers—Syria. |
Women dancers—Syria.

Classification: LCC GV1703.S95 S55 2024 (print) | LCC GV1703.S95
(ebook) | DDC 793.3/195691—dc23/eng/20231117

LC record available at https://lccn.loc.gov/2023047034

LC ebook record available at https://lccn.loc.gov/2023047035

5 4 3 2 1

TO MY PARENTS,

who inspired me to ask questions

and climb mountains

CONTENTS

ACKNOWLEDGMENTS

This book spans many life chapters, individually and collectively. The origin of the research project can be traced to the Hamra neighborhood of Beirut, Lebanon, in 2006, where ongoing conversations with Bassel Kassam and Raed Yassin guided me towards the topic of *dabke*. Each in their own way, they insisted on the invaluable significance of conducting a major research project on this subject for those committed to the histories, cultures, and societies of the Bilad al-Sham region. I am especially grateful to all the Syrians, named and unnamed, who have likewise radiated their warm encouragement, generous hospitality, and steadfast dedication to sustaining Syrian culture throughout the journey that led to this book.

In particular, my efforts have been supported by Dr. Samer Ali, whom I had the great fortune to meet at his birthday party in Latakia, and who immediately grasped the aims of this research such that his contributions have indelibly shaped the fieldwork that grounds this book. Dr. Ahmad Sadiddin has offered acute insights and enduring friendship since we met in 2004. I hold immense gratitude for Wassim Mukdad, Faadi Hardan, Essam Rafea, Hanan Qassab Hassan, Salma Qassab Hassan, Eyas El Moqdad, Ali Hamdan, Noura Murad, Hannibal Saad, Hassan Abbas, Jumana al-Yasiri, Mohammed al-Attar, Ghazi al-Ammari, Yahya Abdullah, Somar Tarabeh, Tarek al-Saleh, Mithkal Alzghair, Medhat Aldaabal, and Ali Hasan, among many others who have each generously extended hearth, community, conversation, and archival materials. Juhaina and Nazir Mawas enfolded me into their family during my years in Damascus, for which I am forever grateful.

Research and studies in Damascus would not have been possible without the patient encouragement of my esteemed Arabic tutors, Issam Eido, Maha Abu Hamra, and Ahmad Karout. I also benefited from Arabic language studies at Damascus University and the Institut français du Proche-Orient, funded by the Critical Language Enhancement Award and language study grants from the Department of Music at the University of Chicago. The generous support of the Fulbright-IIE Fellowship, stewarded by the inimitable Katherine Van de Vate, enabled my residency in Syria, during which I had the privileged fortune to be in community with Eyad Houssami, Emily Robbins, Stephanie Hartgrove, Pouneh Aravand, Kathleen List, and Elyse Semerdjian.

At the University of Chicago, my graduate training was moored by Philip V. Bohlman and Martin Stokes in the Department of Music, and brightly encouraged by Kaley Mason. Noha Aboulmagd Forster and the late Farouk Mustafa pushed my Arabic studies with just the right amount of pressure, while Orit Bashkin, Fred Donner, and others at the Center for Middle East Studies provided welcome fellowship and pedagogy. The Middle East Music Ensemble, directed by Issa Boulos and Wanees Zarour, respectively, was a crucible for friendship and repertoire. I am grateful to my doctoral dissertation committee, which included several of the abovementioned as well as Lisa Wedeen, for their feedback and encouragement. This period was also marked by the vital companionship of Toufoul Abou Hodeib, Laura-Zoe Humphreys, Michael O'Toole, Eun Young Lee, and Carmel Raz, along with my comrades Mike Figueroa, Luis Manuel Garcia-Mispireta, Jim Sykes, Rich Jankowsky, and Andy Greenwood.

Several research fellowships and writing programs granted me the coveted space, time, and resources to draft and revise pages that gradually emerged into a book. I thank Sara Varney for providing support during my Andrew W. Mellon Post-Doctoral Fellowship at the Wolf Humanities Center at the University of Pennsylvania, during which I consorted with Bea Jauregui, Jessica Goethals, and Jason Ward. The Institute for Citizens & Scholars' Career Enhancement Fellowship introduced me to an outstanding cohort of justice-oriented scholars, and a Faculty Fellowship with the Alice Kaplan Institute for the Humanities at Northwestern University enabled me to devote time to my research and writing. Thanks to Joan M. Johnson's thoughtful planning, the Provost's Office at Northwestern University provided an on-site writing group that nudged this work forward. Beyond institutional support, several writing coaches and programs have provided vital interventions and advice that cultivated my writing practice, namely, Michelle Boyd of Inkwell Retreats and Laura Portwood-Stacer of Manuscript Works.

Feedback and dialogue from colleagues across multiple fields of study have propelled my thinking forward and sideways. Portions of this project have been presented at conferences held at Alwan for the Arts, Lund University, Aga Khan Institute, University of Nijmegen, Cambridge University, City University of London, Oxford University, Westminster University, Duke University, the University of Maryland, as well as academic associations including the Society for Ethnomusicology, British Forum for Ethnomusicology, Dance Studies Association, Performance Studies International Association, American Anthropological Association, the Middle East Studies Association, and the World Congress for Middle Eastern Studies. I am grateful for invitations from colleagues to present talks at the University of California Berkeley, Harvard University, Yale University, the University of Wisconsin Madison, the University of Chicago, Charleston College, and the University of Pennsylvania. Funding from the Buffett Institute at Northwestern University supported a book manuscript workshop at which Roshanak Kheshti, Joshka Wessels, and Clare Croft offered copious remarks and confident assurances that together fortified the promise of this project.

The Department of Performance Studies at Northwestern University has been an incredible and unflinchingly supportive academic home as this book project weathered a war and a pandemic. D. Soyini Madison, E. Patrick Johnson, Ramón Rivera-Servera, and Mary Zimmerman mentored my path into new intellectual and ethical terrain. Joshua Chambers-Letson and Marcela Fuentes encouraged me with passion and care. Nadine George-Graves, Thomas DeFrantz, Bimbola Akinbola and Dotun Ayobade sustain our collective work. It has been a joy to work with sparky colleagues in the Middle East and North African studies program, especially Rebecca Johnson, Jessica Winegar, İpek Yosmaoğlu, Wendy Pearlman, Hannah Feldman, Brian Edwards, and Hamid Naficy. I am equally heartened by the camaraderie of Susan Manning, Dassia Posner, Elizabeth Son, Melissa Blanco Borelli, Neil Verma, Jacob Smith, Masi Asare, Inna Naroditskaya, Ryan Dohoney, and Marwan Kraidy. Graduate students whose efforts have helped this project directly or indirectly include Danielle Ross, Tarek Benchouia, Meiver de la Cruz, and Nathan Lamp. Benjamin Zender dedicated his angelic editorial acumen to the final iteration of this manuscript.

Aspects of chapters 3 and 4 appear in "Disorienting Sounds: A Sensory Ethnography of Syrian Dance Music" in the edited volume *Remapping Sound Studies* (Duke University Press, 2019), 241–59.

A portion of chapter 6 is published as "'I Dance, I Revolt:' The Migratory Politics of Syrianness in Mithkal Alzghair's *Displacement* (2017)," *Middle East Journal of Culture and Communication* 16, no. 3 (2023), 1–22.

Parts of chapter 4 and 6 appear in "The 'Barbaric' *Dabke*: Masculinity, Dance, and Autocracy in Contemporary Syrian Cultural Production," *Journal of Middle Eastern Women's Studies* 17, no. 2 (2021): 197–219.

I offer my deepest appreciation to Suzanna Tamminen at Wesleyan University Press for bringing this project to roost, as well as to the Music/Culture faculty series editors Deborah Wong, Sherrie Tucker, and Jeremy Wallach. I also am grateful to the cogent and highly informed comments provided by anonymous readers.

None of this work would be possible without Fay Florence-Steddum and Carmen Cartianu, who have provided care for and forged loving bonds with my children. Moukhtar Kocache and Theodore Levin each respectively guided me towards this work before its inception as an academic pursuit and continue to encourage my life's work. My memory of the late Riad Ismat and his conviviality is a blessing. Roya Shanks, Blair Mclaughlin, Ellen Ko, Rachel Derkits-Gelman, Tullia Dymarz, and Fanny Söderbäck have cheered me on for decades and helped me pursue my lifelong dreams. Walking alongside me in every step of this journey is Mandy Terc, whose sharp wit, compassion, and loyal friendship have buoyed me for decades.

My family are my truest champions. Yoshi Silverstein and Abby Bruell laugh, hug, and high five in equal doses. Paula Jackson is a life force who fiercely supports me, as do Clement and June Jackson. My parents, Pam and Steve Silverstein, inspired me to chart my own course by being pioneers in all that they do. This project is indebted to their love, support, and eagerness to experience the world through their children's perspective. My two children, Kamau and Tayo, have grown up alongside this book and yielded perspective on life's balance. Since the fortuitous day that we met, my anchor has and always will be Kirabo Jackson. I cannot thank you enough for the manifold ways that you have supported my efforts each and every day across the years.

COMPANION WEBSITE

Readers are highly encouraged to consult the website that accompanies this book—shaynasilverstein.com/fraughtbalance—for video and other media materials discussed throughout the book. These materials are organized online by chapters. Readers can also look for cross-references to online media in each chapter's text. For instance, the video discussed on the first page of the introduction may be viewed on the companion website by finding CLIP 0.1 on the Introduction page of the companion website, and the video discussed on the first page of chapter 2 may be viewed on the companion website by selecting CLIP 2.1 on the chapter 2 page.

NOTE ON SPELLING AND TRANSLITERATION

In transliterating Arabic, I generally follow the system employed by the *International Journal of Middle East Studies* (IJMES), with certain modifications. My foremost concern is to maintain the pronunciation of spoken Syrian Arabic. I also wish to facilitate accessibility for readers who are familiar with other spoken Arabic dialects or Modern Standard Arabic (MSA). These distinctions play out in my decision to render *dabke* with a feminine *tā' marbūṭa* ending of "e" rather than the standardized "a" that is employed in transliterations of MSA. The pronunciation of the *tā' marbūṭa* is not standard within the broad range of spoken dialects in countries where *dabke* is practiced. Pronunciation depends on the word's relative position within the sentence as well as the possibility of elision. Thus my transliteration of *dabke* remains more faithful to its local pronunciation in Syrian Arabic. Pursuant to IJMES guidelines, Arabic words that are commonly used in English appear without diacritical markers and in conventional spelling. Given names appear in conventional international media forms, such as Bashar al-Assad (Baṣār al-Asad) and Latakia (al-Lādhiqīya). When citing or referring to published work in Arabic, such as that by ʿAdnan ibn Dhurayl, I adopt the preferred transliteration of author names in accordance with the Library of Congress. All errors are my own.

SEARCHABILITY

For readers interested in learning more about the technical aspects of *dabke* and related dance and music practices, I recommend searching YouTube for any of the following terms: *dabke*, Syrian *dabke*, *daلʿūna*, ʿ*ataba*, *mawwāl*, and *zajāl*.

I also encourage readers to search for any other specific *dabke* genres, related performance genres, and artists mentioned in this book. A concise definition of these genres is available online in the essay "Folk Music," authored by Dr. Hassan ʿAbbas (see https://syrian-heritage.org/folk-music/). For readers interested in learning how to *dabke*, I recommend asking for recommendations for *dabke* teachers and troupes wherever you reside or subscribing to dabkemasters at Zoom Entertainment (https://zoomenter33.com/how-to-dabke/).

Fraught Balance

Introduction

In October 2014, a Syrian friend tagged me on Facebook to share a grainy and low-resolution video of a local *dabke* dance. We had met ten years earlier when I first studied in Damascus, and over the course of our enduring friendship we had discussed local village practices across Syria. I read the video's caption: "Syrian Dabke from Village of Sawran in the countryside of Hama . . . high 'fitness' (kicks?) and fabulous dance [*sic*]."[1] Though I was not familiar with Sawran, a Syrian village located in the inland mountainous region of Hama, I noted that this dance clip had circulated quickly and widely among thousands of Arabic-language users on Facebook.[2] (See CLIP 0.1 on the Introduction page of the companion website, shaynasilverstein.com/fraughtbalance.)

The video opened with bright fluorescent lights beaming across an outdoor courtyard at an evening celebration in Sawran. A young man led a line of fifteen or so male dancers, who repeated codified sequences of footsteps as they moved in a counterclockwise circular direction around the courtyard. They wore *thawbs* (long robes) rather than the shirts and jeans or athletic pants commonly worn at celebratory occasions such as this. The young man clasped hands with another young man to his left; moving together, they grounded each other's balance and rhythm. Flooding the courtyard was the familiar shrill timbre of *mijwiz*, a reed instrument synthesized for electronic keyboard, that repeated melodic motifs for a mystifying electro-acoustic effect. A *ṭabl* (double-barrel drum) player walked around the open dance space, pounding heavy bass rhythms and erratic treble tremolos oriented to the rhythmic movements of the dancers.

At about twenty-six seconds, I watched the young man expand his agile legwork. Sprightly and light, he bounded around the space, still clasping hands with his fellow dancer. Unusually, he seemed to place his weight on the top of his foot rather than the sole. He broke from the line to improvise in the center of the dancers. Here, his knee bends were deep, and his solo work was virtuosic and highly stylized. I had not seen movements such as these before, not during fieldwork and not on social media. The *dabbik* (one who is skilled at *dabke)* lunged, spun, twisted, and rotated, all synchronized with the duple meter groove of the dance rhythms.

Viewers across Facebook delighted in the virtuosic performance by the anonymous *dabbik*. In their comments, they admired him for his rhythmic precision, offering praise with compliments like *"Ḥelwe!"* and *"Yā rayt!"* ("sweet! how awesome!"). Generally, as I argue in chapter 3, *dabke* skills are assessed on the basis of rhythmicity, balance, and an energetic display of feeling conveyed by the dance and accompanying music together. Yet at the same time that the *dabbik's* skills were widely appreciated, most of my friends and interlocutors who chatted with me about this clip were unfamiliar with the style performed by the *dabbik* of Sawran (the music was easily recognizable as the rhythms, melodic phrases, and instrumental timbres of *dabkāt*, or popular *dabke* music).[3] The bounding jumps of the solo performance that took place in the middle of all the participants were particularly fascinating to those I spoke with, who also said they had not seen such movements before. One acquaintance contacted friends in Sawran to find out more about the style. They assured him that Sawran and the nearby village of Morek (separated by about fourteen kilometers) are considered "famous" for their dances.[4]

The sentiments encircling this moment of encounter, from the local sense of belonging and pride to the keen curiosity to learn more about a *dabke* style that was relatively unknown beyond immediate communal circles, were not uncommon among Syrians. As I found out while researching this practice for almost twenty years, people were often unfamiliar with each other's local practices. Many surmised that this lack of familiarity resulted from the expansive heterogeneity of local communities located across disparate regions of the nation. To bridge these gaps, many aimed to understand the distinctiveness of a given local dance tradition in terms of the formal conventions of genre and style, that is, the pace of the dance or specific patterns of movement (Abbas 2018). Though these efforts were generative, they presumed an analytic dissection of style that left me wondering if there were other analytic frameworks that could help explain the aura of exceptionalism surrounding the *dabbik* of Sawran.

In other words, what about this video made it so popular? Ahmad Sadid-din, who first shared the video with me, spoke about its emotional effects on him: "This video makes me wish I could return to my village, where I *dabke*d on my wedding day, and dance again on its terroir."[5] His nostalgia evoked the close association of *dabke* traditions with the joy of weddings, at which *dabke* is practiced for hours upon hours. His sentiment suggests that the *dabbik's* performance encapsulated what was lost and sacrificed in the armed conflict: village life. For many, the village is the locus for collective identity, the nucleus of Bilad al-Sham (the Greater Syrian homeland that encompasses present-day Syria, Jordan, Palestine, and Lebanon).[6] Some say that the importance of the village to spatial imaginaries of al-Sham is evoked by the colloquial interpretation of "sham" to mean freckle, in poetic reference to the numerous villages that dot the "freckled" geography of Bilad al-Sham. The dance clip from Sawran arguably spoke to and for the place of the village in Syrian national mythology, before and during the war, when half the population of Syria was forced into internal and external displacement. Symbolic of traditional ways of life that purportedly remained unchanged over generations, *dabke* evokes an intimate rural sociability associated with the Syrian village. Syrians loved this video, I suggest, because the dance was so clearly local and because Syrians hold *al-rīf* (the countryside) dear to their hearts.

Yet the cognitive dissonance between the popularity of the video and the relative unfamiliarity among Syrian viewers with its formal conventions was still striking to me. How is that which is so deeply constitutive of Syrian life also so unknowable, particularly among Syrians for whom it is an iconic tradition? This book addresses this question on several registers, from the epistemological to the historic and political. In studying one of Syria's most beloved traditions, *dabke*, I ask who has the authority to perform cultural knowledge and how that authority has been strategic for the performance of authoritarian power. Syria is one of the most heterogeneous societies in the South West Asia and North Africa (SWANA) region, home to social groups with numerous and historically specific linguistic, local, ethnic, and religious practices.[7] Though nationalist movements have striven to integrate these social groups into an imagined community, and though state governance has established institutions (e.g., military, security, communications, state bureaucracy, education, health) that bring individuals from different social groups into contact with one another, societal integration remains arguably more superficial than deep (Al-Haj Saleh 2017). Despite or perhaps because of the friction-causing dynamics between the heterogeneity of Syrian society and its governance, performance traditions such as *dabke* are at once "acts of transfer" from generation to generation that "transmit social knowledge, memory, and a sense of identity through their reiteration" (Taylor

2003, 2) and performances of cultural heritage deeply imbricated in the divisive politics of postcolonial difference. While these two registers of performance are interrelated, they are also indicative of the broader politics of identity, difference, and representation that comprise Syria's social fabric.

Fraught Balance: The Embodied Politics of Dabke *Dance Music in Syria* positions issues of body, performance, and culture at the center of the country's political contestations and social tensions. Drawing on almost two decades of immersive, multisituated, and digital ethnography, respectively, as well as textual and archival analysis, this book analyzes the affective, sonic, and kinesic dynamics that constitute *dabke* and situates these dynamics in a heterogeneous society governed by a sectarian and authoritarian state. I present this analysis through a historically chronological narrative that begins with the emergence of Syria as an independent state in the mid-twentieth century (part I), continues with the era of postsocialist neoliberalism in the 2000s (part II), and ends with armed conflict and forced migration in the 2010s (part III). Each of these three parts addresses shifting constructions of gender as well as classist tensions between urban elite and rural nonelite and ethnocentric ideologies and discourses in order to establish the role of embodied politics in negotiating the public domain of authoritarian states.

I trouble the limits of authoritarian power by expressly considering the pleasure and play intrinsic to *dabke* circles as evidence of how performance coheres communal bonds in ways that negotiate the tenets of gender, class, and ethnicity on which state power depends. The story of how these fluctuating dynamics shore up political and social forms of power is neither linear nor evenly distributed. Across the chapters of this book, I focus on various loci—including state-sponsored folk dance, social dance music in everyday life, and cultural reckonings with conflict and displacement—in order to tease out these dynamics and demonstrate their interrelatedness. As there is a kinesic balance in the *dabke* circle between and among participants and spectators, there is a social balance unique to contemporary Syria, a heterogeneous society governed by an authoritarian and sectarian state. Examining the historical, political, and epistemological conditions of *dabke* practice reveals the ways that hegemonic forces of gender and the hierarchies of class and ethnicity shape and are shaped by relations between Syrian state and society. As the title of this book suggests, this balance has become fraught in contemporary Syrian society, where a revolution that challenged forty years of authoritarian rule developed into a decade-long armed conflict that produced the world's greatest humanitarian crisis. Ultimately the book argues that though *dabke* practice sustains social life and solidifies group bonds, it also reproduces the societal divides that are endemic to Syrian authoritarianism because of and through the embodied politics of performance.

ON *DABKE*

Dabke (alternatively transliterated as *dabkah, dabkeh, debkeh, debke*, and *deppka*) is a participatory performance tradition that literally means "to stomp the ground with one's feet."[8] It is widely considered a pre-Islamic, Arab performance tradition practiced across the Bilad al-Sham region, though some debate whether the term *dabke* is itself of Arabic origin.[9] Lebanese folklorist Bassel Kassem related a common myth about its origins: "*Min zamān* (back when), villagers would build a house for newlyweds. All the villagers would come together to pound mud on the roof of the new home. Our *dabke* began with this dance of communal labor, which celebrates marriage, the fostering of kinship and the transfer of property. Like this, *dabke* is of the people."[10] This popular narrative is often reiterated in ways that link performance to kinship, labor, rurality, and infrastructure.[11]

Among those invested in discourses of cultural authenticity, *dabke* is considered ontologically distinct from *raqṣ* (dance) and *mūsīqā* (music) in ways that demarcate the social values and cultural meanings of the practice. *Dabke* is distinct from *raqṣ* for several reasons: it is indigenous to the region, it bears its own etymological form (as Nicolas Rowe [2010, 11] points out, "one does not dance *dabke[h]*, one *yadbeks*"), and it is perceived emically as a communal activity with social value that distinguishes it from other, often sexualized, movement practices. *Raqṣ* is generally associated with Oriental belly dance (*raqṣ sharqiyya*), folkloric dance (*raqṣ shaʿbiyya*), dance theater (*raqṣ masraḥ*), and contemporary concert dance (ballet, modern, jazz, etc.). Oriental belly dance carries a complex set of moral values related to the sexualization of solo dancing (Karayanni 2004; Shay 1999). The other three dance industries are complex spaces of postcolonial cultural hybridity; of these, this book looks most closely at the adaptation of social *dabke* into a staged folkloric dance (*raqṣ shaʿbiyya*), performed for festival audiences in Syria and worldwide as a national tradition.

In popular discourses on music, *dabke* is generally considered a local or vernacular popular music associated with lifecycle events (weddings and circumcisions) and leisure spaces (restaurants, nightclubs, and live music shows). As popular music, it is distinct from the repertoire of classical Arab music beloved by musical connoisseurs across the region (Farraj and Abu Shumays 2019; Racy

2003), especially the *muwashshaḥ* tradition of Aleppo (Shannon 2006). Often stigmatized because of its status as "low culture" or "street music," *dabke* circulates in informal markets not as *mūsīqā* but as recorded (and heavily edited) tracks identified by their traditional song genres, specifically *'atabāt wa dabkāt* (*'ataba* and *dabke* are the singular form of the song genres).[12] Part of the work of this book lies in unpacking the histories, discourses, and politics that paradoxically claim *dabke* as an indigenous movement tradition and song genre while also adapting *dabke* practices for modern stages and contemporary recording industries.

Given these contradictory and overlapping discourses, I approach *dabke* as a performance practice through which participants negotiate shifting social hierarchies. While my analysis of *dabke* is deeply rooted in local Syrian discourses, practices, and sensibilities, it is also grounded in and opens up new conversations between performance studies, musicology, and dance studies. I offer a phenomenological and ethnographic approach that regards *dabke* as an embodied practice firmly embedded in everyday social relations. I therefore consider *dabke* not as a fixed genre of music, dance, or performance—that is, not an object or product—but as a set of participatory actions that performatively enact affective attachments to historically specific relations of belonging. This approach accounts for how *dabke* inhabits a complex moral, affective, and discursive space that exceeds any fixity of meaning. Across the chapters of this book, I translate the totality of the practice as it is experienced, that is, as a world of action in which intersubjective and intercorporeal relations between people emerge through dancing and musicking, as well as through participation and spectatorship.

I am particularly interested in participants' "sonic and kinesic interactions" (Turino 2008, 28–29). Listening to *dabke* is less about the aesthetic structures of music, as I argue in chapters 3 and 4, and more about understanding an intensely somatic environment in which the senses constitute a totality through which the body perceives the world (Ingold 2000). Rather than approach listening as a singularly aural phenomenon or assume that listening bodies are poised, seated, or otherwise still, I assert that bodies that listen move just as bodies that move listen. By showing how movement works as a listening practice and considering the listening and moving body as a distinct object of study, I depart from the visual and aural epistemes that have dominated historical and ethnographic scholarship on the senses (Sterne 2003). My focus on the dancing body as a listening subject also challenges elite discourses on Arab music that tend to focus on musical connoisseurship as a site for the reproduction of social distinction (Shannon 2006; Racy 2003). In contrast to this musical world of serious listeners in which sonority is paramount, I demonstrate how Syrian dance music constitutes a strikingly different "social field of listening" (Kapchan 2017, 1), in which sound, affect, and the participant's body "fold in on one another" (Kheshti 2015, 55) in ways that engender "vibrational affect" (Garcia 2020). By modulating between the sensory perception of sonic and kinetic phenomena in dance music, my work offers a crucial intervention in the current disciplinary turns of ethnomusicology towards both embodiment and sound studies, respectively, by not only pursuing these two lines of inquiry but demonstrating the ways in which they inform each other.

Also important to the embodied aesthetics of *dabke* practice is the art of the *dabbik* (one who performs *dabke* well; fem. *dabbak*). The solo performer in the video of a *dabke* circle in Sawran that I described earlier is an outstanding example of a *dabbik*. He was admired for his ability to improvise footwork and legwork (*ḥarakāt*, literally: movements) with rhythmic precision at the head of the *dabke* circle. One *dabke* aficionado suggested that a *dabbik* is one who floats.[13] Floating is a paradoxical descriptor for a dance practice that is named, literally, for stomping one's foot on the ground. By suspending gravitational force, a *dabbik* sublimates the dominant aesthetics of this movement tradition: repeated steps and footstomps that pound the ground in alignment with percussive and musical rhythms. The unnamed *dabbik* of Sawran certainly defied the physics of gravity, weight, and motion.

However, the art of *dabke* does not generally venerate individual talent, skill, and performance. Rather, as I insist, performance in the *dabke* circle, whether leading the circle or following along, is about a balance between bodies. All *dabbikūn* (plural for *dabbik*) depend on the participant next to them in the *dabke* circle to support their sense of balance, rhythm, torque, and other kinesthetic components of the practice. Balance, or *mīzān*, is arguably central to the aesthetics of *dabke*. It is vital for achieving a "flow state" (Csikszentmihalyi 1990; Bosse 2015), which, as I describe in chapter 3, is a necessary performance condition for the effect of "floating" during improvisatory breaks. It also embodies the intersubjective relationships between participants that emerge through *dabke* practice. I use balance as a concept to probe the dynamics of affect, performance, and subjectivity that occur in *dabke* circles and extend these dynamics to analyses of the social structures and political conditions that comprise Syrian history, society, and culture.

The interactions that constitute the *dabke* circle forge, like other embodied performance practices, "collective flows of affect" that saturate "the fabric of the social" (Born 2013, 44). Studying these dynamics of performance "exposes aesthetics' social work as [an] embodied, processual, rhetorical, and political . . . practice of everyday life" (Hamera 2006, 47). Relationships of power circulate in *dabke* circles in ways that sustain, reinforce, and negotiate the social structures specific to Syrian society.[14] *Dabke* participation, for instance, is highly gendered insofar as the *shakl dāʾira* (*dabke* circle) is valued as a space for the performance of masculinity. This is not to say that women are excluded from participating in the *shakl dāʾira*—there are many contexts in which women's participation is valued and expected—but that *dabke* is perceived as a means to cultivate a normative sense of masculinity in ways that do not have a feminine equivalency. In other words, the choreographies of power and privilege that constitute *dabke* circles construct "hegemonic masculinity" (Connell and Messerschmidt 2005) in ways that "legitimize patriarchy" through playful bonding "between men" (Sedgwick 1985).

The improvisational play intrinsic to *dabke*, often though not always between men, creates a space for reiterative acts of masculinity that generate what I term "relational masculinity." Relational masculinity refers to the social bonding that occurs at weddings, in nightclubs, and in other spaces of festivity and leisure. Through this term, which I develop fully in chapter 3, I advocate for an approach to masculinity that centers the role of play, pleasure, and desire, aspects that are often overlooked in studies of Arab gender and sexuality.[15] In the last part of this book (chapters 5 and 6), I extend the discussion of relational masculinity into contexts of armed conflict and mass displacement to look at, respectively, the role of gender in constituting spaces of violence and the performance of masculinized dignity in migratory spaces outside of Syria. Tracing relational masculinity in *dabke* circles across these different contexts demonstrates how that which facilitates social bonding also polarizes social groups during political conflicts—a key argument in this book.

As mentioned earlier, *dabke* traditions are not solely the province of Syria but are widely practiced across the region. Palestinian *dabke* is a deeply communal and intensively political set of performance practices that are shaped by the struggle for cultural and political sovereignty under Israeli occupation (Rowe 2010; McDonald 2013). *Dabke* traditions in Jordan are relatively sustained in local spaces, while folkloric dance companies stage these traditions in ways that integrate Bedouin identity with Jordanian nationalism (Yessayan 2015). In

Lebanon, *dabke* traverses a local and national dyad in which cultural meaning is generally ascribed through local difference (Abou Mrad 2006)[16] and constructed in nationalizing projects such as the Baalbeck Festival, which historically reinforced Christian cultural hegemony (Stone 2008); dance and music practices in Lebanon have also shifted in relation to a rise in piety practices in Muslim public spaces in the early twenty-first century (Deeb and Harb 2013).[17] Beyond the Bilad al-Sham region, adjacent societies practice similar though distinct dance traditions that encompass repeated footwork in a collective dance circle, accompanied by sung verse, instruments, and percussion. These practices include but are not limited to Iraqi *choubi*, Turkish *horon*, and Kurdish *govend* (also known in Turkish as *halay*). *Horon, govend*, and *halay* are tactics for political activism in the struggle for Kurdish political and cultural sovereignty (see chapter 5 for instances of this in relation to the Syrian conflict) as well as other protest movements in Turkey (Bayraktar 2019).What, then, distinguishes Syrian *dabke* as such? When I posed this question to those I met in Syria, most corrected me that there is no such thing as "Syrian" *dabke*, per se. They insisted that there was no single component or force that connected these disparate traditions into a unified sense of Syrianness. Rather, each village in Syria claims its own local tradition. While I recognize the power of disidentifying with nationalist and other supralocal framings of *dabke*, I complicate this popular perspective in chapter 2's discussion of how state-sponsored cultural production elevated "Syrian *dabke*" into a marker of pluralism and diversity in Syrian nationalist discourses, as well as in chapter 5's analysis of how fighters during the armed conflict strategically positioned "Syrian *dabke*" within ideological contestations as part of their struggle for secular and revolutionary principles. I also argue that embedded in "Syrian *dabke*" is a classist struggle between urban and rural classes that I trace in discourses on authenticity and modernity from the early twentieth century through the twenty-first century and that I situate in the state's neglect of rural communities over the past two decades. I demonstrate that because traditions such as *dabke* are situated in specific political, economic, and historic circumstances experienced by those living in contemporary Syria, these shared experiences of the authoritarian nation-state generate a consensus of meaning around the term Syrian *dabke*. Across the chapters of this book, I take care to position my analyses of *dabke* in ways that account for the historic specificities of the Syrian Arab Republic while also demonstrating how embodied tactics in everyday life negotiate the politics of Syrianness.

ON SYRIA

Though *dabke* is often authenticated as a pre-Islamic, Arab tradition that dates back to biblical times, this book begins in the "modern" era of Syria, which most historians set in the late nineteenth century (Watenpaugh 2006). To better understand experiences of modernity in "Syria," itself an unfixed construct that has shifted over time and through borders, I offer here a concise overview of key historic events and political conditions that have shaped twentieth- and twenty-first-century Syria. In addition to these few pages, I provide more in-depth accounts of context in the "interludes" that precede each of the three main parts of this book.

Located on the Eastern Mediterranean coast of western Asia, Syria is the historic home of numerous communities who identify on the basis of class, kinship, locale, ethnicity, religion, occupation, and politics, among other categories. (Please consult the companion website for a map of Syria, located on the introduction webpage.) For over a century, it has also welcomed numerous groups fleeing persecution, genocide, and conflict from neighboring countries. Both the capital, Damascus, and the other major city to the north, Aleppo, are renowned for their food, architecture, religious landmarks, and history—with Damascus famously retaining its status as the "longest most continually inhabited city in the world." Though a social history can be traced to the ancient civilization of Mesopotamia, the historic events that matter most to many Syrians (and tourists) are those that occurred during the biblical age and the time of the Prophet Muhammad in what is present-day Syria. Fundamentally, Syrians share a deep sense of history that binds them to the neighborhoods, villages, cities, and lands in which they live next to one another and that for some provides perspective on the immediate social, economic, and political issues that they negotiate in everyday life.

Syria is one of the most heterogeneous countries in the contemporary SWANA region. With a prewar population of approximately twenty-two million persons,[18] Syria is a Muslim-majority society with a recognized historic set of Christian communities (10–12 percent) who ascribe to the Syriac Orthodox, Greek Orthodox, and Catholic Churches, among others. Muslim communities are predominantly Sunni (75 percent);[19] highly visible religious minorities whose communities bear historic claims to the region include Druze (3 percent) and ʿAlawite (17 percent), both of whom consider themselves distinct from mainstream Islam.[20] A number of distinct ethnic and religious groups also inhabit

Syria or have migrated into Syria, including Isma'ili, Muridian, Yazidi, Assyrian, and Chaldean communities to a lesser extent. Until emigration stemming from the Arab-Israeli conflict, historic urban Jewish communities resided primarily in Aleppo, Damascus, and Qamishli. Insofar as the dominant ethnic group is Arab, Arabic is the primary language spoken, and local dialects of colloquial Syrian Arabic are important measures of social distinction between local communities. Significant Kurdish communities have historically inhabited Syria; however, because Kurdish cultural expression was prohibited by the state from the 1960s until the formation of Rojava in 2014, Kurdish has not been widely spoken in public life.

The Syrian Arab Republic is organized into governates, or administrative territories, which are each popularly associated with a distinct topography and with historically specific ethnoreligious groups. Beyond the two major cities, a number of smaller cities serve as centers for port trade, industry and manufacturing, and as administrative centers for their respective governate. Syria is primarily comprised of small towns and villages to which most inhabitants trace (or claim to) their origins. It was a middle-class country with strong literacy rates, but a decade of conflict and warfare has forced society into an economic decline that has severely weakened kinship ties, education and health-care systems, local industries, and intellectual and cultural life.

Since gaining independence as a sovereign nation in 1946, followed by a transition period of social unrest and political contestations, the Syrian Arab Republic has been dominated by authoritarian one-party rule that represses political liberties and human rights at the same time that it espouses the socialist, egalitarian ideology of the leading party, the Ba'th Party. The regime is dynastic in the sense that the Assad family has been in power for over five decades, from the 1970 coup by Hafiz al-Assad that mounted his rule to the transfer of power from father (Hafiz al-Assad) to son (Bashar al-Assad) in 2000 upon the former's death. Though the regime and the party are often collapsed together, they have arguably become distinct, with the Assad regime using the party system as a mechanism to perpetuate and legitimate its power. In addition to leveraging party ideology and infrastructure to preserve its power, the regime anchors its preservation through the following three mechanisms: first, an army and security apparatus that prohibits public assembly, encourages surveillance between and among civilians, and detains and tortures dissidents and others without due process of law, all while favoring those loyal to the regime (particularly those of the same ethnoreligious group as the Assad family, who are 'Alawite, along with many Druze communities); second, a state bureaucracy that expanded in the 1970s and 1980s to employ at least a quarter of working Syrians and has penetrated all facets of Syrian life; and third, corporatism, or the organization of different social forces, such as peasants, students, and artists, into state-controlled associations that receive financial support but lack political autonomy (Abboud 2015). These associations were slowly incorporated into the state apparatus in the latter half of the twentieth century and created a large constituency committed to the survival of the state and regime.

Related to corporatism was the social contract between the Syrian regime and its citizens, which was largely based on what some scholars refer to as the "patriarchal bargain" (Kandiyoti 1988). According to this unwritten yet implicit dynamic of state and society, the regime fulfills the role of the authoritative paternal figure who offers protection and national security to citizens and provides social welfare, including subsidies, nationalized industries, and products. In return for such protection and providence, the regime demands the loyalty and public support of all citizens, who fulfill this by performing obedience and complicity in praising the regime and its president, surveilling one another and informing authorities of acts of disloyalty, and (for men only) fulfilling their military service. This social contract began to unravel, however, in the mid-2000s when Bashar al-Assad ushered in wealth and private finance while neglecting rural communities and failing to provide sufficient job opportunities, especially for Syrian youth. These economic and social pressures were exacerbated by drought; forced migration into Syria that stemmed from the US-led invasion of Iraq; and former Lebanese prime minister Rafik Hariri's 2005 assassination, which led to the withdrawal of Syrian occupying forces from Lebanon and increased tensions with the US.

After years of domestic and regional pressures, an uprising against the regime erupted in March 2011. Local protests were inspired by the Arab revolutions that had begun earlier that year in Tunisia and Egypt. Following a brutal crackdown on nonviolent protesters, within a year the Syrian uprising escalated into armed conflict. Conflict actors splintered and proliferated in ways that turned the conflict into a spectacle that was widely documented and witnessed in networked digital spaces. In the absence of moral leadership by the international community, including the UN and the US, the regime (with the support of Russia) committed atrocious war crimes against its civilians, triggering one of the largest humanitarian crises and forced migrations in recent history.

In 2015 the conflict incorporated a significant number of external actors, each of whom supported different factions and groups active within Syria in what became a proxy war of alliances between those conflict actors and external actors writ large. These alliances shifted again with the rise in late 2014 of the Islamic State, an extremist religious fundamentalist movement with aspirations to sovereignty, a weighty recruitment industry, and an intense drive for violence. The Kurdish People's Protection Units (YPG) and Kurdish Women's Protection Unit (YPJ), both trained and highly effective military units, intervened against the Islamic State and won back crucial territory. Over several years of fighting, the autonomous Kurdish region of Rojava was established in what was previously northeastern Syria, and the Islamic State was defeated. Armed skirmishes continue throughout Syria, particularly focused on the province of Idlib, where antiregime militants congregated following the regime's gradual conquest of rebel territories in Dar'a and eastern Ghouta, among other locations.

Casualties, infrastructural losses, a wartime economy, and the scarcity of basic food and medical care provisions, as well as the internal and external displacement of thirteen million persons throughout the conflict, have all fundamentally transformed the social structure of Syrian society. At the time of this writing, approximately one in ten Syrian refugees live in refugee camps, with the majority struggling to settle into unfamiliar urban communities or forced into rural environments. As of 2012, Syrians tended to flee first to neighboring countries (Jordan, Turkey, and Lebanon), where they often encountered hostility and were not able to secure work visas and stable residency permits. Many continued on, some to a different neighboring country and others towards Europe by way of smugglers controlling a high-risk passage across the Mediterranean Sea. The rise in numbers of those seeking politically and economically motivated migration into Europe around 2015 challenged the European Union's (EU's) system for processing, supporting, and incorporating migrants. Political tensions intensified and polarized, resulting in, on the one hand, xenophobic attitudes and closed borders, and on the other hand, an increase in public support, including the opening of borders, distribution of resources, processing of asylum claims, and open dialogue. These tensions somewhat dispersed in the following years, in part due to the urgency of the global Covid-19 pandemic, which slowed the pace of migration due to closed borders and increased economic vulnerability.

As of the early 2020s, Syrians continue to reckon with a host of conflict-related social and political issues whether they live within the Syrian Arab Republic or elsewhere. International relations with the Assad-led regime are beginning to normalize despite the continuation of assaults on antiregime opposition forces in

Idlib and Darʾa. The agricultural sector has collapsed due to the effects of climate change, inflation, currency devaluation, Western sanctions, and the damage to crops inflicted during the conflict. Cultural production suffers from many of the same economic issues, forcing some to consider migration. The global remittance economy that has kept Syrian families afloat in recent years is shrinking due to global economic repression and regime policies that hinder and extract from remittance streams. These stacked social, political, and economic crises are predicted to remain unresolved for years to come.

METHODS

What started out as a classic ethnographic study of performance culture conducted through in situ, immersive, and multisited fieldwork for an extended period of time (2004–8) was radically transformed by revolution, war, displacement, and a global health pandemic. The ethnographic methods that support this project are by necessity fluid modalities that together aim to address central research questions while pivoting in response to political conditions and global crises. Given these shifting circumstances, this project encompasses a wide range of methods that generally fall under the umbrella of ethnography while expanding what ethnography contains. I briefly introduce here the key ethnographic modalities that inform the book: immersive fieldwork, archival/ text analysis, and digital ethnography. I revisit and elaborate on each of these modalities in the interlude essays that introduce each of the three main units of the book. I also describe here my positionality in the social spaces imbricated in this project and reflect on the ethics of conducting ethnography during the abovementioned crises.

The primary research method of in-situ fieldwork provided the overall structure and ethos for this project. Trained in ethnomusicology's techniques of participant observation, discourse analysis, bimusicality (studying and performing music as a form of research), interviews, and sociocultural immersion in specific communities and social spaces, I designed my initial research efforts around approximately two short-term and long-term periods of fieldwork in Syria (and Lebanon, to a limited extent) between 2004 and 2007, at which point I moved to Damascus for doctoral fieldwork. I prepared for fieldwork by studying Arabic (colloquial Syrian and Modern Standard Arabic) intensively and by performing with the University of Chicago's Middle East Music Ensemble (2003–12). From 2007 to 2008 I focused on mapping out cultural production and culture industries related to folkloric dance, folk music, and popular music. This involved attending numerous festivals and shows across Syria that ranged from world music and folkloric dance to experimental multimedia productions and entertainment. I interviewed musicians, dancers, choreographers, composers, directors, teaching faculty, culture ministers and secretariat, record shop owners, and other persons formally and informally invested in cultural production. I attended rehearsals with dance companies and orchestras and studied music privately with 'ūd (Arab lute) and violin players. I also gathered archival and educational materials from personal contacts, private collections, libraries, bookstores, music shops, record stores, and cultural centers, all of which constituted a "shadow archive" (Simon 2022) outside of any official national archive. I also requested and was granted access to specific materials from the Ministries of Culture and Radio and Television.

Though based in Damascus, I conducted a significant amount of fieldwork in village communities across Syria. Motivated by popular claims that sited *dabke* in rural spaces and enabled by invitations from village residents who embraced an outsider's interest in wedding traditions, I regularly made social visits to and developed research networks in the following villages, each in a different region: Jable (Latakia governate), Jaabat Khashab (Qunaytra governate), Saddad (Homs governate), and Qraya (Suwayda governate). During repeated visits, I conducted open-ended interviews with village residents and collected (with consent) video footage of weddings and other celebratory occasions. I documented how families constructed place and performed ethnic and local forms of belonging through ritual and heritage practices. My ethnographic engagement with rural areas provides a much needed yet often overlooked perspective on prewar rural Syria and state neglect of rural communities during this period, especially because most ethnographic studies of contemporary Syrian culture have tended to focus on Damascus and Aleppo.[21] My work also helps to account for the transformations that occurred among these communities as rural areas increasingly became the epicenters of opposition movements.

In addition to talking to people about performance, I learned technique from performers. "Technique," insists Judith Hamera, "organizes socialities" and "facilitates interpersonal and social relations as it shapes bodies" (2007, 5). Though my prior training in ballet (ten years) and concert violin (more than fifteen years) disciplined my bodily disposition and aptitude, learning *dabke* technique disoriented and disrupted my sensibilities in ways that generated practical and theoretical outcomes. Professional and recreational *dabke* dancers and musicians instructed me on the basics of their craft, sometimes directly through one-on-one sessions and at other times more indirectly through social events at which I "picked up" technique through observation and imitation. Perhaps one of the most important insights gained from these encounters is that the academic pursuit to identify lexicon, style, and genre is not the only epistemological relationship to the practice.[22] People maintain various relationships to the lexical aspects of performance practice; some converse at length about many styles in terms of their names and distinguishing features, while others practice skillfully without an expressed need to discuss aesthetics. Several professional artists stressed the improvisatory nature of the practice by performatively refusing to affix formal aesthetic markers, such as footwork sequences, to *dabke*. While the bulk of these issues is addressed in part II, I revisit issues of embodied pedagogy, representation, and technique at the end of chapter 6 when discussing my experience with leading and teaching *dabke* workshops in the US.

Despite the overwhelming generosity and warmth of innumerable Syrians towards my project and myself, the mid-2000s was a fraught period to conduct fieldwork and reside in Syria as an American citizen. As suggested in the historical background narrated earlier, there were general risks involved in conducting fieldwork in a state with a repressive security apparatus, entrenched intelligence service, and controlled access to limited information, such as national archives or communication media. People were eager to discuss the arts but wary of sharing political and personal information and viewpoints or interacting in spaces that might raise suspicion. Due to restrictions on movement and heightened surveillance of Kurdish-identified regions (historically perceived as a political threat to Syrian Arab nationhood), I was unable to conduct ethnographic research within Kurdish social spaces. Similarly, I did not gain access to Bedouin communities, who have both assimilated into Syrian society and largely been forced to abandon mobile pastoralism. Stemming from the US occupation of Iraq, diplomatic relations between the US and Syria had deteriorated in ways that impacted students, including myself. In September 2007, US-based educational and exchange programs were targeted by the Syrian state, including Amideast, the Damascus Community School (reopened in 2010), and the Fulbright program, forcing staff and Fulbright fellows to depart the country. Unable to stay in the country legally and banned from reentry due to the diplomatic tensions that implicated my Fulbright-IIE fellowship, I bid friends and contacts farewell and hoped to find a way to return in the future.

In March 2011 Syrians protested the detention of minors by security forces as well as corruption and economic insecurity. The regime responded with state violence, triggering a civil and international conflict with global repercussions and irreparable damage to Syrian lives and society. Unable to visit the region during the 2011 revolution and war, I turned to digital ethnography. In 2011, digital ethnography was perhaps comparable to the "remote" interactions popularized during the Covid-19 pandemic, in the sense that social activity depended more heavily on mobile communications technology (such as Skype and WhatsApp, as Zoom was not widely available at the time) due to warfare, war economies, and displacement. However, as opposed to being a means to work from home and communicate directly with one another, digital ethnography in the context of the Syrian conflict refers to my attempt to identify and interact with social spaces specific to digital media platforms, primarily Facebook, Twitter, and YouTube. In 2017 and 2019 I conducted short-term fieldwork in Berlin, where many Syrians resettled during an intense period of mass displacement and migration to Europe. Extending the geography of the project into spaces of displacement enabled me to reconnect and meet old and new interlocutors through copresent and in situ exchanges after years of forced distance as well as to better account for the considerable social and cultural transformations that occurred in the 2010s.

Positionality

Recognizing the role that gender, ethnicity, and nationality play in forging relationships with my interlocutors, I identified myself as a cisgender, nonwhite, female American researcher. Many welcomed me as an American; whatever their political opinion about American foreign policy during the War on Terror (2001–21), people tended to distinguish between state policies and individuals. I was often racialized as nonwhite; people asked "but where are you really from" when they learned my nationality, likely because they imagined America as a hegemonic white space. To my surprise, they frequently and accurately identified my ethnic background as Chinese, occasionally with additional warmth due to imaginaries of China as a model for postsocialist economic development that circulated in the 2000s. At the same time, some individuals racialized my phenotypic features as Asian, suggesting that I add cat eyes to my makeup to enhance my Chineseness and making light jokes about my Chinese American background.[23] Though I also identify as a secular Ashkenazi Jew, close Syrian friends whom I met during fieldwork advised me to avoid disclosing my Jewish background out of concern about the risk posed by decades of anti-Jewish rhetoric stemming from long-standing political and military hostilities between Syria and Israel. I navigated this aspect of my background cautiously, especially during brief interactions with acquaintances, and relied on close friends' advice for specific situations.

Being a young, unaccompanied, single, cisgender *hapa* woman affected how I negotiated public spaces and built networks of trust and support. Though my nonwhite appearance helped me to blend in with others passing through public spaces, I experienced sexual harassment as a young woman in urban public spaces. This harassment was at times racialized when I was assumed to be Iraqi. Well-meaning men occasionally sought to protect me from their anticipation of harassment by offering to accompany me to my destination. Sexualized encounters were also an issue when conducting some interviews, especially with male interlocutors for whom the boundaries between work and desire were malleable (Appert and Lawrence 2020). At times I was integrated into kinship networks (e.g., being more like someone's "daughter" or "sister" than a "guest"), which afforded some privileges of social intimacy but also meant that I was expected to conform to local gender roles and expectations that differed from my own progressive American viewpoint. At other times I was excluded from male-dominated sites of research in ways that required me to pivot away from those and identify spaces more welcoming of female participation, observation, and socialization. My experiences reinforce the fact that gender-based exclusion from musical performance and production remains a salient but buried issue for artists, producers, and scholars in musical spaces worldwide, including Syria.

Intersecting with the social construction of gender and ethnicity that emerged during ethnographic encounters were the privileges of class and mobility attached to my status as a Western "foreigner" (*ajnabī*). My academic work and personal background as a postmigrant subject are entangled with a noncontiguous history of colonialism, empire, and modernity that makes available material resources such as fellowships, residencies, and other institutionalized forms of support.[24] Intellectual authority, legitimacy, and visibility are ascribed to my efforts because of my institutional affiliations and nationality.[25] Moreover, the category of the foreigner is a racialized construct that "embodies proximity to white power and delimits the boundaries of such power" (Silverstein and Sprengel 2021). Responses to this project, my subject position, and the overarching politics of Western scholarship in the SWANA region were varied. Many embraced the attention that this project illuminated on their work and culture heritage, likely because of the power of Western modernity, while others were indifferent. However, Syrian attitudes towards Western interest in their lives shifted significantly when I engaged in fieldwork in Germany in 2017. Whereas people had extended incredible generosity in Syria before the war, it was more difficult to gain trust in 2017. I explore this shift more deeply in the interlude in part III, but suffice it to say that the failure of the international community to respond to the Syrian revolution and humanitarian crisis, the politics of border crossings as Syrians sought refuge, and the fetishization of Syrian asylum seekers once they arrived in Europe fundamentally transformed the politics of foreignness.

BOOK NARRATIVE

In poetic homage to the predominant choreosonic patterns of *dabke* practice, *Fraught Balance* is organized into three units, each of which comprises two chapters. The book is designed to be read through in its entirety; alternatively, individual parts can be selected for specific reading and teaching aims. Interludes serve as brief essays that introduce each of the three parts, offer background on relevant historical and political contexts, and discuss the methodologies that support the work of a given unit. I offer here a broad overview of each part of the book, followed by a chapter-by-chapter summary for those interested in more details about this book's claims and narrative arc.

The first part, "Folkloric Dance," looks at the gendered, ethnocentric, and classed discourses entangled in cultural heritage practices as part of the formation of secular, territorial nationalism and the political ideologies of the authoritarian state. I ask what "Syria" means, and for whom, through a history of how social *dabke* became a national folkloric dance that projected specific visions of cultural citizenship in the newly independent Syrian nation-state (chapter 1) and in the Assadist regime (chapter 2). "Everyday Performance," the second part, examines gender and class dynamics in everyday practices and social spaces. I unpack the embodied and affective dynamics of *dabke* practice by focusing on the sonic and kinesic interactions that animate the social space of the live performance event, the *hafla* (literally: party). Based on fieldwork conducted in prewar Syria (2004–8), this part portrays the dancing body as a listening body (chapter 3) and details how musicians craft a digital sonic aesthetic attuned to listeners' desire for loud and distorted forms of live sound (chapter 4) that energize dancing. The third part, "Conflict and Displacement," extends the analyses of gender, class, and cultural difference from the earlier essays to the polarized politics of revolution, war, and forced displacement. I consider the role of *dabke* during these cataclysmic conditions, insisting on the tension between the affective capacity of performance to both forge and fragment social bonds. These final chapters employ digital ethnography (chapter 5) and in situ ethnography (chapter 6) to identify gendered spaces of power and reckon with the power of representation in precarious conditions of migration.

The first chapter, "Virtuous Figures," draws on archival documents, extant manuscripts, and images to demonstrate how nation-building efforts in the mid-twentieth century invented *raqṣ shaʻbiyya* (folkloric dance) as a staged art shaped by the political and aesthetic ideologies of postcolonial modernity, Arab nationalism, and state feminism. It analyzes the gendered and classed transformations that occurred in the process of making *dabke* folkloric, namely the construction of the fellaha (peasant woman) as the archetypal *dabke* dancer, in order to articulate the formative role of nation-building elite in developing models of cultural citizenship that valorized nonelite, rural, and feminine subjects.

Chapter 2, "Staging Difference," continues examining folkloric dance as a site for the pedagogical performance of nationhood but shifts the focus from the homogenizing approach to cultural nationalism elaborated in the first chapter to late twentieth-century projects that envisioned nationhood through a "unity in diversity" framework. Looking at live performances, scholarly publications, and television media produced in the 2000s, I situate contrasting usages of the "mosaic" as a rhetorical figure for this framework in relation to different audiences and cultural projects. The representational politics of the mosaic reveal, I argue, strategies of statecraft that are foundational for the Assad regime: the exclusion of specific ethnic groups from the Syrian polity, the failure of nationalist pedagogy to offer deep cross-cultural engagement between social groups, and the exacerbation of class tensions due to the privileging of neoliberal spaces in state cultural policy. Together, these chapters address the shifting role of the state in controlling and managing subnational cultural difference across the twentieth century.

"Floating Rhythms," chapter 3, discusses the sensory and spatial dynamics between dancers and musicians that yield "flow states." In contrast to Western understandings of flow as a phenomenon predicated on an autonomous sense of self enveloped in solitude (Csikszentmihalyi 1990), I identify flow states in this project as an intercorporeal, immersive, and participatory experience suffused with pleasure. Flow states, I argue, are not immune from but rather indicative of relationships of power that circulate between bodies playing in the event space. Drawing on theorizations of corporeality from dance studies and performance studies, alongside vibrational affect from sound studies, I examine how the "flow states" specific to *dabke* construct hegemonic and nonhegemonic masculinities—or "relational masculinities," as I suggest—through the mechanics of bodywork and sociality.

Chapter 4, "Sonic Spectacularity," addresses the question of how digital audio technology mediates listening experiences by extending the previous chapter's attention to dancing as a form of listening to a focus on musicians and the production of sound. Based on ethnographic exchanges with studio producers and performers who play the digital synthesizer (org), I define a digital sonic aesthetic specific to *dabkāt* and characterized by the primacy of sonic vibrations and "live" (Kim 2017; Auslander 1999) performances of spectacular excess. I situate this spectacularity in the making of "communitas" (Turner 1977) at ritual wedding events in kinship-based communities. I conclude by analyzing a satirical television show, *Spotlight*, that places the male dancing body at the heart of the social contradictions of gentrification in neoliberal Damascus. In so doing, I demonstrate how this digital sonic aesthetic of *dabkāt*, indicative of a growing wealth divide in urban spaces in prewar Syria, simultaneously brings guests together at live parties while also alienating those who consider *dabkāt* excessive.

"Conflicting Movements," chapter 5, locates *dabke* in the protest events, media worlds, and ideological contestations of the decade-long armed conflict. I unpack contradictory political claims articulated through and as *dabke* practice across three different sites of digital research, including popular political songs, videos of dancing soldiers on the front lines of war, and Kurdish women's dance circles at the geopolitical edges of the conflict. Applying chapter 3's concept of relational masculinity to the complex gender dynamics of the war as these emerge in situ and online, I identify the role of play and pleasure in perpetuating power across the spaces, institutions, and bodies enmeshed in conflict.

Following pathways of displaced artists, chapter 6 reorients the geographical focus from contested conflict zones to Europe, where contemporary Syrian dance has flourished since 2015. "Translating Syrianness" considers the performance of Syrian difference on European stages through two projects: a choreography imagined for European audiences that adapts social *dabke* into a postmodern critique of masculinity and institutional power, and community *dabke* workshops led by Syrian dancers that bridge cross-cultural difference in Berlin through *dabke* pedagogy, as well as workshops led by myself in the US. This chapter frames these projects as political and social interventions in which *dabke* performers disidentify with state-sponsored nationalist projects by translating Syrianness on their own terms. In this chapter I recognize the radical directions and risky movements of Syrian dancers by grounding their work in the historical, political, and social structures in which Syrian *dabke* is ensconced.

ETHICS OF ETHNOGRAPHY

This project has emerged in contiguity with the reality of political and social conditions in Syria. As an ethnographer, I privilege immersion and lived experience as fertile grounds for building long-term relationships and investing in collaborative networks of exchange. However, my aspirations have been confounded by political realities and militarized conflict, which dissolved social stability and foreclosed opportunities for in-person, copresent exchanges. With the turn to armed conflict in 2012, the ethnographic spaces represented in this book became murkily dark. Syrians suffered from chemical attacks, while parents clutched their young children taking their final breaths. World leaders fumbled to respond. I have remained betwixt and between conditions of witness, empathy, solidarity, and helplessness. I cannot save children or provide solace to grieving parents whose tragedy is consumed by strangers, such as myself, engaging with the conflict on social media. What does it mean to write in the temporal presence of violence, yet be privileged to be distant from its spatial and physical proximity? What salvages a writing imperative, if anything can be salvaged, in the face of the impossible tragedy that is "Syria"?

Ethnographic writing, for me, is a representational strategy that questions colonial and imperial relations of power by unpacking how bodies are rendered (in)visible, (in)audible, and (il)legible through performance and research on performance. There is a history of scholarship in the region that colludes in the erasure of minority status and ethnic difference (Shami and Nagiub 2013). This ethnography is not immune to such collusion, as I have narrated with respect to my difficulties gaining access and proximity to Kurdish and Bedouin communities. To the extent that nationhood is produced by exclusions and inclusions, this ethnography reflects a historically contingent reading of who is most visible and accessible within the modern state. This ethnography is therefore situated between imperialisms of the past and hegemonies of the present. I hope that as readers encounter the subjects of this book, including myself, they attend to how processes of representation constitute power relations and how their own performativity is enmeshed and constituted through shifting fields of power. I approach writing about Syrian *dabke* as its own performance, one that strives to speak with and for the millions living through this moment and that negotiates my own positionality as a contemporary American researcher.

This book aims to portray the grace and vitality of performance in Syrian lifeworlds. While I do not romanticize music, dance, and performance as cultural acts that resolve conflict and inspire unity (indeed, I argue that performance is instrumental to the hegemonic forces that have fragmented Syrian society), I do focus on subjects and spaces that are often flattened by media narratives or overlooked by studies that focus on political power and foreign policy. The power of writing hinges on what acts of writing make legible. In these pages, I hope to make legible the affective attachments that root Syrians to a place where they belong.

PART I

Folkloric Dance

Modern Syrian Society and State

The 1950s and 1960s were an unstable period distinguished by Arab nationalist movements and the rise of Baʿthism in Syria. The political ideologies of these distinct yet overlapping movements substantively shaped the formation of folkloric dance. Though the mechanisms and institutions that support authoritarianism began in the late 1950s, the systemic forms of rule that constitute authoritarian Syria today were cemented in 1970 with former president Hafiz al-Assad's seize of power. In this interlude, I provide an overview of the social, political, and economic dynamics that shaped the Syrian state and society from the mid-twentieth century into the twenty-first century in order to set the stage for chapters 1 and 2's respective queries into the cultural expediency of folkloric dance in authoritarian Syria.

Most historians place the social roots of contemporary Syria in the late Ottoman Empire (1860–1917). With its seat of power in Istanbul, the Ottoman Empire controlled a vast territory that was home to communities of many different ethnicities and religions. While maintaining the superiority of Islam over other religions, the Ottoman Empire also developed a system that protected ethnoreligious groups, primarily though not exclusively Christian and Jewish, through a covenant that offered protection and safety in exchange for taxation. Due to conflict with other empires, namely the Austro-Hungarian Empire and the tsarist Russian Empire, many local Muslim populations living outside of the Ottoman Empire's contested boundaries fled into the Ottoman Empire to seek refuge. Other groups that migrated included Bedouin tribes, who had arrived in the eighteenth century from Saudi Arabia and continued to practice mobile pastoralism in the eastern steppe region of Syria. Genocidal persecution and occupying forces in neighboring countries also forced people to seek refuge in Syria over the course of the long twentieth century, including Armenians (1904), Palestinians (1948), Iraqis (2003), and Yazidis (2014).

Class structure and divisions were consolidated during the nineteenth century as agricultural sectors expanded, especially crops for European export. Though there was recognition of inequalities in private property and agricultural labor vis-à-vis the Land Code of 1858 that granted access to land for peasants, this law ended up concentrating land among urban families. Landowners also gained political power in the late Ottoman Empire due to the centralization of power in the expanding Ottoman state. As a result, conflicts between peasants and land-owners increased, especially in the Hawran region, in ways that would later ignite popular support for Arab nationalist movements in the early twentieth century.

By the early twentieth century the region known as Bilad al-Sham was con-sidered a relatively stable haven of coexistence. It was home to communities that spoke Arabic, Ottoman Turkish, Armenian, Circassian, Kurdish, and many other languages. Religious life was diverse, particularly in the cities, where Christian quarters were adjacent to historic Jewish quarters in the old cities of Aleppo and Damascus, as well as Sunni mosques. Some villages were dominated by a single religion, such as the Syriac Orthodox villages of Saadnaya and Maalula to the north of Damascus, while other villages were mixed, such as those in the agricultural Hawran region of southern Syria that were Christian and Muslim. Meanwhile, some areas were recognized as predominantly inhabited by a sin-gular community, especially the Druze community of Suwayda, in what is now southwestern Syria, and the 'Alawite community of Latakia, now a governate in northwestern Syria. This heterogeneous web of linguistic, ethnic, and religious groups inhabited distinct urban and provincial areas in modern Syria.

With the collapse of the Ottoman Empire in 1917, Ottoman power transitioned into the establishment of French Mandate authority over what is present-day Syria in 1923. French authority endured for roughly two decades (1923–36), during which the power of the elite landowning class was reinforced. Class structure was significant to the economic, political, and social dynamics in the region, particularly agricultural production. Society was generally divided into three social strata: the landowning class, merchant class, and lower classes, which included urban artisans and rural peasants. French authorities intensified these divisions by distributing collective land to landed elite and to Bedouin tribal lead-ers in exchange for political power, alliances, and favors for the colonial power.

Also significant to power alliances during this period was the French authority's "divide-and-conquer" policy between ethnoreligious groups. Seeking to weaken Arab nationalism, which the French saw as a threat to their authority, the French carved Aleppo and Damascus into separate political units while making Latakia and Suwayda into compact states for 'Alawite and Druze minority groups, respectively. These geographic separations and communalist segregations had a lasting impact, eventually shaping the "minoritarian" ethos of the modern Syrian state that purportedly protected religious minorities from a Sunni religious majority (White 2011). French authority weakened in the 1930s, when the Syrian elite saw French interests as inimical to Syrian nationalism. National strikes and student protests, to which French authorities responded with violence, led to the eventual negotiation of the Treaty of Independence.

After Syria ratified independence in 1946, the struggle for power led to numerous coups and turnovers in political leadership, which eventually favored Arab nationalist and socialist movements. The Ba'th Party began to gain key momentum with its ideological tenets of socialism, Arabism, and anti-imperialism. Those who favored Nasserism (a political movement based in Egypt and led by then Egyptian president Gamal Abdel Nasser) tended to be more nationalist and urban Sunni middle class, as well as some middle- and lower-class actors who favored pan-Arabism over Ba'thism. Those who did not were largely rural and from minority communities. They turned towards class struggle, especially Marxism and socialism, which they sought to achieve through mass political mobilization and social revolution. These latter political actors would shape the future of the Ba'th Party and the authoritarian state in Syria.

On March 8, 1963, a military coup seized control of the Syrian Arab Republic. Considered a "bloodless revolution from above," it instilled the Ba'th Party as the ruling party by purging Nasser loyalists and establishing leadership drawn from a core of rural and minoritarian military officers (primarily 'Alawite and Druze). Other key policies enacted during this initial period of Ba'th Party rule included the nationalization of industry and finance, the redistribution of property and wealth from landed elite to nonelite actors, and the strengthening of anticapitalist and anti-imperial foreign policies and relations. The state also continued the trajectory established in the 1950s that strove to make society more egalitarian by providing access to education, health care, and rights for personal status to women. It also strengthened its resolve to push for "the people" (al-sha'b), who became recognized in political propaganda as a new social order comprising peasants, workers, intellectuals, professionals, state capitalists, and the army.

Yet at the same time that the Ba'th Party consolidated a political platform of egalitarianism, class equity, anti-imperialism, and anticapitalism, party leaders also displaced populations within Syria in the name of industrialization, development, and modernization. Cities were growing rapidly in the 1960s and, like other developing nations worldwide, Syria sought to boost infrastructure, mechanization, and other facets of modernization. As part of this agenda, party leaders encouraged Bedouin tribes to abandon mobile pastoralism and settle. During and in the aftermath of the formation of the United Arab Republic, Bedouin tribes had already lost a significant amount of the political privileges they had initially negotiated with French Mandate authorities, who sought to appease them because they perceived Bedouin tribes as politically powerful. Wealthier and stronger Bedouin shaykhs lost significant property holdings during the Ba'th Party's redistribution of land in 1963, while poorer Bedouin families received some land. Some tribes were resettled to the "Arab corridor" region of Hasakah. The long-term effects of these changes were to disrupt the patronage and leadership relations that sustained Bedouin tribal life. A sense of Bedouin belonging began to dissipate as successive generations assimilated into the broad contours of Sunni Arab life in modern Syria, while Bedouinness itself became an index of Arab authenticity, especially in the 2000s.

The repression of Kurdish identity and political organizing in Syria, perceived as a threat to pan-Arab and Syrian Arab nationalism, respectively, dates to this period of early statecraft as well. In the early 1960s the Syrian government revoked the citizenship of hundreds of thousands of Kurds, rendering them stateless, while also forcibly resettling Kurdish communities in the northern Djajira region (Arabic: Hasakah) to establish an "Arab corridor" that would turn the Kurdish majority in the region into a minority. Displaced persons largely moved to cities, where they were marginalized and lived on the urban periphery because, as "foreigners," they could not own land, work for the government, or access education, and they experienced disenfranchisement from other civil rights. Since 1967, Kurdish identity has been erased in official Syrian documents, including the mention of Kurdish minorities in Syria in school textbooks (notable in a regime that legitimizes its rule on the basis of minoritarianism), at the same time that the Kurdish language has been restricted in oral and written practice, and Kurdish festivities are banned, most visibly Nowruz, the traditional Kurdish New Year. Government surveillance of political activity and gatherings increased during Bashar al-Assad's regime, following a crackdown on a 2004 event in Qamishli and a 2009 edict that prevents people without Syrian nationality from working in the private sector.

In 1970 a young ʿAlawite army officer from Latakia, Hafiz al-Assad, seized power to become president and secretary general of the Baʿth Party, as well as commander of the Syrian Armed Forces. Assad quickly established "absolute" rule through several "pillars of power" (Abboud 2015). To ensure his political legitimacy, he inculcated a "cult of Assad" that enforced obedience; induced complicity; and set guidelines for public speech and behavior that revolved around constant praise of Assad, Syria, and God. He projected himself as a father figure who maintained a paternalistic set of expectations towards and from his citizen-children, though people generally remained ambiguous in their negotiation of the "cult of Assad" by "acting *as if* they revered their leader" (Wedeen 1999, 19). His policies were largely a continuation of the Baʿth Party's, in which he maintained socialism yet did so with the privileging of rural and minoritarian communities while promoting an authoritarian-populist rhetoric whose main aim was to ensure regime preservation. Other key mechanisms to ensure regime security included the Baʿth Party, state bureaucracy, corporatism, and the army and security apparatus. The realities of living under this regime were sober, involving tactics of repression (detainment, imprisonment, torture, murder), tactics of coercion (threats, bribery, rampant corruption), and tactics of clientelism in the 1970s and 1980s that benefited the business and political elite rather than distributing wealth in accordance with the socialist rhetoric of the Baʿth Party.

Repression and surveillance were managed by the security apparatus, officially registered as the Ministry of the Interior, which enforced authority through arbitrary detention, imprisonment without trial, and torture. In addition to the constant presence of the "secret" agents of the *mukhabarāt* (intelligence officers), a surveillance culture emerged over generations in which citizens constantly gathered information on each other to report to the *mukhabarāt* for self-gain and self-preservation (George 2003). These tactics, writes Panagiotis Geros, induced an embodied sense of fear that "inscribe[d] the meanings produced by the relations of power on people's bodies" (2010, 99). The "constant and excessive display of agency" by the regime engendered a fear in ordinary people that convinced them of its "absolute strength" (97). Dissidence was not tolerated, and coercion was commonplace. The most significant challenge to the regime was an armed insurgency in the late 1970s mounted by the Muslim Brotherhood, who had been expelled from formal politics in the 1963 coup. The insurgency (and the presence of the Muslim Brotherhood in Syria) was defeated by tactics of indiscriminate collective punishment by the regime, most prominently in the massacre of tens of thousands in Hama in 1982 in response to a major insurrection in that city by the Muslim Brotherhood.

The governance of difference was also a tactic of rule and domination, similar (though perhaps counterintuitive) to Western liberal democracies that espouse "multicultural forms of recognition" as a strategy of statecraft (Povinelli 2002). In public rhetoric, the regime legitimated its power by linking the country's communitarian identities to regime stability. It presented itself as a minoritarian government, of and for minority communities, in ways that harnessed the minority consciousness that was the legacy of French colonialism and manipulated it towards regime legitimacy. Accordingly, the state promised to ensure protection for religious minorities (including Christians, Druze, Isma'ili, and Twelver Shi'i groups) from persecution and discrimination. However, this guarantee depended on the perpetuation of the myth of "majority [Sunni] rule as an existential threat to the state and to minority groups" (Dajani 2015, 2527). Relatedly, the cultural arm of the regime espoused a liberal model of religious and cultural pluralism that played into the celebration of sanctioned forms of difference.

Some scholars suggest that at the same time that the state utilized minoritarianism and celebrated pluralism, the regime practiced sectarianism in its everyday management of persons and groups. Calling sectarianism "an invisible system of discrimination from above," Yassin al-Haj Saleh (2017) argues that the regime favored certain ethnoreligious groups over others in ways that secured power, privilege, and loyalty while sowing divisiveness and isolation.[1] Through a focus on the politics of cultural heritage, the following two chapters show how social isolation and the cultural erasure of specific groups (especially Kurdish communities) were exacerbated by the regime's management of subnational difference in the domain of cultural heritage.

With the death of Hafiz al-Assad in 2000, regime leadership transferred into the hands of Bashar al-Assad, son of the former president. Bashar al-Assad introduced economic policies (known collectively as "social market reform") that neoliberalized Syrian culture and economy while maintaining the rhetorical principles of Ba'thism as well as authoritarian tactics of state repression and intimidation. Chapter 2 argues that the long-standing but faded promise of Ba'thism to provide social welfare for "the people" was compromised by the particularly egregious economic effects of neoliberalization, leading to a split between those reassured of a "good life" under neoliberalism and those reassured by the symbolic platitudes of Ba'thism.

RESEARCH NOTES

Conducting historic research in an authoritarian regime required me to blur distinctions between archival and ethnographic work. Despite Bashar al-Assad's pledges to open society, in many ways twenty-first-century Syria remained the same heavily bureaucratic and opaque research site that it had been for decades under Hafiz al-Assad's rule. Legal files, such as residency permits, were completed by hand and stored in tall, flimsy stacks in dusty offices where fatigued personnel smoked. I once tried to find an office of records to address my residency status only to stare at a line of emaciated, imprisoned men shackled together, shoulders bent low as they passed by the office where I waited for most of the day on a broken metal chair.

In a state that strives to conceal its workings from the public eye, there were no repositories for performance traditions, no archive of recordings, and no images from past dance performances (at least my best efforts did not locate any).[2] It is not that the state found those items necessarily suspicious, as most had to pass the committee on censorship in order to be performed or published. Rather, the logic of the surveillance state foreclosed the capacity and the desire for a national archive of such items. The official state archives, known as Al-Assad National Library, for example, did not have any holdings relevant to my search. Surprisingly enough, I was able to successfully request and receive a copy of a television program produced by the Ministry of Radio and Television. The process for acquiring this media was highly secured and monitored and required a letter of introduction from a known reference in addition to multiple security checks and an escort through the ministry's building.

Archival work was made possible through ethnographic relationships in the field. Instead of surveying official state archives, I located archival materials in the "shadow archives" (Simon 2022) that emerged from social and research networks. Many interlocutors would suggest a particular resource to me, such as Ibn Dhurayl's manuscript on Syrian folk dance, but would not be able to identify where I could find the manuscript. A young musician in his early twenties spotted it at the Adawi Cultural Center and photocopied it for me as support for the research project. A shop owner in Latakia shipped me a parcel of books to the central post office in Damascus, because he thought these might benefit this research. I surveyed the shelves of every music shop and bookstore I passed, purchasing items of potential interest. Occasionally artists and intellectuals would gift me copies of their collections and scholarly projects, such as the archival images of the Omaya Ensemble for Folk Arts discussed in chapter 1, and sheet music books of Latakia folk song collections from a music director based in Latakia. Another scholarly resource was shared with me in the late stages of this project, with pages from a relevant publication photographed, uploaded, and sent over social media in 2019. These decentralized and relational dynamics of archival work are far from ideal because they are exceedingly partial and incidental. However, they do suggest how building relationships with interlocutors and consultants can fill archival silences and gaps created in the absence of institutional resources.[3] They also facilitate a collaborative mode of scholarship that grounds my authority in presenting and representing Syrian traditions for academic study.

Chapters 1 and 2 are also based on tens of interviews conducted with artists, performers, and artistic directors. Interviewing in a "closed context" (Koch 2013)—that is, in environments in which coercion, surveillance, and closed doors impact the power relations embedded in research—required me to navigate certain constraints and dynamics peculiar to these circumstances. Interlocutors, for instance, posed specific constraints on the interview process, from scheduling the interview to analyzing the "meta-data" of a given interview session (e.g., moments of silence, refusals, reverse questioning, and half-truths; see Fujii 2017). I often encountered "half-commitment" (Janenova 2019), such as when a research participant initially agreed to be interviewed but repeatedly postponed a meeting without formally declining the request. These strategies are more likely than not indicative of the ways that Syrians have learned how to manage themselves while living in a state of constant surveillance, not only by intelligence officers but by neighbors, coworkers, and others who inhabit every social space. In general, I approached interviews as open-ended, semistructured sessions that were part oral history (though I did not ask interviewees to share personal histories beyond what was relevant to their creative pursuits) and part reflection on artistic expression, its meanings, and its process.

One effect of scholarship in an authoritarian state is that the gaps and unanswered questions that unintentionally appear in these chapters reveal much about the historiographic process of tracing performance in an authoritarian society. There are histories that I did not have access to and could not account for in this iteration of this project. Folk dance is a theater for an archive that does not exist except in embodied acts of performance. This history cannot be written without the state as a specter, both in the historic moment that is performed and written about and in the act of writing. But it does speak to the ephemerality of performance as something that the authoritarian state (even one that has mastered the power of performance to ensure complicity and obedience) cannot preserve.

FIGURE 1.1 Solo female folk dancer. Omaya Ensemble for the Folk Arts, 1961,
from the private collection of Salma Qassab Hassan.

ONE

Virtuous Figures

In this archival image (figure 1.1), a solo female dancer performs folkloric *dabke* center stage. She cocks her right hand to her ear as she extends her left arm frontward. She moves towards stage left, with one foot following the other in a light footwork motif. She wears an embroidered dress, headcap, and character shoes typical of Arab folk dance attire in the 1950s. Around and behind her, young women clap their hands while seated in a semicircle formation. They appear demure, with their legs folded sideways while sitting on their hips. Three men smile pleasantly and clap from their position behind the row of seated women. Behind the dancers is a painted drapery of a bucolic landscape with verdant rolling hills, blooming trees, and houses. The theatrical personas, attire, and landscape together construct the performers as rural subjects, or fellahin. The solo female dancer herself portrays a fellaha, a rural, female peasant subject who embodied the Syrian homeland in performances of embodied cultural heritage.

This image documents a performance of *raqs shaʿbiyya* (literally: folk dance), an invented national performance tradition of Syria that has graced folk festival stages since the 1950s. During this seminal period for arts and cultural institutions, leading dance and music directors adapted everyday *dabke* practices into folkloric *dabke*. Referred to as *raqs shaʿbiyya*, this stand-alone choreographic genre was related to, yet distinct from, local *dabke* practices across Syria. Efforts to cultivate a space for national dance stemmed from and contributed to the nation-building visions of Syrian elite, some of whom sought to foster political sovereignty and cultural citizenship during this seminal period of Syrian independence through their patronage of the arts. Newfound political independence in the 1940s ushered in opportunities to build not only political, economic, and social institutions, but also cultural institutions such as folkloric dance ensembles and music institutes that could realize the long-standing aspirations of Arab nationalists who had resisted Ottoman rule and French colonialism for decades. Nationalist elites, most famously Fakhri al-Barudi, actively supported the study, practice, and showcasing of dance, music, and other cultural traditions as part of a collective effort to inculcate a unified national identity by reviving, preserving, and teaching traditional practices between and among Syrians.

The nation-building project to develop folkloric dance during the 1950s and 1960s was part of broader efforts to forge a collective national identity grounded in territorialized notions of homeland. Folkloric dance, along with other forms of cultural heritage, staged the homeland as a timeless and eternal space that legitimized claims for nationhood through "acts of transfer" (Taylor 2003, 2) that transmitted social knowledge, cultural memory, and a sense of identity through reiterated acts of performance. Yet the invention of folkloric dance as an embodied tradition was complicated by an anxiety, particularly among the intellectual class, that rural Syrian traditions would disappear in the wake of urbanization and modernization. Ironically, what remained of Syrian perfor-mance traditions after their intervention was an entirely new repertoire—com-posed of original choreographies, performed by state-sponsored ensembles, and integrated into theatrical productions—all of which became codified as *raqṣ sha'biyya*, or folkloric dance. The story of Syrian folkloric dance is also a story of how elites shaped the way Syrians saw themselves and their place on the world's stage. Syria was one among many nations that established professional state folk dance ensembles in the post–World War II era as a response to ethnonationalism (Shay 2002).[1] In Syria, folk dance followed a trajectory similar to its develop-ment in other nations, including Lebanon and Palestine. A close cadre of artists and intellectuals dedicated to developing the performing arts collaborated with Soviet folklorists and dance directors to craft dance as an expression of national identity and mode of cultural citizenship that found form in the international folk aesthetics of this period. This small but dedicated group of scholar-artists founded the Omaya Ensemble for the Popular Arts in 1958, which adapted *dabke* into a new, modern style of dance—*raqṣ sha'biyya*—that sought to elevate social dance traditions through a flair for theater and a commitment to socialist realist aesthetics. Over several generations of dancers, *raqṣ sha'biyya* consolidated into an autonomous genre with its own distinct repertoire and choreographic history. Energetically performed, wholesome in character, and executed with theatrical gaiety, *raqṣ shaʿbiyya* constructed ideals of Syrian citizenship and sovereignty through performance.

The process of inventing *raqṣ shaʿbiyya* as a cultural tradition necessitates situating "*shaʿbiyya*" in the specific historical, political, and social conditions of postcolonial Syria. The materials presented in this chapter suggest that though *raqṣ shaʿbiyya* emerged in step with international folk dance movements, what is considered *shaʿbiyya* does not neatly translate as folk, that is, as a cultural practice transmitted from generation to generation that upholds a sense of collective memory. Rather, I propose that *shaʿbiyya* refers to a range of practices, expressions, and discourses, the meanings of which shift over time, through which institutions and actors position themselves. Most saliently, the figure of the *shaʿb* resonates as a contested political figure of Syrian Arab nationalism and, relatedly, the populist authoritarian Assad regime. The figure of the *shaʿb* hails from rural, lower-class origins and, as the proletariat class, is paramount to the socialist mandate of Baʿthism. The Baʿthist mobilization of this social class in the 1940s and 1950s succeeded in securing political power for leaders from Syria's minority communities and rural areas, including those who seized power in the 1970 coup d'etat that established the Assadist regime. The figure of the *shaʿb* plays a significant role in the rhetoric of Baʿthism and Assadism because, following Tarik Sabry, it is "part of the workings of a discourse through which feelings of unity, harmony, reconciliation and stability are constructed" (2010, 55). The *shaʿbiyya* component of *raqṣ shaʿbiyya* is, I propose, part of a powerful political ideology whose efficacy is far more expansive than that typically associated with the anachronistic, neutralizing moniker of the "folk." At the same time, however, the nonthreatening status of that designated "folk" has time and again been activated, and manipulated, by state actors and institutions to legitimate and perpetuate political power.

Folkloric dance in Syria is illustrative of the broader postcolonial struggle to control symbolic forms of representation that structure how people see themselves and their role in the world; in Syrian folkloric dance, I argue that this served to tout the rural class and elevate women as symbols of the homeland. Consider, again, the figure of the solo female dancer, the fellaha, in the image above. She marks a major transformation that occurred in the historic development of *raqṣ shaʿbiyya*, namely, the participation and performance of female dancers onstage. Female participation in staged folk dance culture was hardly unique to mid-twentieth-century Syria: from Jordan to India and Iran, female dancers mediated nationalist visions of postcolonial modernity that aimed to assimilate heterogeneous communities and their rich cultural resources into a single unity by coupling womanhood with homeland (Purkasyatha 2014; Chakravorty 2008; Yessayan 2015; Meftahi 2017). As stated earlier, national imaginaries were an important component of bringing together communities—long divided by French colonialism, and before that, Ottoman rule—through a sense of homeland. These imaginaries constructed "the past, tradition, and nature" as feminine, while notions of change, progress, and futurity were rendered masculine (Chatterjee 1993). Male bureaucrats and intellectuals were generally perceived as the principal drivers of the administrative project of nation-building (Baron 2005; Yuval-Davis 1997) at the same time that male bodies were also disciplined and controlled by military and political systems in ways that "reproduced colonial forms of socio-political order" in postcolonial nation-states (Mitchell 1991, 38). In mid-twentieth-century Syria, a nation newly emerging from French colonial rule, the inclusion of young women in folk dance groups was part of these larger nation-building projects that gendered the nation. As I argue in this chapter, these projects were embroiled in discourses of modernity, selfhood, and gendered virtue in ways that fundamentally transformed the status of *dabke* in modern Syria.

In what follows, I trace the historic emergence of *raqṣ shaʿbiyya* to the gendered and classed dynamics of the French Mandate period, examining how heteronormative constructions of masculinity and femininity as well as elitist endeavors to valorize peasant life shaped writings on local dance practices by Syrian folklorists in the 1930s. I then turn to the peak of *raqṣ shaʿbiyya*'s popularity in the mid-twentieth century, a buoyed moment of nationalistic ardor that forged new forms of cultural citizenship in the modern nation. Here also gender and social class played a key role. Choreographic adaptations of local practices privileged imaginaries of the village and the fellaha in their stage productions. Furthermore, these performances were primarily intended for urban audiences within and beyond Syria for whom the folk resonated as a unifying mechanism that bridged internal difference during a period of urbanization, modernization, and nation-building. Folk dance thus embodied elements of *al-shaʿb* critical to the formation and political legitimacy under Baʿthism: ruralization, Arabization, and a feminized glorification of the homeland. Born out of colonial encounters and developed in the era of postcolonial nationalism, *raqṣ shaʿbiyya* would become one of the dominant aesthetics for that which is considered authentically and politically Syrian in public life.

MODERN ENCOUNTERS

The story of how everyday practices of social *dabke* transformed into *raqs sha'biyya* can be traced within the historic emergence of Arabness as a social construct that bound together a distinct group of people. Many historians locate the beginnings of modern Arab identity in the *nahda* (literally: renaissance), a literary, linguistic, scientific, and theological movement that emerged in the mid-nineteenth century among Arab intellectuals living in the Ottoman Empire that would later undergird ideologies of Arab nationalism and expressive culture (Sheehi 2004). Key to this movement was Butrus al-Bustani (1819–1883), a scholar and teacher who dedicated his life's work to establishing Arabic as a tool for the modern world, including the revival of literature and scholarship in Arabic. One of his many projects was an Arabic encyclopedia, *Muhit al-Muhit* (Ocean of oceans, 1869), in which he inscribed a reference entry for *dabke* that marks the epistemological moment in which *dabke* emerged as an object of scientific inquiry. Al-Bustani wrote: "One who *dabkes* stomps on the ground in the particular manner of *dabke*, and he renders *dabke* by stomping the ground of the village with his foot, or by other means" ([1870] 1977, 624). This entry is significant for at least two reasons: first, by translating embodied praxis into written knowledge, al-Bustani was the first to ascribe narrative and historical potential to *dabke*; and second, by gaining empirical value, *dabke* became a definable, bounded object that could be contrasted with other similarly defined and bounded objects of study.[2] The possibility of representing *dabke* as a thing in and of itself thus emerged within a movement to build modern Arab identity and forms of expression that gained political traction in the late Ottoman era.

One of those who continued al-Bustani's work in preserving Arabic language and Arab customs as cultural heritage was Muhammad Kurd Ali (1876–1953), an early nationalist reformer recognized today as an icon of Arab nationalism.[3] Kurd Ali's writings on *dabke* can be found in his major work, *Kitab Khutat al-Sham,* a six-volume encyclopedia published in 1926 that offered a social geography of the region. In this work, Kurd Ali introduced *dabke* as a "natural art found [in the] Arab countryside." He offered a historical perspective on the practice, noting that "dancing *dabke* in the past is similar to what is found now in the Arab countryside and among Arab travelers" (Kurd Ali 1926, 141–42; cf. Ibn Dhurayl 1996, 74). By delimiting *dabke* as Arab in terms of geographical space (the countryside) and practitioners (Arab travelers), his observations clearly echoed al-Bustani. Like his predecessor, Kurd Ali ushered *dabke* into nationalist debates on heritage, modernity, and tradition by presenting visions of *dabke* as a rural practice that embodies Arabness and articulates social spaces as Arab.

Leading the first waves of Arab nationalism, al-Bustani and Kurd Ali advanced visions of collective identity that consolidated Arab communities differentiated by class, locale, and religion into a singular ethnic and linguistic group, albeit problematically excluding other ethnic communities, including Kurdish, Armenian, Circassian, and Assyrian, among others. Though their writings on *dabke* are hardly extensive, even bordering on marginalia, their attentiveness is reflective of their ethnographic impulse to document Arab culture, specifically rural village culture, as part of advancing Arab society and contesting Ottoman rule. As a consequence, they solidified the objecthood of *dabke*. Yet it could be argued that in the process of formulating *dabke* as distinctly rural and Arab, their work reinforces a European worldview in which that which is "authentic" and "traditional" is distant from the colonial center of modernity. The later adaptation of *dabke* into a codified folk dance that represents Syrian nationhood would echo this colonialist formulation of nonmodern difference.

Their work is also indicative of how *dabke* would become valorized as a popular tradition with intrinsic moral value that advanced scholarship and cultural heritage rather than be dismissed as a form of popular entertainment that appealed to a growing desire for stage culture in the fin de siècle era.[4] The emergence of stages and performance halls during this time "enabled and nurtured innovations" (Ward 2018) in dance, music, and theater, most notably through the work of Abu Khalil al-Qabbani (1841–1902), a Syrian playwright and director now considered a national treasure. However, *dabke* was conspicuously absent from the popular stages that al-Qabbani and his contemporaries invigorated.[5] The study of *dabke* would later beckon to Syrian folklorists working in the 1930s, including Wajih Wabih al-Khoury and Yusuf Musa Khanashat, who located the promise of Arab nationalism within performance culture. Their French Mandate–era projects were shaped by collective efforts, spearheaded by the nationalist elite, to "save the peasant" in response to the unprecedented mass migration into cities in the 1930s. Writing about Egypt, Omnia El Shakry writes of a paradox that applies equally to Syria: "At the same time that [the peasantry] were localized by the nationalist elite as the repository of cultural authenticity, they were also demarcated as a locus of backwardness to be referred and reconstituted as modern moral subjects of the nation-state" (2007, 91). Figures of a romanticized, idyllic past, fellahin constituted the "temporal Other" (Bhabha 1994, 217) of the modern urban Syrian citizen. Projects that engaged *dabke*, along with other closely linked performance traditions, fulfilled this classist desire to reform society through the "classicization" (Chatterjee 1993) of traditions into folk culture.

Working within this milieu, several Arab scholars of music, dance, and society launched research projects that mapped out the region in terms of traditional arts and customs, including *dabkāt*.[6] Their surveys provided a crucial link between earlier intellectuals, namely al-Bustani and Kurd Ali, who identified *dabke* as a uniquely Arab cultural tradition situated in rural villages, and later Syrian Arab nationalists, who vaulted *dabke* onstage to represent Syria on the world's festival stages. In particular, Syrian scholars Wajih Wabih al-Khoury and Yusuf Musa Khanashat focused their efforts on a geographically enclosed set of local village practices. Around 1936, al-Khoury surveyed *dabkāt* in the town of Zaydal and the surrounding Homs area in central Syria (see table 1.1).[7] Khanashat focused his efforts in the countryside northeast of Damascus, specifically the city of al-Nabak (his birthplace and to which he dedicated his efforts) and the surrounding Qalamoun area.[8] Khanashat (1877–1980s) was born to a Christian family in al-Nabak and pursued artistic interests in painting, music, and photography alongside working as a municipal clerk and treasurer.

Unlike al-Khoury, whose study extracts *dabkāt* from their social context to categorize distinct practices according to stylistic features, Khanashat's study situates everyday *dabke* practices in the ritual spaces of weddings and other life events in al-Nabak. Despite their different approaches, al-Khoury's and Kha-

TABLE 1.1 Eight *Dabkāt* of Zaydal and the Greater Homs Region
(Wajih Wabih al-Khoury, ~1936)

1. *Gharbiyya* requires stomping with the right foot and shaking the abdomen continuously.
2. *al-Lawha al-Wa'riyya* is a lifting of the waist to the front while stomping.
3. *Niswāniyya* is a women's circle that turns around itself; each woman puts her hand on the next woman's shoulder.
4. *Ṭabīla* is a combination of dancing and jumping.
5. *Badāwiyya* involves jumping upwards and pushing the foot towards the floor while shouting "*dahaj*" (to look, pay attention, and walk).
6. *Dandashiyya* is a quiet dance.
7. *Nashla* involves jumping upwards and forward.
8 *'Uthmāniyya* requires the dancer to turn around slowly in full circles in the yard while walking sideways for one hour.

nashat's projects are together indicative of broader efforts during this period to valorize the fellahin, or peasant subject, as a locus of authenticity through their documentation of ways of life in rural areas. Their focus on Arab village practices is contiguous with the perspective of their predecessors, al-Bustani and Kurd Ali. Moreover, their work tracing specific styles to specific locales certifies a sense of national belonging through the mapping of place and identity. They affix meaning to *dabke* through the sociospatial logic of the homeland. Their work continues to be recognized as pioneering in popular accounts of Syrian *dabkāt* and more broadly as historical accounts of Syrian ways of life during the Mandate era.

Yet their work is also indicative of the social divides between class, geography, and communitarianism that were compounded in the 1930s, divides that were in large part due to the "divide-and-rule" policies enacted by French Mandate authorities. In terms of class, their efforts to make legible local village practices were not immune from the class tensions between nationalist elite and rural peasants that turned the latter into an object of reform and development at the same time that rural lifeworlds were elevated into and as spaces of authenticity. Regarding the juncture of geographical and communitarian boundaries, both projects focused on Sunni and Christian Arab villages in the Damascus-Homs corridor, to the exclusion of more distant regions such as Suwayda or the northern coast of Latakia, which were largely inhabited by Druze and ʿAlawite communities, respectively. Their selection of research sites among specific Sunni and Christian communities in the Damascus-Homs corridor is likely reflective of the French authority's division of the Mandate territory into several states. French authorities intentionally divided Greater Syria into communitarian-based administrative zones to prevent the growth of Arab nationalism, protect alliances with Syria's Christian communities, and protect against challenges to their colonial rule (White 2011). The fact that these projects took place in the state of Damascus and did not extend into other states—namely the ʿAlawite state centered in Latakia, the Druze state centered in Suwayda, and the state of Aleppo—is symptomatic of the geopolitical conditions of Mandate-era governance. Finally, the fact that studies did not attempt to position local traditions as exemplars of a broader nationalistic project is also indicative of how nationalist activities at that time were more focused on resisting French presence than on unifying local villages, cities, and states into an imagined national community.

Of the two studies, Khanashat's work stands out for the ways in which he accords *dabke* value as a form of both physical activity and expressive culture. More specifically, his characterization of *dabke* as physical activity resonates with discourses on gender that circulated among middle-class youth during this period. Gendered dynamics in public spaces were generally transforming during the 1920s and 1930s, following the impact of World War I on labor and households and extending through feminist movements as these converged with nationalist movements that galvanized in these decades. Mass male fatalities due to war efforts and male anxiety over the effects of French occupation on local structures of patriarchy compounded with women supporting their families through employment, demanding political rights, pursuing increased educational opportunities, and participating in public forms of leisure and entertainment to generate a "crisis of paternalism" (Thompson 2000). Stemming from this crisis, young men were encouraged to exercise and strengthen their bodies as part of collective efforts to elevate Arab masculinity towards ideals of heroism and virility (Jacob 2011). Middle-class Syrian boys and men cultivated sports, bodybuilding, and scouting as part of this physical culture movement that valorized the body as a site for physical discipline and political ideology.

The disciplinary and gendered dynamics of scouting and related activities associated with physical culture arguably structure Khanashat's descriptions of male participation in *dabke* practice, which he links to the display of masculinized competence and embodied authority in an extended passage on the role of the *dabke* leader. The head of the circle (*al-sundah*), details Khanashat, is "the most skilled and knowledgeable of the young men . . . one who moves his feet and body with mastery." His role in the performance space is akin to that of a lynchpin between the participants in the *dabke* circle and the musicians. The *dabke* leader, according to Khanashat, communicates transitions to the musicians that determine shifts in tempo, pace, and energy. He also facilitates dancers' participation by guiding and adjusting their movements and steps to establish a common flow, or conversely, by "adjusting his movements so that other dancers can follow him" (Khanashat [1936] 1982, 345; cf. Ibn Dhurayl 1996, 85–86).

In this passage, Khanashat approaches *dabke* as a performance of masculinity between men, specifically young men, in ways that echo discourses on masculinity, discipline, and physical culture that circulated across the region. By carefully delineating the role of the leader as one who "guides" other young men and "orders" accompanying musicians, Khanashat arguably suggests that the leader possesses the power to command other young men. The social choreographies of *dabke* practice, according to Khanashat, mediate relationships between young men more through an imperative and hierarchical mode of leadership than a sense of playfulness, which as I argue in chapter 3 is fundamental to the embodied ethos of pleasure that suffuses *dabke* practice. By underscoring the hierarchical and gendered dynamics between male *dabke* participants, as well as by endowing the *dabke* leader with an authoritative "mastery" of embodied knowledge, Khanashat arguably reinforces the valorization of young male bodies as an act of empowerment against anxieties over shifting gender roles in the public sphere in the Mandate period.

Also indicative of an increased public awareness of the role of gender in everyday life is the appearance of female subjects in Khanashat's descriptions of social traditions. In another passage, Khanashat organizes performance genres into two categories: "men's" and "women's" *dabke*.[9] Here, Khanashat qualifies the tenor of women's movements as "quieter and faster" than those of men. He opines that "girls are generally better than young men at *dabke*, as they are lighter in leaping, jumping, skipping and stomping" (1936 [1982], 341 and 345; cf. Ibn Dhurayl 1996, 83). The practice, he continues, provides "an opportunity for women to dance, sing, and get some enjoyable exercise." This utilitarian attitude demonstrates his encouragement of physical activity for young women during a period in which the role of women in the public sphere was both more visible and contested. On the one hand, women increasingly worked outside of the home and pursued education while being criticized for ignoring their domestic responsibilities. On the other hand, public discourse on patriotism and domesticity encouraged women to continue their dual (albeit mediated by male guardians) roles at work and at home in order to cultivate a sense of virtue that was at once national and filial. Though Khanashat's emphasis on *dabke* practice as an opportunity for young women to "exercise" as well as his comparison of "girls" as "better than young men at *dabke*" is likely not an overtly political contribution to debates on women's public roles that circulated at this time, his perspective nevertheless offers insight into the saliency of heteronormative forms of gender as a means to encode value within embodied cultural practices.

In many ways, Khanashat and his colleagues' work during the Mandate period sowed the seeds from which folkloric *dabke* as a staged performance genre would spring. Their work is also demonstrative of the modern colonialist impulse to archive and preserve embodied practices through techniques of observation, selection, description, and classification. Yet Khanashat takes care to praise the "young people" who "dance *dabke* to flaunt their bodies, their youth, and their artistry, as well as convey their versatility and mastery of a virtuous dance" ([1936] 1982; cf. Ibn Dhurayl 1996, 83). By labeling *dabke* a "virtuous dance," as well as by elevating its status as artistic, Khanashat dignifies the young men and women who perform *dabke* and imagines the practice, as a whole, as a platform for the greater social good. This ethics of virtue would become central to discourses of gender, class, and nationhood in the decades that followed, especially in the domain of national cultural heritage. Importantly, the ways that nationalistic virtue later resonated with and as folk culture can be traced to these Mandate-era accounts of *dabke* as a gendered and classed tradition in which male and female peasant bodies in motion encoded newly emerging forms of cultural authenticity.

CULTURAL CITIZENSHIP

Upon attaining political sovereignty as of 1946, Syrian nationalists faced a pivotal moment in defining the terms of their struggle. Some found footing in the ideological aspirations of Nasserism, pan-Arabism, and later, the short-lived United Arab Republic, while others agitated politics in alignment with the Ba'thist and communist movements. At the heart of these competing political visions between elite and nonelite was the question of which political subject would gain the power of the state in the struggle for Syrian sovereignty. For a few, *dabke* became a container for this question, a cultural practice of "the people" on which nationalists pinned their political aspirations and ideologies. Shining a brief spotlight on this period reveals the many ways in which performance inscribes nationhood and sovereignty in the contested moment of political autonomy.

Political life in the 1950s was significantly shaped by urbanization and industrialization. Many people moved from their villages, to which they had a deep sense of historical attachment, to cities (primarily Damascus, Aleppo, Homs, and Latakia) in search of economic and educational opportunities that were not available in struggling agricultural regions.[10] Not everyone was at ease about the flow of people into urban areas and what this meant for political stability and the political future, especially at a moment when political parties vying for control of a nascent state emerging out of French colonial rule into self-determination were competing for political traction. While some political leaders, such as Akram al-Hawrani, argued that all Syrians were ready for political autonomy and self-governance without the need for education, reform, and moral investment, most nationalist elites believed that people, especially the peasantry, were not ready to participate in a sovereign state without a formal education in how to participate in civil society. These modernizing nationalists, identified by historian Kevin Martin (2015) as male, urban, and bourgeois, perceived their urban environment to be under threat by political and social disorder. They considered protests, strikes, and demonstrations disruptions to public space and advocated for programs and organizations that educated and aided "the people" (*al-sha'b*). Those who did not fit their mold of citizenship as Arab, male, urban, literate, and heterosexual were generally perceived as objects of development.

One of the primary domains for public tutelage was official national culture, or *thaqāfa wataniyya*. As the dominant mode of state-sponsored cultural production, *thaqāfa wataniyya* incorporated an "educational function" that encouraged the public to act "as social and moral agents rather than as mere consumers" (Boëx 2011, 140). Artists affiliated with or supported by official national culture were encouraged to "deal with 'serious' (*jaddiyya*) issues within the nationalist ideological framework . . . and consider themselves a distinct group endowed with the particular task of enhancing a moral conception of aesthetic value" (140). This elitist lens, however, suffered from classist prescriptions for a preferred social hierarchy that privileged those who were male, urban, literate, heterosexual, and Arab (Martin 2015). Promoting secularism, Arabism, and socialism, *thaqāfa wataniyya* disseminated these principles through literature, poetry, film, and the performing arts. The strategies that the nation-building elite used to inculcate such citizenly virtue in the mid-twentieth century were a continuation of the gendered and classed ideals that had shaped earlier elitist efforts, especially those of the Mandate period, to reform society.

Folkloric *dabke* emerged within this ideological domain of official national culture that was less about entertaining the masses and more about instilling citizenly virtue in audiences. Like other forms and expressions of *thaqāfa wataniyya*, folkloric *dabke* inscribed nationhood by constructing *al-sha'b* as a rhetorical figure of a national past. Consider, for example, the following passage, composed by Nijat Qassab Hassan (1920–1997), a lawyer who advocated strongly for the arts and cultural heritage as cornerstones of nation-building:

> When we challenge the preservation of our artistic heritage in the present, our work is not merely to preserve its ancient image such as how archaeological objects are preserved in museums. When artistic heritage lives in the spirit of the people, in their eyes, and in their ears, its value is accorded a renewed life. It follows that the civilization of the motherland in her post reaches a position of artistic value in the bygone arts. . . . Therefore we gather ancient heritage and record it anxiously in our present moment. Then we make it an issue of polishing and cultivating it in order to present it in a new condition that

awakens our yearning for sight and sound. (Nijat Qassab Hassan, dedication to Al-Manini 1961)[11]

As Qassab Hassan's dedication suggest, folkloric *dabke* was a means to mythologize the past on which the nation was to be built. A form of cultural memory, folkloric *dabke* gave expression to the eternal timelessness of the nation, itself a temporal construct that served to legitimize territorial claims for sovereignty. One of the principal myths of Syrian nationhood was, relatedly, that of quiescent village life anchored by agricultural life and seasonal cycles. The figure of the fellahin and the construction of the village as a site of collective memory appeared both in the staging of folkloric *dabke* and in the methods books and research studies that supported its production.

In 1961 the well-regarded artistic director and choreographer ʿAdnan al-Manini (1933–1989) published a manual, *Qawaʾid Tadween al-Raqs al-Shaʿbi* (Folk dance notation method), that stemmed from his experience as an artistic director working with young folk dancers to train, rehearse, and perform Arab folk dances for local, national, and international audiences. Al-Manini was native to the Midan neighborhood of Damascus, where he started out as a textile weaver before pursuing pathways in music and dance. He studied the folk dance genre known as *raqs al-samāḥ*, traditionally accompanied by *muwashshaḥāt* musical repertoire, with the renowned artist ʿUmar al-Batsh (1885–1950) during the latter's brief period in Damascus.[12] Al-Manini was appointed by the Ministry of Education as a professor of *raqs al-samāḥ* to the Arab Music Institute. In this book, one of seven that he published and the only one to focus on folk dance per se, al-Manini sustains earlier folklorist efforts to emplace *dabke* traditions in rural spaces. He defines *dabke* as a set of rural dances (*raqṣāt rīfiyya*) practiced among distinct village communities (*ahl al-qraʿ*, literally: people of the village).[13] He lists approximately forty distinct *dabkāt*, annotating each in relation to its place of origin. He also devises a list of eight movements that he saw as characteristic of Arab *dabke*, including the footstomp.[14]

Like most of his contemporaries, al-Manini attributes the origins of *dabke* to the village, a long-standing object of identity and authenticity across the modern Middle East (Slyomovics 1998). However, unlike Khanashat's and al-Khoury's studies that grounded *dabke* practices within a locale without explicitly gesturing towards nationalist imaginaries, al-Manini specifically inscribes *dabke* as of the "Arab" village. Rather than introducing *dabke* as local to a specific village, or as Syrian from a nationalist standpoint, al-Manini positions *dabke* as an Arab dance among other Arab dances (*raqṣāt al-ʿarabiyya*) located across the SWANA region. In so doing, he attaches Arabness to movement in ways that both echo his predecessors, especially Mohammad Kurd Ali's observations of Arab life that privileged that village as an Arab social space, and speak to the pan-Arabist sentiment in which a shared Arab language, culture, and history are a unifying force for groups across the broader region.

His desire to enact pan-Arab imaginaries through folk dance was shared by many, most prominently Fakhri al-Barudi (1887–1966), one of the founding leaders of the prestigious National Bloc coalition and a prominent Damascus politician who instigated anti-French actions in late 1935. After 1946, al-Barudi dedicated his efforts to building arts and cultural institutions in newly independent Syria, including Radio Damascus and the Oriental Music Club (later the Arab Music Institute). A lifelong patron of the arts, al-Barudi invited Nijat Qassab Hassan to head the Arab Music Institute and asked ʿUmar al-Batsh, al-Manini's teacher, to relocate from Aleppo to Damascus to direct music and dance there. A decade later, in a 1957 interview with the Syrian magazine *Al-Jundi*, al-Barudi professed his aim to document folk dances across Syria and "choose the most beautiful to be a national dance for the Syrian people."[15] After stating that Syrians were not knowledgeable of each other's regional folk dances, al-Barudi pledged to teach children their cultural heritage from a pan-Arabist perspective. He promised in the interview that after ten years, "all our youth will have mastered a general Arab dance and the national dance of each Arab country." While his vision was not fully realized, in part due to the collapse of pan-Arabism after 1967 as well as the Assad regime's gradually dwindling level of support, the transformation of *dabke* from a local practice into a national folk dance can be attributed to this generation, swept up in the nationalist dreams of the 1940s and the pan-Arabist visions of the late 1950s.

Al-Manini's findings and approaches were debated vigorously by his contemporaries and colleagues, especially on issues of transcription and notation. One of his contemporaries, ʿAdnan ibn Dhurayl, would go on to publish several books on folk dance (one of which I discuss extensively in chapter 2). Their work—as published authors, folklorists, choreographers, and artistic directors—constitutes the corpus of knowledge on Syrian *dabke*.[16] Along with Qassab Hassan and al-Batsh, they were raised in artisan and trade class households, rather than elite notable estates, and pursued educational degrees and artistic opportunities that emerged in step with the growth of Syrian civil society through the 1950s. Together, their work approaches *dabke* as a practice that originates in local villages, reinforces place-based identities, and tethers the performance of Syrian nationhood to the idealized Arab village. Perhaps counterintuitively, these projects made *dabke* more mobile through the act of transforming the practice into a nostalgic representation of the idealized Arab village and inserting this cultural tradition into the translocal and transnational domain of folk dance. The genealogy of their projects can be traced from the *nahda* (the late nineteenth-century intellectual and artistic Arab movement) and early Arab nationalism to the Mandate period. These writings can also be read forward into the twenty-first century as the authoritative texts on which a variety of projects, from educational documentaries for the general public to folk festivals, were based.

INVENTING *RAQṢ SHA'BIYYA*

The year 1958 was a key historic moment in which dance became part of national imaginaries that connected Syria's past to its present. Following the establishment of the United Arab Republic, Egyptian president Gamal Abdel Nasser established the first Syrian Ministry of Culture in 1958 (Al-Saleh 2016). Though its leadership turned over rapidly due to political instability, the ministry acquired and controlled theaters, cinema houses, and cultural centers that had been built prior to and during the 1950s (Adwan 2016). Working with the Ministry of Culture were artists and intellectuals that included Qassab Hassan, the first director of arts in newly independent Syria, who supervised theater, fine arts, music, cinema, and folk culture, as well as 'Adnan al-Manini and 'Adnan ibn Dhurayl. They were not alone. Folk dance had arrived in the Levant (Rowe 2010) by way of the Soviet dance director Igor Moiseyev, who trained Lebanese directors Marwan and Wadia Jarrar Haddad (Racy 1981). The Haddads immersed themselves in Moiseyev's signature style of character dance—a synthesis of folk dance, ballet, and theater—and also trained Lebanese students in how to document local traditions in local villages. Their work was influential throughout the region, from the Rahbani Brothers' productions at the Baalbeck Festival to El-Funoun Palestinian Popular Dance Troupe, the premiere *dabke* troupe of Ramallah. While there is no indication that the aforementioned Syrian directors worked directly with either the Haddads or Palestinian directors (although Qassab Hassan was friendly with the Rahbani Brothers, who regularly collaborated with the Haddads), there was a synergy in how these arts visionaries envisaged the role of folk dance in building a national community.

Raqṣ sha'biyya was officially established with the formation of the Omaya

Ensemble for the Popular Arts in 1960. Initially an amateur folk dance troupe, Omaya was directed by Qassab Hassan, who traveled around the greater Syrian countryside to document local dance practices. By 1964 Omaya was considered Syria's leading folk dance company, performing regularly at political events, domestic festivals, and international folk festivals. As an opportunity to travel worldwide, folk dance became a path for social mobility for members of the troupe.[17] By the late 1960s, Omaya was participating in the "golden age of theater production" (Joubin 2013, 94).[18] Dancers performed at popular theaters in central Damascus, including Theater al-Hamra, Azem Palace, and the Damascus International Fair Theater. In the 1970s, folk dance was an integral part of festivals presented by the Ministry of Culture, with members of Omaya also joining theater and television miniseries to present "song and dance with biting political critique" (94). (See CLIP 1.1 on the companion website.) In 1973 Omaya officially became part of the Ministry of Culture and gained membership to the National Syndicate for Artists, the primary professional association for visual and performing artists, whose credentials are mandatory for participation in state-controlled cultural industries.[19] The first generation of dancers with Omaya cultivated successive generations of dancers, many of whom launched their own dance companies.

It is not incidental that Omaya was established during a period of urbanization, when many arrived in the city from agricultural regions. As I suggested previously, the appropriation of rural dances into and as raqs sha'biyya was geared towards the emerging urban popular class in mid-twentieth-century Syria. Omaya's target audiences were primarily urban residents who attended political events and folk festivals. Omaya's performances for urban audiences had a didactic function, namely, to sustain urbanites' connection to rural spaces and abate the anxiety that residents of mid-twentieth-century Damascus were not exposed to village life. These anxieties can arguably be linked to earlier desires for public tutelage. In an interview with me, former Omaya folk dancer Salma Qassab Hassan recalled that "in Damascus, there was no dabke at all. Not on television, or anywhere. If you were invited to some village to see a wedding, ok you go, you see, but otherwise, [if] you don't go to the village, you don't see it, you don't think about it [sic]."[20] For many Damascenes, their "first contact" with folk music and dance "came with [radio] broadcast and TV, not before." Cultural leaders, including Qassab Hassan, father of Salma, were therefore determined to educate Damascenes about life beyond the city and prevent Syrians from losing a sense of historical attachment to the village. This anxiety also typified the politics of folk dance beyond Syria, particularly in post–World War II countries politically influenced by the Soviet Union that developed state-sponsored folk dance companies modeled after Moiseyev's ensemble (Shay 2002). In Yugoslavia, for instance, folk dance "events [tended to be] aimed at urban, national and international audiences, for whom dance and music stood for the 'ubiquitous' and anonymous folk. Models created for performance serve both as a social experience, that is, of integration in a common experience of performance for the performers, and as a form of public entertainment for audiences" (Maners 2006, 80–81). In the making of the peasant into an object of spectatorship, urban audiences arguably affirmed their shared urban perspectives in ways that, paradoxically, reinforced urban and rural distinctions.

Adapting Raqṣ Shaʿbiyya

The question of which artistic and pedagogical projects to model was foremost for artists and intellectuals leading the first efforts to adapt and present Syrian folk dance. Syrian directors and choreographers were keenly aware of the ideological values embedded in aesthetics and navigated competing ideologies through their choreographic strategies. They also accepted that staging *dabkāt, raqṣ al-samah,* and other folk dances demanded methods of adaptation and devising that would fundamentally alter the practices and create "parallel traditions" (Shay 2002). They looked outward to Lebanese, Yugoslavian, and Soviet directors for inspiration, collaboration, and training while striving to maintain ethnographic fidelity to local practices and visions. Seminal to these efforts was Qassab Hassan. The challenge of folk dance, he wrote, rested in how to preserve the "love" and "excitement" (1994) for dance that characterizes Syrians as a people.

Inspired by the Rahbani Brothers' adaptation of rural ways of life for the stage, he invited them to speak on his radio program in Damascus.[21] Recalling their visit years later, Salma, his daughter, shared that "the Rahbanis brought to us the aesthetics and classic materials of the West (we learned Bach from them). But more than that, they gave us the idea of taking our life to the stage. Otherwise we just look at something and note that it exists. It doesn't occur to us to stage it. To be clear, we were not interested in appropriating folk practices into Western art forms. No, we preferred to adapt 'folk into folk.'"[22] Salma's reflections suggest that Qassab Hassan and his contemporaries approached *raqṣ shaʿbiyya* as an "authored tradition" (Wilcox 2018, 96) in which choreographers and dancers creatively craft the performance and representation of traditions.

At the same time, the attribution of such authorship was often "muted" (Shay 2002) rather than recognizing a specific individual or group of persons, largely because folkloric dance was intended to reproduce "the fiction that the choreographies that [audiences] view[ed] onstage reflect[ed] actual dances as they would be experienced in a typical field setting" (Shay 2002, 39, cf. Wilcox 2018, 105).

Qassab Hassan directly addresses the question of how to adapt *dabke* movements for the stage in his collection of essays, *al-Hina wa al-Sanabal* (1994). Central to his approach was the concept of innovation. This was in part driven by the practical desire to avoid monotony. He suspected that the repetition of a particular movement more than three or four times, such as occurs in social *dabke*, might "bore the audience" (34). At the same time, he conceived innovation as "from within" (33) the tradition. Folk dance, he asserted, was to be adapted from the peasant (fellah) who dances with ingenuity and skill at the "*ras al-dabke*," or head of the line. Adaptation workshops were organized with the aim to preserve and honor the "spontaneous" dynamics of the practice. A distinguished "peasant dancer" was chosen (presumably by a director such as Qassab Hassan, al-Manini, al-Batsh, or Ibn Dhurayl) to teach the troupe. Individual movements were extracted from the *dabbik's* improvisations and taught to the amateur folk dancers. "Extraordinary steps became normal steps" (33) in ways that both celebrated innovation from within the practice and significantly developed *dabke* movements for theater audiences.

Directors tussled with the question of who to consult in the nascent development of folk dance. Their impulse to look outside of Syria towards the Soviet Union and invite international experts with experience in the field of folk dance was hard to ignore, given the oversized influence of Soviet folk dance director Igor Moiseyev on state-sponsored folk dance companies worldwide (Shay 2002). However, these experts were given a mixed reception. One Yugoslavian consultant was dismissed because his work was not amenable to the specific urban-rural dynamics of Syria in the late 1950s, which differed substantially from Yugoslavia's more urbanized population (Qassab Hassan 1994). Though another foreign consultant, the Soviet director Georgy Pataraya, spent considerable time in Damascus helping to develop *dabke* and *raqṣ al-samaḥ*, several folklorists critiqued his *raqṣ al-samāḥ* choreography as inauthentic (Ibn Dhurayl 1996).[23] Thus even as *raqṣ sha'biyya* gradually incorporated the choreographic strategies of international folk dance, the early pioneers of folk dance tended to eschew foreign influence in favor of local and regional expertise.

Despite the preference by arts directors for locally authentic forms, the adaptation of social *dabke* into *raqṣ shaʿbiyya* ultimately transformed three domains of movement: bodily comportment, upper body work, and floor formations. All of these domains were strongly influenced by classicized Soviet ballet discipline and a Moiseyev-based folk aesthetic, both of which were reinforced in warm-ups, rehearsals, and performances that adopted Soviet ballet techniques. Led by trainers, such as Safouh Qassab Hassan, dancers practiced standardized warm-up routines that isolated specific gestures and developed their individual technique. Their training helped them to theatricalize their movements for the stage. They lengthened their postures and exaggerated their gestures in order to expand the size and scale of their actions. For instance, they dramatized the rhythmic character of *dabke* by performing highly emphatic shoulder raises. A pronounced bend at the waist or upright, erect posture added dramatic effect to poses and figuration. Dancers exaggerated the footstomp by raising their feet to knee height. They reoriented their torsos to face the audience directly. They also softened their bodies to produce a lyrical affect.

These character portrayals are evident in archival images of Omaya, where a group of folk dancers pose onstage. In figure 1.2, women dressed in traditional embroidery stand in one line, while men dressed in peasant clothes stand behind them. The women hold their chins high, with bright smiles, effusing a "wholesome" and "optimistic" mood (Moiseyev, quoted in Chudnovskii 1959, 23; cf. Shay 2002, 74). Their hands are on their hips, with feet close together, facing front. The men are staggered behind them, with their right hands held straight up high, fingers pointing to the ceiling at a slight angle. Behind them is a painted drapery of a bucolic landscape with verdant rolling hills, blooming trees, and a village in the distance. The theatrical personas, attire, and landscape clearly construct the performers as rural subjects, or fellahin.

In addition to dramatizing bodily carriage and exaggerating their gestures, dancers substantially changed the upper body work of *dabke* by making it into a domain for choreographic authorship. In social *dabke*, arm movements are generally constrained by the formation of the *shakl dāʾira* (dance circle), in which dancers clasp their hands together at their sides or embrace fellow participants by the shoulders. Some participants may emphasize a particular rhythm or moment with a shoulder raise or a forearm raise, but these remain ornamental gestures in a practice dominated by lower body work and footwork. In the adaptation of social *dabke* into *raqṣ shaʿbiyya,* folk dancers did not interlock hands and arms to form a *shakl dāʾira.* Instead, their bodies moved autonomously onstage, and their upper bodies became a domain for choreographic inscription. Much of the arms

FIGURE 1.2 Folk dancers. Omaya Ensemble for the Folk Arts, 1961, from the private collection of Salma Qassab Hassan.

choreography in *raqṣ shaʿbiyya* was derived from ballet technique, from port de bras to arabesque, though adapted for the caricature aesthetic of folkloric dance.

Finally, folkloric *dabke* demanded new spatial configurations, as social *dabke* was reimagined for the proscenium stage. Rather than an open-ended *shakl dāʾira* that maintained a consistent dance circle in a casual performance space, the group formations of *raqṣ shaʿbiyya* were designed to offer novelty for audiences facing the performers. Arrangements included rows of front-facing dancers, interweaving lines of performers, and dozens of other floor formations. Rather than ambulating in a pedestrian range of limited and repetitive motion typical of social *dabke*, performers traversed the breadth of the stage with a sense of theatricality that embellished their motions. Other dance techniques were directly imported from international folk dance, including a sashay between two dancers with their arms interlocked (see figure 1.3).

With the adaptation of *dabke* for the modern theatrical stage, gender roles were also reconfigured. Decades earlier, Khanashat had described gendered participation in *dabke* circles in terms of male competence, authority, and the privilege to lead, dynamics that continue today (discussed in chapter 3). Rather

FIGURE 1.3 Two female dancers perform a character dance. Omaya Ensemble for the Folk Arts, 1961, from the private collection of Salma Qassab Hassan.

than maintaining fidelity to a dance circle that privileged male leaders, Qassab Hassan, al-Manini, and other folk dance directors ensured that folkloric *dabke* featured both young women and young men. The inclusion of women onstage in performance was an important gesture that signaled commitment to the role of women in building the modern nation-state and participating in the public sphere. To accomplish this, the directors hosted workshops in which they invited an accomplished *dabbik* (often male) to perform, observed and documented his techniques, and disseminated these techniques into group choreography among male and female dancers, respectively (Qassab Hassan 1994). In so doing, they redistributed the male cultural authority associated with the figure of the *dabbik* onto the corpus of dancers, male and female. Arguably one of the most pronounced effects of reconfiguring gender roles was to displace male bodies, and male cultural authority, from the heart of the performance.

Separated into same-sex groups, each group of men or women performed distinct roles onstage and maintained distinct group formations with separate rows, circles, timings, and more (see figure 1.4). Many aesthetic and technical figures in this groupwork incorporated ballet and Soviet-influenced folk dance. Men's choreographies, for instance, featured the rapid, athletic repetition of high jumps and kicks, whereas women's choreographies featured softer movements, such as *chassé* and *pas de valse* footwork. By inserting gendered difference as a fundamental axis of choreography that intersected with globally circulating hegemonic forms, folkloric *dabke* embraced modern understandings of gender in ways that further distanced what occurred onstage from how *dabke* was practiced in local social spaces. New roles for male and female performers promoted the visions of citizenly virtue imagined by modernizing nationalists. However, a closer look at the specific choreographic choices made available for female dancers, as well as social attitudes towards female participation in stage culture, complicates what may have appeared to be an egalitarian embodiment of cultural citizenship.

Staging the Fellaha

In a charismatic portrait (see figure 1.5), a female folkloric dancer affiliated with the Omaya troupe poses in a courtyard. Her body pivots towards the camera, with her upper body leaning over to the left, right hand raised, while balancing on her right leg. She drops her left arm and looks straight at the camera with a congenial smile. She wears an intricately embroidered dress (*thawb* or *jillaya*)

FIGURE 1.4 Omaya Troupe performs in Chile in the early 2000s.
Photo courtesy of Ghazi al-Ammari.

FIGURE 1.5 Young woman dressed in a *thawb* in the courtyard of *bayt ʿarabī*.
Omaya Ensemble for the Folk Arts, 1961, from the private collection
of Salma Qassab Hassan.

with a bedazzling headdress (*wuqāyat al-darāhim*) evocative of ceremonial wedding garments in village spaces, along with knee-high leather dance boots common to folk dance troupes in that period. Behind her in the courtyard of a *bayt 'arabī*, or traditional urban dwelling, is a landscaped background of black-and-white, Mamluk-era stone architecture. Her playful confidence in this image captures the highly visible, and likely fulfilling, role of female participation in folkloric dance.

The opportunity to serve the nation through embodied cultural expression was a significant advancement for women. Supplanting the young male *dabbikūn* traditionally at the head of the *dabke* line, this female folkloric dancer projected not only tradition but also shifts in the status of women in the independent Syrian republic. Women's participation in nation-building processes, and more broadly in public life, was indicative of modernity's progress and the future horizons of the young nation-state. Socialist and Third Worldist political ideologies circulating around many postcolonial nation-states promoted universal liberation, including that of women, and encouraged women to participate in the public sector through education, work, and creative expression. Policies of "state feminism" (Hill 1997) granted women protections and benefits with regard to marriage, divorce, children, and other aspects of family law (ratified as personal status law in Syria in 1953). However, there were major discrepancies between state rhetoric that accorded "equal status" to women; personal status laws based on *shari'a*; and the actual negotiation of family, state, and kinship dynamics at the individual level. Though many women pursued and created new opportunities, the lived realities for women in patriarchal societies dictated that they were also expected to maintain the law of paterfamilias at home (Boehmer 2013; Gandhi 1998).

This tension was particularly fraught in the world of folkloric dance. At the same time that women were encouraged to cultivate themselves in service to their family, community, and nation, and as they became increasingly integrated into social institutions, they were expected to uphold moral codes that valued female modesty. Folk dancing as a profession was particularly vulnerable to moral equivocation because of the "culture of dishonor associated with women's professional dance" (Yessayan 2015, 64). Though these contestations of morality generally centered on *raqṣ sharqiyya* (belly dancing), performed solo by women for nightlife audiences, they also extended to the question of whether women should participate in other fields of professional dance, including folkloric dance. For some, performance onstage of any kind was deemed dishonorable for the female performer and her family, particularly male kin. For others, folkloric dance was an ideal space for young women because of postcolonial nationalist perceptions of women as the "natural" agents for the transmission of embodied traditions from generation to generation (Chatterjee 1993). *Dabke* was, after all, a cultural expression of "young men's enthusiasm on the one hand and women's femininity and innocence on the other hand" (Ibn Dhurayl 1996, 84), according to 'Adnan al-Manini. Thus, even as women were encouraged to practice "virtuous" forms of citizenship (Martin 2015) through folkloric dance and were likewise protected by accusations of shameful behavior because of the virtue attached to folkloric dance, they were also constrained by the gendered expectations of virtue.[24]

The pressures translated directly into choreographic choices regarding how to position women's bodies onstage, a question always at stake in dance worlds (Banes 1998). The first photo presented in this chapter (figure 1.1), for instance, presents a young female dancer moving across the floor. Three male dancers stand in the background, clapping their hands, while young female dancers sit in a row on the floor against the painted backdrop of a mountain village. What is notable about this photo is that the young woman is accompanied by other dancers onstage rather than commanding the stage with her singular presence. Additional images from the same collection of Omaya shows confirm that female dancers were always accompanied by male performers (with the exception of figure 1.5, which is likely a staged portrait rather than a live show). In figure 1.4, for instance, the two female folk dancers sashaying together are accompanied by a row of male folk dancers in the background who clap their hands, with one holding a *qānūn* (zither) in his lap. Similarly, in figure 1.6 a female folk dancer performs with a *riq* (tambourine) player accompanying her in the center of the stage. Her fingers take on the classic staggered port de bras hand comportment of ballet. Her arms are raised and elbows bent, with the right arm extended higher than her left. The posture is evidence of how upper bodywork is a domain for choreographic inscription. Moreover, she performs with the male *riq* player, turning her head back towards him to present a cheerful smile. Folk dancers of both genders sit on the floor behind them, also smiling broadly and clapping in participatory collective performance. Their display of youthful gaiety and virtuous modes of pleasure mediate performances of gender.

Though young women performed with expressions of gaiety and innocence that affirmed virtuous citizenship, the social obligations of citizenly virtue included male guardianship onstage. Figure 1.7 depicts this vividly. A row of female

FIGURE 1.6 *left*
Male percussionist on *riq*
accompanying female folk
dancer. Omaya Ensemble for
the Folk Arts, 1961, from the
private collection of Salma
Qassab Hassan.

FIGURE 1.7 *below*
Seated rows of folk dancers.
Omaya Ensemble for the
Folk Arts, 1961, from the
private collection of Salma
Qassab Hassan.

dancers sits inside a row of male dancers. The male performers rest their forearms on propped right legs and generally keep their hands open in a paternalistic posture that emphasizes the chest and shoulders. The female dancers sit demurely with legs tucked behind them and covered by full skirts in ways that emphasize the embroidered pattern of the *thawb*. They place their hands on the floor in a soft resting position. Whereas men look directly ahead, women tilt their heads as if performing for (or smiling back at) the male gaze (Mulvey 1975). Though vital to the myth-making processes of nationhood that valorized the fellaha, female presence onstage remained subject to outstanding sensibilities of virtue that delimited the parameters of their participation.

The gendered dynamics of staging female bodies with the accompaniment of male bodies are significant because they convey how social forces of paternalism and male guardianship are transmitted through performance culture. More often than not, women who travel alone are frowned upon, and elder male kin mediate women's terms of employment or family disputes (Thompson 2000) in accordance with the patriarchal codes of paterfamilias. Neither, according to this collection of images, may they dance alone onstage. The choreographic instantiation of male guardianship is indicative of how the social aesthetics of folkloric *dabke*, as a nation-building project, were gendered in ways that were congruent with everyday experiences of gender, family, and public life. The rural utopias created for the stage, in other words, were not separate from but rather circumscribed by patriarchal structures of power in Syrian society.

———

By the time I encountered the fellaha subject in private archival collections shared with me in 2008, she was a vestige of past glory, her performances relegated to the archive. Women's participation in folkloric dance had not diminished, in fact it had expanded in terms of numbers, with many folk dance ensembles working across the country, and in terms of aesthetics, with an entire performance genre dedicated to *raqṣ niswāniyya* (women's dance). But the specific figure of the fellaha as the embodiment of the Syrian nation dissolved over the course of the four decades that passed between the establishment of Omaya and my engagement with *raqṣ shaʿbiyya*. Choreographers working in *raqṣ shaʿbiyya* largely preferred group work over individual solos, though they chose to retain the segregation of groups by gender in their stagings. The reasons for the fellaha's dissolution are not clear. Writing a complete cultural history of folkloric dance during this period faces numerous challenges. Archival materials such as directors' stage notes, program bills, images, and recordings are (to the best of my knowledge, after concerted effort) not held at publicly accessible institutions, including but not limited to the National Assad Library, but may be found in private collections. Access to private collections depends on social networks, which have been ruptured by the conflict and mass displacement. The lack of archives in Syria, not only for performance culture but in general, can be attributed to the fact that the ephemerality of performance is political in an authoritarian regime, and likewise, that the power of authoritarianism thrives in the ephemerality of its performance.

These dynamics between authoritarianism and performance were poignantly articulated by the celebrated Syrian playwright Saʿdallah Wannous (1941–1997) in his highly regarded play, *An Evening's Entertainment for the Fifth of June* (1968). Set on the first day of the 1967 war, the play addresses "how government-sponsored artists use theater to alienate the public, perpetuate the status quo, and prevent public debate" (Wannous, Myers, and Saab 2019, 190). At its heart, the play provokes discontent and frustration between the play's director, whose weak attempts to appease the audience evoke the hollow rhetoric of the post-Nasserist state, and the audience, which consists of both invited guests and actors who antagonize the conflict with the director. State-sponsored folkloric dance shows up in the director's attempts to placate the audience with state-sponsored program content in lieu of the programmed feature. Making an appearance at the play's climax, when the director has lost all semblance of control, folkloric *dabke* is offered as a substitute for the canceled play. Performers offer a lackluster performance of folkloric *dabke* that is abruptly interrupted by a Palestinian refugee from the Golan Heights talking about his village and the politics of statelessness. What Wannous accomplishes in this brief insertion of folkloric *dabke* into a play that critiques the hollow rhetoric of the post-Nasserist Syrian regime is an account of how the tenor of folkloric dance more or less shifted from a socialist realist affirmation of "the people" to a cultural expedient for Baʿthism in Assadist Syria. Thus whereas folkloric dance originated as a form of virtuous citizenship that imbued performance with "moral and social value," to repeat Cecile Boëx's apt phrase, it later became fodder for authoritarian rhetoric.

Aside from this critique, which likely did not circulate much beyond the intellectual class, folkloric dance remains to today an industry enthusiastically supported by most Syrians. Those who actively participate in Omaya, which continues to perform on domestic and international stages, as well as other folkloric ensembles such as Firqa al-Hamami, approach folkloric dance as an avenue for employment, social mobility, and opportunity for travel. Perhaps most importantly, they view themselves as professional artists who contribute meaningfully to their society. At the same time, however, ensembles that rely on state funding have limited budgets and have not seen significant investment in terms of supporting the ensemble or supporting festival venues since the early 1970s (Kastrinou 2016). For whom folk dance has stagnated and for whom it is meaningfully vital in light of these changes is the subject of the next chapter.

This chapter has demonstrated how *raqs sha'biyya* served as a site for the modern inscription of the nascent postcolonial Syrian nation as young, female, and rural.[25] Performed for international and domestic audiences, *raqs sha'biyya* was a platform for modern visions of state and society that sought to stabilize society in the midst of ongoing political, economic, and social upheaval. Gendered colonial ideologies and Western aesthetics became embedded in *raqs sha'biyya* in the same moment that Syrians claimed it as quintessentially Syrian. This was manifest in the spatial organization of bodies on the proscenium stage, the emphasis of upper body work in choreography, and the training regimens maintained by dancers. These techniques created a new dance genre alienated from everyday practices of *dabke*. Also significant within the process of adapting local practices for the stage was the redistribution of gender in performance, from dismantling the role of the male line leader to privileging the fellaha in solo performance. *Raqs sha'biyya* was paradoxically imbricated in a geography of cultural imperialism at the same time that it enacted sovereignty through gendered movement.

TWO

Staging Difference

In July 2008, a friend and I made our way to Idlib, a town in northern Syria known at that time as a small industrial urban center that attracted few foreign tourists.[1] My interest in Idlib was to explore a site of domestic tourism relatively distanced from the main arteries of international tourism—Damascus, Aleppo, Bosra, Palmyra—because I was keen to learn how Syrians presented their cultural heritage to one another. Established in 2007, the annual Idlib Festival for the Popular (Folk) Arts invited artists and entertainers from across Syria to perform in a Roman-era amphitheater in the main public park for residents of Idlib. This particular evening's program was titled a "Festive Evening with a Mosaic of Popular Arts from the Province of Hama." The *fusayfisāʾ*, or mosaic, was a popular motif for state-sponsored cultural production that generally symbolized cultural pluralism within the Syrian nation, though its specific meanings depended on the event and occasion. On this particular night of the state-sponsored folk festival, the mosaic represented the cultural traditions of Hama, a neighboring province of Idlib to the south.[2]

After the opening act, which featured a troupe of acrobatic performers who entertained the audience with panache, the main act of the evening began their program. Firqa al-ʿAsi, a children's folkloric dance troupe from Masyaf, a city in Hama, presented "The Wedding Season," a dramatic reenactment of a rural summer wedding celebration. Performed by children ranging in age from eight to fourteen years, as well as an accompanying orchestra (of adults), "The Wedding Season" was a story about a young girl and young boy who fell in love, encountered family conflict, and resolved the conflict by the tale's end, with the support of their families and village community. It offered song, music, and dance traditions local to Masyaf yet adapted into *raqṣ shaʿbiyya* vis-à-vis group formations, port de bras arms, and other choreographic techniques typical of Syrian folkloric dance. Against a painted stucco backdrop, and costumed in festive headdresses and robes, the young performers emulated Arab peasant life with the theatrical gestures and folkloric dance aesthetics that comprised *raqṣ shaʿbiyya*. (See footage of this performance at CLIP 2.1 on the companion website.)

The presentation of Firqa al-ʿAsi at the Idlib Festival for the Popular Arts was indicative of the continuing popularity of folkloric troupes in prewar Syria.[3] Children participated in folkloric song and dance at afterschool programs nationwide. These programs began in the 1960s and 1970s, when the nation-building elite developed folkloric culture as an opportunity to preserve cultural traditions, teach Syrians about one another's cultural heritage, and catalyze the integration of diverse social groups within the framework of the nation. These school programs also exposed students to the performing arts. Opportunities to perform for festival audiences, such as those at the Idlib Festival, encouraged youth to participate in artistic modes of cultural citizenship. Local folkloric dance troupes were thus a vehicle for sustaining engagement with local cultural traditions and for engaging with audiences beyond local communities—not only urban and international audiences, but also local audiences in other towns and provinces. State-sponsored folkloric dance, along with other forms of the "popular arts," served to educate Syrians about each other's local (and regional) cultural heritage in ways that recognized cultural heterogeneity within Syrian society through a sense of place.

"Place-making" is a complex process in which social actors enact cultural discourses and negotiate local social hierarchies in order to situate themselves in, and produce, space (Gupta and Ferguson 1997; Lefebvre 1991; Massey 1994). On the one hand, a sense of place has long structured belonging for individuals, families, and communities across Syria. As I traveled around Syrian villages and cities and met people from different social strata, I noticed that people largely introduced themselves, and strongly identified, with the village or city in which they were born or to where they traced family lineage (though, as Christa Salamandra [2004] and Faedah Totah [2014] have pointed out in their studies of gentrification in Damascus, claims of origin and descent often negotiate shifting social hierarchies, such as urban-rural binaries, in complex and nonlinear ways). Throughout my fieldwork, local, place-based identities were often privileged as much as (and in some cases, more than) other vectors of identity, including religion and ethnicity. People typically marked their identities through the perception of local dialect as well as speaking about different ways of life, including culinary traditions, artisan crafts, and performance (song and dance) traditions. In this chapter, I focus on how locality is the dominant means by which the Syrian state, working through the Ministry of Culture as its main apparatus for cultural production, recognizes cultural diversity among Syrians in the 2000s.

In the same year as the Idlib Festival, a major cultural initiative took place throughout Syria's capital, Damascus. The 2008 Damascus Arab Capital of Culture (DACC) festival was a yearlong, multi-million-dollar platform sponsored by the United Nations Educational, Scientific, and Cultural Organization (UNESCO) in partnership with the Syrian Ministries of Culture and Education. While the festival itself rotated annually among Arab cities across the region, each host city, designated as such by UNESCO, curated its own vision for how to best represent Arab urbanity. In Damascus, curators commissioned a wide range of projects from Syrian artists and presented innovative programs throughout the year that centered on the past heritage and future horizons of Damascene culture. The festival aimed to "offer opportunities for social inclusion and cohesion, business, education, tourism, heritage and urban regeneration at every level."[4] These included investment opportunities for an emerging generation of artists and arts administrators, increased resources and capacity-building for established arts centers and institutions, and a roster of high-profile international artists invited to Damascus to work with emerging Syrian artists. The DACC festival was part of a longer process of urban renewal and gentrification, centered in the Old City of Damascus yet impacting neighborhoods citywide, that began in the early 1990s and peaked in 2008 (Totah 2014).

It is significant that these two contrasting festival programs occurred in the same year, 2008, the end of a decade in which symbols of nationhood had been shifting rapidly due to the transfer of political power from father to son and the economic liberalization policies enacted by Bashar al-Assad. The DACC festival was part of these policies insofar as it stimulated new streams of wealth and spending in the domain of cultural production and enabled proximity to Western artists and culture by dismantling barriers to tours, live performances, and other events. It had the look and feel of twenty-first-century global cultural capital. The Idlib festival, in contrast, maintained the socialist realist aesthetics of folk culture that had characterized state-sponsored cultural production for decades and that continued to appeal to the taste of many working- and middle-class families. Yet despite its more provincial scale, it was also relatively well-funded through the Ministry of Culture and visible across Syria due to national media coverage

(Kastrinou 2016). Most importantly for my discussion here, the two festivals both privileged cultural diversity among Syrians in their program selections.

Perhaps the most conspicuous indication of the role of cultural difference in thematizing and structuring the DACC festival was its logo. The curatorial team behind the DACC festival, led by executive director Dr. Hanan Qassab Hassan (daughter of Nijat Qassab Hassan), selected a rosette as the festival's logo (see figure 2.1). The rosette was prominently displayed on all event banners and posters, on billboards throughout Damascus, and in television promotions that broadcast the festival's message of tolerance and openness. (See a television promotion at CLIP 2.2 on the companion website.) A common decorative motif across Syria prior to the DACC festival, the rosette typically evoked commemorative rituals of ancient Mesopotamia. In the context of the DACC festival, the rosette referred to the pluralist and diverse backgrounds of Damascenes and their histories of contact. Workshops, commissions, and exhibition series presented throughout the year explored these open-ended themes. In one concert series held in September 2008, the rosette referred to the spiritual and religious diversity of Damascus. "Spiritual Music Days" presented traditional and spiritual ensembles at the Azem Palace courtyard in Old Damascus. Distinguished Sufi performers from across the region were featured, including the Aleppo Heritage Band (of the Qadiriyya [Sufi] Order), Shaykh Ahmed Al-Tuni (Egypt), and the Ibn Arabi band (Morocco). While Syrian (and other) Sufi music ensembles have long been naturalized as "sacred" in Western world music venues (Shannon 2003), their appearance at the 2008 DACC festival hailed spiritual diversity in ways that resonated with the regime's pivot at that time towards recognizing religious difference as a state-sanctioned category in official state culture (Pinto 2011).

The rosette of the DACC festival was not entirely dissimilar to the mosaic of the Idlib Festival. Both were visual metaphors for cultural pluralism that depended on the logic of parthood relations, that is, how parts (place-based or other forms of cultural difference) relate to each other and to a distinct whole (the nation). Both festivals staged difference in ways that reinforced the public-facing embrace of multiculturalism encouraged in official national culture. However, the types of sociocultural difference on which nationhood was predicated diverged substantially between the two festivals. The Idlib Festival's focus on regional diversity embraced a territorial paradigm of nationhood bounded politically and geographically by its composite sum of regions. Maintaining the long-standing model of secular, territorialized nationhood was, I argue in this chapter, a critical tactic of regime power that emerged in the mid-twentieth century and continued

FIGURE 2.1 Wassim Muqdad performing on *ʿūd* in front of the rosette logo of the Damascus Arab Capital of Culture Festival. Downtown café, Damascus, 2008. Photo by the author.

through the 2000s. The DACC festival, by contrast, reoriented nationhood to be inclusive of multiple forms of difference, including but not limited to spiritual and religious diversity.[5] Some DACC festival projects animated the past within the present by considering historical change, while other projects spotlighted the Old City of Damascus as a historic site of religious and ethnic coexistence. The DACC festival was part of a larger "renew and refresh" (Donati 2013) shift in authoritarian discourse and strategy to accommodate changing demographics and economics, particularly a rise in piety practices and religiosity in the public sphere. That these two apparently divergent yet structurally similar approaches to cultural diversity and pluralism took place in the same year is indicative of the uneven shifts occurring in the cultural sector as part of broader processes of neoliberalization.

This chapter critiques the construction of national imaginaries through the "unity-in-diversity" logic of cultural heritage, specifically *dabke* traditions. As evidenced through the mosaic and rosette figures that thematized state-sponsored cultural production, this logic informed how Syrian citizens learned "to recognize themselves and articulate self-recognition within the terms of liberal national discourse" (Mahmood 2005). This logic also, I argue, shaped the exclusion of non-Arab ethnic minorities and religious forms of belonging from national imaginaries. As a practice that emplaces communities within a specific locale, *dabke* traditions became a site for "multicultural domination" (Povinelli 2002), that is, a domain in which social actors "perform and authenticate their difference within the moral and legal frameworks determined by," in this case, the regime (Tambar 2010, 652).[6] The effects of tethering sociocultural difference to territorialized forms of identity embodied by *dabke* traditions, rather than to religious or ethnic identity formations, were to suppress the latter configurations from attaining visibility in the public sphere (Kastrinou 2016; al-Haj Saleh 2017).

Drawing on in situ fieldwork and archival documents, I look at three state-sponsored projects that construct *dabke* traditions as immutable expressions of local and regional identity within Syria. These, I contend, served as techniques of statecraft that reinforced territorial forms of nationalism as well as exclusionary policies against Kurdish communities. I then briefly situate these state-sponsored projects in the context of neoliberalization in prewar Syria in order to examine an ambivalence towards *dabke* held by a generation of emerging choreographers seeking new trajectories for Syrian dance. This chapter demonstrates how performances of cultural heritage perpetuated and were subject to the Assad regime's political calculus at the same time that they upheld liberal models of cultural pluralism—in other words, how *dabke* traditions were imbricated in and for the most part upheld the balance between the regime and society.

"THE WEDDING SEASON"

In 2008, local residents of Idlib perceived their home as a "nice mosaic" of mostly Sunni Muslim groups with some Christian communities that lived alongside one another.[7] The Idlib Festival extended this pluralist sentiment of the mosaic through the festival programming by projecting the festival as a contact zone between different regional cultures, each a component of the Syrian mosaic. How did these cosmopolitan dynamics resonate for the festival performers from

Hama and local audiences of Idlib? Did the programming address the histories of contact and shared experiences common to the two regions?

The cities of Masyaf (home of Firqa al-ʿAsi) and Idlib are only 150 kilometers from each other. They have historically occupied the same political and economic corridor that stretches between Damascus and Aleppo. Masyaf is located in the foothills of the Jabal Ansariyya mountain range, near to Al-Ghab plain, and Idlib is an agricultural zone in the Qwayk River basin. This corridor has been inhabited and farmed for centuries; today, in twenty-first-century Syria, it serves as a major transport conduit between Syria's major cities, Damascus and Aleppo. Prior to the revolution, both areas supported agriculture and were historic centers for manufacturing; Masyaf developed a carpet-weaving industry and Idlib produced soap and olive oil. Their prewar demographics were generally more similar than different: Sunni Arab majority and Christian communities inhabited Idlib, while Sunni, ʿAlawite, and Ismaʿili Shiʿi communities along with some Christian communities inhabited the city of Masyaf and its surrounding villages. But the conflict polarized relations between the two areas. Idlib generally supported antiregime efforts, and Masyaf generally supported the regime. Islamist control of Idlib since 2015 has forced the near-total displacement of Christian Syrians from the area at the same time that the regime has isolated and continually attacked Idlib, considered by many the last rebel stronghold.[8]

Whether these histories informed performer and audience experiences at the festival, which occurred years before the conflict, remains unclear. Approximately four hundred spectators, mainly families, attended that evening's performance. The audience generally expressed light-hearted appreciation for the good-humored sketches performed by the young artists. Several men started dancing with each other despite the narrow space of the amphitheater rows. Balloons were released into the clear skies. They did not appear to be attending or participating out of regime-mandated citizenly duty.[9] To me, "The Wedding Season" appeared to be a continuation of the social and cultural projects developed since the 1930s that attempted to reform the fellahin while upholding rural life as the historic groundswell of Syrian society. Like the national Omaya troupe, the performance represented the life of rural peasants through a purportedly objective lens that in fact portrayed this life as purposeful, dauntless, and tethered to socialist values accorded to agricultural labor.

Most of Firqa al-ʿAsi's program was dedicated to folkloric dance choreography. After the introductory scene, the next two scenes featured song, music, and dance in same-sex group choreographies that advanced the romance narrative.

The group choreographies offered a wide range of codified folkloric dances, presumably local to Hama. As a cultural outsider, I was generally not able to discern exactly what made these social dance practices local to Hama or how the social dances precisely related to their staged adaptations; neither could my friend, who was from a town near Aleppo. Whether audiences consider folkloric dance to be an imitation of social life or a "parallel tradition" (Shay 2002) that is not directly bound to ethnographic fidelity remains open to subjective interpretation, but my friend and I were keen to identify meaningful links between place and its embodied representation.[10] Of the movements that we could identify, one *dabke* set emphasized a knee bend (*thanī al-rukba*) with a torque (*fitla*), a gesture particular to Hama according to Syrian folklorist ʿAdnan ibn Dhurayl (1996). Other styles included a slow, swaying *dabke* that alternated with more quick styles, and a group wedding dance (*raqṣ zawjiyya ʿarabiyya*) in the style of *lawḥa ḥamawiyya,* in which pairs of dancers place the left foot in front of a bent right foot in a quasi-limping, syncopated motion. These folkloric dance idioms folded into intricate same-sex group floorwork, in which young male and female dancers moved through staggered, intersecting, and encircling patterns.

There was a complex politics of representation at play in "The Wedding Season." The complexity resulted from not only the performance of a Hama regional identity for audiences in a different region but also the construction of a collective identity purportedly representative of social life across the Hama governate. The performance techniques through which Hama, as a putative cultural whole, was constituted reveal acts of internal Othering that are endemic to cultural heritage industries. Like many folk productions, this show reenacted a rural wedding. It opened with an orchestral overture played by an accompanying ensemble (of adults) positioned on risers at the back of the stage. The young performers entered the stage in character, walking out as if they had just arrived at a wedding party. They greeted and embraced each other with hand gestures, shoulders thrown back to make way for faux-rotund bellies, and general posturing that dramatized mature adulthood. After their theatrical entrance, two of the performers lip-synched a *mawwāl* (vocal improvisation) and pretended to play a *taqsīm* (instrumental improvisation) on *rabāb* (spiked fiddle). The vocal and instrumental parts were not performed live but lip-synched along with prerecorded audio tracks, including one that featured adult male vocals.[11] (See CLIP 2.3 on the companion website.) I was struck by the multiple registers of mimesis taking place onstage, from the theatricalization of gestures imitating the social codes of adulthood to the imitation of vocal and instrumental playing.

The efficacy of mimesis, insists Michael Taussig (1993), is that within the desire to imitate lies the capacity to usurp the power of that which is imitated and imbue the imitated subject with a sense of alterity, or Otherness,. Youth imitating adult life placed the bride, groom, and other nuptial subjects in an anachronistic sense of time that rendered village life eternal and unchanging.

The performance also constructed collective regional identity through its renderings of a mythical past that drew upon Bedouin culture. Nomadic pastoral communities have historically inhabited the steppe areas of the present-day Hama province since the eighteenth century (Chatty 2010). Markers of Bedouin culture appeared in "The Wedding Season," particularly the *rabāb*, the traditional headdress with an *'iqāl* (rope), and the *thawb* (robe). Though these ethnographic objects likely indexed local Bedouin traditions, they were also indicative of the slippage between Arabness and Bedouinness.[12] The latter has often been designated as "the origin and pillar ('Once we were all Bedouins') of a sedentarised and urbanized [Arab] society" (Prager 2014, 74). Bedouinness frequently embodies the mythical origins of Arabness. Yet there remains a "profound ambivalence" (Lange 2015) over Bedouin social identities and their representations. Whereas Bedouin persons are often dismissed as "fundamentally non-modern" (whether they herd sheep or drive taxis), Bedouin culture is associated with Arab authenticity, which is itself actualized in part through the "Bedouin ethos" of "nobility, courage, and generosity" (Lange 2015). The effects of these slippages and contradictions within "The Wedding Season," as a representation of social life in Hama, are to detach the storyline from a concrete historical, political, or territorial context and to place it in a vaguely premodern time and space through Bedouin tropes. Absent the "complex realities of intertribal relations and stratified hierarchies of social status" (Lange 2015), as well as the contested political histories between Bedouin shaykh authority and the Syrian Arab Republic, this representation of Hama culture and society emplaced Bedouinness within discourses of cultural heritage and Arab authenticity.

It is also noteworthy that this insertion of Bedouin identity markers into a folkloric performance occurred in 2008. Bedouin culture became a popular commodity in Arab tourism in the 2000s, especially in theme parks and other spaces of exhibition (Cole 2003; Peutz 2011). One effect of this regional market, which extended beyond Syria into Egypt, North Africa, and the Gulf, was to shift popular perceptions of Bedouinness. Historically, Bedouin worlds have been attached to nomadic pastoralism as an industry dependent on livestock, climate, and migratory lifeways. However, the regional tourism market transformed representations of Bedouinness from a contemporary "way of life grounded in ecology and economy [towards an] identity [based] in heritage and culture" (Cole 2003, 237) that attached Bedouinness to the Arab past. The 2008 Idlib Festival and the broader Arab heritage tourism industry produced, as Natalie Peutz articulates in conversation with Barbara Kirshenblatt-Gimblett, a "'Bedouinness' positively transvalued through its emphasis on 'pastness, exhibition, difference, and, where possible, indigeneity'" (Kirshenblatt-Gimblett 1998, 50; cf. Peutz 2011, 338). By claiming a Bedouin past, "The Wedding Season" displayed the authentic Arab heritage of the Hama province at the same time that it appealed to early twenty-first-century transnational desires for Bedouin identity production.

The construction of provincial identity also occurred through conditions of spectatorship. As I have demonstrated, in its initial development in the 1950s, folkloric Syrian dance was presented to domestic audiences as part of nationalist efforts to teach urban male citizen-spectators about the rural Arab heritage of their newly emerging postcolonial nation. This pedagogical mode shifted in the twenty-first century, as stagings moved away from depictions of ruralness for primarily urban audiences to intraprovincial performances, in which distinct provinces staged local traditions for other provinces to generate a sense of "local, state-bound cosmopolitanism" (Kastrinou 2016, 151). The cultural logic supporting this shift remained the same: through the performance of the folk, spectators encountered the "cultural memory of a time and a place" that they "may not have experienced personally" (Maners 2006, 86). Importantly, these contemporary performances positioned audiences as external to ethnographic subjects represented onstage in ways that constructed a boundary between provinces. Performances of folkloric dance therefore reinforced these imagined boundaries between provinces as fixed, immobile, and stable, in contrast to the lived realities of internal migration that generations of Syrians experienced throughout the twenty- and twenty-first centuries due to urbanization, drought, and state neglect (Totah 2014; Abboud 2015).

This performance of territorialized and immutable forms of subnational difference is arguably an explicit strategy of regime statecraft precisely because it makes place-based identities visible and legible and because it occludes ethnic and religious forms of belonging. In her study of power, sect, and state in Syria, Marie Kastrinou argues that the "substitution" of sectarian or class-based differences among Syrians for "regional cultural variation" can be attributed to the avowedly secular constitution of the Ba'th Party and its monopoly on regime power (Kastrinou 2016, 150). Public rhetoric that celebrates secularism and regional forms of difference, she insists, stands in contradiction to the socioeconomic networks of the political power that are based on sectarian relationships as well as the refusal of the regime to disrupt these networks and provide opportunities for social and class mobility.[13] Using such rhetoric, the state maintains regime power through "the legitimate governance of and over difference" (Kastrinou 2016, 152).

Regime control over public rhetoric and the cultural representation of place matters greatly for those who live in and care about Hama. The regime has yet to account for one of the major national traumas of the Assad regime that occurred in Hama. In 1982, then president Hafiz al-Assad ordered a massive military attack in the face of insurgency from the Muslim Brotherhood and unsparingly massacred thousands of civilians in Hama as a tactic of collective punishment against the faith-based political movement. This event and its political aftermath were largely responsible for coercing several generations into compliance with the regime out of fear of retribution. Given how much the "events," as they are popularly referred to, have scarred the collective Syrian psyche, bucolic productions like "The Wedding Season" that enact the dominant state-sanctioned representation of collective identity in Hama are arguably a means to sanitize political trauma and suppress other forms of belonging that the regime perceives as a threat to power. Folkloric culture as a domain of regimecraft is effective not only because it perpetuates political power but because it does so through the affective dimensions of performance—people have strong attachments to a sense of place to which they attribute kinship ties, and performance animates these desires by embodying them onstage in larger-than-life recreations. The "events" slip deeper into the psyche in the immediacy of beholding the folkloric present.

In its longtime support of local folk festivals each summer across the country, the Syrian state continually demonstrated its investment in the preservation and performance of cultural heterogeneity among Syrians, but in specific terms that it managed and controlled. By privileging the territorialization of cultural difference over other forms of difference, namely ethnic and religious, state-sponsored folk culture arguably neutralized difference into a status quo, or balance, tethered by the fixity of place. The secular and territorialized constructions of difference presented at the Idlib Festival were in compliance with Ba'thist ideology and its valorization of rural, Arab subjects, imagined in this performance as explicitly Bedouin. Another aspect of statecraft that occurs through performance is pedagogical—the moral imperative to teach Syrians about each other through folkloric dance, an imperative that stemmed from the mid-twentieth-century projects to cultivate cultural citizenship. As I discuss in the next section, the stage was not the only medium for state pedagogy through folkloric dance.

BALANCING CULTURAL GEOGRAPHY

The Idlib Festival was one among numerous performance spaces that sought to educate Syrians about their cultural heritage by ascribing distinctions in *dabke* style to specific geographic places, a sociospatial logic that structures cultural practices as historical givens. In this section I continue to examine this geographic mode of cultural representation by considering how the nation as a whole is territorialized through cultural mapping. Looking at two state-sponsored projects that survey *dabke* practices across Syria, I expose the influence of Arabist and place-based ideologies on nationalist discourses of cultural heritage. One is a comprehensive scholarly study of folk dance in Syria, published in 1996 by scholar-artist 'Adnan ibn Dhurayl, who dedicated his life's work to the performing arts of Syria. The other is a documentary feature produced by the Ministries of Culture and Radio and Television that presents song and dance traditions across Syria with detailed descriptions of specific regional practices. As I demonstrate, the privileging of geographic space as a category for distinguishing between performance traditions is consonant with the secular, territorial modes of nationalism that prevailed in Syria in the second half of the twentieth century. These projects insert *dabke*, as a Syrian folk dance, into the national mythology of Syrian territory as the basis for political sovereignty. However, these projects also problematically reproduce the exclusion of Kurdish and other non-Arab groups from the Syrian polity by not including them, or the regions in which they primarily reside, in these accounts of Syrian cultural heritage. By upholding the marginalization and erasure of difference through a partial cultural geography of the nation, studies of cultural heritage are, I argue, not immune from the politics of statecraft that ensure the preservation of regime power. Instead, they sustain the political balance between the embrace and suppression of difference.

As a researcher in Syria, what I was able to access depended heavily on individual interest and willingness to support my research agenda. Word of mouth and individual recollection of past encounters with relevant research materials or events were key strategies for me to learn about possible sources. This was mostly due to the fact that archival collections of materials since the 1960s were not generally supported by Syrian state institutions, and most existing archival sources and cultural artifacts were part of private libraries, collections, or, occasionally, bookshops. As I asked around for materials on folk dance, the two sources most often recommended to me (by word of mouth) were those introduced earlier. The academic study by Ibn Dhurayl, largely published for his colleagues in the arts and humanistic sciences, was recommended by leaders in the arts, such as the director of the dance department at the Higher Institute of the Arts. The televised documentary, a state-sponsored documentary feature broadcast on state television as public education for viewers across Syria, was recommended to me by working artists and laypersons for whom the program was an authoritative source on folk culture. This difference is important for understanding the politics of researching and representing folk culture in the Syrian Arab Republic as well as how ethnographic authority is constructed and transmitted. The book and the televised program approach folk dance from similar perspectives, namely as an immutable cultural practice comprised of formal stylistic idioms that territorialize embodied performance to a fixed locale.

ʿAdnan ibn Dhurayl (1928–2000) was a widely respected scholar and performer who published several books and numerous essays on music, theater, art, and philosophy. He served in the Ministry of Culture, taught in Damascene schools, worked as a journalist, and actively participated in stage life as a folkloric dance director, choreographer, and musician.[14] His lifelong efforts centered on dance in ways that were indebted to al-Bustani and Kurd Ali's earlier writings on society and culture that provincialized social life as Arab (see chapter 1). Like his intellectual forefathers, his research conveys the value he places on knowledge production as a mechanism for establishing Syria's place in the history of civilization. His anthology of folk dance bears considerable weight as the most extensive study of Syrian *dabke* by a Syrian scholar and arts practitioner.

Ibn Dhurayl published *Raqs al-Samah wa-l-Dabkah: Tarikh wa-Tadwin* [*Raqs al-Samah* and *Dabke*: History and method] in 1996 with the Syrian Ministry of Culture. At once an intellectual history, ethnography, and cultural history, the publication is organized into two main sections that present *raqs al-samāḥ* and *dabke*, respectively. Each section begins with a historiographic overview of oral and written sources that situates each folk dance in broader discourses of Arab modernity, heritage, and authenticity. In the first half, Ibn Dhurayl presents *raqs al-samāḥ* as a Sufi-inspired genre adapted for the stage; in the second half, he situates *dabke* as a social dance practiced at wedding celebrations in village life across Syria. Important to the social function of *dabke*, according to Ibn Dhurayl, are the ritual events at which *dabke* is typically practiced. Though an in-depth analysis of the role of *dabke* in specific social rituals is not provided, nor is an account of which rituals include *dabke* and which do not, Ibn Dhurayl carefully denotes the ritual order of who leads, closes, and participates in the *dabke* circle. He documents the use of ritual objects such as kerchiefs or weaponry (swords, batons, etc.) in these ritual spaces. Also provided is a comprehensive lexicon of the movement idioms and techniques that constitute each genre, as well as transcriptions of modern choreographies of *raqṣ al-samāḥ* and local practices of *dabke*, respectively. By documenting the history and practice of these Syrian folk dances as such, Ibn Dhurayl affirms the value of movement as an expressive form of culture that engenders local and national identities.

In his account of *dabke*, Ibn Dhurayl ascribes the authority of the tradition to those who practice it in daily life, rather than to the staged folk dance troupes that he directed. This ascription of ethnographic authority, especially to the lead dancer, is commonplace — Nijat Qassab Hassan viewed *dabke* expertise similarly, as did many of the researchers cited in Ibn Dhurayl's study. Ibn Dhurayl describes the practice as "individual and spontaneous" (1969, 76; cf. 1996, 84), noting that "what gives one particular dance or *dabke* its unique quality and essence goes beyond the dictation of steps or of the footstomp" (1996, 99). Despite this prefatory remark, however, the study does not frame *dabke* as a dynamic, emergent, and iterative practice that is malleable in form and meaning. Rather, his objective is to catalog set patterns of footwork and describe the social function of *dabke* practice.

Ibn Dhurayl provides a catalog of fifty-eight styles of *dabke* practiced across Syria. Each entry provides the title and locale of the given *dabke* style, followed by a transcription of the footwork pattern (including variations). These transcriptions expand on an earlier summary of the primary idiomatic figures that characterize Syrian *dabke*, including the following: to set the foot in place (*zuḥun*), to tap (*niqra*), to cross (*badal*), to extend (*madd*), to raise (*rifaʿ*), or to pause (*ḥatt* or *iss*). In addition to identifying and naming specific movements, Ibn Dhurayl provides an annotated description of the characteristic features and attributes of each style, as well as their social function. He specifies, for example, when particular styles are considered men's or women's practices in ways that echo the work of Khanashat and al-Manini in moralizing *dabke* as a practice that cultivates personal virtue (as discussed in chapter 1). Relatedly, Ibn Dhurayl characterizes *dabke* styles as sober, happy, simple, and hoppy, respectively, in ways that affix emotional states onto movements in and of themselves, rather than situating affect in the social relations and structures at play in the *dabke* circle. What these various categories of analysis suggest is that the author approaches *dabke* as a definitive feature of Syrian culture to study, observe, and document.

One of the primary organizing principles of the catalog is that of place. Ibn Dhurayl was neither the first Syrian folklorist to ascribe specific locales to a given *dabke* style nor the first to organize a study of cultural traditions on the basis of regionality. In his extensive literature review, he cites Yusuf Musa Khanashat and Wajih Wabih al-Khoury's study of *dabke* on the Homs-Aleppo corridor (see chapter 1) as well as later studies that focused on the cultural traditions of specific provinces, such as Jabal al-Arab or Dayr al-Zur.[15] In contrast to this earlier scholarship, Ibn Dhurayl's anthology aims to comprehensively map out *dabke* styles across Syria. Among the fifty-eight entries, all but four include a reference to a specific town or a province in which the style is documented.[16]

The correlation of *dabke* style to locale is not a precise one-to-one relationship. Some communities are attributed with multiple styles, and some styles are documented in multiple locations. Tartous (a coastal city), for example, is associated with three distinct styles: *shiba al-tartous*, *shina al-tartous*, and *kurja al-tartous*. The *kurjat* style is documented in both Shaykh Badr and Midal (outside of Homs), in addition to Tartous. Likewise, the *walda* style is linked to Raqqa (*walida al-raqawiyya* and *walida al-raqqa*) in eastern Syria as well as Aleppo, a major city in northern Syria. Unfortunately, Ibn Dhurayl does not provide an explanation of his methodology or an interpretation of these findings that accounts for mobility in either naming practices or *dabke* styles. For him, what is important to convey is that "for the regions related to Syrian folk dance, especially *dabke*, these types are diverse and distinct" (Ibn Dhurayl 1996, 98).

Notably omitted from these regions of Syrian folk dance, however, are Damascus (the capital city of Syria) and the Hasakah province (the northeastern region bordering Turkey and Iraq). The omission of Damascus from an anthology of Syrian *dabkāt* is not altogether surprising. It reinforces the popular opinion that *dabke* is not indigenous to Syria's capital city, even though *dabke* is widely practiced in Damascus as a consequence of rural-urban migration as well as the historical development of urban leisure spaces. The reasons for the omission of Hasakah from a comprehensive anthology of Syrian folk dance are very likely political in nature and indicative of the pressure of regime politics on what is or is not published and presented in academic and cultural production.

In 1996, Hasakah was widely considered the most heterogeneous region in the Syrian Arab Republic, a border zone adjacent to Turkey and Iraq inhabited by mainly Arab and Kurdish communities who speak various dialects of Syrian Arabic, Kurdish, Turkish, and Iraqi Arabic. In the 2000s, it was under strict regime surveillance due to political strikes and riots by Kurdish activists and dissidents supporting the transnational struggle for Kurdish political and cultural sovereignty. These contestations were a continuation of the long-standing persecution of Kurdish communities, including their relocation and cultural dispossession by the regime. Somewhat paradoxical in this systematic repression was the inclusion of Kurdish folk dance at folk festivals across the country (Kastrinou 2016).[17] Perhaps reflecting this paradox, many individuals expressed to me, in private, their respect for the rich culture of Hasakah. Time and again, people recommended that I travel to the province to learn local folk dances (one arts instructor even facilitated an introduction to a Kurdish acting student), specifically *govend* (known as *halay* in Turkish), a social dance similar to but distinct from Arab *dabke*. Though their recommendations and the inclusion of Kurdish folk dance on national stages indicate widespread public awareness of Kurdish culture in 2008, Ibn Dhurayl neither mentioned *govend* nor included Hasakah in his 1996 survey of folk dance in Syria.

The reasons for this exclusion remain speculative. Perhaps Ibn Dhurayl committed this project specifically to Arab cultural traditions, implicitly or explicitly adhering to Arab nationalist ideology that excluded non-Arab ethnic minorities indigenous to the region. Perhaps he was beholden to the political exigencies of his publisher, the Ministry of Culture, led by the well-respected Najah al-Attar in the year of its publication (1996).[18] This branch of government maintains some degree of independence from the Ba'th Party and does not necessarily serve as a "mouthpiece" that "legitimates" regime power "in exchange for institutional support" (al-Saleh 2016). Nevertheless, there may have been some censorship criterion that the Ministry of Culture was obliged to uphold, specifically the prohibition on Kurdish cultural expression, intended to curb Kurdish sovereignty. Though the reasons for the occlusion of Hasakah from this anthology remain unknown, the effects are clear. The absence of Kurdish culture in this study perpetuates the erasure of Kurdish subjects within the national space demarcated as "Syria."

Beyond the specificities of the Kurdish predicament in Syria, there are other peculiar absences, erasures, and appearances in the study, particularly with regard to the representation of ethnicity and religion. Like Syrian Kurds, non-Arab ethnic groups with a historical presence in Syria, along with those who migrated into Syria in the early twentieth century (including Circassian, Armenian, and Jewish communities, among others), are omitted or at least not identified in terms of ethnicity. Religious identity is similarly not included as a category for *dabke* traditions. When religion does appear in the manuscript, Ibn Dhurayl explicitly links Sufism to *raqṣ al-samāḥ* as the historic antecedent of the devotional performance genre. By rendering religion as a historic influence rather than a contemporary social force (Shannon 2003), Ibn Dhurayl rehearses a maneuver common to secular nationalism, especially within Syria.[19] It is worth repeating that popular perceptions of the nexus of ethnicity, religion, and geography within Syria tend to associate specific ethnoreligious groups with distinct regions, even though microhistories attest to migration within and between these regions (Chatty 2017). Readers of the text familiar with Syria would likely extrapolate ethnoreligious identity from the markers of place that occur throughout the manuscript. Nevertheless, the opacity of ethnicity and religion in juxtaposition to the privileging of geographical difference attests to the secular and territorial constructions of nationalism that inform this scholarly work.

These representational politics further raise the broader question of whether and how the geography of Arabness extends beyond Syria in this project. The study is bereft of a sense of pan-Arabism that might ideologically link localities across Bilad al-Sham through performance traditions. Though *dabke* is practiced extensively across present-day Palestine, Jordan, and Lebanon, Ibn Dhurayl makes no mention of *dabke* practices beyond Syria or of how political borders and their crossings potentially shape knowledge and performance of *dabke* practice. In contrast to al-Manini's methods book on "Arab folk dance" that frames the "Arab village" as a unit of study (discussed in chapter 1), Ibn Dhurayl considers each "Syrian" village to be a distinct unit. This in and of itself is not surprising. Pan-Arabism had declined in its appeal following the end of Nasserism and the 1967 war with Israel, particularly in Syria, where there were political tensions between Arabists and Baʿthists. By the time that Ibn Dhurayl developed this project, the ideology of a pan-Arab subject or spaces promoted through shared linguistic and cultural heritage had generally been dispelled.

Nevertheless, Syrian *dabke* appears isolated in relation to its neighbors and their cultural heritage and anachronistic in relation to the political histories that delimit national boundaries and their crossings. For instance, several artistic directors of dance and entertainment companies referred to their own Palestinian identity and commented on the fact that multiple generations of dance directors were more often than not Palestinian.[20] They suggested that Syrian folkloric dance was indebted to the contributions of Palestinian dance professionals, a provocative suggestion given that Palestinians living in Syria (including those born and raised in Syria) do not receive full citizenship and are relegated to second-class residency status.

The study used empirical methods to essentialize social groups as historic givens that have a fixed relationship to place, a framework that I challenge in my approach to everyday *dabke* practices in chapter 3. It therefore performs a kind of cultural nationalism bound to the paradigm of the mosaic yet blind to the limits of that paradigm. Those limits are the exclusion of religious and ethnic minorities (especially Syrian Kurds); the occlusion of those with second-class political status (Palestinians); and a general approach that does not account for migration, historical change, and other social forces that shift the nexus of difference. In so doing, the project crafts a balance of representation that problematically perpetuates the status quo of how difference is managed in state-sponsored cultural production and that legitimizes territorial claims to political sovereignty. This is a balance that makes the nation seem eternal and unchanging, itself a cultural myth that fundamentally contributes to the preservation of regime power.

TELEVISED TRADITIONS

Turning now to a televised documentary on regional Syrian *dabke* traditions, I detail how this documentary continues the central ideological tenets of Ibn Dhurayl's scholarship while staging these performance practices in settings that further complicate the work of ethnographic authority. In the mid-2000s, Syrian state television broadcast *al-Ughaniyya al-Sha'biyya wa-l-Raqsat al-Sha'biyya* (Traditional songs and traditional dances), an educational program on traditional Syrian performance culture. Targeting urban, middle-class viewers across Syria, it appeared on a series dedicated to cultural heritage, *Safhat min al-Turath* (Pages from heritage) on the channel Syria Tanni (literally: Syria Two), under the administration of the Ministry of Radio and Television.[21] The television program stemmed from the pedagogical impulse to teach the Syrian public about their common yet distinct forms of cultural heritage and to inculcate citizenly virtue through the exhibition of cultural heritage. It assumed that, as Nijat Qassab Hassan and his contemporaries in the 1950s had predicted and as Salma Qassab Hassan insisted decades later, urban Syrians needed "to get in touch with the folk, especially when they no longer experience it or have access to it."[22]

The program was the single (to the best of my knowledge) official presentation of *dabke* traditions that strove to represent cultural practices in the context of in situ social spaces rather than as theatricalized adaptations into folkloric dance. Indeed, explicit attention was brought to the influence of folk dance troupes on *dabke* traditions when the program's narrators contrasted several traditional styles with the development of "derived" forms presented by folklore troupes, which they framed as expressions of "modern" identity based on the "scientific" study of song and dance forms (*tashkīl*). The program was part of broader efforts to catalog and display everyday practices through a "logic of exhibition" (Kirshenblatt-Gimblett 1998) that dominated displays of Syrian cultural heritage. Spaces such as the National Museum for Popular Culture, located in Al Azem Palace in Old Damascus, exhibited ethnographic artifacts such as Arab coffeemakers (*dalla*) and embroidered dresses. However, by detaching artifacts from their lived contexts and placing them in ahistorical displays, the museum failed to communicate the vibrancy of cultural meanings and social values that enmeshed the life of the coffeemakers and dresses. These "poetics of detachment," elaborates Barbara Kirshenblatt-Gimblett, reveal a process by which ethnographic display "accepts the inherently fragmented nature of the object . . . which stands in contiguous relation to an absent whole that may or may not be recreated" (1998, 18). This logic structured most (if not all) state-sponsored productions of cultural heritage in Syria, from the Idlib Festival to this television documentary.

The documentary organized Syrian performance traditions into three sections: *al-Ughaniyya al-Shaʿbiyya* (Traditional songs), *al-Raqsat al-Shaʿbiyya* (Traditional dances), and *al-Dabkat al-Shaʿbiyya* (Traditional *dabkāt*). The *dabke* program presented twelve styles practiced across Syria through a combination of narration and staged performances set in a "real" mis-en-scène. The narrators (male and female, speaking in Modern Standard Arabic) provided brief ethnographic descriptions of each traditional style, summarized in table 2.1. In general the descriptions adhered to the same empirical framings of style and genre demonstrated in Ibn Dhurayl's anthology. The descriptions presented *dabke* styles as fixed patterns of codified movement that emphasized signature idiomatic figures and formations as well as pace and accompanying song genres and instruments. A place of origin was ascribed to half of the twelve styles and was generally presented on a regional scale. Like Ibn Dhurayl's anthology, it was a partial list of regions that occluded ethnic and religious identity markers. The narrators did not provide information about the curatorial process through which these particular traditions, out of dozens practiced nationwide, were selected for exhibition.

TABLE 2.1 Twelve *Dabkāt* Featured in *al-Ughaniyya al-Shaʿbiyya wa-l-Raqṣāt al-Shaʿbiyya wa-l-Dabkāt al-Shaʿbiyya* (Traditional songs and traditional dances and traditional *Dabkāt*)

1. *Dabke al-Umayya* (Greater Syria): This authentic *dabke* is from Syrian heritage. A light *dabke* for girls and boys, it is accompanied by *mijwiz*, *aghūl*, and *ṭabl*.

2. *Dabke Fatuma* (unspecified locale): This *dabke* is accompanied by song in 4/2 meter until the wedding processional begins, after which it conforms to the natural rhythms of processional movement.

3. *Dabke al-Anaba* (unspecified locale): This *dabke* is simple and traditional and correlates with the meaning of musical phrases in 4/4 meter. Dancers begin in two lines facing each other, form a half-circle when the vocals enter, then return to the line formation. It is performed for family events or festive occasions.

4. *Dabke al-Marfudh* (Dayr al-Zur): This is a heavy, slow style that resembles the hextuplet sequence of *dabke al-ʿarabiyya*. It is accompanied by *mizmār* or *ṭabl* and performed in a half-circle formation.

5. *Dabke Shams* (unspecified locale): This *dabke* is distinctive for the movement in the torso, belly, and shoulders.

6. *al-Asmar al-Lawn* (Aleppo and Idlib): This *dabke* occurs in various formations. It is often performed with the traditional *qudud* songs of Aleppo.

7. *Dabke al-Zawja al-ʿArabiyya* (Aleppo): This is an Aleppo-based style based on *raqṣ al-ʿarabiyya* and *shaykhānī* styles. It is performed at marriages and considered agile, quick, and wide.

8. *Dabke al-Hawrani* (unspecified locale): Perhaps the most widespread and ubiquitous style known, this *dabke* occurs as a simple hextuplet pattern that occurs in two formations, processional and with a knee bend. It starts to the front and may include shoulder contractions.

9. *Dabke Daʿuna* (Greater Syria; possibly Damascus): Widespread throughout all regions of Syria though its origins are likely from Damascus, this *dabke* occurs in a hextuplet pattern in correspondence with the song "ʿAla Daʿuna" and is distinguished by the foot stomp figure as well as steps in place.

10. *Dabke Shaykh Badr* (unspecified governate): This is a slow, hextuplet pattern performed in half-circle or opposing line formations among girls and boys. It is distinguished by a knee bend that resembles the *nakha* figure.

11. *Dabke Hamawiyya* (Hama): This *dabke* is performed with 8/8 meter and features knee bends, footstomps, and occasionally walking in place.

12. *Dabke Farq* (unspecified locale): Girls and boys participate in this choreography, in which instrumentalists and percussionists perform in the middle of the dance circle.

Animating each of these descriptions were short demonstrations of each *dabke* tradition, performed by a group of men and women dressed in traditional attire, that aimed to be congruent with the place of origin (if provided). (For excerpts from the documentary, see CLIP 2.4a, CLIP 2.4b, and CLIP 2.4c on the companion website.) *Dabkāt* from Aleppo, for instance, were presented in the traditional courtyard of a *bayt ʿarabī* (Arabic house), a historic style of architecture specific to urban Syria. Others were staged in outdoors environments, such as the performance of *dabke hamawiyya* (of Hama) on a hill overlooking a valley. The narrators explained that stylistic distinctions between *dabke* traditions are strongly correlated to the climates in which each tradition is practiced. They stated, for example, that the cold mountains of Hama yielded "quick" movements, whereas the warm desert of Dayr al-Zur yielded "steady" or "heavy" movements. This evolutionary paradigm assumes bodies are naturalized to their physical environments in ways that shape intergenerational cultural practices, and remains a popular theory (Traboulsi 1996). Despite these claims, the actual locations of some of the demonstrations were incongruent with the stated place of origin. Of particular note was a demonstration staged in the ruins of Apamea, an ancient Greek and Roman city that overlooks the Orontes River valley near Hama. The archaeological site is generally valued for its lengthy colonnade and theater, one of the largest in the Roman world.[23] The dancers performed against the backdrop of an archaic stone wall in ways that juxtaposed dance and archaeology as forms of Syrian cultural heritage, albeit incongruently. In so doing, this demonstration echoed one of the central pedagogical tenets undergirding the performance and presentation of folk dance, that of Syria's unique contribution to the history of world civilization. This lesson was aimed at Syrians as much as the global community.

Frequently recommended to me as the authoritative source on Syrian *dabke* by people from different social circles, this documentary carried weight and authority as a project sponsored by the Ministry of Culture and broadcast on state television. It was a continuation of the public educational programming on cultural heritage that Nijat Qassab Hassan, ʿAdnan al-Manini, and ʿAdnan ibn Dhurayl began cultivating in the mid-twentieth century. Like the Idlib Festival, it strove to bridge social and cultural boundaries by teaching Syrians about each other's traditions. The program also elevated and classicized *dabke* traditions by emplacing regional *dabke* practices within UNESCO World Heritage Sites. Yet the official narrative that it transmitted fundamentally upheld the logic of multicultural domination that this chapter has probed. The projects discussed throughout this chapter varied in terms of their medium and their audience, including a live embodied performance for local audiences, an academic study that archived movement practices for intellectuals and artists, and a television program that presented these practices for the mainstream public. Despite differences in the mode of communication, they reinforced the same ideological biases and exclusions and perpetuated the balance of subnational difference that avoided making mention of ethnic, religious, and other identity markers that potentially destabilized political power. Together, they rehearsed the secular and territorial forces of nationalism on which Ba'thism was predicated and ensured the terms of public discourse through which Syrians recognized their differences.

The broader context in which these projects were distributed and performed bears further examination, particularly in the domain of cultural production and cultural heritage. As described in the introduction of this chapter, the regime undertook a significant investment in boosting the tourism industry as well as the arts sectors of urban Syria, primarily Damascus. From the ancient temple of Palmyra to Old Damascus, the state rehabilitated heritage sites and installed infrastructure to support international tourist routes. At the same time, the state also pursued the development of cultural heritage through festivals such as the 2008 DACC festival. Given the state-led directive to reimagine historic sites and cultural practices from contemporary perspectives and interests, to what extent did Syrian choreographers working during this period consider new interpretations of *dabke* traditions? I now return to the DACC festival as a case study in the directions and horizons of contemporary cultural production to ask if and how *dabke* was presented on the festival's stages.

THE INVISIBILITY OF DANCE HERITAGE

In the early 2000s, dance worlds in Syria were caught up in the struggle for new cultural horizons under emergent neoliberalism. In a 2005 interview with the *New York Times*, First Lady Asma al-Assad "winced" when asked about a dance theater (*raqs masrah*) production presented at Dar al-Assad (the Opera House): "I think there was a lot of talent . . . [but] I don't think it portrayed what Syria is, in any era."[24] Dance theater was beloved by many Syrians, for whom its mélange of gymnastics, acrobatics, ballet, and folkloric dance, along with its spectacular light, sound, and set designs, appealingly narrated epic myths of ancient Arabia. Despite the strength of the dance theater industry, Assad's hesitation to mark Syrian national identity through dance theater (and by extension, dance) conveys the ambivalence among the political and cultural elites over how to uphold symbols of cultural heritage while also conceiving new national imaginaries. Some choreographers chose not to pursue the question of national identity; others recognized that national identity was shifting but failed to envision how that shift might take place in terms of dance.

When I interviewed contemporary choreographers based in Damascus in the 2000s about whether and how they drew on *dabke* for artistic material, they explained that they were more interested in art for art's sake and turned to modern dance, jazz, and ballet styles. They tended to eschew local expressions and traditions in favor of Western dance styles that positioned contemporary dance on the Syrian stage and contemporary Syrian dance on the Western stage.[25] Generally, dance was seen by this generation less as a means for cultural tutelage or public service for audiences (the older Baʿthist model) and more as a domain for personal expression and artistic talent (the more contemporary neoliberal model). Choreographers were careful to differentiate their work from the state-sponsored folkloric dance ensembles associated with official national culture and seemed to measure the distance between their work and this culture industry through *dabke*, thereby refusing to engage with *dabke* on an artistic or social register. Young dancers who trained during this period were similarly alienated by *raqṣ shaʿbiyya*, noting that it lacked innovation and creativity.[26]

Though the rising stars of the contemporary dance world generally lacked a cohesive vision about how contemporary dance might best represent a national community and who might be represented by contemporary Syrian dance, this world reached its zenith in the years immediately prior to 2011. Trained in classical ballet, dance theater, modern, jazz, and tango, among other contemporary styles, choreographers Alaa Krimid, Eyas Al Mokdad, and the late Lawand Hajo came of age during the period of economic liberalization, founded their own dance companies, and toured their productions regionally and internationally.[27] They represented the first generation of graduates who studied with Metaz Malatialy, then director of dance at the Higher Institute of Dramatic Arts in Damascus.[28] They were influenced by world-class artists such as Akram Khan, who offered workshops and exposure to international dance networks during his visit to the DACC festival. These visionaries built a diverse landscape for dance that reflected their training in Europe and Russia, respectively, and that sought to both inspire and entertain audiences. The scene expanded further when artistic director Mey Seifan launched the Damascus Contemporary Dance Platform in 2009. This festival cultivated emerging local talent while strengthening regional connections with artists working in Lebanon, Jordan, Palestine, and North Africa. By jumping onto the world's stage and suggesting a veneer of cosmopolitanism in the creative economy, contemporary dance reinforced the neoliberal imaginaries of Bashar al-Assad's economic reform.

While the country underwent a cultural renaissance, however, this surge in creative output arguably retained cronyism that, as in other sectors of economic liberalization, helped to make authoritarianism resilient to change. As Caroline Donati writes, the regime "convey[ed] the impression of openness but in reality penalize[d] reformist aspirations . . . viewed as a threat by the ruling coalition" (2013, 26). Donati argues that economic liberalization "renewed" rather than "reformed" existing patronage networks, including those that sustained authoritarian frameworks for repression and co-optation. Cultural production, like other economic sectors, reinforced and consolidated wealth and elitism. For instance, cultural entrepreneurs established arts organizations and initiatives that politically profited the regime, and the regime supported artists who helped to convey a positive image of Syria that corresponded with Western social and cultural norms (Weiss 2013). Neoliberal expansion in entertainment, fashion, and leisure enabled increased access to mass media and transnational networks of cultural production while also consolidating media wealth among the business elite (Haddad 2011). And though cultural production generally performed the liberal ethos of multiculturalism, it continued to be censored by the state (Della Ratta 2018).

As first lady, Asma al-Assad supported many of the efforts in the 2000s to revitalize cultural production, especially in the tourist sector. Old Damascus in particular was the site of major renovation as part of efforts to attract international tourism. Historic homes were renovated into popular restaurants and boutique hotels, and infrastructure was rehabilitated to construct the aesthetic of the late nineteenth-century Ottoman era. In 2006 Assad formed a planning team made up of artists, writers, poets, the minister of culture, and the minister of education to brainstorm the 2008 festival.[29] The DACC festival curated values of balance, harmony, and tolerance that extended geographically as far as Iraq and historically as deep as Mesopotamia. The curatorial team (composed of executive director Dr. Hanan Qassab Hassan and several emerging artist-curators, including Jumana al-Yasiri and Mohammad al-Attar) embraced an ethics of inclusivity for ethnic groups typically excluded from the main stage.

Given the breadth of cultural traditions, geographies, and histories articulated at the DACC festival, one particular performance tradition remained strikingly absent from the festival stages: *raqṣ shaʿbiyya*. According to the festival's executive director, Dr. Qassab Hassan, folkloric dance, specifically *dabke*, was in a "crisis" that forced her to strike it from her ambitious efforts to integrate Syrian cultural heritage into music, literature, film, and drama.[30] (She did not suggest that *dabke* was omitted because it is not considered indigenous to Damascus.) The crisis, she elaborated, emerged during the curatorial process. Despite their deep family history of engagement with folkloric dance, Dr. Qassab Hassan and her sister, Salma, maintained that then-current productions of *raqṣ shaʿbiyya* were not authentic representations of social dance in Syria. She tried to identify a choreographer who would accept a commission to reimagine *dabke* for the DACC initiative, but these efforts were futile.[31] Stigmatized and avoided by artists, *dabke* was clearly an object of ambivalence in what some called the "Golden Era" of Syrian cultural production. The national performance tradition of *dabke* was ultimately excluded from the yearlong program of a festival that celebrated and honored Syrian arts and culture.[32]

This exclusion is indicative of how much the Baʿthist promise of populist socialism had faded for those who came of age in the era of economic liberalization. The populist aesthetics of socialist realism were fatiguing for young choreographers with professional aspirations grounded in concert dance and oriented to Western cultural modernity. Leaders in the arts and culture sector looked to refresh cultural production with sophisticated and cosmopolitan aesthetics that projected the image of a country opening up to an increased flow of capital in a more liberal market economy. Ultimately, however, this period was more fleeting than anyone could have predicted. With the rapid collapse of social stability after 2011, this generation of choreographers largely dispersed. Some moved to the Gulf, others to neighboring countries and later to Europe, with some remaining in Syria or moving back once this became a viable option for them. What set of meanings and opportunities *raqṣ shaʿbiyya* will offer to those living in postconflict Syria remains to be seen.

———

Symbols of nationhood were under intense debate in the 2000s as the Syrian regime enacted economic liberalization policies and as regional tensions exacerbated economic and political precarities. Syrian political and cultural elites aspired to update their national image with sophisticated and cosmopolitan forms of cultural expression that projected the image of a country opening up to an increased flow of capital and a new repertoire of aesthetic constructs. They distanced themselves from territorial and fatigued models of cultural national- ism, even though these models continued to be widely popular among the general public. Part of the struggle to generate national imaginaries that appealed to all sectors of Syrian society was due to the fact that, as Yassin al-Haj Saleh (2017) argues, nationalist propaganda in general was monopolized by the regime and there was a dearth of ideas about how to approach national imaginaries. The regime, he continues, presented nationalist ideology in "vague" rhetoric that "conceal[ed] and suppresse[d] a generally divisive atmosphere" (225).

Performances of cultural heritage were not immune to these issues. As I have demonstrated in this chapter, dominant forms of nationalism rippled through folk dance at the local and national levels, reproducing colonialist ideologies of identity and difference. Performances constructed national imaginaries of Syria as a collection of territorialized communities whose cartography neatly reinforced the association of political administrative units (governates) with entrenched forms of minority consciousness. Through staged performances of *raqs sha'biyya*, as well as in educational materials that surveyed *dabke* traditions across Syria, *dabke* became an ethnographic object for display and consumption by the citizen-subjects of the Syrian polity. Though state-sponsored folkloric dance provided opportunities for Syrians to relate to one another across their geographical differences, as the singular model for cultural nationalism through dance it foreclosed the possibility of finding alternative ways of imagining dance heritage. These possibilities have recently emerged as an effect of forced migra- tion, as I explore in my final chapter.

Part I of this book has traced the historic formation and continued develop- ment of folkloric dance, situating these histories in the political ideologies that inform them. At stake with these performances and archives of performance were the ideological constructions of subnational difference and internal Otherness that underpinned them. Whereas the first chapter considered the role of the female peasant subject in relation to Ba'thist Party ideology and the efforts of the nationalist elite to manage practices of cultural citizenship in public life, the second chapter has focused on the role of folkloric dance in reinforcing which social groups are legitimate within Assadist ideology and statecraft. Aligning cultural difference with provincial regions, as evidenced at the Idlib Festival and in educational materials, is, I argued, part of the regime's strategy for statecraft that espouses a territorial model of pluralism within Syria while occluding mar- ginalized and discriminated against religious and ethnic communities.

PART II

Everyday Performance

INTERLUDE

Syria in the 2000s

In 2000 Hafiz al-Assad passed away, and the mantle of authoritarian leadership was transferred to his son, Bashar al-Assad. Many welcomed this transition because they viewed Bashar and his British-born wife, Asma al-Assad, as a modern, young couple with children who would bring fresh perspectives to a stagnant and beleaguered society. Syria was in an economic crisis when its father figure passed. Poverty had increased while the standard of living had decreased in a sluggish economy with insufficient employment opportunities. Though attempts to reduce dependence on oil revenue had been initiated in the mid-1980s, the economy was still oil dependent. Those who thrived in these conditions were the political and business elites, whose relationship had become increasingly cozier due to the regime's approach to economic policies in the three decades under Hafiz al-Assad. Specifically, the regime turned to the private sector in the mid-1980s to generate revenue, promising to drive it out of stagnancy through patronage relations with the political elite (including seats in parliament and increased access to that elite). Over two decades, political and business interests became more aligned and dependent, as the political elite needed the private sector to create jobs, generate foreign exchange to compensate for lost oil revenues, and stimulate the economy. Yet the private sector was not autonomous. It faced complicated regulations, fear of asset seizure, and suppressions by the regime for not following through on bargains with politicians.

After Bashar al-Assad became president in 2000, he expanded existing economic liberalization policies that made wealth more mobile and transnational yet still consolidated among the business and political elites (Haddad 2011). Though not new, kinship between the regime and business partners, including but not limited to the Sunni business elite, was doubly secured. In addition to increased wealth, the Assad regime redistributed political, economic, and security privileges to benefit prominent government officials, members of the upper and upper-middle classes, and modern-day technocrats (Siham 2022). The regime relied on these businesspersons, who in turn demonstrated their loyalty to the regime. While ordinary Syrians struggled to stretch their *lirāt* (Syrian currency) to accommodate the rising cost of food and housing staples, with many taking second jobs to cover the increasing cost of living, those who benefited from economic liberalization invested their wealth in luxury lifestyles and properties. Not only did the "new neoliberal elite" (Terc 2011) aspire to a cosmopolitan lifestyle that maximized pleasure through acts of conspicuous consumption, they also sought to achieve it through political networks that assured them of "domestic security and a sovereign national identity" (Wedeen 2013, 843). Some members of this social class would later become the "silent middle," or those who quietly supported the regime in the face of protests and war in the 2010s (Wedeen 2019). The entanglement of business and politics, and the seemingly contradictory trajectories of business and politics, wherein market freedoms expanded and political freedoms became more constrained, produced a number of disjunctures in the everyday life of Damascene residents and displaced many to the urban periphery.

In addition to policy changes, the state refreshed the fatigued rhetoric of socialism and Arab nationalism by rebranding the newer generation of the Assad family as reform minded, contemporary, and enlightened. Newly chic party slogans such as "God, Syria, and Bashar" served as vehicles for love and devotion to the young autocrat. A "new appetite in the country for celebrating 'Syrianness'" found audiences through reality television shows and *musalsalāt* (television dramas), which boomed in the mid- to late 2000s (Al-Ghazzi 2013). Nostalgia for the late Ottoman era took form in the renovation of numerous restaurants, hotels, and tourist retail shops in Old Damascus, intended to recreate this nostalgic sheen and boost the international tourist sector (Salamandra 2004). Meanwhile, new wealth appeared throughout the city and its suburbs as Assad expanded the market for luxury goods, internationalized finance, opened the stock exchange, and generally recalibrated consumer expectations towards global forms of neoliberalism. At the same time that he reformed the economy, however, Assad faced resistance to opening up political dialogue from within his Ba'th Party. He negotiated this resistance by concentrating his presidential powers and relying on the coercive tactics of the security apparatus and the army to dispel the "Damascus Spring," a brief period in which political salons and declarative mandates were allowed to circulate. This economic-political dyad pinned individual desires for socioeconomic mobility to the cronyism and repressive tactics of the regime, asserting "two contradictory logics of rule" that Lisa Wedeen critiques as "neoliberal autocracy" (2013).

Neoliberalism redefined the relationship between state, society, and the economy. The older populist-authoritarian model represented an alliance between the army, peasants, workers, the Baʿth Party, and the public sector. It also formulated a layer of protection from market fluctuations by nationalizing industries and the distribution of goods. These policies and regulations produced a strong middle-class sector with a robust state bureaucracy and public sector. The regime could neither extract wealth from these groups nor accumulate capital. The newer model favored the economic interests of the urban classes, economic elites, and regime officials. It attempted to maintain compatibility with, or at least to not discredit, the Baʿthist social policies of the previous decades (1970–2000). The regime attempted to establish continuity by designing a set of public narratives about the economy intended to help ordinary Syrians make sense of the rapid economic changes that they experienced. These narratives focused on issues of personal responsibility, the central role of the private sector in economic development, decreasing dependence on the state for social welfare, and greater integration of Syria into regional and global economies through trade liberalization (Abboud 2015). The narratives paired the rhetoric of social welfare and protections that was paramount to Baʿthism with the benefits of liberalization and marketization. One major difference, however, was that instead of promoting the redistribution of wealth (as the land reform of the 1950s did), these policies stressed capital accumulation.

Economic liberalization was not in and of itself a new policy—Hafiz al-Assad had already accommodated a stronger private sector since the mid-1980s. These newer policies of economic liberalization continued his efforts to shift Syria's fiscal independence away from oil revenues (which had been nearly half of all budgetary revenues in the 1990s). But the rapidity and degree of change that brought the private sector parallel rather than secondary to the public sector were significant. Some of the more impactful policies included the rapid decline of agricultural subsidies, new land laws that reoriented ownership and usage rights away from the cooperative models of previous decades, and government incentives for "strategic crops" instead of a diverse production of crops. The effects of these policies were detrimental. Agricultural productivity declined, and government attention turned towards nonagricultural sectors of the economy, especially communications and tourism.

Many Syrians were negatively impacted by economic liberalization. Many actively felt a sense of neglect, especially those with ties and dependencies in rural areas and agricultural production. Along with others, they felt betrayed as these had historically been the Ba'th Party's primary social and economic basis of support. Many turned to nongovernmental sources of social welfare, primarily offered by religious establishments and organizations. Expressions of piety, primarily Muslim but also Christian, became increasingly part of public life and strengthened the political power of religious authorities, forcing the regime to accommodate a stronger role for Islamic religious leaders in political administration.

Exacerbating these conditions and responses was the gradual movement of rural migrants into urban peripheries, leading to an internal migration of 1.5 million people between 2006 and 2010. About 20 percent of the Syrian population lived in urban slums by the late 2000s, with urban populations increasing by 50 percent during this period. Many moved to escape the effects of long-term drought, which especially affected Eastern Syria. Due to warming (0.2 degrees Celsius change) and 10 percent less precipitation over the course of the century, groundwater was depleted. Meanwhile, cotton exports were encouraged, which meant that irrigation was prioritized for export crops over domestic agricultural products. These conditions led to the loss of livestock, a plunge in the amount of crops, and doubling of food prices throughout the country.

In addition to crises within Syria, regional and global dynamics also strained everyday life for most Syrians. When Bashar al-Assad inherited the presidency, Syria had just emerged from a collapsed peace process with Israel. Relations with its neighbors Turkey and Iraq were somewhat hostile, and Syria maintained influence in Lebanon through military occupation initiated at the start of the Lebanese Civil War in 1975. After 9/11, some of these dynamics shifted. Syria entered into "brotherly" relations with Turkey. The regime supported opposition to the US-led occupation of Iraq, especially as 1.6 million Iraqis crossed the border into Syria to flee the occupation and ensuing conflict. Though they were welcomed in official state discourse as well as by local communities, their displacement raised rent prices in urban areas and stressed already high prices for everyday groceries and household needs. Following the assassination of former Lebanese prime minister Rafik Hariri on February 14, 2005, Syria withdrew its occupying forces from Lebanon while deepening its ties to Hizbullah. The Hariri assassination frayed US-Syrian relations, prompting the departure of the US ambassador several days later and triggering tensions that lasted for several years. In 2008 American teachers, students, and exchange programs were pushed out of Syria because of these strained relations.

The suppression of political dissent continued throughout this decade. With the transition in leadership in 2000, casual political forums sprouted up in private homes and a manifesto of political demands was released. The short-lived "Damascus Spring" was quickly suppressed by Bashar al-Assad's regime, which closed the salons and imprisoned forum organizers and participants. The regime also increased surveillance of Kurdish political activity, including a crackdown on a 2004 event in Qamishli, a city near the Turkish border in Syria's northeast governate of Hasakah. In addition to quashing political opposition, the regime maintained repressive tactics towards its civilians, whom it continued to intimidate and manipulate into complicity.

Syria in the 2000s was a globalizing nation eager to embrace the circulation of goods, markets, and ideas from which it had long been isolated. It was also an autocracy, one that advanced the "good life" under the condition that political liberties and civil rights would remain severely compromised. To reiterate, this brand of "neoliberal autocracy" was not entirely novel for Syrians in the 2000s, as there had been a slow trickle of liberalization for fifteen years or so prior with no changes in the security and intelligence branches of the regime. But what was exceptional about this decade was the erosion of the fundamental principles of Ba'thism that had ensured loyalty to the state by its citizens. Without the solidity of the cultural and belief system of Ba'thism, especially the provision of social welfare in exchange for paternalistic authoritarianism, Syria became poised for unrest.

RESEARCH NOTES

Whereas the previous two chapters were primarily based on interviews, rehearsals, and performances with those in the dance and music industries, the next two chapters are primarily based on social events in everyday life in a period from 2004 to 2008. My research benefited directly from neoliberalization because I was able to observe and participate in what some have called a "Golden Age" of cultural production. State-directed support for new projects, initiatives, and performance spaces catalyzed a fresh creative synergy among artists and performers across artistic disciplines. The growth of the entertainment sector provided new opportunities for professional music and dance, both in theaters and in the booming restaurant sector. The Ministry of Culture permitted performance in public spaces with the celebration of the Francophone Fête de la Musique and with a performance series, "Music on the Street." Even as these changes stimulated cultural production in Damascus and other cultural hubs, social dance and popular music occupied a separate industry, which was generally referred to as *sha'bī* (popular or street culture).

I was based primarily in Damascus and made regular extended visits to specific village communities. All of these visits were made possible by invitations through friends and acquaintances. A few rare encounters began in a taxi or *servees* (shared van service) and ended up in open-ended interviews and music sessions or invitations to wedding events. The *sha'bī* industry is the primary focus of chapters 3 and 4, with the other efforts and activities remaining in the background of these chapters, though I do address in chapter 4 the tension between the commercial music favored by gentrifying Damascus and the *sha'bī* music that was muted in these neoliberal spaces of consumption. It is in these two chapters that the methods of bimusicality and technique factor most prominently, as I draw extensively on my experience as a participant on the dance floor as well as on my experience as a musician and listener.

THREE

Floating Rhythms

"What a pleasure to be with all of you. Okay everyone, now it's time for *dabke!* For those girls and boys who love the dance floor, please come on down. *Yalla!* [Let's go!]" With a flourish, the *muṭrib* (wedding singer and, often, the MC) invited participants to start the dancing segment at a November 2007 wedding *ḥafla* (literally: party, typically with dance music and refreshments) in Latakia, a coastal region in northern Syria. Behind him, musicians started an instrumental *taqsīm* (improvisatory musical form) that would establish the atmosphere for the dance session, held in the banquet hall of a restaurant. The keyboardist added a drone, above which floated melodic motifs in the shrill timbral register of the *mizmār* (reed instrument), played as a digital preset on the org in the upper register pitches of *maqām rāst*.[1] The *ṭabl* (double-barreled drum) player pounded his drum with a steady beat and ornamental fills as he strode around the dance floor. My host (the brother of the bride) and friends grinned as we sat at our banquet table, all of us excited to share in the celebrations and experience the dance music set. (View footage of this event on the companion website at CLIPS 3.1a–c.)

As people joined the dance floor, I turned my attention to the front of the *shakl dāʾira* (*dabke* circle). A young man, sharply dressed in a popular urban street style of jeans, collared shirt, and pointy leather shoes, raised his arms high. His right hand clasped a *misbaḥa* (chain of rosary beads), and his left hand joined with the hand of another fellow next to him in line. Each of them was clearly a *dabbik*, skilled in the arts of the movement tradition. Together, they shook their shoulders back and forth (*hiz*) in synchrony with the *ṭabl* drummer, who accelerated the pulse of his drumming as he moved forward in the *ḥalqa* (open space of performance) to improvise *ḥarakāt* (movements) with them. The *muṭrib* noticed their energy and called for people to turn their attention to the leader (*awwal*, literally: first) of the *dabke* line: "Hey look! The *awwal* is going! Look, everyone!"

I was mesmerized by the ensuing performance, especially how the *dabbikūn* dissolved my sense of rhythmic time through their interpretation of the drummer's strokes. The *awwal* suspended his movements across multiple beat patterns, creating a series of dramatic poses. He dropped excessively low to the ground, then raised his body up high—all in a slow, deliberate pace that generated a liminal sense of time while entrained to the beat of the *ṭabl* drummer. The *dabbik* next to him, in a role known as *tānnī* (literally: second), accompanied him by shadowing his movements without executing them in their full realization. The relatively slow pace of the *mizmār* and *ṭabl* instruments were typical for the start of the dance set, which tends to begin with slower performance genres before gradually building towards faster ones. Together, they generated a sense of adrenaline, focus, and anticipation that quieted the atmosphere of the event as everyone turned to watch their performance.

Similar to but different from the *dabbik* of Sawran that I described in the book's introduction, the *awwal* and *tānnī* at this wedding party in Latakia floated over and across the rhythms of the *ṭabl* drummer. The synergy of their performance emerged from how they aligned movements with the beat patterns and yet exceeded the bounds of rhythmic precision through the flow of one movement to the next, all of which created a floating effect. A trope that evokes the energetics of the practice, floating embodies what performance studies scholar Mady Schutzman describes as "the paradox of 'flow,' [in which] a complex pleasure derives from effortless movement just on the brink of a breakdown" (2006, 278–95). Western understandings of flow states, popularized by Mihaly Csikszentmihalyi (1990), consider this a psychological experience that occurs when the self loses consciousness in the very process of expanding its boundaries, typically while doing an activity such as reading, painting, or physical exercise. The flow states of *dabke*, I counter, are intersubjective, that is, between and among participants.[2] Flow states are less about the talent and skills of the individual *dabbik* and more about how *dabbikūn* move in relation to one another, such as how the *awwal* and *tānni* balanced with one another as well as the drummer. They are also about how dancers position their bodies in relation to the sounds of *dabkāt*. How *dabbikūn* achieve a flow state is therefore not so much about individual footwork or rhythmic patterns as about the "corporeal conditions of possibility"

(Wells 2021, 9) that emerge through listening, moving, and negotiating bodies in a given social space.[3]

In what follows, I explore how flow states emerge through the tensions and dynamics of corporeality in performance, from a sense of balance and the distribution of weight between dancers to the ways that improvisatory interactions take place through sensorial listening to dance rhythms. I also account for my own corporeal experiences on the dance floor as I listen and move alongside others, a sensation that dance ethnologist Deirdre Sklar theorizes as "empathic kinesthetic perception," or noticing how it "feel[s] . . . to be in the other's body moving" (2001, 32). Corporeality is a means to understand the experiential and sensory forms of cultural competence and embodied knowledge possessed by others, a key objective pursued in the fields of ethnomusicology (Spiller 2010) and dance ethnography (Reed 1998), among others that privilege ethnographic fieldwork.[4]

My phenomenological approach to *dabke* practice draws on and is informed by music and sound studies that approach listening as a corporeal and affective set of interactions with vibrational sounds that mediate social structures (Eidsheim 2015; Kapchan 2017). Inspired in part by percussionist Evelyn Glennie, whose deafness encouraged her to embrace tactility and visuality as grounding sensations in her percussion practice in ways that unsettle the primacy of aurality in listening, I account for the many sensory domains through which sonic vibrations are perceived.[5] Following this turn in music and sound studies also helps to dislocate a Eurocentric emphasis on visuality in dance studies by asserting that dancing is a listening practice. Sound and performance studies have also reckoned with how the sensate body is not a universal subject, but rather differentiated by long-standing discourses on the body as well as the politics, economics, and histories that subjugate certain bodies while privileging others (Brooks and Kheshti 2011). My framing of *dabke* as an embodied "choreosonic" (Crawley 2017) practice, one that delights in rather than stigmatizes the complexity of bodily phenomena, strives to amplify the corporeality of rhythmic aesthetics as these map onto the moving body. *Dabke*, in turn, is significant for modeling approaches to embodied performance and cultural expression that play with the relationality of the senses.

Embedded in the embodied poetics and playful pleasures of *dabke* circles is the "social life" of performance (Turino 2008). In particular, this chapter attunes to the gendered dynamics of performance that emerge in *dabke* circles, focusing on the performance and production of masculinity. While these dynamics vary widely across social spaces (each differentiated by region, religion, social class, and local codes of conduct, among other social forces), young men display and flaunt their bodies through *dabke* performance in ways that produce a masculine subject as distinct from feminine subjectivity.[6] Comparable techniques of embodied masculinity include paying attention to hair and bodily care, displaying fashion sense, walking with an "alert and aware" disposition, and other acts of self-expression that locally and historically situate the "male body as a social product and producer of social life" (Ghannam 2013, 5).

In my approach to the construction of gender through embodied performance (Butler 1990), I locate masculinity in terms of its "bodily, affective, socially constituted, symbolic, and performative dimensions" (Mahadeen 2016, 450).[7] Similar to Jane Cowan's seminal work on social dance at Greek weddings (1990), this approach is critical of essentialist depictions of manhood that reinforce gendered codes of honor and shame in ways that stereotype Arab, Muslim, and Mediterranean persons and societies. Ebtihal Mahadeen problematizes these discursive constructions through a linguistic distinction between two grammatical conjugations: *rujūla* (literally: masculinity or manliness) and *marjala* (literally: masculinity; plural: *marājil*, masculinities). Whereas *rujūla* perpetuates patriarchal forms of gender domination, *marjala* is a situated, relational, embodied, and contradictory construction that shapes both hegemonic and nonhegemonic social relations in public and private domains. Both formulations of masculinity are deeply embedded in the lived experiences and social institutions of the region (Cowan 1990; Herzfeld 1997; Gilsenan 1996; Ghannam 2013). During my extended fieldwork in Syria, for instance, I experienced moments when this "code" was broken by individual men, only to be restored by interventions from other men who sought to "protect" me from what they perceived as sexualized attention. In what follows, I privilege experiences of *marjala* to affirm masculinity as playful, pleasurable, and intimate and to intervene in discourses that problematically focus on Arab masculinities only as a facet of patriarchal domination and gendered aggression.

In this chapter, I locate *marjala* specifically in the embodied techniques of *dabke* practice and the embodied social relations of *dabke* circles. These dynamics realize what I call "relational masculinity," a concept that underscores the ways in which masculinity is a social phenomenon constituted between and among participants, who are themselves subject to gender, age, class, race, and other social hierarchies (Sedgwick 1985; Connell and Messerschmidt 2005; Johnson and Rivera-Servera 2016). I situate relational masculinity in corporeal interactions, from listening to dance rhythms to balancing the weight of each other's bodies in motion, that are crucial for understanding and critiquing the gendered choreographies of power that take place in *dabke* circles. This critical approach builds on Suad Joseph's concept of "intimate selving" (1999), by which Joseph challenges Western frameworks that assume the autonomy of selfhood to instead argue that a sense of self emerges between male and female kin, particularly through patriarchal "kinship idioms" developed during childhood through the intimacy of growing up in the same family unit. Her emphasis on the role of patriarchal family structure in shaping social life and social institutions in Lebanon provincializes how social actors negotiate "hegemonic masculinity" (Connell and Messerschmidt 2005; Segal 1990) across the SWANA region, in comparison to European or North American societies. Recognizing the role of patriarchal dynamics of kinship in organizing selfhood and social life in Syria, I expand on her concept of "intimate selving" by considering *dabke* an embodied kinship idiom that engenders homosocial bonding at weddings and other communal events. Relational masculinity aims to situate *dabke* practice as a (non)hegemonic form of embodied masculinity that is within and constitutive of local kinship dynamics in order to deprivilege Western tendencies to approach the dancing body as an autonomous subject and to construct masculinity as independent from family institutions.

I locate relational masculinity in small moments—an interaction here, a missed cue there—in order to animate the choreosonic social life of *dabke* as socially and locally meaningful. One of these moments occurred at the wedding party in Latakia, where the drummer and the lead dancers, all young men, continued to improvise their movements, musical and dancing, with each other. (View footage of this moment on the companion website at CLIP 3.1b.) The *ṭabl* player flicked his *ʿaṣā* (mallet) between *dum* and *tak* strokes to thicken the percussive texture. In response, the *awwal* dancer lowered into a deep knee bend, sustaining this low position for a charged moment. He raised his arms high into the air and twisted his knees, still bent, to the right and left, coordinating each movement with each rhythmic stroke of the *ṭabl* player in acts of empathic kinesthetic perception. He moved his right arm in and out, as if waving a sword in slow motion. Then, in a moment of synergetic flow between performers, he looked up at the *ṭabl* player, who looked right back at him. Together they effortlessly suspended time, seemingly floating above the rhythmic timeline they had established through deep legwork and exaggerated drum strokes.

In the background, the org player cued the end of the instrumental introduction and beginning of the main song. The *ṭabl* drummer usually plays a key role in this transition, as he is responsible for the downbeat that launches musicians and dancers into the groove. In anticipation of the first key downbeat, the drummer repeated *tak* strokes in the same tempo, using two deliberately heavy eighth notes on the downbeat to steady the pulse. In response, the *awwal* dancer shook his shoulders vigorously, with panache, then suspended his movements as he waited—body poised, posture upright—for the downbeat. Still waiting, he lowered his knees to the ground and extended his arms higher. The *ṭabl* player looked to the other musicians for a cue for the transition, while continuing to maintain the pulse. Meanwhile, the *awwal* dancer rose from his knee bend and lifted his right heel on the offbeat. He repeated the same motion with his other leg in the second measure. He then anticipated a step exchange from left to right.

But he was early. He missed the cue for the main song and the re-entrance of the other participants. Raising his eyebrows, he acknowledged the misstep by looking directly at the *ṭabl* player, who returned the gaze, as if to reassure him of recovery. The missed cue and subsequent disorientation did not seem to affect the experience of flow between the drummer and the lead dancer. Rather, it heightened their awareness of each other and intensified their sensorial connection and nonverbal communication. Their flow state did not depend on a perfectly realized enactment of repertoire but could incorporate communicative disruptions and failures. This was an act of relational masculinity in which their listening, watching, and moving male bodies bonded through homosocial, intercorporeal actions.

Dabke is an embodied listening practice that can fail or be disrupted in small moments that produce social life. Like this momentary disruption to the flow state, sensory disorientation, however fleeting, is crucial to the performance methodology that guides this chapter. "Sensory disorientation" (Silverstein 2019) is a method of performance ethnography in which, I propose, fieldwork-based encounters are critical for disrupting and disorienting the ethnographer's sensory modes of perception. This phenomenological approach to perception recognizes that our bodies are entrained to perceive the world around us in culturally specific ways rather than to universalize acts of perception as constitutive of a uniform sense of personhood (Larkin 2014). This chapter, then, unfolds through a series of episodic encounters in which I narrate several experiences of sensory disorientation as well as provide descriptions of social choreographies that I witnessed in performance spaces. These encounters, I suggest, "slanted" (Ahmed

2006) my habituated modes of perception such that my interpretation of spatial, kinesthetic, visual, and auditory phenomena became more of an open-ended rather than naturalized process. By accounting for my experiences of sensory disorientation while immersed in the ethnographic field, I aim to underscore how body techniques, such as listening and dancing, are contingent, situated in, and constitutive of social distinctions between researchers and their object of study. As a method of performance ethnography, sensory disorientation engages in and disrupts our relationships to each other in order to better understand the cultural logics and performative processes that shape ethnographic subjectivity as well as how our methods imbricate our own bodies.

In general, my descriptions of dance attend more to movement as physical bodywork and social choreography rather than attempting to translate a specific cultural repertoire for an English-language readership primarily based outside of the region of study. This choice is influenced by debates on cultural representation that argue for a decolonizing approach to cultural studies, namely, to translate dance, among other cultural repertoires, into writing without depending upon and reproducing forms of analysis external to the culture of study (Foster 2011). Importantly, then, my approach to *dabke* in this chapter does not attempt to provide a complete catalog of repertoire or to analyze performance as a signifying practice. Similar to how Alexandra Vazquez "listens in detail" to Cuban music, I do not presume *dabke* is an "object [that] can be known" (2013, 7). Colleagues in the field of Arab dance support this position.[8] *Dabke*, they concur, is fundamentally an embodied tradition that is passed down from generation to generation through social immersion in performance spaces. Though there are some terms to refer to specific footwork, there is no commonly shared lexicon for the many idiomatic movements that comprise this relatively codified and yet vastly heterogeneous set of regional traditions.[9] Rather than insist that embodied repertoires become scripted into the archives of academe, a maneuver that Diana Taylor notably critiques as colonialist (2004), what follows is my venture to honor embodiment as epistemology and praxis.

RHYTHMIC PRECISION

The rhythmic sensibilities of *dabke* have fascinated listeners for decades. Legendary jazz player Duke Ellington, for instance, was deeply affected by his experience of *dabke* performed at a private party held during his 1957 Damascus tour as a cultural ambassador for the US Department of State. All he "could remember afterwards was the kick on the sixth beat."[10] Ellington would go on to compose a chart entitled "Depk" (*Far East Suite*, 1967) that rendered his recollection of this key rhythmic motif into a complex passage featuring a pattern of six beats, the last of which was accented. He most likely encountered standard *dabkāt* rhythms and the folk dance style of *dabke al-shamāliyya* (literally: Northern dabke), a ubiquitous sequence consisting of several crossover steps that alternate left and right feet and end with a kick—the *dabke*—on the last beat. By arranging a footwork idiom into a rhythmic jazz motif, Ellington unlocked the rhythmic aesthetics of *dabke*. Crucially, he listened to the dance kick itself, that is, to movement as much as, or perhaps more than, sound.

Ellington was deeply attuned to the possibilities of the choreographic and the sonic being linked through live embodied performance, even as his artistic career was committed to elevating jazz into a musical art rather than social dance music at a moment of historic transformation for jazz in the mid-twentieth century (Wells 2021). Though Ellington faced accusations of cultural appropriation for his "travel suites," inspired by tours across Asia and South America,[11] he was acutely aware that listening is a "location for producing difference" (Kheshti 2015, 712). As Roshanak Kheshti argues, the power of the "aural imaginary," an affective site of attachment, is harnessed through corporeal engagements with sonic Others. Ellington engaged with *dabke* performers by listening to and imagining their dance kick as a patterned rhythmic gesture.[12] Here, I take seriously Ellington's act of memory in which he conveys that listening is an embodied act that ascribes meaning to sound through movement—in other words, that dancing is a listening practice.

What does the "kick" refer to, and what is the significance of the "kick" among local understandings of *dabke* practice? The kickstep is a "*dabke*" (literally: footstomp) step that ranges from a highly exaggerated stomp to a relaxed placement of the ball of the foot on the ground, depending on local practice and the individual performer. The "firm-footed" stomping step bears weight and holds pressure, quite literally, allowing the dancer to sense "the whole earth from under the feet" ("*bi-haythu taḍhal al-wadmān*"), as popular lore suggests.[13] This poetic phrase underscores the physical tactility of the step from the perspective of the participant rather than an external observer. When Ellington recalls the "kick," he associates it with a metrical rhythm, the "sixth beat." In fact, the rhythmic placement of the stomping step is variable in practice, depending on how the practice is situated in a geography of local idiomatic styles. In local codified styles closely related to *dabke al-shamāliyya*, the stomp occurs on "the fourth step, the third, or any other steps depending on the musical phrase and the accompanying song."[14] It may also occur more than once in a given pattern. Though nonstandardized in its aesthetic and energetic form, as well as its rhythmic placement, the *dabke* step remains central to the aesthetics of the practice, including the choices that participants make on the dance floor.

More than the construction of the kick as an object of performance, what is most compelling about Ellington's impression of *dabke* is that he understood what local practitioners and spectators appreciate about the practice: that a sense of rhythm is clearly manifest through physical movement. Being able to convey a sense of rhythm through variation and alignment is a highly valued skill among practitioners as well as spectators. When assessing whether a *dabbik* displays a sense of rhythm, speakers of Arabic use the adverbial phrase "*ʿāl maḍbūṭ*," which approximately translates to "with precision; in an exact manner."[15] This phrase denotes a sense of rhythmic timing that is precise, or "on the beat," with reference to embellishments, improvisatory movements, and general skill in the *shakl dāʾira*. *Dabbikun* tend to be praised for their rhythmic sensibilities through statements such as "he is precise in *dabke*" ("*huwa maḍbūṭ bi-dabke*"). Conversely, practitioners tend to deflect praise or critique their skills with the phrase, "I don't know [how to do it] exactly" ("*mā baʿrif ʿāl maḍbūṭ*").

The improvisational choices that participants make are usually unscripted yet emerge from a codified set of gestures, movements, and patterns, all of which ideally strive to convey a sense of rhythmic phrasing to other participants and spectators. An *awwal* often maintains fidelity to the *dabke* step while improvising. Whereas some line leaders maintain a limited stepping area, others embellish the footstomp with a raise, jump, attack, stress, or other ornamenting gesture. These footwork techniques double time, suspend, and otherwise shape rhythmic phrasing. One common embellishment is a *tahwiya*, or an extension-retraction of the left leg and foot that requires a shift of balance and division of the rhythmic pulse (Ibn Dhurayl 1996). The *tahwiya* often occurs on the fifth pulse of *dabke al-shamāliyya*, as well as the first pulse of the sequence. Other footwork embellishments include acrobatic and rhythmic movements, such as a "scoop," squat, raise, or jump. Participants broaden their movements to cover more ground and add height with extended steps, leaps, and jumps. They may also rotate their torsos in towards the *shakl dāʾira* and angle their legwork to play with directionality in bodily movements. These performances typically occur during an instrumental break between vocal refrains, which participants listen for in anticipation of an opportunity to improvise. Where and when embellishments occur is important for the realization of rhythmic aesthetics and the display of technique. (View examples of these techniques on the companion website at CLIP 3.2.)

Dabke is not the only dance practice in Syrian (and more broadly Arab and Middle Eastern) performance culture in which dancing is considered an act of musical interpretation. *Raqṣ sharqiyya*, popularly known as belly dancing in the West, is an expressive performance practice in which predominantly female dancers perform choreographies set to *ṭarab* (traditional art music) repertoire, from recorded film music to live improvisatory sets. Dancers translate their listening experience of particular musical voices, such as a solo instrumental improvisation (*taqsīm*) or a melodic motif, into a movement motif, such as a hip shimmy or figure eight movement (Bordelon 2011). *Raqṣ sharqiyya* performers may also layer their movements in ways that make kinesthetic the multivocal arrangements of *ṭarab* repertoire—from Abdel Halim Hafiz and Umm Kulthum's recordings to popular songs such as "Lamma Badda Yutathanna"—by, for instance, articulating through movement the shift of an instrument to the foreground of the musical arrangement. By translating their cultural knowledge of *ṭarab* musical structure and theory into choreography, *raqṣ sharqiyya* dancers present themselves as musical connoisseurs for whom dance is a means to express their interpretations of the dominant musical arts canon in the region. In contrast to the studied and closely attuned interpretive work of *raqṣ sharqiyya*, *dabke* dancers are less wedded to the metonymic adaptation of musical arrangements, structures, and vocalities into choreographic techniques and more about improvising with and around rhythmic sensibilities.[16]

How to correlate bodywork with musical rhythms is not only a matter of distinction between popular performance traditions but also a debate that scholars of dance, music, and performance have and continue to wrestle with (Power-Sotomayor 2020). The most common approach to the rhythmic relationship between *dabke* music and dance has, in the past, emphasized pulse groupings, in which each dance step is paired with a single rhythmic beat and then grouped into corresponding patterns (Ibn Dhurayl 1996). The issue with grouping steps according to their metrical and sequential patterning is that, as an abstract aesthetic ideal, this framing assumes a fixed and linear relationship between *dabke* movements and metrical pulses. This framing is common among those seeking to document, record, and analyze the practice. In their study of Palestinian *dabke*, Cohen and Katz (1996) reduced the analysis of rhythm to "beats per minute" rather than asking how dancers perceive the beats.[17] Syrian folklorist Ibn Dhurayl, trained in empirical positivism, was also keen to maintain fidelity to the fixed ratio of one step for each metrical pulse in his transcriptions of local *dabkāt*, published as an anthology in 1996 in Syria. In each of his detailed descriptions of Syrian *dabke* styles, Ibn Dhurayl "specified [the] duration [of each style], along with its movements and metered steps."[18] He identified each style's "pulse grouping," by which he correlated each *dabke* step (*khaṭwa*, sing.; *khaṭwāt*, plural) to a rhythmic beat, or pulse (*naqra*, sing.; *naqrāt*, plural). He determined that pulse groupings ranged from two or three to seven, ten, or twelve units, depending on the style.[19] Ibn Dhurayl's work on duration and pulse groupings was commensurate with similar studies of folk dance taking place across the region in the 1960s and 1970s in which meter, rhythm, and pulse groupings were considered empirical units that could be analyzed and notated in order to distinguish between distinct ethnonational traditions.[20]

As a theoretical structure that infers how dancers listen and phrase, however, the pulse grouping does not always materialize neatly in the messiness of social dancing. Moreover, the concept of pulse groupings does not, I argue, sufficiently account for how rhythmic expressions enliven the dance floor, that is, the embellishments, improvisations, and variations that emerge in practice. Many dancers, for instance, stress the second and fifth beats through ornamental footwork gestures and in more complicated improvisational sequences. Others suspend the forward momentum of the beat by holding a pose across several beats. By not accounting for how dancers, as listeners, make choices that convey distinct rhythmic expressions, the emphasis on pulse groupings reinforces the tendency to make dance autonomous from music as well as the priority often placed on the visual perception of danced movements. Redirecting "somatic modes of attention" (Csordas 1993) away from the visual and towards the auditory and kinesthetic, I locate in *dabke* practice an opportunity to consider dance an embodied and affective process of listening to popular music.

Locating rhythmic precision in *dabke* footwork remains, ironically, an imprecise exercise. Practicing *dabke* with precision is not about entraining movements to metrical beats, that is, of moving on the beat, off the beat, with the downbeat, or otherwise aligning footwork with metrical structures.[21] Rather, the musical aesthetics associated with *dabke* practice are located in the affective, embodied, and intersubjective conditions of flow states wherein *dabbikūn* play with and around phrasing. Thus, while rhythmic precision may involve a "kick on the sixth beat," it more often emerges when *dabbikūn* improvise on the second and fifth beats, moments that are often temporally suspended through movement work. Rhythmic precision may also happen when *dabbikūn* displace the *dabke* step entirely through performance-based choices in footwork and legwork. Finally, rhythmic precision is about moving within the constraints of the overall tempo — *dabbikūn* do not fall behind, slow down, or quicken footwork in ways that would create a parallel tempo autonomous from that of the music. Arguably more significant than a *dabbik*'s footwork choices are the sensory modalities, including balance and weight, that *dabbikūn* need in order to attain a flow state. Rhythmic precision, in other words, is less a skill to be observed and more an embodied affect to be felt, lived, and experienced.

At the wedding party in Latakia, I joined the *shakl dāʾira* upon the invitation of my friend. Clasping hands with those who made room for me in the line circle, I tried to synchronize my steps with those moving around me. People danced *dabke al-shamāliyya* in a quick and light variation.[22] Entraining each of the six steps *(khaṭwāt)* to the metrical pulse, their footwork coalesced into a triple meter rhythmic unit. Participants more or less coordinated each of their steps to the metrical pulse while emphasizing the first, third, and fifth steps, which each correlated with the downbeat of the duple meter rhythms. The rhythm, I would learn later at *dabke* workshops, could be felt as either six independent steps or three sets of paired steps.

After falling into step, I began to listen more attentively to the band to try to discern whether there was a distinct musical cue for either the beginning of the six-step dance sequence or the *dabke* kick. What I heard was mainly a repetitive and additive melodic and rhythmic arrangement in a driving duple meter. The dominant rhythmic structure was a *mālfūf* dance rhythm (transcribed as [D--t--t-]) streaming from the org (electric keyboard) through the party speakers. The keyboard player textured the repetitive rhythmic unit with *ayyub* (transcribed as [D--t D-t-]) and other closely related dance rhythms to generate a wall of sound. A percussionist added fills with the *darbukka* (goblet-shaped drum). Together they accompanied the vocalist, who sang in *bayt* (poetic lines) of approximately four bars' duration that strictly adhered to the rhyming pattern of the song form, *ʿataba*. The *mijwiz* (reproduced digitally on the org) also accompanied the vocalist by playing short melodic motifs (*lazīm*) in between *bayt* that responded to, elaborated on, and filled in the vocal melodic material. Melodic phrases repeated every four bars in a consistent 2/4 meter, with occasional breaks for instrumental riffs. Amid the unvarying repetition of the band's improvised arrangement (see chapter 4 for an analysis of musical practices), I failed to identify an audible cue for when to start the sequence or when to place the *dabke* step in the ongoing repetitions of *dabke al-shamāliyya* around the dance floor. I would later come to understand that in *shaʿbī* music spaces, musical form is generally considered less significant for the construction of musical meaning than the material qualities of sound, such as timbre, frequency, and distortion (see chapter 4 for an elaboration of these issues).

Despite the metrical consistency and rhythmic alignment between the dance pattern and the musical form, I experienced sensory disorientation in the *shakl dāʿira* when I tried to integrate what I heard with what I saw and with what I was doing. Though each dance step of *dabke al-shamāliyya* aligns with a metrical pulse, and though dancers tend to (though not always) stress the downbeat of the duple meter rhythms, the lengths of their overall cycles differ. Whereas the musical melody maintains a four-, eight-, and sixteen-measure cycle, the dancers repeat a six-step pattern (some divide the pattern into three sets of two steps). The metrical organization of the dance and music parts adheres to a 3:2 structure wherein dancers practice a triple meter feel while musicians entrain a duple meter groove. What this means for dancing participants is that the first step of the dance sequence and the *dabke* stomp do not consistently occur in the same part of the melodic units. The rhythmic cycles of the dance were staggered with those of the music in ways that cycled in and out of sync with one another.

How does one listen for the kick on the sixth beat, to refer back to Ellington, when the "kick" step varies according to *dabke* dance style, when the "kick" step is not always at the end of the melodic phrase, and when the rhythmical units for musicians and dancers are staggered across several cycles rather than occurring in parallel modalities? Ellington also noticed this "grouping dissonance," wherein musicians and dancers are "in phase but oddly out of synchrony" (Jackson 2013, 525), which he found compelling enough to insert into his "*Depk*" composition.[23] Ellington's keen attention to the choreosonics of meter arguably converges with my disorientation as a dancing listener trying to parse metric cycles of music and dance in terms of how we listen for and hear a 3:2 relationship between the dance and the music, respectively. Part of my disorientation could be attributed to my training in ballet and other studio dance forms. I was accustomed to learning dance movements in sets of eight, with each set correlating with the beginning of a clearly discernible musical sentence. Listening, to invoke Kheshti again, involves a reiterative series of embodied acts that produce and perform social difference because these acts are situated in aesthetic ideologies specific to each listener.

At the wedding's dance session, I stopped trying to correlate the start of the sequence or the footstomp with a musical cue. Instead of analyzing rhythmic phenomena through a "close listening" method, I began to listen differently.[24]

I fluctuated between a duple and triple rhythmic feel that, I insist, constitutes the "choreosonics" (Crawley 2017) of *dabke* practice. If I turned my auditory awareness towards the band, I became attuned to the duple meter groove. If I turned my kinesthetic awareness towards the *shakl dāʾira*, I became immersed in the triple figure sequence. To flow in *dabke* practice is arguably to experience a state of perceptual flux between triple meter and duple meter rhythmic sensibilities, as each continuously displaces the other.[25] This fluctuation, I suggest, is a generative tension from which swells the flow state of *dabke*. Rather than something that produces "dissonance," this tension animates the multisensorial modes of perception that constitute the embodied experience of rhythmic flux. Moreover, rhythmic precision (*ʿāl maḍbūṭ*) emerges from, not despite of, this tension because *dabke* aesthetics are less about entraining movements to pulse groupings and more about a sense of floating between auditory and kinetic rhythmic fluctuations.

How are these aesthetics transmitted between participants, especially in spaces of pedagogy? Is there a codified language that communicates rhythmic phrasing in *dabke* practice? That is, how do *dabke* teachers verbalize rhythm to their students? To what extent do pulse groupings shape how dancers phrase and group their steps in relationship to the rhythm? Many *dabke* teachers, as I have found over the course of taking workshops in Europe and North America, begin tutorials with *dabke al-shamāliyya*, the most ubiquitous of *dabke* styles. However, they do not all teach this style with the same approach to rhythmic phrasing, instead offering distinctive approaches that vary according to the cultural and educational capital of the instructor.

At a teaching workshop in New York City in 2010, two experienced Syrian American and Palestinian American *dabbikūn* from the Bay Ridge neighborhood of Brooklyn introduced *dabke al-shamāliyya* to a group of students entirely unfamiliar with *dabke*.[26] They subdivided the six steps into three pulse groupings in which each group was comprised of two beats, or 2-2-2. Their phrasing reinforced the downbeat of the duple meter rhythm with the dominant left cross-steps (*zuḥun*) occurring on the downbeat and the passing right foot occurring on the offbeat. They also instructed students to use hip motions on their left side to stress the downbeat. The left hip thrust, they suggested, would help students plant the left step flat and firm on the ground and, likewise, retract the foot on the offbeat. In summary, they instructed students to subdivide the six steps into three duple figures that emphasized the downbeat of each rhythmic measure.

In contrast to that approach, Rotterdam-based Syrian dancer Jol Alholo drew on a set of metric techniques derived from his extensive dance training with Enana, the preeminent dance theater company of prewar Syria. I first noticed how his training influenced his approach to teaching when he counted off "5, 6, 7, 8" to start his rendition of a *dabke* sequence. This counting technique is commonly practiced among professional dancers in class or when rehearsing choreographies designed of eight-movement units. Alholo then counted the *dabke al-shamāliyya* sequence as two groups of four, where count one correlated with the left and right steps of the grapevine figure, repeated again as a grapevine on count two, and counts three and four occurred at twice the tempo in correlation with the *dabke* step and final step in place. While this apportionment aligned the six *dabke* steps with the eight-movement rubric used when rehearsing choreographies, it did not maintain a fixed relationship between each count and the duration of a metered beat. Rather, a count could refer to either a beat or a half-beat.

Though each instructor organized footwork into a triple meter dance pattern that can be readily mapped onto the duple meter rhythm groove, what none of the instructors mentioned is that this three-to-two rhythmic relationship between dance and music does not neatly align.[27] Rather, the felt pulse and sensed movement retains a tension that, as I have demonstrated through my experience of sensory disorientation, is fundamental to the affective experience of *dabke*. Rhythmic precision, one of the primary aesthetic categories of *dabke* practice, is not about landing the "downbeat" in the step sequence, nor is it about the position of the *dabke* step in a particular footwork sequence. Neither is it about executing a particular step, a specific timing, or an ideal form. Rhythmic precision is about a choreosonic flux that modulates fluidly between bodies in spaces of performance. Rhythmic precision, as I elaborate in the rest of this chapter, is also about differentiation between these bodies in gendered social spaces that tend to reproduce hegemonic forms of masculinity.

ON BALANCE

Towards the end of our Skype session, both Alholo and I lamented that the lack of in situ, copresent experience was a major barrier to getting into a flow state. Neither the digital communications technology nor the ad hoc arrangement of the home dance studio bothered us. Rather, we were referring to the disorienting effects of moving around as autonomous bodies rather than being attached to another (or several) bodies that would ground and balance our movements. Unanchored, our bodies in motion could not quite feel each other's movements or bridge empathic kinesthetic perception as we moved across screens and oceans. Palestinian *dabke* artist Mohammed Tamem, born and raised in the Yarmouk camp of Damascus, Syria, affirmed in a virtual university workshop, held in June 2021, the necessity of more than one dancing body to practice *dabke*. He and his partner, Hidal, informed dance students at Cologne University that the minimum number of participants needed to *dabke* is "two or more," and that it is nearly impossible to *dabke* by oneself.[28] What Tamem, Alholo, and many other *dabbikūn* underscore is that participation in *dabke* is intercorporeal, that is, that dancing with others is axiomatic for the practice.

Intercorporeality is a precondition for flow states because of the role of *mīzān*, or balance, in grounding bodies in motion. This complex somatic phenomenon, that I argue is central to *dabke*, emerges through auditory, proprioceptive, kinetic, and other sensory modes of perception.[29] It is crucial for navigating rhythmic flux among dancers[30] and necessary for improvisation — relatedly, its absence or failure to be achieved can thwart attempts to flow, improvise, and move in the dance circle.[31] *Mīzān* impacts the affective dynamics and social choreographies of the dance circle, particularly, as I describe later, because it structures dynamics of relational masculinity.

Though balance in motion is of course experienced to some extent by everyone participating in the dance circle, *mīzān* is most intimately associated with the *dabke* leader, located at the head of the dance circle, whose function is not only to establish group footwork but also to improvise. The *dabke* leader, referred to as *awwal* (literally: first) depends on the skills of the participant next in line, referred to as *tānnī* (literally: second), for improvisation. Those who assume these highly visible and often spectacularized positions are usually accomplished and experienced practitioners, referred to in Syrian Arabic as *dabbik* (masc.) or *dabbak* (fem.).[32] *Dabke* teachers typically emphasize the role of the *awwal*, also commonly referred to as *lawwīḥ*, in leading the *shakl dāʾira*. The *awwal* maintains the sequence and also performs improvisational legwork and footwork, drawing on an unscripted repertoire of codified movements to display some degree of virtuosity that both plays with and is constrained by dance rhythms. The *awwal* may break off from the line and dance in the center or switch positions with the next dancer, the *tānnī* (also known as *tāllī*). The *tānnī* offers rhythmic support for the *awwal*, improvising alongside the lead dancer with idiosyncratic figures that similarly suspend, emphasize, and attack the beat (see figure 3.1).

A chant traditionally sung by older women at wedding *ḥaflāt* hails these key dance roles, as well as the "last" dancer, in the *shakl dāʾira*:[33]

FIGURE 3.1 Lead dancer and dance circle at a wedding in Jable, Syria.
October 8, 2008. Photo by the author.

Hā-gha awwal-kun	To the first among you all
Hā-gha tāllī-kun	To the next among you all
Hā-gha akhīr-kun	To the last among you all,
Illa lī m-zayinn-kun	who make all of you look beautiful
[*zagharīt*]	[vocal ululations]

Relatedly, this traditional chant identifies and names the "first," "next," and "last" positions in the *shakl dā'ira* as at once conspicuous sites of spectacular performance and constitutive of the overall performance aesthetics of a *shakl dā'ira*. Importantly, those who perform in these positions affect the aesthetics of the collective, making not only themselves but "*all* . . . look beautiful" (my emphasis). The chant thus portrays these performer-subjects in synecdochic relationship to the *shakl dā'ira*, a relationship that is vital for understanding how *mīzān* resonates across all bodies in the *shakl dā'ira*. If and when the leaders of the dance circle attain a weighted balance with one another, a physical force necessary to realize the rhythmic aesthetics of the practice, their balance affects the performance aesthetics of all those participating in the dance session. Embodied interactions at "dance-events" affirm a "collectivity bound by shared knowledge, skill, and physical connections" (Cowan 1990, 20). In other words, *mīzān* is not only a physical experience that enables rhythmic precision between dancers but also a "dicent indice" (or body language) (Cowan 1990; Turino 2008) that, when and as perceived by others, contributes to the collective experience.

Embedded in the social relations of *mīzān* are the gendered politics of privilege — that is, whose bodies are granted the authority to perform first, next, and last — and influence the overall performance aesthetics of the event. For instance, this traditional chant is also significant for how it voices the gendered relations of *dabke* performance. Though the gendered identities of the "first," "next," and "last" dancers are not explicitly named in this chant, it is notable that older women are the presumptive subjects who vocalize this chant (at least, as this chant was narrated to me). As spectators of the dance, those who simultaneously bear witness to the dance and voice the aesthetics of performance, they construct spectatorship as feminine. Female spectatorship is more common than not at *ḥaflāt*, where lead dancers of the *shakl dā'ira* are typically male, a gender divide that I address in a moment. Female spectatorship, as well as nonperformative refusals to perform (Silverstein 2016), is an important part of how relational masculinity emerges at *dabke* sessions, where performance and spectatorship in ritual wedding spaces reproduce kinship relations.[34]

What this chant suggests is the primacy of performance aesthetics in wedding *ḥaflāt*; that is, it is not only the presence of bodies in collective ritual formations and practices, but also the synergetic movements of specific bodies, that construct a sense of beauty. This synergy was palpable to me at the wedding that I attended in 2008 in the village of Jaabat Khashab. Not long after I arrived, the last four dancers in line broke out into a complicated sequence (see CLIP 3.3 on the companion website). All *shabāb* (youth), they repeated the sequence several times, each time with perfect coordination. Their virtuosic sequence consisted of high leaps, deep bends, and syncopated steps. On the fifth beat, they jumped (*wathab*) high in the air with both feet tucked underneath. They landed on the sixth beat in a deep squat (*qirfaṣa'*) with the left leg extended straight out. They repeated these two movements at the end of each cycle. No one cycle was performed the same: the *shabāb* added a twist (*fitla*) as they rose from the squat or switched sides in their held position, footwork in which the right heel extended front and the left toe extended back. At other times they added a double time step on beat two that emphasized the first eighth note with a rapid exchange of the feet. Each time, the six young men fanned out into a *rīsh* (literally: feather) formation, a metaphorical term that likens their collective contraction and expansion to the light movement of feathers.

When Ramzi El Idlibi, a professional folklore dancer based in New York City, watched a recording of this *rīsh* sequence, he described it enthusiastically as *nashīṭa* (literally: lively, active). El Idlibi elaborated that *nashīṭa* "is exciting. If the music is a fit, fast people get crazy. The four people at the end are just an example. I remember myself with friends of my age when I was like eighteen, we really used to get very crazy so that our feet used to fly."[35] El Idlibi's evocation of flying seemed apt for what I had the privilege to watch in Jaabat al-Khashab: buoyant acrobatics that maintained the rhythmic precision of the practice as they flew around the *shakl dāʾira*, dropping to the ground, jumping into the air, all in playful and graceful synergy.

———

While El Idlibi expressed his appreciation for technique and vigor, not all participants are granted the politics of privilege to perform equally. Whose bodies, then, are granted the opportunity to perform in the "first, second, and last" position of the dance circle? A gender divide structures participation and spectatorship in the *shakl dāʾira*, and more broadly in spaces of leisure and entertainment. This gender divide between male participation and female spectatorship is deeply embedded in and indicative of family relationships, particularly those between siblings. Learning about *dabke*, as I would find out when trying to learn *dabke* from female friends, was also a lesson in how kinship dynamics and relationships uphold gender barriers.

Early in my research I reached out to female interlocutors to learn how to advance my *dabke* skills and improvise. My rationale was that it would be more socially acceptable to learn this performance tradition among those of the same gender due to social norms and conventions that emphasize same-sex sociability, especially with regard to embodied practices. However, with the (significant) exception of one, none of my female contacts expressed deep interest in becoming a *dabbak*, nor did they demonstrate skills that extended beyond basic footwork sequences, a fundamental for social participation.[36] Instead, they referred me to their brothers, insisting through much (and well-deserved) praise that their brothers possessed the requisite skills for my perceived needs and interests. For instance, a good friend of mine invited me to her village in the central Homs valley, so that I might observe the local *dabke* practices of her Syriac Christian community at weddings and a baptism ceremony. Despite countless visits to her family homes, in the village and in Jeramana (a suburb of Damascus), she and I never *dabked* together. Rather, she deferred all matters of *dabke* to her youngest brother Ahmad, whom she and others considered to be *"āl maḍbūṭ"* at *dabke*. She said that he practiced at home in the salon by watching video CDs of *ḥaflāt*.

It is not incidental that she perceived her brother as the *dabbik* of the family. Across innumerable *dabke* sessions in different social contexts throughout Syria, I generally found that women refrained from leading, improvising, and elaborating during participation in *dabke* sessions. Yet these approaches to *dabke* practice did not mean that women excluded themselves from the tradition; rather, they related to the practice through their relationships with their brothers and other male kin. This construction of self through perception of another is enculturated, according to Suad Joseph (1999), in Arab families. Brothers and sisters, Joseph argues, learn to see themselves in each other through a process she terms "intimate selving." Sisters gain a sense of dignity and security tied to their brother's selfhood. Likewise, brothers view themselves in relation to their sisters' attributes and behavior. Joseph views these dynamics as instantiations of both love and power, forms of relationality constituted by "gendered and aged forms of domination" and "moralized by kinship rules, moralities, and idioms." The brother-sister relationship, Joseph argues, is central to patrilineality and patriarchy because sibling relationships eventually map onto conventionalized gender roles within marriage. Intimate selving produces healthy senses of self, though it may also perpetuate coercive, and at times violent, dynamics of power (as I describe in chapter 5's discussion of the Syrian conflict).

What Joseph's concept of intimate selving means for how *dabke* is perceived between family members is that my friend's deference to her brother's *dabke* skills was not just a matter of shyness or lack of experience. Rather, his skills connected her to a broader sense of kinship through the dynamics of relational masculinity. She felt a sense of pride as a sister when her brother displayed his *dabke* skills at village weddings, small gatherings, and other occasions. His performance as a *dabbik* became gendered not only as an act of masculinity that flaunted skills in front of his male peers and older male figures, but also on behalf of his female kin and friends. Improvisational performances by *dabbikūn* are therefore not only an expression of individual selfhood. Rather, performance in the *dabke* circle, as well as the acts of spectatorship that construct value, constitute acts of intimate selving that cultivate family relationships. Through *dabke* practice and spectatorship, norms of masculinity and femininity are rehearsed among brothers and sisters and extended to other gendered kinship relationships, from spouses to extended family. Though not being able to learn from female friends felt initially like a methodological and social failure, what I learned from this impasse is that becoming a *dabbik* is an overwhelmingly masculine endeavor, a *marjala* (Mahadeen 2016) formation of masculinity constructed by both sisters and brothers. From sibling dynamics to the aunties who chant about the beauty of the (presumably) male dancers, these acts of intimate selving demonstrate how *dabke* is deeply embedded in and upholds patriarchal kinship structures when it enacts relational masculinity in Syrian society.

In addition to heteronormative sibling relationships, *dabke* practice mediates relational masculinity in terms of generational differences between youth and older men. *Dabke* remains an important avenue for young men to cultivate selfhood, as demonstrated in my descriptions in the opening act of this chapter of the ludic improvisations performed by the young man who led *awwal*. For young men who are physically able, *dabke* is considered a rite of passage, among other forms of play (Schechner 2006), that is part of their adolescence and young adulthood.[37] This sense of self shifts, however, as the body ages. Older men often explained to me that they were no longer as keen to *dabke* as they had been when younger. Though they assured me that they were "good at *dabke*" ("*kunt maḍbūṭ bi-l-dabke*") when they were young, their aging bodies experienced physical restraints, particularly weak knee joints that prevented the twists, drops, and other agile movements associated with *dabke* footwork. What a generational shift in *dabke* technique and ability suggests is that *dabke* practice becomes an object that mediates masculinity in relation to physical ability and processes of aging. Whether an active pursuit or an object of nostalgia among those who have aged beyond youth (Inhorn 2012), *dabke* play is part of a "masculine trajectory" (Ghannam 2013) that moves across lifespans.

———

At the same time that *dabke* practice mediates gendered kinship relations and shapes masculine trajectories in closely knit lifeworlds, it also facilitates more public forms of social cohesion precisely because persons of varying generations, genders, and skill levels all participate in the *shakl dāʾira*. What kinds of ethnographic encounters emerged when I, as a non-Arab, American woman, joined the dance circle? Approaching *mīzān* as a means to engage with the experiential and sensory forms of cultural knowledge possessed by others, what Deirdre Sklar theorizes as "empathic kinesthetic perception," I turn to the first (and long-anticipated) moment in which I experienced a flow state in *dabke* and generated a sense of *mīzān*.

As a female cultural outsider who was exempt, in ambivalent and opaque ways, from some of the gendered standards expected of Syrian young women, I was occasionally able to meet with a *dabbik* willing to share his expertise. Usually these *dabbikūn* were cosmopolitan young men already socializing with *ajānib* (foreigners) through educational or arts networks. As I described earlier, I found it surprisingly challenging to find a flow state in these sessions—though we practiced "empathic kinesthetic perception," more often than not we could not integrate all the performance dynamics into a fulfilling *dabke* experience. It was in one of these sessions, with Ahmad, that I finally learned how to properly fulfill the role of a *tānnī*. In a small flat in a Kurdish neighborhood of Aleppo, Ahmad demonstrated several variations to the popular six-step sequence of *dabke al-shamāliyya*. "Sometimes I cross the left over rather than keep it directly in front. Or I extend my right foot far back. Here, in the *baṭʿa* (slow) style you can tilt your hip to accent steps two and four." Yet he stumbled slightly when trying to *dabke* on his own. For increased stability, he asked me to join him on his left and maintain a sense of the beat, as a *tānnī* would. However, we could not sync our movements and felt disoriented. Recalling how disorientation could destabilize my rhythmic entrainment, I hoped to turn my "sensory disorientation" into an opportunity to learn about the practice as well as myself. The body, following Deirdre Sklar's cogent framing (2001), is a means to explore physical knowledge through the phenomenology of movement, including that of the researcher as well as the interlocutor.

I could not pivot out of sensory disorientation on my own. Fortunately, as an experienced teacher of Arabic for foreign students, Ahmad was accustomed to helping students overcome moments of cognitive dissonance and sensory disorientation. He asked me to anchor him by reinforcing the duple meter rhythm with crossover steps. In particular, he emphasized how the left foot anchors the rhythm:

> The movement starts from the hip, from the waist, which is the basis of all the movements in *dabke*. You start with the left foot and place it over the right foot. The right foot follows and you repeat these steps. Clasp hands with the other. . . . No, don't turn your hips, but stay in a straight line. The hips are in

line with the person next to you. Kick the left foot out on five and bring it back to place on six. Practice these [six steps] over and over. The anchor is the left foot because it keeps the rhythm and you always return to it.[38]

We resumed our dance session. I thought I was anchoring well with my left crossover step, but Ahmad said that he needed more of "something" in order to feel *mīzān*. I responded with enhanced proprioception—my handgrip, length of my arm, shoulder attachment—on my right side, the one that connected me to Ahmad. Finally, I flowed. With a sense of *mīzān*, I could let go and feel the rhythm, float around it rather than seeking to entrain every step to a beat. And locating rhythmic precision and stability as a *tānnī* is crucial for an *awwal* to perform at their best—to embellish, individuate, stylize, and improvise. With a shared sense of *mīzān*, Ahmad could improvise, playing around with the rhythmic placement of the footstomp, adding legwork and suspending the beat, yet never fully displacing the footstomp from its rhythmic position in the sequence. With the balance flowing between us, I realized that our connectedness is central to the coveted aesthetic of rhythmic precision for a *dabbik*. "*Āl maḍbūṭ*" is dependent on the actions of other participants, rather than entirely on the skills and talent of the individual. Weighted and balanced movements between dancers are, paradoxically, the conditions that yield floating rhythms, or flow states between and among participants.

The experience of *mīzān* is important for actualizing an embodied sense of self that, as I have argued, is situated, relational, and "intercorporeal" (Weiss 1999). *Mīzān* is constituted through proprioceptive and kinesthetic modes of perception between participants, similar to how skin and other bodily surfaces, boundaries, and systems generate modes of "being-with and being-for" (Ahmed and Stacey 2001, 1). The weighted rhythmic balance that is *mīzān* is also constituted through "empathic kinesthetic perception," introduced earlier as a combination of mimesis and empathy that transfers embodied experiences and forms of knowledge between participants. "The temporary joining in empathy" that occurs as "empathic kinesthetic perception," notes Deirdre Sklar, may "produce not a blurry merger but an articulated perception of difference" (Sklar 2001; cf. Albright 2013, 11). In my tutorial with Ahmad, for instance, empathic kinesthetic perception generated through *mīzān* bridged our many relationships—as teacher and student, cultural insider and outsider, male and female, experienced *dabbik*, and trained movement artist learning a new movement tradition. Moreover, this approach to the social and embodied relations embedded in *dabke* practice reinforces my earlier critique that flow states do not universally generate the autonomous and individuated experience of selfhood theorized by Csikszentmihalyi (1990). Rather, flow states are experienced as an intersubjective and intercorporeal phenomenon situated in gendered (and other) social structures.

The concept of *mīzān* and its weight, so to speak, in anchoring rhythmic sensibility lends itself to metaphors of selfhood and sociality that posit selfhood in Syrian society as relational rather than autonomous, similar to Susan Foster's critique that dance "summons other bodies" rather than hails an "autonomous inner self" (2011, 2). Though I stress relationality, I hold back from suggesting that *mīzān* is what constructs the sense of collectivity often imparted on the *shakl dāʾira*. Rather, I want to hold up *mīzān* as a fluctuating, dynamic, and incredibly inconsistent condition of performance, one that occurs with missteps, mis-hearings, and missed cues. In this way, *mīzān* is indicative of how different bodies depend on and relate to each other through emergent and indeterminant embodied interactions. By leaning on each other and sensing each other's weight, performing bodies enter an intersubjective flow state that is the groundswell for social relationships, intimate and public.

Embodied, situated, and relational performances of Syrian Arab masculinity, that is, of *marjala*, occur through men dancing together (improvising as *awwal* and *tānnī*, or tuning into the *ṭabl* drummer's percussive strokes while leading the dance circle) as well as masculine performance constructed in relation to female spectatorship, among other patriarchal modes of kinship. *Mīzān* is socially and culturally significant not only for its vital function in *dabke* practice and as an embodied practice of masculinity, but also as an approach to performance that de-essentializes toxic notions of Arab masculinity and patriarchy in Arab societies. At the same time, however, it is important to recognize that hegemonic masculinity and structures of patriarchy persist on the dance floor, not despite but because of *mīzān* and other embodied phenomena.

PERFORMING MASCULINITY
IN THE DANCE CIRCLE

In many popular dance practices, choreographic codes of embodied participation on the dance floor are comprised of culturally specific repertoires of gestures, movements, speech, and positions that mediate and configure identities (Foster 1998). What takes place on the dance floor are both everyday negotiations of membership and status within local communities (Cowan 1990) as well as broader contestations of class, gender and sexuality, race and ethnicity, religion, nationalism, and migration. The floor choreography most specific (though not exceptional) to *dabke* practice is the *shakl dāʾira*—an open-ended line formed by participants circling around the performance space.[39] It is a highly participatory space without distinctions between artists and audiences, in comparison to presentational spaces where performers dance or play music for spectators,[40] in which embodied participation and spectatorship often co-occur as participants both dance and watch others dancing. Yet there is a range of codified positions in the *shakl dāʾira*, such as the lead dancers as I have indicated, that are coveted as more visible and privileged. In addition to these positions, an enclosed space created by participants as they circle around in a linked chain is occasionally a site for improvised and often uncodified dance performances. (For an example of solo improvised performance, see CLIP 3.4 on the companion website.) This enclosed space is mainly occupied by solo instrumentalists (on *mijwiz, ṭabl*, and vocals, respectively) who interact with the participants in the *shakl dāʾira*, as I describe in more detail in chapter 4. Because it is a participatory space constituted through individual acts of performance, the *shakl dāʾira* is not a fixed form; rather, it is a situated assemblage of bodies, movements, timings, balancing acts, and other embodied interactions that constitute the social space of the *ḥafla*.

From *ḥaflāt* to informal gatherings, the *shakl dāʾira* is undeniably recognizable in its appearance. For many Syrians, this signature formation is associated with wedding customs wherein, like the institution of marriage, the "circle of *dabke* embodies a truism in which the beginning is the end."[41] For others, the poetry of synchronized bodies in motion and clasped hands has spawned political metaphors of populism, proletarianism, collectivism, and solidarity. The *shakl dāʾira* has also inspired contemporary dance and theater that aim to critique state and society through choreographic reimaginings of this configuration: *Alf Mabruk!* (Noura Murad, 2009), a performance about gender and marriage, subverts the participatory and spectatorship roles embedded in *dabke* practice by directing performers to *dabke* around audience members, who are enclosed by the *shakl dāʾira*, rather than watching from outside the dance space (Silverstein 2015). *Displacement* (Alzghrair, 2017) situates the *shakl dāʾira* differently. This dance production, discussed extensively in chapter 6, envisions the *shakl dāʾira* as a form of social support that bolsters individuals, particularly young men, against the hegemonic forces of state, religion, and the military.

Yet for others, the *shakl dāʾira* has unambiguously solidified into a hegemonic social ritual that reproduces patriarchal forms of domination. A male friend

FIGURE 3.2 Elders dancing at a wedding celebration
in Jaabat Khashab, Syria. July 2008. Photo by the author.

in his thirties likened the *shakl dāʾira* to a "wall of people that inhibits social progress . . . by literally stepping in the footsteps of generations before you, the *shakl dāʾira* reinforces village traditions."[42] One of these traditions is embedded in the social choreography of the *shakl dāʾira*, through which participants negotiate social status at community events. In figure 3.2, for example, an older man in a red and white *kaffiyeh* (traditional checkered headscarf) leads several other male dancers in the *shakl dāʾira*. Next to him, in the *tānnī* position, is the bride's father, taking an honorary position of distinction at the dance circle of his daughter's wedding. Behind the men leading the dance circle cluster a group of veiled women who observe their male companions. Their spectatorship echoes the chant included in the previous section, in which elder female vocalists hail the beauty of the *dabbikūn* at the head and end of the *shakl dāʾira*.

This image, of course, is a moment frozen in time that is not indicative of the complex gender relations at this mixed-gender event of several hours' duration. Nevertheless, this image captures how male elders of status occupy the most honorific positions in the *shakl dāʾira* in contrast to female spectators, who (in this image) gaze from behind the dance line, beholding figurative male honor. It demonstrates how social hierarchies "privilege the [systemic] authority of males and elders" and reinforce the "patriarchal connectivity" (Joseph 2005), or gendered forms of socialization that privilege family structures, that perpetuates and is perpetuated by paterfamilias. By extension, these and other forms of patriarchal kinships become embedded in state and religious institutions through "an implicit and legally encoded kin contract" (Joseph 2005) in which elder male kin serve as guardians and mediators for women's education, employment, and household affairs. By reproducing the patriarchy through the ritual performance of certain bodies in honorific positions of the *shakl dā'ira*, this image embodies the problematic *rujūla* mode of Arab masculinity, which essentializes manhood in terms of a binary code of honor and shame.

What would a relational masculinity look like beyond this image? How is an embodied and affective masculinity constituted through and embedded in the everyday social hierarchies of the *shakl dā'ira*? In which ways do gendered contestations and disruptions to these hierarchies emerge through the "pleasures, sensual intensities, and public socialities" (Cowan 1990, 4) of performance? At the heart of these questions is a feminist approach to affect and corporeality (Ahmed and Stacey 2001; Sedgwick, Barale, and Goldberg 2003) that undergirds this chapter: the sensate body performs iterative and repetitive bodily acts that enact the intercorporeal and kinship-based relationality of *marjala*. Analyzing the social life of *marjala* demands situating gender in relation to shifting political, social, and religious conditions. It also merits recognition that, because *dabke* is practiced across a multitude of social and moral spaces, not only in Syria but also in Palestine, Lebanon, Jordan, and the broader diaspora, questions about gender roles evade any singular definitive analysis.[43] To better understand how relational masculinity is constructed through participatory choices and by how other participants engage and react to such choices at a given event requires, first, an overview of the spatialized dynamics in the *shakl dā'ira*.

The *shakl dā'ira* consists of any number of participants, from several to dozens, who together form a circumlinear, open-ended chain of participants. Dancers casually enter and exit the dance circle throughout the dance session, where they collectively repeat a sequence of codified steps that circle counterclockwise around the performance space. Generally participants clasp hands together and extend their arms straight and firm alongside their torsos. Some consider this close physical contact erotic; for others, it is an indication of "romantic interest" between members of the opposite sex, although most typically normativize (and de-eroticize) such contact as codified behavior within the *shakl dā'ira*.[44] Participants may also link elbows or grab each other by the shoulders. Their hips face towards the center of the circle rather than rotating towards another dancer. This provides for a tightly knit and cohesive line that follows the lead of the *awwal* and *tānnī* dancers at the head of the line (see figure 3.3). Participants may expand and

FIGURE 3.3 Example of a tight-knit *shakl dā'ira*. Wedding celebration in Jaabat Khashab, Syria. July 2008. Photo by the author.

contract the spacing between bodies in the *shakl dā'ira* as they embellish their movements, with a shoulder lift in time with the duple meter rhythms, a deeper knee bend, or heavier footstomp, among many possible gestures.

Small groups of three to four dancers occasionally initiate brief episodes of codified variations. These impromptu intervals typically take place during instrumental breaks in the music. One of the most vivid breakout episodes I observed was in the middle of an extended session of *dabke al-shamāliyya* at a wedding in the village of Jaabat Khashab. (See footage of this session at CLIP 3.5 on the companion website.) About five or six male participants in the middle of the *shakl dā'ira* (of at least a hundred participants) broke out from the repetitive pattern and began to *dabke* in a related style, *dabke al-sha'arāwiyya*. What initiated this breakout moment is unclear; there was no specific musical cue such as a shift in rhythm, melody, or arrangement. They grasped each other by the shoulders rather than clasp their hands below waist level. In contradistinction to the counterclockwise flow of *dabke al-shamāliyya*, in this pattern they stepped broadly to the left on the downbeat, leaning their bodies into a clockwise direction. They marked the offbeat with a pulsing knee bend that, depending on the individual, was more or less pronounced. They repeated this figure on beats three and four. The cycle ended with another duple figure comprised of a left leg raise that circled back to center and an assertive footstomp towards the left that led into the strong downbeat of the first duple figure of the next cycle. Some further embellished this variation with hops on beat five or by leaning their torsos into the line to increase the angle and pivot of their bodies. They noticeably shifted weight from side to side, at a brisk upbeat pace. A sense of balance, of *mīzān*, distributed across their five or six bodies as they leaned energetically into their movements.

Admiring this breakout episode from the section of the *shakl dā'ira* in which I was participating, I was particularly struck by the rhythmic effects of this variation within the broader aesthetics of *dabke al-shamāliyya*, which others, including myself, continued to practice. In *dabke al-shamāliyya*, there is a 4-2 rhythmic subdivision of the stepping pattern that consists of two crossover steps on the first four steps, followed by a *dabke* footstomp, and a final step in place before repeating. The breakout dancers similarly maintained a strong duple meter alignment of the downbeat with the left foot. But rather than making crossover steps that moved counterclockwise with each pulse, they leaned clockwise with a left step on the downbeat and a double knee pulse on the offbeat. In addition, they maintained accent patterns that emphasized beats six and one but shifted these footstomps to the left rather than as crossover figures, again a clockwise directionality in *dabke al-shamāliyya*, rather than stomping in place or in a slight counterclockwise direction. The shift in directionality opened up different interpretations of the rhythmic phrasing of these two steps at the end of the repeating pattern. The step's rhythm could be felt either as a leading step, or a pickup note, into the firmly planted downbeat step that marked the beginning of the next cycle, or as a double-stomp pattern on beats six and one that stresses both equally. However interpreted by the spectator, the rhythms of the breakout episode playfully disrupted the repetitive movements of the *shakl dā'ira* and contributed to the festive and participatory ambiance of the event.

Also important to note about this breakout episode was the relatively unmarked status of the dancers within the social hierarchy of the wedding and the choreography of the *shakl dā'ira*. They were not at the head or the end of the dance line but deeply sandwiched in the middle of dozens of participants. All middle-aged men, they did not attempt particularly agile or adept footwork, in contrast to the young guys at the end of the dance line (the *rīsh*) described earlier in this chapter. Rather, their playful buoyancy emerged from the episodic and unscripted modality of performance as well as the aesthetic contrasts in directionality and rhythm generated by their version of *dabke al-shaʿarāwiyya*. Episodic variations or embellishments tend to be fairly common in a *shakl dāʾira* of extended duration, with many *dabke* sessions continuing for many hours as the evening progresses. Though these gestures are less conspicuous than improvisations by the *awwal* at the head of the line, and likewise less of an indicator of social privilege and rank, they remain acts of self-presentation that draw attention and generate a sense of play. In this vein, breakout episodes such as this make legible a masculine subject that remains relatively unmarked within the gendered and aged hierarchies of communal and familial spaces.

As dancers circle around, their linked bodies enclose an open space. This open space in the center is informal and permeable—people often pass through it when traversing from one end of the room to another, and children play by imitating adult behavior. It is a performance space where, as discussed earlier, the *ṭabl* drummer, *mijwiz* player, and *muṭrib* (vocalist) circumambulate throughout the live event and interact with dancers. It is also a space in which some participants perform solo or with one another.[45] Most often the solo performer is the *awwal*, who at times breaks away from the *shakl dāʾira* to improvise at length, as described in the introduction of this book. More uncommon is a performer, or two, who enter the center from a nonmarked position in the *shakl dāʾira* to show off their skills and rhythmic sensibilities—to perform the splits, for instance—or otherwise express themselves in a (more or less) virtuosic manner.

In everyday *dabke* practice, this unmarked yet enclosed center is a space in which relations of pleasure, desire, and power often circulate. This space affords possibilities for gendered acts of performance that bear indeterminate meaning, particularly between men. Two such moments occurred at the double wedding in Jaabat al-Khashab. First, a skinny young man cruised the *shakl dāʾira* from inside the line. Facing the predominantly male participants in the dance circle, he shimmied his hips and undulated his wrists. His provocations did not target individuals; rather, his erotics were multivalent and fluid in ways that were perhaps protective of his vulnerable subject-position in this libidinal economy.[46] His playfulness suggests that the spatial and sexual boundaries of heteronormativity at weddings are, much like the line of dancers that comprise the *shakl dāʾira*, permeable. Less than a minute later, two older men of social distinction (the father of the bride and the wedding singer) danced around each other in the center of the *dabke* circle. They ended their playful banter with a brush across each other's lips. Was this performance a demonstration of how older men with social privilege may "bend the rules" (Herzfeld 1997) of *rujūla*—that is, they may express embodied acts of pleasure without the risk of public shame? Or does their provocative play refuse to conform to any fixed code of honor and shame in ways that invite hesitation and a "caution to name" (Al-Kassim 2013) gendered and sexualized expressions? Whether and how bodily performance sexualizes ritual spaces raises broader questions about the indeterminacy of embodiment, desire, and power in the Arab Middle East.[47] Though these questions are beyond the scope of this chapter, they are indicative of how moments of improvised play, pleasure, and performance "unravel [any] certainty" (Al-Kassim 2013) about the construction of gender and sexual norms.

As described in these ethnographic episodes, there is much about the poetics and politics of performance and spectatorship in the *shakl dā'ira* that links *dabke* to the "male body as a social product and producer of social life" (Ghannam 2013). Of course femininity is also negotiated in this arena; as I have written about elsewhere (Silverstein 2016a), young women negotiate the gendered privileges of participation in public domains through the moral politics of dance. Yet the *shakl dā'ira* remains a predominantly heteronormative arena for "embodied acts of self-presentation"[48] (Chambers-Letson 2013, 6) that negotiate male privilege and status within patriarchal hierarchies of gender and age. By focusing on the construction of *marjala* as a bodily, affective, and relational construction of masculinity, I hope to have demonstrated how male physicality, sexuality, and morality are situated in and mediated by the spatial, participatory, and embodied dynamics of dance circles.

———

Flying, floating, flowing—flow states, or the process of attuning one's self to other moving bodies to actualize a culturally specific experience of playful pleasure, emerge from how individuals negotiate fluctuations in the dynamic space of performance. Drawing on my ethnographic participation in everyday social occasions and ritual performance events, I have explored how and why *dabke* is considered a "rhythmic" practice by pivoting to the sensate body—one that moves, listens, and feels—in order to probe the modes of perception and performance dynamics that engender flow states. I have demonstrated how flow states are dependent on intersubjective and intercorporeal relations with other bodies, such as *mīzān*, in the performance space. Disruptions to or failure to flow create moments of sensory disorientation that impact the sociality of embodied encounters. Flow states are not immune from but rather indicative of relationships of power that circulate between gendered bodies. In particular, relational forms of masculinity are constituted through distinct roles of performance, namely *awwal* and *tānnī* dancers, *awwal* dancer and *ṭabl* drummer, and collective participation within the *shakl dāʾira*. Furthermore, these performances comprise a culturally distinct set of codes and values that mediate gender, age, and kinship in ways that (more often than not) sustain the heteronormativity of wedding *ḥaflāt* and, more broadly, the patriarchal norms and conventions of Syrian society.

This chapter's close attention to bodywork and relational masculinity in prewar Syria sets the groundwork for understanding the complex body politics of the Syrian conflict, war, and displacement examined in the last part of this book. In chapters 5 and 6 I build on my analyses of masculinity and dance that dwell in the playful, pleasurable, and intimate spaces of social life and contribute to efforts to problematize hegemonic constructions of Arab masculinity. I also draw out the broader implications of the scholarship presented in this chapter, namely how the relational dynamics of gendered performance in everyday life are foundational for understanding the role of masculinity in negotiating the hegemonic forces of state and society.

At the outer limits of this chapter remains the question of how the music associated with this dance practice sounds. I address this topic in chapter 4, which focuses on a particular field of popular music known as *dabkāt*. Though *dabkāt* is not the only music to which people *dabke*, this particular music industry is based in the same performance spaces described in this chapter. Together these two chapters form a performance dyad that is at the heart of *dabke*—a dyad in which listening practices and subjects are foregrounded in the performance of *shaʿbī* movement and sound.

FOUR

Sonic Spectacularity

I first met the "King of *'Ataba*," aka Abu 'Atef aka Ibrahim Saqer,[1] at an 'Alawite wedding in Jable, a coastal mountain town in the Latakia region.[2] Saqer is a well-respected *shā'ar* (poet-singer) who, at the time of our introduction in 2008, performed regularly at local weddings. He began his lifelong career performing *sha'bī* music in the village of Shayr al-Nahal (literally: beehive), located just outside of Jable, where he still continued to receive visitors, such as myself, for informal *jalasāt*, or musicking sessions. He established his local and national career in the late 1950s, during which he traveled regularly to Damascus to perform at weddings and other private parties (*haflāt*). When I met Saqer in the fall of 2008, he was still very much in demand around Jable and held in wide esteem as a *fanān* (artist) of sung poetry (including the traditional song genre of *'ataba*) for his skills in improvising wordplay and rhymes, his vocality, and his charisma. Saqer attributes his talent and fame to his ability to perform *sha'bī* speech and song idioms that are *"kadīm min al-rassa"* ("old from the head," or from the original source). He theorizes that because he is from the coastal region that "gave birth" to the *dal'ūna*, he performs this folk song genre in its most authentic version. His style stands in contradistinction to those who modernized folk music in the mid-twentieth century by arranging it for urban audiences and recording industries (Asmar and Hood 2001; Racy 1996). Since social media became accessible in Syria in 2011, the circulation of Saqer's numerous historic and contemporary recordings of the coastal repertoire (featuring *mawawīl* and *'atabāt*,[3] as well as *zajāl* and *muḥāwara* ["duels"] with other well-regarded poet-singers) have further locked in his legacy as one of the most well-regarded poet-singers of modern Syria.[4] (View Saqer performing in a *muḥāwara* at CLIP 4.1 on the companion website.)

Saqer constructed a sense of musical authenticity through dominant identity paradigms that imbue these performance traditions (collectively known as *al-mūsīqā al-shaʿbiyya*, or popular music) with local, place-based senses of tradition, or "*maḥalī*" (place). Notwithstanding the significance of performing locality, it was immediately apparent upon my arrival at the wedding that Saqer's career was also built on extraordinary charisma. At the entrance to the wedding venue, a restaurant with a sizable banquet hall, Saqer greeted me and my colleague Samer Ali (who facilitated the invitation) with an enthusiastic handshake and warm embrace. Saqer had arranged for us to attend the wedding as his guests, a privilege indicative of Saqer's *wasta* (social capital) as well as his role as MC of the event. After we settled down in the back of the hall, the band began tuning up and checking their audio levels. The synthesizer player stationed his double decker Korg under the obligatory banner decorated with an image of President Assad (see figure 4.1).

Wedding singers tend to be adaptable and flexible in how and what they sing, with the main goal being to establish a party atmosphere, or *mazaj*, which is generally assessed by the extent to which party guests participate on the dance floor. As MC and lead vocalist (*muṭrib*), Saqer was responsible for pacing the event and recruiting participants to the dance floor. He began warming up the wedding guests by circling around the banquet hall and schmoozing with guests before the entrance of the bride. After the bridal processional (set to Lebanese singer Majda al-Roumi's "Nashid El Zafaf"),[5] Saqer gave a rousing toast that praised the bride and groom as well as their extended families. He then transitioned into the dance session with a *mawwāl*, an extended vocal improvisation that warmed up the *mazaj*. Over the course of the wedding *ḥafla* (which went until the early morning hours), Saqer progressed through a repertoire of popular songs familiar to this Jable community. He continually assessed the energy of the party guests, determining when to pick up the tempo with a *dabke* or, as a *shaʿbī* music producer put it, "take a big *mawwāl*" that allowed participants to return to their tables for a break.[6] Meanwhile, people ate, drank, smoked *narjīla* (a waterpipe with flavored tobacco), and celebrated the ʿAlawite nuptials.[7]

The wedding appeared to be full of *mazaj*—young men flaunted their moves while a *ṭabl* drummer encouraged participation in the dance circle (see figure 4.2). It was more theatricalized in comparison to outdoors weddings that I attended in other regions. In addition to the dramatization of the bridal proces-

FIGURE 4.1 *above*
Muṭrib Ibrahim Saqer
performing at a wedding in
Jable, Syria. October 8, 2008.
Photo by the author.

FIGURE 4.2 *left*
Ṭabl player and *dabke*
participants at a wedding in
Jable, Syria. October 8, 2008.
Photo by the author.

sional, there were a lavish bridal throne, full band, and professional cameramen who projected their video on a large screen mounted near the band. In the midst of this mediatized spectacularity, Saqer gave a dynamic and charismatic performance befitting a seasoned performer. The day after, however, he expressed disappointment with the event. Chatting at his home in the mountains of Jable, Saqer blamed the wedding guests: "They're not so good," he observed, referring to what he perceived as the relative lack of responsiveness by the audience to his live performance. Likewise, a few of the wedding guests were also disappointed by their experience, among them my colleague. He admitted that he had not understood most of the lyrics sung by Saqer, even though he was raised in the area and was a native speaker of the local dialect.

Both Saqer and my colleague attributed the faulty listening experience to the low-grade quality of the PA system and the venue's acoustic signature. Saqer in particular was displeased with the venue's acoustics—long reverberations and muddy frequencies that, according to him, reflected off the concrete walls of the restaurant. The acoustics obstructed the more subtle expressions of melody, timbre, and poetry that Saqer executed in his vocal improvisations. These artistic expressions have long been a measure of taste and appreciation among musical connoisseurs of *ṭarab* in the region (Racy 2003; Shannon 2006), but at this event, party guests overlooked such connoisseurship for the acoustic pleasures of the sound systems, specifically loud and distorted sounds.[8]

Sound systems are integral to listening experiences, not only at Syrian weddings but at dance parties worldwide, where "sonic bodies" (Henriques 2011) are constituted through the physical effects of acoustic vibrations and audio technologies on listeners. Relatedly, Kurdish musicians noted that they have to turn up the volume and distortion to offer guests the listening experience to which they are accustomed (Mürer 2020.) Every Syrian wedding that I attended featured a PA system, the quality of which varied according to the financial resources of the hosts. At outdoors events held in rural villages, speakers were hoisted high onto lampposts and other pieces of infrastructure in parking lots that had been converted into event spaces. At indoors events hosted at restaurants, the guests were barraged by high-impact acoustics from multiple speakers. Speakers provided the kind of atmosphere that appealed to listeners of *al-mūsīqā al-shaʿbiyya*, within which *dabkāt* (and its adjacent genre, *ʿatabāt*) is a stand-alone genre.

The preponderance of loud, distorted, and persistent sounds from the speakers suggests that listeners of *dabkāt* experience audibility as part of a greater sensorium—a world of haptic, olfactory, and proprioceptic sensations that engulf bodies over extended periods of time. More pointedly, listeners of *dabkāt* credit an event as having atmosphere (*mazaj*) when the audio is loud and distorted, that is, when bodies are placed within sound. Loudness and distortion, as I elaborate on throughout this chapter, are part of a theater of sound in which audio systems generate a mediatized sense of presence (Auslander 1999) and through which bodies become spectacularized through acts of listening. I name this phenomenon "sonic spectacularity" in recognition of the intensity and immediacy of sonic matter in shaping experiences of performance. Sonic vibrations produce a collectively shared experience that generates a ritualized sense of "communitas" (Turner 1977) at parties and renews community (Garcia 2020). By emphasizing the collective effects of embodied listening, I do not mean to suggest that the phenomenology of vibrations is a normative experience. As Michele Friedner and Stefan Helmreich note, "Vibrations may produce shared experience, [but do] not therefore produce identical experience" (2012, 77). Rather, my emphasis on audibility aims to shift scholarly focus away from the traditional role of the *muṭrib* in managing the social atmosphere of a *ḥafla* (Schade-Poulsen 1999) and towards the effects of corporeal experiences of listening on generating social bonds within local and kinship-based communities.

Among the musicians and studio producers that I interviewed, industry professionals of *al-mūsīqā al-shaʿbiyya* privileged the affective relations of musical performance. One music producer emphatically declared to me that a vocalist's reception by audiences is entirely "related to *mazaj* (mood, or atmosphere). Form is not a question." In other words, the affective experience of vocal (and instrumental) performance is central to the social and aesthetic significance of *al-mūsīqā al-shaʿbiyya*. These dynamics are not exclusive to popular music. Affective relations between musical performers and their listenership have long been celebrated as exceptional to Arab music, especially in studies that focus on *ṭarab* traditions. Scholar-artist Ali Jihad Racy introduces *ṭarab* (literally: enchantment, ecstasy) as a specific affective state associated with performing and listening to modern Arab art music repertoires, many of which are referred to as *ṭarab* because they are associated with the exceptional emotional experience.[9] He attests that artists and audiences of *ṭarab* music seek to attain a "higher plateau of creativity" (Racy 2003, 130) through their interactions.[10] For many connoisseurs of this musical world, the affective dynamics of *ṭarab* provide a "counter-narrative to European Enlightenment ideologies that stress the autonomous rational self" (Shannon 2006, 9). Important as these debates are to understanding the politics and value of *ṭarab* traditions, they do not animate *al-mūsīqā al-shaʿbiyya*, which generally inhabits a different social space. In the words of a record label owner, performer-spectator dynamics in the world of *al-mūsīqā al-shaʻbiyya* depend mainly "on what the *muṭrib* smoked."[11] At the risk of reproducing a false binary between modern art music and popular music, what arguably separates these different listening publics from one another are the long-standing politics of taste and social class (Simon 2022) that emerge from and reproduce discourses on morality, gender, sexuality, and modernity (van Nieuwkerk, LeVine, and Stokes 2016).[12] These politics inform the direction that critical studies of *al-mūsīqā al-shaʻbiyya* have undertaken insofar as these tend to focus more on the class and gender politics of popular music rather than on their affective force (Gilman 2014; Grippo 2010).

I challenge this academic genealogy of musical cultures in the SWANA region by insisting that *dabkāt* (as a specific genre in the broader industry of *al-mūsīqā al-shaʻbiyya*) has been overlooked and underappreciated, mainly because it is a dance music that speaks to acoustic pleasures rather than an elevated arts tradition predicated on musical knowledge of theory and repertoire. According to the music producers who control much of the *shaʻbī* music industry, wedding singers "play *dabkāt* to get people excited to go and dance."[13] Building on how performers and music producers in the popular music industry approach their audiences, I position the dancer-subject as an imagined listener towards whom musicians project their aesthetic choices. In so doing, this chapter aims to dismantle classist boundaries that have excluded the dancing body from musical spaces and musical scholarship of SWANA while also building on the previous chapter's discussion of dance and listening as an embodied social experience. Furthermore, this chapter's focus on dance music—that is, music for which a dancer is the imagined listener—generally sustains my theorization of embodiment in/as performance culture by analyzing the particular balance of sound and sociality that emerges in live embodied musical performances and that is considered necessary for the flow states of *dabke* practice.[14]

Complicating issues of liveness and sociality is the fact that *dabkāt* are what Eliot Bates calls a "digital tradition" (Bates 2016), that is, a cultural practice that sustains a sense of tradition through performance techniques that are entangled with the "analog-digital hybridity of contemporary life" (34). The digital tradition of *dabkāt* resonates in this hybrid space, particularly through live, embodied, and digital techniques of performance—which I refer to as *improvised arranging*—which together produce the digital sonic aesthetics associated with *dabkāt*. Improvised arranging, I suggest, is a process in which instrumentalists continually arrange and repeat codified units of traditional repertoire in live performance in ways that sync the aesthetics of liveness with the technological practices of playing instruments, especially the digital keyboard. Based on interviews with musicians and music producers, as well as my participation in live performance events, this chapter turns an ethnographic ear to the particular nexus of affect, aesthetics, and digital music production that constitutes *shaʿbī* musical spaces in prewar Syria.

This chapter argues for and details the transformative effects of digitalization on the politics of class and taste in popular music. In the 2000s, neoliberal spaces (from radio and television to cafe culture) increasingly excluded *dabkāt* in favor of Arab pop music produced by transnational media conglomerates and broadcast over satellite television. The sensory excessiveness associated with *dabkāt* (and with *al-mūsīqā al-shaʿbiyya* in general) became a matter of class politics in the context of these gentrified urban spaces, where *dabkāt* were often muted because they were considered excessive. By locating shifts in music consumption not in discourses on popular music but rather in an analysis of listening experiences, I center sonic bodies at the heart of everyday social life in prewar Syria. More specifically, I spotlight the role of digital audio technology in making the listening experience spectacular and situate sonic spectacularity in the negotiation of social relations at ritual wedding events. However, I also destabilize the sociality of *dabkāt* by illustrating how, because of its spectacular sonic excess, it became a marker of taste and class in ways that divided listeners between newly emerging neoliberal urban spaces and long-standing spaces for musical consumption. Listening to and for *dabkāt* reveals the fraught balance of class relations that afflicted Syria in the decade immediately prior to the revolution and war.

SITUATING THE DIGITAL IN *DABKĀT*

Developments in audio and digital technology have significantly transformed *dabkāt* over the twentieth century, like many popular musics worldwide. In the 1970s in Lebanon, a single *darbukka* (goblet drum) was sufficient for guests dancing at smaller weddings.[15] More common than a single percussion instrument was a wedding singer and band who performed a range of traditional song genres including but not limited to *ʿataba*, *daʿūna*, and *dabke*. Musical creativity in *dabkāt* finds expression through the improvised and emergent arrangement of repeated vocal, melodic, and rhythmic motifs, situated in a repertoire of popular traditional music that is distinct from (though at times overlaps) the repertoire of *ṭarab*. Since the 1970s, these practices have been digitalized, a process of integrating digital technology into musicianship, performance, and recording practices. Rather than being perceived as inauthentic to traditional musical culture, digital technology sustains the musical creativity of *dabkāt* and related popular musics. Here I briefly outline the main performance roles and history of digital music as they relate to the performance and production of *dabkāt*.

Currently, vocalists perform improvised, often rhyming, repertoire in a number of traditional song genres, including *'ataba*, *dalʿūna*, *dabke*, and *ruzana*, among others (Abbas 2018). Vocalists also play a key role in facilitating social interactions and dance sessions at events. Similar to the role of MCs and DJs in electronic dance music culture, they actively curate the musical material of the event, which in turn shapes the performed behaviors and social interactions of the event. Because of this role, wedding singers remain accountable for whether and when *mazaj* coagulates or dissipates among those present, although, as I describe later, this accountability has somewhat shifted with the predominance of the digital keyboard synthesizer.

Among the range of instruments that accompany the vocalist, those most often associated with *dabkāt* include the *mijwiz* (double reed pipe), *rabāb*, and *ṭabl*. Local performance practices and traditions vary in terms of which of these instruments, and many others, are considered indigenous; across Syria, however, these three dominate in performance, production, and national imaginaries. The *mijwiz* has a shrill, nasal timbre that is, according to Racy (1994), associated with states of ecstasy and elation as well as *dabke* dance.[16] Whereas the *mijwiz* remains the most popular melodic instrument, often serving as an indexical signifier of *dabke* across popular music genres, the *rabāb* has become a cipher of authenticity that is strategically deployed to signify sanctioned forms of nostalgia. These forms encompass staged folklore and Bedouinness (as described in chapter 2), as well as a general sense of pastness for live performances of epic poetry (to which *rabāb* is linked [Racy 1996]), which have not been an active performance genre in everyday life for decades. Finally, the *ṭabl* is performatively linked with the *nawari* dance rhythm [tD-t D-t-], which the drummer often plays while walking around the *shakl dā'ira* (dance circle) and helping to keep dancers in time with the music (see figures 4.3 and 4.4).[17] Within *dabkāt*, rhythms are a bricolage of common Arab dance rhythms, with no singular dance pattern signifying *dabkāt*. Through performance practice, these three instruments engender senses of place, tropes of memory, and affective registers that construct, in complex ways, the musical authenticity of *dabkāt*.

FIGURE 4.3 *above*
Mijwiz player at a
wedding in Jaabat
Khashab, Syria. July 2008.
Photo by the author.

FIGURE 4.4 *left*
Ṭabl player performing
at a wedding in Saddad,
Syria. August 2008.
Photo by the author.

Like many other regional practices, *dabkāt* are anchored by a "place-based sense of tradition" (Bates 2016, 24), specifically rural traditions. The construction of *maḥalī* (literally: place) occurs through the signifying practices of local vocal dialects and instrumental performance techniques (Silverstein 2013). The authenticity paradigm of *dabke*, upheld as much by performers as by listeners, is also linked to repertoire and its performance as "acts of transfer" (Taylor 2003) that connect peoplehood to a sense of rurality across generations. Latakia, for instance, is claimed by many, including Ajjan and Ibrahim Saqer, as the "birthplace" of the *daḷūna* (a song and a song genre) and a haven for *dabkāt*.[18] Folk song traditions, writes Ziad Ajjan (2008), a musicologist based in the coastal city of Latakia, "reflect everyday life in local contexts and express the joys and sorrows of husbandry and manual labor."[19] These claims for cultural authenticity situate Latakia within a sociocultural corridor that runs along the coastal mountainous areas of the eastern Mediterranean, mainly in present-day Syria and Lebanon.[20]

Though these claims for Latakia's role in song heritage appear to reinforce the "sociological solidity" (Bhabha 1994) of place in ways that more broadly reproduce the seeming durability of the homeland, these and similar signifying practices have shifted significantly in the twentieth and twenty-first centuries. During the urbanization and modernization of the 1950s, urban composers and singers adapted rural song repertoires to appeal to urban audiences. For instance, Wadiʿ al-Safi is famous for collapsing the song form of "*mijana*" into the "break" of the urbanized *daḷūna* song genre (Asmar and Hood 2001). Other composers arranged song practices of repetitive form, such as *dabke*, into short (three-minute) songs capable of being pressed onto LP records (Asmar and Hood 2001). In so doing, these rural repertoires were reimagined as "folk" at a historic moment in which a modern music industry emerged through the establishment of major recording and movie industries and festivalization (Stone 2008). A second major shift occurred in the 1990s, when a new generation of vocalists (dubbed "new wave *dabke*" by some fans) began releasing albums that were essentially recordings of live performances edited with digital audio technology (Silverstein 2013). These editing practices integrated audio technology and digital culture in ways, on which this chapter focuses, that have had a significant impact on the performance and production of *dabkāt*. Finally, a third historic moment is currently being shaped by the mass migration of Syrians that occurred in the 2010s as a result of armed conflict, in which musical artists are creatively hybridizing *dabkāt* with other popular musics, especially electronic dance music. From the invention of the folk to global cultural flow, *dabkāt* are a practice infused with imaginaries of place and tradition.

Starting in the 1980s, musicians, producers, and audiences of *dabkāt* began adopting digital forms of music technology for their performing, recording, editing, and listening practices. The digitalization of *dabkāt* was not exceptional or unique to the West, but rather occurred worldwide in popular music practices as developments in computer technologies and audio culture converged with corporate industries and mass consumers. The "watershed" moment for the digitalization of popular music, according to Paul Théberge (2015), was 1983, when Yamaha released a DX7 synthesizer, and the Musical Instrumental Digital Interface (MIDI) was introduced to consumers, mainly amateur and professional musicians. Prior to this moment, synthesizers and other music technologies had been primarily housed in the research centers at universities and corporations. The impact of this technology was to make popular musics more editable, mutable, and malleable. With content more "copyable" and "ripe for manipulations" (Hesmondhalgh 2009), there was a sea change in how creativity was perceived and carried out. New definitions of musicianship emerged as the relevance of traditional performance skills shifted, increasing anxiety that digital technologies might "deskill" (Reyes 2010) musical labor, especially that of drummers. At the same time, the role of the producer became more significant in recording studios as MIDI technologies, especially digital sampling, sequencing, and multitrack recording, became more widespread (Warner 2003).

Digitalization was not the first historic moment in which technology impacted music production, performance, and reception. The development of the phonograph enabled listeners to listen repeatedly to recorded tracks, a phenomenon that shifted the object of listening such that timbre, intonation, and microtiming came to be considered part of the composition process rather than individualized artistic interpretation in live performance (Zak 2001; Gracyk 1996). Digital audio technology has similarly shifted what listeners attune to and how musicians and music producers approach musical aesthetics. Comparable to "phonographic effects" (Katz 2004) on listening practices, sonic elements of music have been pushed to the foreground by MIDIs, synthesizer keyboards, samplers, and, as of the mid- to late 1990s, the digital audio workstation (DAW) and its associated software (Pro Tools, Ableton, Fruity Loops, etc.). Central to digital sonic aesthetics are "clear audible traces of digital technology," which forge "digital signatures" out of unique combinations of audio effects, including "digital reverb, delay, MIDI and sampling, digital silence, virtual cut-and-paste, digital glitches, micro rhythmic manipulation, [and] attuning" (Danielsen and Brøvig-Hanssen 2016, 2). These audio effects, argues Eliot Bates, are produced through "digital logics," that is, an "object-oriented" (2016, 277) process that mediates "entanglements between studio professionals, technological objects (analog, digital, instrumental, and acoustical), and musical aesthetics" (17).

What characterizes *dabkāt* today is a digital sonic aesthetic that integrates all of these traces, effects, and logics through creative acts that sustain a place-based sense of tradition. Musical creativity is generated through digital technology via *improvised arranging*, or emergent aesthetic choices that continually arrange and repeat codified units of traditional repertoire. The performer most essential to these processes of improvised arranging is the keyboard player. The digital keyboard synthesizer, popularly known as the org, quickly came to dominate *ḥaflāt* in Syria and across the region after its introduction in the 1990s.[21] Some refer to org players as "one-man shows" in acknowledgment of how the technological capabilities of the synthesizer have reconfigured and depreciated musical labor at live events. According to Khaled, a *muṭrib* from Hama, org players can "make a complete party (*ḥafla kāmil*)."[22] Though org players offer "all [the] possibilities," they have not altogether displaced other instrumentalists from the wedding and entertainment industry—larger *ḥaflāt* continue to feature players on acoustic *mijwiz, mizmār, kamān* (violin), *buzuq* (long-necked lute), *ʿūd*, and percussion, typically *riq, darbukka*, or *ṭabl*. Nevertheless keyboard players are overwhelmingly considered the most indispensable instrumentalists to be hired for live music sessions.

Org players reconfigured performance practice by integrating digital technology with live performance through the practice of improvised arranging. Such integration does not necessarily imply that there is a binary between technology and live performance (Kim 2017). The relationship of technology, liveness, and performance is a widely debated issue, particularly in the field of performance studies. The question of whether the value of "bodily co-presence" (Fischer-Lichte 2008) is privileged as something that cannot be reproduced (Phelan 1993) because it is situated in a particular place and time, or bodily presence is mediated by historically contingent forms of technology and media (Auslander 1999), centers the immediacy of "presence" (Dixon 2007) in the "here and now" (Fischer-Lichte 2008) of performance. These debates on the significance of presence have accounted for digital technology by recognizing that "what counts culturally as live experience changes over time in relation to technological change" (Auslander 2012, 3). However, they remain predicated on assumptions about liveness that are not universally upheld (Muñoz 1999; Nyong'o 2022). Perhaps akin to these critiques that question the social biases that shape debates on presence and liveness in academia, those who perform and consume Syrian *dabkāt* do not necessarily attribute value to the question of whether a particular sound is technologically mediated. For instance, digital reproductions of a melody in a *mijwiz* timbre are considered as valuable as acoustic performances by a *mijwiz* player rather than the latter being privileged as the source, or original performance event, on which the former is based. I argue that instead of rooting liveness in the presence or absence of acoustic or digital instruments, *dabke* performers and listeners locate this phenomenon in the material effects of sonic vibrations in the event space.

LIVENESS

Dabkāt producers recognize the powerful somatic relationship between listeners, bodies, and audio technology through a relationship that they identify as "*ḥayy*." Translated as "liveness," this socio-aesthetic construct refers to both a copresent experience in which performer and listener share the same physical space and the audio simulation of that experience. *Ḥayy* is intermedial in the sense that it refers to embodied and technologically mediated sounds (acoustic, analog, electronic, and digital) that mutually constitute the listening experience of the *ḥafla*. *Ḥayy* is also an important factor in the production of recorded sounds. Studio producers describe *ḥayy* as a socio-aesthetic construct that they consider valuable for the participant's experience. When musicians and producers aim for *ḥayy* as a desirable sonic aesthetic during recording and editing time in the studio, they imagine the sensory experience of their listeners; that is, they recognize that sounds are a material acoustic force that impact bodies on the dance floor in ways that make those bodies aware of their own and each other's presence.

The materiality of sound, in this discussion, refers to acoustic vibrations, or the physical movements by which sound travels through air (among other mediums, such as water; see Eidsheim 2015). Sound studies has broadly theorized how these vibrations shape listener-centered experiences by decentering the role of the ear and hearing functions in notions of what constitutes listening, and by expanding vibration-oriented listening (Eidsheim 2015; Holmes 2017) to include the whole bodily apparatus through multisensorial processes, including tactility. The pivot to the materiality of sound has been especially attentive to the effects of rhythm, percussion, and beats in musical experience. The impact of acoustic vibrations "across the human body's sensory modes," argues Luis-Manuel Garcia

(2015, 61–63) in the context of electronic dance music, is that beats "do not only play an associative or representational role in relation to touch but are impactive and tactile in themselves." Participants expect that their bodies' "flesh, skin and bones" (61–63) will be impacted by acoustic vibrations as part of their musical experience. As mentioned in this chapter's opening pages, listeners have come to expect high volumes and distorted frequencies as part of the digital sonic aesthetic experienced at live ḥaflāt. This suggests that the impact of acoustic vibrations is crucial for the phenomenological sense of embodied presence that is associated with these events. Indeed, one might speculate that the rhythmic precision that *dabke* dancers aspire towards is related to how dancers transduce their haptic experience of acoustic vibrations into dance movements.

Underpinning and shaping these listening and dancing experiences is the digital logic of *dabke* production and performance. Studio producers are motivated to produce samples and presets that make people "excited" to "dance," that is, to anticipate and desire the haptic experience of acoustic vibrations. The musician key to facilitating listening and dancing experiences during the performance event is the org player. How the phenomenon of *ḥayy* emerges through the improvised arranging practice of org players is a complex practice that circulates between the recording and mixing studio and the social choreographies of musicians, dancers, and other participants on the dance floor. Based on several interviews with org players and studio producers active in the *sha'bī* music industry, I detail this culturally specific practice of liveness as *ḥayy*, aiming to decenter and deprivilege academic assumptions about the value of sonic and other modalities of presence in performance.

Digital synthesizers have the capacity to generate any instrumental sound or rhythmic pattern, play audio samples, and accommodate individual musician preferences through choices in sequencing and programming. Org players arrange heterogeneous melodic and rhythmic parts through a process that begins before the show and continues into live performance. They acquire digital material from local music studios, where digital presets, samples, and recordings are produced and mixed. They program and sequence their synthesizers in advance of a show. For instance, an org player who collaborates frequently with Khaled, Abu Hassan (also a pseudonym), programmed his synthesizer to play vocal trills when pressing down on the A# (or another key) in the upper register of his keyboard. He also programmed a *taqsīm* in a *rabāb* timbre by pressing down on the F# black key in the middle register.

Once org players have programmed their instrument to suit their individual preferences, needs, and habits, they improvise with the timing and selection of digital material in the course of performance. In contrast with musicians who play a distinct and singular part of the arrangement, org players arrange as they improvise with musical material that includes melody, rhythm, pitch, vocables (such as vocal trills, exclamations of hurrah, or singing parts), and nonmusical material (such as handclapping). Because the org player has the capacity to introduce these different elements into the musical experience, he is essential for generating *mazaj* and a sense of presence among event participants. Hiring an org player is therefore not only about economic efficiency—that is, that one keyboardist can guarantee a "*ḥafla kāmil*"—but also a recognition of the primacy of the org player in motivating people to enter the dance circle, that is, in generating the affective experience desired of the *ḥafla*.

Instruments are programmed and sequenced into org synthesizers in at least two ways: first, as a live keyboard performance in which pitches are rendered in the timbre of the selected instrument (Rasmussen 1996), and second as "presets," or digital audio files that contain samples of previously recorded tracks from past live events or studio recordings. All the traditional instruments mentioned earlier are typically sequenced into the synthesizer, including *rabāb*, *mijwiz*, *buzuq*, *kamān*, and *ʿūd*, among others. What guides the selection of a given instrumental timbre in the course of improvised arranging is an amalgamation of what the org player judges is appropriate for the *mazaj* and which sonic markers of place listeners prefer. Of the traditional instruments, none is arguably more affect-rich than the *mijwiz*, which for many is synonymous with the *dabke* genre of music (Racy 1994).

In addition to considering affective responses to timbre, keyboardists negotiate discourses of tradition in their selection of instruments. For instance, the *rabāb* is a spiked fiddle associated with Bedouin lifeworlds that traditionally accompanies a *shāʿar*. Distinguishing between the *rabāb* and the *kamān*, Khaled notes that he prefers the former because it is considered *shaʿbī*. "You just can't do the *ʿataba* with the *kamān*. It's not *ḥelwe* (sweet), not representative of heritage. The *rabāb* is prettier. I prefer the *rabāb* because it's *shaʿbi*. It has one string and it goes with *ʿataba*. Where there is *ʿataba* there is *rabāb*." Khaled's remarks inflect a correlation between song genre (*ʿataba*) and instrument (*rabāb*) that itself substantiates the discursive construction of musical tradition through performance practice.

Notably, in Khaled's exaltation of the *rabāb*, he did not distinguish between the digitally reproduced sound of the instrument and the acoustic instrument itself. Nor did he grant the privilege of authenticity to the acoustic instrument, that is, to the instrument as sound source. This struck me as peculiar given how much Khaled upholds the *rabāb* as a musical signifier of authentic Arabness. Similar to Khaled's appreciation for this folk instrument, the *rabāb* figured prominently in the children's folk dance performance at the 2008 folk festival in Idlib, where they opened their wedding scene with a young boy singing epic poetry while accompanying himself on the *rabāb*. Both vocal and instrumental parts were prerecorded and lip-synched, effectively enacting the "art of mimesis" (Kirshenblatt-Gimblett 1998, 20) and, through staged in situ performance, turning the *rabāb* into an ethnographic object. In the context of live entertainment such as a *ḥafla*, by comparison, the org is considered a sufficient medium for the sound of the *rabāb*.[23] I never saw the *rabāb* played as an acoustic instrument in live performance during my fieldwork, and I only occasionally heard it played as a preset or timbre option on the org. The shift from acoustic *rabāb* to digitalized *rabāb* has led to the construction of a new category, "*rabāb ḥadīth*" (modern *rabāb*), according to Khaled. For most listeners at *ḥaflāt*, however, there is little perceived need to distinguish between digital and acoustic sounds so long as listeners recognize distinctions between timbres, motivic constructions, and rhythmic patterns.

Outside of a folk festival setting, listeners generally do not ascribe more value of authenticity to the "real" body of the instrument than to its digitally reproduced sound. What is valued is the production of sonic liveness through digital music production. Recorded audio tracks are mixed and edited at digital audio workstations in professional music studios to simulate liveness, before being sold as a preset to org players. Liveness, in other words, is constructed through the digital material and digital logics of *shaʿbī* musicians and producers. A studio producer based in Beirut, Walid Baghdadi, told me that though a *mizmār* melody may sound "live on the face" at an event, the melody and timbre are more often than not generated from samples arranged at a studio.[24] This process contrasts sharply with other popular musics in which liveness, tradition, and authenticity emerge through a fidelity to instruments as sound sources.[25] Syrian producers of *dabkāt* eschew this approach to traditional popular music, instead opting for a digital sonic aesthetic that values spectacular modes of listening.

Nonmusical sounds also contribute to sonic spectacularity. Org players strategically use material known as "the *ḥafla* track"—audio recorded from a live performance event that is arranged and edited into samples, clips, or even a full track by music studios for purchase by org players who incorporate this digital material into their practice. I had heard samples from these tracks played at weddings, from Suwayda to Qunaytra and Greater Damascus. They were comprised entirely of 2/4 rhythmic patterns, usually a combination of *mālfūf* and *ayyub* with handclapping. The handclapping occurred on the beat and reinforced the downbeat drive of the groove. Also common to the "*ḥafla* track" were *zagharīt* (vocal ululations, usually performed by older women at weddings).[26]

In his informal demonstration of org techniques, Abu Hassan played these two effects from his "*ḥafla* track." (View Abu Hassan's session at CLIP 4.2 on the companion website.) He used the handclapping and *zagharīt* samples differently—the handclapping was part of the rhythmic texture and reinforced the downbeat of the 2/4 meter and the persistent, unwavering pulse. He kept it running throughout the duration of the session. The vocal trills were an effect that he programmed into the synthesizer on the F# of the middle register. Every time he pressed down on F#, vocal trills cascaded out the synthesizer's built-in speakers. He explained that he "used this as an ornament whenever he felt like it," in other words, that his timing was improvisational. He liked it because it enhanced the live party feel that he was going for. Importantly, he did not deploy the *zagharīt* as an authenticating strategy that might, for instance, serve as a sonic trace of the event at which the *zagharīt* originally occurred. These kinds of archival traces are important for recordings of traditional Turkish folkloric recordings, according to Eliot Bates (2016), which include diegetic sounds, such as the sounds of dancing feet, in order to make recordings sounds more "live."[27] The *ḥafla* tracks of *dabkāt* differ insofar as nonmusical audio material is not intended to mimic an in situ experience but rather to theatricalize the listening experience through the digital production of audio spectacle.

Arguably the component of this digital tradition that is most fundamental to the theater of live performance is rhythm. Many keyboardists prioritize rhythm as the key to generating the performance conditions appropriate for *dabke* dance circles. After all, rhythmic sensibilities are vital for the movement aesthetics of *dabke*, as discussed at length in chapter 3. *Dabke* rhythms are neither precomposed nor arranged, nor is there any one specific rhythm prescribed for the practice.[28] The repetitive and dense percussive texture characteristic of *dabkāt* is generated by how musicians alternate, switch, overlap, embellish, double-voice, and above all, repeat duple meter rhythms.[29] Keyboardists typically sequence a heterophonic arrangement of multiple electronic tracks that comprise a composite of duple meter dance patterns. These most often include 2/4 styles, primarily *ayyub* [D--t D-t-] and *mālfūf* [D--t --t-], along with 4/4 styles such as *ṣaʿīdi* [Dt-D D-t-] and *nawari* [tD-t D-t-], set to tempos ranging from 104 to

132 m.m.[30] Some rhythms, such as *mālfūf* and *ayyub*, are more often performed electronically on the org, while others, such as *nawari*, are more often performed acoustically on the *ṭabl*.

Abu Hassan suggested to me that the overall rhythmic "vibe" (Garcia 2020) is more important than the specifics of the rhythmic patterns. In other words, he linked sonic affect as primary to collective experience. He created the appropriate vibe through the production of "ʿiqa ḥayy" (live percussion). The aesthetics of ʿiqa ḥayy, according to Abu Hassan and studio producers, are unparalleled in production and performance and considered essential to the danceability of *dabkāt*. Counterintuitively, however, ʿiqa ḥayy is not dependent on the live, embodied presence of percussionists.[31] Exemplary of the digital logics of *dabkāt*, it can be produced in the studio and integrated into live shows through the improvised arranging practice of org players, who sequence and program rhythmic tracks and samples throughout their playing. By creating a theater of sound through improvised arrangements of beats, samples, and audio effects that boom from speakers, org players mold the digital sonic spectacularity of *dabkāt*.

The production of ʿiqa ḥayy begins both in the studio and at the live party. Production studios source edit and mix recordings of live parties that they sell as recorded music or to produce presets and samples for purchase by org players. Studio producers are deliberate about how they manufacture liveness through recording and editing processes. One Beirut-based producer, Abu Husayn, often hires a percussionist to augment what is "not heard very well in the recordings" of *ḥaflāt* and to make the *ṭabl* more "powerful in the studio." "Sometimes," he continues, "we really need to add live *darbukka* just to excite people to go and dance." By recording additional *darbukka* sounds in the studio, what producers such as Abu Husayn amplify is the concept of live digital sound as intermedial, such that recorded sound incorporates an aesthetic of liveness, and live performances incorporate recorded sounds. In other words, ḥayy is not considered a referent to the authenticity of the live acoustic listening event (in contrast to other popular musics such as Nashville-based country music or South African *mbaqanga*) but rather indexes the loud aesthetics of *dabkāt*.[32]

The production of ʿiqa ḥayy depends on a complex and multifaceted process that shifts in relation to what music producers create in their studios, how org players play with digital material at the live show, and whether and how many live percussionists are hired to boost the ʿiqa ḥayy for a given event. With the integration of digital tools and logics into performance practice, musicians and producers have come to consider sound itself, as opposed to the musical construction of genre, style, melody, and rhythm, an affective component crucial to the process of experiencing music. The slippage between liveness and digital sound production is enmeshed in the tastes of those who sustain the *sha'bī* music industry. However, just as loudness is a sonic experience whose intensity is relative to the individual perception of the amplitude of soundwaves, listeners respond differently to the vibrational intensities of *'iqa ḥayy*. Some listeners register the somatic intensity of *'iqa ḥayy* in ways that facilitate danced participation, while others do not. The politics of frequency, to echo Steven Goodman (2010), differentiates between those who desire *dabkāt* and those tormented by *dabkāt* (there is rarely a middle ground). Taste politics notwithstanding, the digital sonic aesthetic is integral with and constitutive of live performance in ways that have made liveness more sonically spectacular.

SPECTACULAR NUPTIALS

Related to the variegation of listening experiences is the question of what the performative effects are of *ḥayy* on the social relations of the *ḥafla*. Though digital technology has transformed much about *dabkāt*, parties have long been theatrical spaces in which musical performances of sound dominate. The sonic spectacularity of *ḥayy*, I argue, intensifies the social dynamics of these communal events by dramatizing participants' sense of presence through loud and excessive vibrational listening to a digital sonic aesthetic, similar to the visual effects of multiple large screens at live concerts. By expanding the scale and intensity of technology and media, the immersive experience of the event becomes more intense (Dixon 2007). Such intensity becomes a social force when it is imbricated in the "structured actions that naturalize wider power relationships" (Couldry 2004, 356; cf. Kim 2017) in rituals such as weddings and other *ḥaflāt* performatively associated with *dabkāt*.

In Syria, like elsewhere, weddings bear the ritual function of engendering the heteronormative reproduction of kinship from generation to generation. Though specific ritualized processes vary between communities, the participant-spectator relationship between wedding guests and the bridal couple is crucial to enacting the ritual transformation by which the bridal couple is incorporated into the "social body-politic" of communities (Kastrinou 2016). Moreover, spatial choreographies of performance and spectatorship enact ritual subjectivities through the spectacular, argues Marie Kastrinou. She suggests that brides and grooms aspire for a spectacular presence that is at once glamorous and regal.

The bridal couple are spectators—they sit still and apart from their guests, often on a bridal throne adorned with roses, to watch their guests enjoy themselves.[33] By watching wedding guests participate and perform in nuptial activities, such as dancing, Kastrinou maintains, the bride and groom's nuptial subjectivity extends onto and is extended by the bodies of their guests. These intersubjective relations, constituted through performed behaviors, are crucial for the ritualized integration of the bridal couple into broader kinship relations between families and, often but not always, within sectarian communities.

Other performative elements of the wedding are also spectacularized in ways that enhance the performer-spectator dynamics. For example, the Jable wedding described at the outset of this chapter hired two *ṭabl* drummers to perform rather than the customary single *ṭabl* player (if additional live percussionists are desired, they usually join on *darbukka* or *riq*). The two *ṭabl* players paraded behind Saqer as he mingled with guests at the beginning of the wedding party, banging *nawari* and other popular rhythms on their large double-barreled drums (see figure 4.5). Not only was the doubling of *ṭabl* players unusual, but the effects of two drummers parading around the banquet hall in the opening stages of the party was multifold: their playing propelled acoustic vibrations onto the bodies of guests as they mingled, their parade theatricalized musical performances, and they boosted the immersive spectatorial experience on which presence is predicated.

Kastrinou's interpretation of nuptial subjectivity is helpful because it reinforces the role of *dabke* performance at weddings in facilitating spectatorship, by the bride and groom as well as other guests, thereby mediating the integration of the bridal couple into the larger community. It is also helpful for understanding the role of the spectacular at these ritual events, where a "larger-than-life" presence is aspired to by all involved. For instance, the fluid social and spatial dynamics at the Jable wedding were magnified by screen technology, which Kastrinou notably does not mention in her analytic focus on performance as embodied social behavior. The entrance of the bride was announced with a flood of light onto a projector screen that continued to video-broadcast the wedding activity throughout the evening. A disco ball bounced light around and across the room throughout the dance sessions, which lasted all evening. Meanwhile the professional cameraman and his lighting assistant dazzled the dance floor as they moved around with their bright lighting effects. They relayed their videos onto projection screens that displayed participants as "large-scale telematic images" (Kelly 2007, 118). These images impacted the immediate sensory environment with the bigness of the screen and enlarged the presence, symbolic and real,

FIGURE 4.5 Two *ṭabl* players parading around a banquet hall at a wedding in Jable, Syria. October 8, 2008. Photo by the author.

of those appearing onscreen. Spectatorship, liveness, and technology became "somatic forces working on the spectator's body" (Kelly 2007, 117) that impacted the lived experience of the event. I later wrote in my field notes that "it was a nice touch to have the video camera going live so we could see all the action as it happened."[34] The visual spectacle also arguably enhanced a sense of voyeurism, which, as Steve Dixon (2007) suggests, enabled the viewer (the wedding guests) to glance at the performing subjects on the screen in ways that situated the viewer as a specific kind of spectator who overlapped with the ritual participatory dynamics that generally characterize these nuptial events.

In addition to the big screen, wedding guests took recordings and pictures of intimate and playful moments with their mobile phones. The cumulative effect of numerous video activities and of the engorged screen presence was to amplify and enhance the sense of visual presence and the experience of liveness, both of which mediated the sociospatial relationships between performers and spectators on which the ritual process of a wedding hinges. Syrian weddings often incorporate "technologies of the spectacular" (Kelly 2007) that are visual, sonic, and tactile (and even olfactory, depending on the lavishness of the wedding banquet). As I have demonstrated in my discussion of the performance and production of *ʿiqa ḥayy*, among other specific modalities, these technologies of the spectacular

Sonic Spectacularity **153**

are key components that intensify the social theater and immersive world making that occur at weddings, restaurant shows, nightclubs, and other live events.

SHIFTING POPULAR MUSIC INDUSTRIES

Despite the proliferation of musical recordings in the region since the advent of the phonograph in the 1920s (Denning 2015), and despite the "Golden Age" of the 1950s during which Wadiʿ al-Safi, Zaki Nassif, and Fairouz, among others, adapted and recorded rural repertoire for urban audiences (Asmar and Hood 2001), there is still much that is unknown about the history of recorded music in Lebanon and Syria. One could speculate that the popularization of the digital audio workstation in the mid- to late 1990s impacted the aesthetics of commercial recordings, particularly recordings of street music that circulated as "cassette culture" (Manuel 1993) in informal markets. When I began to visit Syria in the early 2000s, *dabkāt* and *ʿatabāt* sung by local *muṭribīn* (vocalists) were available in the form of low-grade CD recordings, sold at the same street side stalls where vendors displayed pirated copies of the latest pop music hits. Often these products were either recordings taken from live events or compilations of other pirated tracks.

In contrast to this local and informal sector of *al-mūsīqā al-shaʿbiyya*, a transnational market for contemporary Arab pop music (*shabābī*) that first emerged in the 1970s began to grow more rapidly in the 2000s due to the rapid expansion of the satellite media and telecommunications industries (Abdel Aziz 2010). Produced mainly in Egypt, Lebanon, and Algeria, Arab pop music blended Arabic lyrics, melodies and dance beats with Western harmony and rhythms, all in a digestible three-minute format. Some singers occasionally worked in both of these recording industries; they typically started out in local *shaʿbī* scenes before making it big in transnational Arab pop. Lebanese megastars Fares Karam and Melhem Zein, among others, forged a market for *dabke*-style Arab pop music within this industry.[35] The pop music industry expanded significantly through the broadcasting of music videos on satellite television channels, namely Rotana, Melody, and Mazzika. These chic, contemporary videos attested to the accumulation of wealth in the upper classes of Arab societies in the ways that they featured groomed singers as they frolicked in luxury villas; on coastlines; on mountainous overlooks; and in other spaces of leisure, recreation, and heterosexual romance.

Overall, the mass-mediated pop music industry diverged substantively from *al-mūsīqā al-shaʿbiyya* in terms of finance, studio production, distribution, and reception. One of the most important effects of this rapidly transforming industry was the muffling of *al-mūsīqā al-shaʿbiyya*, especially *dabkāt*, in leisure spaces that were increasingly dedicated to Arab pop music.[36] *Al-mūsīqā al-shaʿbiyya* had a minimal presence on satellite television channels, which were generally oriented towards advertising and marketing for the transnational media companies.[37] An important exception was Sawt al-Shaʿb, which offered television programming with socialist and populist overtones, including *al-mūsīqā al-shaʿbiyya* by Syrian (rather than Lebanese or Egyptian) singers. Aside from this channel (itself on the periphery of the mediascape), satellite music video channels were a crucial part of lifestyles of conspicuous consumption, particularly cafe culture. Cafe culture transformed in the late 2000s from traditional Arab coffeehouses frequented by men who sipped tea while playing backgammon to new chic luxury spaces with modern furniture, decorative art, espresso menus, and Arab pop playing on flatscreen TVs mounted on the walls. Musical selections were considered an important element of this environmental design that appealed to the taste of savvy, aspiring neoliberal elite youth (Deeb and Harb 2013). Specifically missing from this leisurely environment was *al-mūsīqā al-shaʿbiyya*.

Another effect of the heavily favored promotion of Arab pop over *dabkāt* was an increased homogeneity of the market. Some lamented that these changes contributed to a "loss of *ruḥ*" (e.g., authenticity or soul). Society, grieved *muṭrib* Mustafa Simasim, has gone "from a million words at a party to covers of Fares Karam and Bous al WaWa."[38] Anxieties over the loss of original musical material, particularly by vocalists, due to transnational corporate media were not misplaced. Local *muṭribīn* and local *dabkāt* styles remained on the streets as "cassette culture" in an informal economic sector, while popular music production shifted from primarily networks of local and regional producers and distributors to transglomerate media companies that distributed music videos over satellite television channels and consolidated fandom around star singers. A notable exception to these trends was "ʿAloush," a *dabke* music video featuring and produced by Ali El Dik that nostalgically portrayed rural life from the perspective of a successful urban go-getter, El Dik. (See "ʿAloush" at CLIP 4.3 on the companion website.) "ʿAloush" broke through the *shabābī* barrier on music videos by introducing a *shaʿbī* music video to the satellite television market (Silverstein 2013).

What, specifically, charged the polemics of *dabkāt* in Syria during the neoliberal autocracy of the 2000s? The dismissal of popular songs as cheap (*rakhīs*) and vulgar (*shaʿbī*) dates back to at least the 1950s (Al-Husami 1954). These culture wars are not specific to Syria, as the politics of popular culture are and have been in constant agitation across the region (van Nieukwerk, LeVine, and Stokes 2016). On what basis, then, did people rationalize their distaste for *dabkāt*, and what do these rationalized logics reveal about Syrian society in the early twenty-first century? Some have labeled *dabkāt* as material and discursive "noise," or aural chaos in the public sphere that demands some kind of intervention and/or legal ordinance. However, I suggest that the abjectification of *dabkāt* is less about the politics of sound and more about the bodily politics of movement. If *dabkāt* are performed and mixed for an imagined dancer as the ideal listener, then listeners who cultivate a certain kind of bodily disposition shaped by "enclaves of new wealth" in neoliberal urban spaces would tend to find these sounds abject. The disdain for *dabkāt* is therefore about which sensorial forms of pleasure are deemed (in)appropriate, and who has the authority to control pleasure (their own and others), in neoliberal urban spaces.

THE *DABKE* "DISEASE"

These cultural politics take the spotlight in a satirical television show, *Spotlight* (*Buqʿat Dawʾ*) that plays with the uncanny power of *dabke* to unravel finely cultivated dispositions of social class and gender in Damascene society of the 2000s. *Spotlight* was a wildly popular show known for its sharp satirical critiques of Syrian state and society.[39] One episode, aired in 2011, took aim at the elite business class, who demonstrate their loyalty to the regime in order to secure the benefits of new forms of wealth consolidated in urban centers, which boomed in housing, construction, and tourism sectors. In "Dabke" (written by Hazim Suleiman), the protagonist is a former general manager of a government company living a luxurious retired life in a suburban development just outside of Damascus. In this episode, Ahmed (played by Bashar Ismail) struggles with his uncontrollable urge to *dabke* any time he hears an "*ughniyya shaʿbiyya*" (pop song). (View excerpts at CLIP 4.4 on the companion website.) Despite his best efforts to disparage and avoid *dabkāt*, Ahmed ironically becomes the imagined listener for whom *dabkāt* is produced. His struggle to maintain the airs of class in the face of affective ties to popular culture and place is further bound up by the fact that Ismail the actor is from Latakia (and stages a Damascene dialect to play the character Ahmed on television). Ahmed's "inappropriate" dancing to *al-mūsīqā al-shaʿbiyya*, seen as symptomatic of psychological affliction for affluent businessman in Damascus, more broadly serves to satirize neoliberal autocracy.

The episode opens with the hit *dabke* song "'Aloush" (sung by Ali El Dīk in an unapologetically Latakian dialect), filtering into Ahmed's bedroom from another part of the house. Ahmed's hand emerges from the bedcovers with a waving motion that emulates the *awwal*, the leader of the *dabke* circle. His body, still under the covers, contorts in rhythmic movements to the beats. His right arm emerges out of the covers, twirling an imagined *misbaḥa* (rosary beads) to the rhythms. He gets out of bed, turning the sash of his silken pajamas into a *misbaḥa*, and leisurely *dabke*s through the house with different dance movements, each recognizable and idiomatic yet not quite codified into a known sequence (see figure 4.6). Ahmed approaches the television set, which is airing a choreographic production of folkloric *dabke* (*raqṣ shaʿbiyya*) set to "'Aloush." Grabbing the remote, he turns off the program with a sigh. When his wife asks why he turned off the music, he complains: "I don't want to listen to these *shaʿbī* songs in the house!" She gently differs: "They are sweet, and most people really love them!"[40]

The subsequent two scenes make clear that Ahmed is unable to resist dancing any time he hears a *shaʿbī* song—whether shaving at home or navigating traffic in Damascus. A *dabke* track featuring digitalized *mijwiz* and *ṭabl* starts up

FIGURE 4.6 Ahmed dancing at home, 2011. Still image from the
TV program *Spotlight* (*Buqʿat Dawʾ*).

while he shaves. As his wife joins his dance, a sample of vocal trills (*zagharīt*) cuts through the recording, perhaps reinforcing the presence of femininity in the scene. Their dancing is humorously out of sync as they pivot away from each other rather than anchor each other through a sense of balance, or *mīzān*. The scene ends in another quarrel. Ahmed is frustrated that he *dabke*s every time he hears a pop song and accuses his wife of enabling and encouraging the situation. He casts shame on his wife in ways that produce relational masculinity within the boundaries and expectations of heteronormative marriage. The next scene occurs at a traffic roundabout. A couple of men in a car one lane over chuckle jestingly, or perhaps in camaraderie, when they see Ahmed dancing behind the wheel of his SUV to "Sabiya" (2010) by singer Wafeek Habib. As he rotates his right hand in a fluttering motion while seated at the wheel, they raise their shoulders up and down in time with the *nawari* beat of "Sabiya," gestures that signal the relationality of Syrian Arab masculinity. They encourage him, exclaiming "*Aywa!*" (Yes!), clapping, and mirroring back his wrist rotations and hand waves, as male spectators do. Ahmed gets out of his car and dances *dabke* in the street. He hops on his right foot, extending his left out and back at the knee, while twirling a *misbaḥa*. When he eventually emerges out of his reverie, he is embarrassed that his *dabke* event stopped traffic entirely.

Listening to *dabke*, for Ahmed, produces a somatic response that disorients him. He is frustrated, unable to trust the physiological consequences of listening to music that he finds distasteful and in conflict with his class pedigree and his perceptions of his own masculinity. His disorientation and loss of control produce a gendered and classed anxiety that most palpably manifests in the urban traffic scene. Instead of signaling a playful and intimate masculine bond with their hand and shoulder gestures, as often happens at weddings, the younger fellows next to him both cajole and ridicule Ahmed's *dabke* movements.[41] They invert the normative expectations of how men behave with one another in public spaces and destabilize masculine relations. Ironically, however, Ahmed's hypnotic urge to dance is the very response that the producers behind *sha'bī* music aim for in their imagined listeners. His dancing exposes his vulnerability to *sha'bī* music, a vulnerability that clashes with his desire for the carefully cultivated composure of the Damascene elite (Salamandra 2004), and that elicits shame.

Later, by the fountain of a restaurant courtyard, a friend counsels him to see a psychiatrist, despite social taboos that stigmatize therapy and counseling services.[42] Frustrated, he responds: "What do I want to say to the doctor? O Doctor, I have *dabke* disease?" When he does chat with a well-regarded psychiatrist, who happens to be dining at the next table over in the restaurant, he confesses: "I have a *dabke* problem. . . . I am a general manager, and it is necessary in my position to join in every national, popular, and humanitarian event . . . as you know, we have many events, Doctor, sometimes there is more than one in a day. I can say that . . . for something close to forty years I have been *dabke*-ing." The psychiatrist replies: "So I understand sir, that for all of your life you have *dabke*-d as you work."

Ahmed commits to visiting the psychiatrist. He arrives in the waiting room of the psychiatrist's office, where, as it turns out, he is surrounded by four other men of his social class who similarly suffer from the same psychosomatic affliction: they are all general managers who cannot control their physiological response to *dabke* songs. Attendance at state functions at which *dabke* is routinely programmed is considered essential to their professional livelihood, a means to signal their service and loyalty to the regime. As they wait to see the psychiatrist, a mobile phone rings, playing Melhem Zein's "Ghībī Ya Shams" (Set oh sun, 2008). The sketch ends as the group of male retired general managers *dabke* around the psychiatrist's lobby, finding company in their misery. The retired general managers, all male, are all rattled by their seeming inability to control their bodies whenever they hear *shaʿbī* songs. Ironically, however, the collective response to the mobile ringtone—no one is able to resist dancing *dabke* to the tinny frequency—helps resolve their anxiety. *Dabke* transforms stigma into a therapeutic exercise in which the male participants lean on each other to work out their shame and trauma. Crucial to this transformation is a framing of masculinity as relational, both among participants in the *dabke* circle and in relation to the state, in which each has a shared history of *dabke* as state-sanctioned service.

The *Spotlight* episode satirizes *dabke* as a means of collusion between business elites and the regime (Haddad 2011). This satirical commentary manifests through a theory of embodiment in which autocratic power works on and is carried out through the bodies of citizens. Though Ahmed's generation of business elites have retired and are no longer contemporary actors in business and politics, their bodies continue to bear the traces of their collusion, one of which is *dabke*. Kinetic, spatial, and temporal disorientation—here of male subjects of the state—is a subversive trope by the show's writers that exposes how, qua Sara Ahmed (2006), elite male bodies acquire their shape and directionality through a lifetime of service to the neoliberal autocratic state. In so doing, the episode reveals that *dabke* is not immune from neoliberal autocracy and the business relations that have historically shaped it, but rather is an active cultural mediator that structures and shapes the very bodies who perpetuate autocracy. The brilliance of *Spotlight*'s work lies in the use of listening practices as a diagnostic for performances of gender, class, and neoliberal autocracy. That *dabke* is music to which one dances and a source of pleasure is a social fact the *Spotlight* writers manipulate to deride the Damascene business elite at a moment when these elites are buoyed by neoliberal autocracy. Listening to *dabkāt* induces shame, embarrassment, and frustration in ways that reveal the fragility of elite performances of class and gender.

The writers behind *Spotlight* are not the only creative intellectuals to forge ties between state ideology, *dabke,* and masculinity. In the novel *No Knives in the Kitchens of This City* (*La Sakakin fi Matabikh Hadhihi al-Madina*, 2016), author Khalid Khalifa portrays *dabke* as a propagandistic tool by which Aleppo's intellectual class demonstrates its allegiance to the regime. One of the main characters, Jean, an intellectual who has returned to Aleppo after significant time abroad, encounters his fellow high school teachers singing party slogans and performing *dabke* at a political event. He reacts with an ambivalent negotiation of performances of authoritarianism that Lisa Wedeen (1999) argues is reproductive of that power, refusing to participate. Though there are important contextual distinctions between the Aleppine intellectuals of this novel and the Damascene businessmen depicted in the *Spotlight* episode, both works stand out for their powerful critique of *dabke* as a form of state propaganda. This critique is not altogether revelatory in and of itself; as I have pointed out elsewhere (Silverstein 2021), there are other creative works that likewise develop this critique. Where both works converge is in the construction of an ambivalence towards *dabke* expressed by both male protagonists and the ways that this gendered ambivalence mediates their affective relationship to the state. Both Ahmed and Jean are, in short, ashamed of what propagandistic *dabke* reveals about their sense of masculinity.

————

This chapter has examined the relationships between musicianship, performance, and technology by focusing on musicians as social actors whose particular aesthetic choices are intended for an imagined embodied listener in specific social spaces. I first explored the assemblage of digital and nondigital aesthetics, objects, and processes associated with *dabkāt*. I then described the intermedial forms of media and technology that facilitate participation, enhance participatory experiences, and dramatize the ritual actions and processes that occur at wedding *ḥaflāt*. These effects, I have argued, are felt in and as *mazaj*, that is, as experiences of sonic sociability that facilitate social bonding at communal events. Rather than posit a false binary between digital technology and live performance, I have suggested that the sense of liveness that animates these performance events is technologically mediated in ways that amplify the social relations of the *ḥafla*. The digital, I have argued, is co-constitutive with live embodied performance.

What these arguments offer to the broader field of popular dance music is an orientation that centers dancers as imagined (and actual) listeners while specifically engaging with musicians and their aesthetic choices. I also ground the analyses of dance that take place throughout this book in the specificities of musical performance practice and digital audio technology. In so doing, I aim to avoid presenting social dance as somehow autonomous from music. Rather, I attempt to bridge a gap that often occurs in studies of dance music that tend to focus on either dance or music, but not both at once, while also maintaining fidelity to the ways that *dabke*, as categorically neither *raqṣ* (dance) nor *mūsīqā* (music) (Rowe 2010), is locally understood and practiced.[43] The aesthetics of *shaʿbī* music are not only about the semiotics of voice, timbre, melodic motifs, and rhythmic patterns, but also about worlds of sonic affect made meaningful through intermedial practices of technology.

Moreover, the integration of digital aesthetics and processes has changed how musicians approach and realize live performance, such that the "balance" of digitalized *dabkāt*—accounting for the sono-musical, the acoustic-digital, and distribution of musical labor—is significantly distinct from predigital practices. Musicians and studio producers have reimagined performance practice and the sonic ontology of instruments while sustaining the semiotic and affective meanings of locality, place-making, and authenticity in traditional music. To return to the ontological questions about *mazaj* posed at the beginning of this section, I argue that this phenomenon is at once embodied and mediatized. At the same time, the digital sonic aesthetics of *dabkāt* have spectacularized listening spaces through preferences for louder, distorted, and high volume audio that fashion desires for a theater of sound. These digital aesthetics are part of what has led to a twenty-first-century schism in popular music taste-making, in which *dabkāt* are often considered excessively loud and inappropriate in gentrified spaces of music consumption.

This chapter's focus on popular music is also important for broadening the scope of analysis beyond the classist attributions of modernity, authenticity, and representation that have saturated entanglements with *dabke* as a form of *raqṣ shaʿbiyya* in modern Syria. In chapter 1, I detailed how the nationalist elite sought to classicize social dance practices by elevating *dabke* into a form of cultural heritage. Moreover, they viewed folkloric dance as a mode of virtuous citizenship that could educate audiences and promote female participation in nation-building processes. The class politics of *dabkāt* as social dance and popular music discussed in these two chapters stand in contradistinction to those of *raqṣ shaʿbiyya*. They are forged and informed by nonelite social actors working in popular music industries who prioritize their listeners' desire for sensory excess over seeking to edify their audiences. These class politics intersect with the performative politics of gender, for instance, in the case of Ahmed's "*dabke* affliction," in which he is embarrassed by his inability to control his dancing body when he hears *dabke* songs, which he finds distasteful and inappropriate for his carefully cultivated image as a patriotic man of wealth.

Beyond this satirical sketch, the social distinctions between *raqṣ shaʿbiyya* and *dabkāt* are indicative of the contradictory classist hierarchy that often plays out in the study of popular culture, wherein *shaʿbī* (popular) stands for both the classicization of the folk and the unrefined tastes of the masses. This hierarchy of taste and cultural capital is not only a discursive construction, it is imbricated in and raises questions about the gendered politics of the dancing and listening body. Future research might look at, for instance, the limits of virtuous citizenship and female participation in dance culture. Since the late 1950s, women have been encouraged (to some extent) to perform *raqṣ shaʿbiyya* onstage as part of a civic duty to the nation. Have their collective efforts impacted their participation and the gendered perceptions of their participation in social *dabke* circles in everyday life, where the performances of relational masculinity dominate? Or is their participation limited to the stage and has limited to no impact on social norms and conventions in everyday spaces of kinship, friendship, and sociality that are penetrated by the body politics of gender and class? Their performances are indicative of the broader dynamics of class and gender that contour the social life of *dabke* in modern Syria.

PART III

Conflict and Displacement

INTERLUDE

Conflict, War, and Displacement

The Syrian conflict is a multisided armed war between domestic and foreign conflict actors that has continued for over a decade since an antiregime, nonviolent uprising in 2011 was violently suppressed and escalated into military combat. Social and political conditions that factored into the uprising include the regime's neglect of rural and lower-class populations, viewed as a betrayal of support at a period in which economic anxieties were exacerbated by neoliberalism and climate change, specifically drought conditions, which threatened agricultural industries. Analyses of the conflict and its dynamics vary widely in ways that suggest how much the conflict challenges the world systems in which it is imbricated. Among these narratives are sectarian opposition to a secular modern state that protects religious minorities; a war on terror that pits the regime with its Western allies against the Islamic State and against Islamist militant factions; and a proxy war between Iran, Russia, Turkey, and the West. In this interlude before chapters 5 and 6, I offer a condensed overview of the Syrian revolution and the armed conflict that illuminates key dynamics, events, and conflict actors.

On March 15, 2011, local residents of Dar'a marched in the village streets to protest the arrest of fifteen children who had marked up their school wall with graffiti that challenged the authority of the Assad state. Security forces opened fire on the local demonstration, initiating a crackdown on protests that persisted until early May. During and beyond these initial two months, "Friday protests" were organized across the country by pro-revolution activists demanding an end to the nearly five-decade-long state of emergency, the release of political prisoners, an end to corruption, and civil freedoms. Demonstrations and marches took place in village streets and squares. Local coordination councils sprouted up as an output of grassroots organizing, later pivoting into a lifeline for social services. Creative tactics abounded, seizing public spaces with graffiti, performing mock weddings, and subverting regime propaganda with satirical rhetoric.

Many marches began from inside mosques, with a single voice shouting "*Allahu Akhbar!*" in a rhetorical register that shifted from worship to political protest. Mosques served as covers for some activists to organize, which led to the targeting of mosques by the regime. Pro-revolutionary activists also organized online through Facebook, prompting a surge in networked activity that triggered a backlash of "networked authoritarianism" (MacKinnon 2011), meaning that the regime intensified its online surveillance and developed digital strategies for identifying and threatening political targets. Other pro-revolutionary forms of public assembly included funeral processionals, which bear a long history as a nationalistic and counterhegemonic performance tactic in the region (Khalili 2005; Ziter 2013). Funeral processionals were a key tactic by which pro-revolutionary protesters in Syria, adept at using online media to advance their agenda, could be seen and heard by witnesses situated worldwide (Silverstein 2020). Using corpses of the deceased as "embodied evidence of state violence," activists used the processional as a "tool to hold the state accountable" (Mittermaier 2015, 586). The dissemination of this political theater in networked public life not only elicited outrage and mobilized political sympathy as a collective memorialization of death, it also made possible a political afterlife by making death repeatable and durable on social media platforms.

Women protested frequently, organizing and joining many nonviolent public actions (Stephan and Charrad 2020). They negotiated and subverted gendered norms in the midst of protest events, at times covering their faces to avoid identification and arrest and, in another instance, convening at a market for housewares generally frequented by women (L. Saleh 2020). Several women-only protests received international visibility, particularly the 2011 demonstrations in Bayda and Baniyas that centered on the effects of arbitrary detention on family life.[1] Beyond these specific events, women led at least 120 demonstrations, organized countless others, and devised creative actions (Asha 2013). Women served as leaders of local coordination councils and generally contributed to organizing activist efforts. Uniquely the targets of gender and sexual violence, women were also detained, arrested, and tortured by the regime. While not a homogenous group, nor necessarily unified around any particular vision or history of Syrian feminism, women's variegated participation in antiregime political actions was fundamental to the ethos and experiences that comprise the Syrian revolution.

In July 2011, activists struggling with resources, regional support, and coordination, and confronted with brutal, violent crackdowns by the regime's security apparatus, began to consolidate under the umbrella coalition of the Free Syrian Army (FSA). Meanwhile, opposition leaders formed the Syrian National Coalition (SNC) as a political entity that advocated for a pluralist and democratic nation. Neither the FSA nor the SNC got their feet underneath them. Both suffered from competing priorities and a lack of cohesive vision that would have helped gain support from potential major allies. As these organizations were debilitated by an internal lack of cohesion, their efforts were further eroded by external dynamics. Gulf-backed Islamist brigades began to seize local opportunities for power, persuading one mosque congregation at a time that they would better protect them from the political and military chaos, and drawing in fighters against the regime with their weapons and funds. All the while, the regime stoked sectarianism by delegitimizing the revolution, assigning blame to Sunni "terrorist" groups, and delivering precise exercises that pitted local communities against one another (Munif 2020). At the same time, a "silent middle" remained ambivalent and uncommitted to ideological positions or political affiliations—this group would arguably weaken antiregime political movements and prove to be a receptive target for the regime's disinformation campaigns (Wedeen 2019).

By 2014, activists shifted from a focus on protests that demanded political change to documenting war crimes in the pursuit of justice, global awareness, and international intervention. The spectrum of "direct and indirect violence" that enveloped Syria (Munif 2020, 28) was more than a litany of human rights abuses; it was, according to Yasser Munif, a "logic of cruelty" (29) distributed heterogeneously across bodies. Whether and how persons crossed checkpoints, for instance, varied according to their family name or gender, with women often being sexually harassed and raped. Other techniques included the regime's siege and starvation of neighborhoods that participated in revolutionary political activity, most prominently the siege of Eastern Aleppo in late 2016. The regime targeted social services to terrorize communities, often bombing hospitals with chemical weapons and arresting doctors who provided medical care or prescription drugs for civilians, all producing "slow death" (32).

In 2014, with its defeat of Mosul and other cities in western Iraq, the Islamic State emerged as a major force. Espousing an extremist ideology centered on militant Salafi jihadism and a violently conservative interpretation of *sharīa* law, the Islamic State embraced sensationalist propaganda, including public beheadings and destruction of cultural heritage sites, to recruit fighters and devotees. Over the next year, it quickly amassed territorial gains in eastern Syria and garnered substantial financial support and recruits worldwide. At the same time as the rapid expansion of the Islamic State in 2015, the conflict escalated into a multinational war. In support of the regime, Russia began air-based military actions in September 2015 while also exercising veto power in the United Nations Security Council (along with China) that prevented resolutions being passed for humanitarian aid, the regulation of arms sales and distribution, and accountability for war crimes and genocide. Iran also supported the regime with its Basij paramilitary voluntary troops, Shi'i militias, and military counsel, while tacitly supporting Hizbullah's participation in pro-regime, ground-based military action. The FSA received some support from a US-led coalition that included France and the United Kingdom, though this support was limited in terms of both actual resources and commitment, especially when then US president Barack Obama failed to follow through on his "red line" ultimatum regarding the use of chemical weapons and instead negotiated a deal with Russia that crushed the morale of the Syrian revolution. Also providing support for Islamic militias against the regime were Qatar and Saudi Arabia. At the same time that external support increased the efficacy of domestic actors, this support hinged, at least for some political actors, on the global existential threat posed by the Islamic State. The Islamic State was therefore a major influence in turning the conflict's trajectory towards the preservation of the Assad regime. While Western and Gulf-based external support ultimately did not provide adequate resources for pro-revolutionary actors, it facilitated the weakening of the Islamic State at the same time that Iranian and Russian support provided a vital boost for regime survival.

The first major setback for the Islamic State occurred in Kobani, a predominantly Kurdish city in Syria, in 2015. The YPG defended Kobani against the Islamic State, which resulted in the initiation of US arms and air support for the YPG and related Kurdish militias, including the YPJ. US support was primarily channeled through the Syrian Democratic Forces (SDF), a predominantly Kurdish coalition with Arab and other ethnic fighters that promotes ethnic and sectarian pluralism. Due to long-standing political tensions between Kurdish nationalists, the Turkish state, and the Syrian state, US support of Kurdish militias served mainly to dismantle the Islamic State and fell short of bolstering efforts towards Kurdish political autonomy and the transformation of the Rojava region into western Kurdistan. In the fall of 2019, the US maneuvered out of its support of the SDF and stood by while the Turkish state aggressively attacked Kobani in a move that many interpret as intended to weaken Kurdish political autonomy. The border region of northern and eastern Syria, respectively near Turkey and Iraq, and considered by some part of contested Western Kurdistan, continues to suffer from low-level conflict as dominant states and nationalist movements pursue armed and political contestations.

Part of what emerged in the confrontation between the Kurdish forces and the Islamic State is considerable media coverage of women's roles in the Syrian conflict. The difference in ideologies of gender between the two groups could not be more stark. The Islamic State promotes an extremist agenda that endorses child brides, enslaves women, perpetuates sexual violence, and generally restricts female movement outside the home. In contrast, Kurdish political movements have strongly advocated for feminist and egalitarian forms of governance and society as concomitant with Kurdish sovereignty, grounding these platforms in the political philosophy of Abdullah Öcalan, one of the founders of the Kurdistan Workers' Party (PKK). They pursue these goals by supporting women's participation in politics and armed combat (women comprise up to 40 percent of the armed forces; they serve alongside men as commanders of mixed units), among other public domains. Feminist liberation ideology can be traced to the leftist origins of the Kurdish nationalist movement and to some extent to the Turkish Left in the late 1970s, as well as to the influence of women's leadership in Kurdish organizations in their early years. Meanwhile, the Syrian army and the FSA, as well as Islamist militias fighting across the region, signaled their position on women's social status as a tactic to strategically situate themselves in relation to other conflict actors.

Over the many years of conflict, at least thirteen million Syrians (half the country's population) were forced to leave their homes in pursuit of refuge. In what is considered the largest refugee and displacement crisis in recent world history, approximately half of these individuals left Syria, and half have been displaced within Syria. The majority of those who left Syria survive in neighboring countries, primarily Turkey (3.6 million refugees), Lebanon (830,000 refugees), Jordan (675,000 refugees), Iraq (260,000 refugees), and Egypt (140,000 refugees). Conditions in these countries vary, but most are exceptionally difficult as most refugees have no clear pathway to stable residency, legal employment, and access to basic services. Due to these circumstances, over one million Syrians have entered Europe in pursuit of better economic and political conditions. Of these, roughly seven out of ten Syrian asylum seekers and refugees have resettled in Germany and Sweden, with most incorporated into the former due to German chancellor Angela Merkel's leadership in responding to humanitarian needs at a time when Germany's workforce was diminished and other member states of the EU were unable or unwilling to process asylum claims and effectively manage migration flow.

RESEARCH NOTES

After the region destabilized, it became clear to me that I would not be able to return to Syria and continue fieldwork as an immersive and copresent mode of ethnographic research. This challenged me as an ethnographer who values embodied experiences as a critical mode of engagement and inquiry. It also posed the critical issue of how to represent ethnographic subjects in ways that accounted for the fluidity and complexity of their experiences. As I bore witness to the revolution and war through networked digital media, I eventually shifted to digital ethnography as my primary research method for the period between 2011 and 2017. Digital ethnography is a method that accounts for how we live and research in digitally mediated and networked environments, in which the presence of networked digital media shapes the techniques and processes of ethnography (Pink 2016; Della Ratta 2018). Rather than approach social media platforms through discourse analysis, digital ethnography underscores how everyday social media practices are a site for world making and lived experience.

Social media practices have been central to both my ethnographic participation in networked publics and to how I perform my positionality as an ethnographer within these publics. Throughout the conflict, I actively participated in social media platforms, primarily Facebook and YouTube, and cultivated my digital presence among interlocutors and their constantly (re)assembling social media networks. Similar to how performance ethnography critiques the positionality of the ethnographer in relation to their interlocutors, digital modes of performance ethnography account for how the researcher participates in social media sites (Silverstein 2020), rather than assuming that the researcher is a neutral outside observer. These ethics of participation are especially crucial during social movements and armed conflict, when passive and/or active spectatorship may straddle a thin line between the fetishized consumption of mediatized events and a politics of solidarity with specific conflict actors. My use of social media shifted over the course of the conflict in step with how many Syrians shifted their practices. In 2011, there was a rapid and immense expansion of social media and internet usage due to governmental easing of controls and restrictions in response to protestor's demands. Social media was increasingly viewed as an opportunity to generate awareness of human rights abuses, document such abuses, and build political movements. However, this illusion was shattered in the mid-2010s as users recognized the "tragedy of the digital commons" (Della Ratta 2018), in which the algorithmic structure of social media polarized political views, spread disinformation, and increased the ability of states and regimes to surveil and spatialize movement. Algorithmic control of content is one of the biggest challenges facing social media users, including ethnographers.

Another challenge of working with digital networked media is the "enduring ephemerality" (Chun 2008) of content. Often I would hear "about" certain performances or recurring patterns of performance (such as the practice of *dabke* at local protests in 2011) but was unable to find the content in search engines (Rasha Salti mentions the same barrier in her 2012 essay on revolutionary practices). Some content would no longer be available despite the promise of everlasting accessibility offered by the interwebs. The inability to control access to content, along with the pathways to such access, limits the digital archive on which chapter 5 is based. But like in situ ethnography, it is also revealing of the ways that research is partial and biased in ways that are out of the researcher's hands.

In 2017, I was able to shift away from digital ethnography and resume in situ research efforts with networks of displaced and migrant artists. I visited Berlin twice (in 2017 and 2019), where I reconnected with old friends and introduced myself to new friends and interlocutors. I attended performances, conducted interviews, and became familiar with Syrian migrant life in Berlin. Because these were short-term visits, I was not able to immerse myself in diasporic communities and develop an ethnography of daily life that might track changes in *dabke* as a social practice in displacement. I hope that future researchers will be able to carry out projects that compare and contrast the role of embodied cultural traditions in the many experiences of displacement co-occurring in refugee camps and urban neighborhoods in the SWANA region, Europe, the US, and other locations. Nevertheless, ethnographic encounters inform chapter 6, where I also reflect on shifts in my ethical role as a teacher of Syrian culture in a moment when advocacy and self-representation for Syrians can intervene in dominant media narratives and political sentiments that make Syrian life vulnerable.

FIGURE 5.1 "The Holiday of Cursing Hafiz's Soul," Kafr Rouma,
November 2011. Still image from YouTube video.

FIVE

Conflicting Movements

At a November 2011 demonstration named "The Holiday of Cursing Hafiz's Soul" (a reference to the late president Hafiz al-Assad), approximately ten men staged a *dabke* performance with live accompaniment by a singer, reed player, and two drummers (*darbukka* and *ṭabl*). The ensemble costumed themselves in robes dyed green, black, and white, the colors of the pre-Baʿth Syrian flag (see figure 5.1).[1] Their use of the flag made an appeal for a kind of Syrian unity unsullied by corruption and state terrorism. A long green, black, and white band tied around his head, the *awwal*, or dance leader, burst into the center of the circle to perform deep knee bends. The corps dancers clasped hands tightly in an upright posture and repeated a standard six-step line pattern while spectators cheered from balconies and waved banners. The joy and exuberance of the dance circle was transmitted from Kafr Rouma, a town of about twenty thousand people in the Idlib governate,[2] to viewers worldwide as the video of the demonstration circulated online and contributed to the making of the Syrian revolution. (View this demonstration at CLIP 5.1 on the companion website.)

In situ, local cultural performances such as this dance circle helped catalyze the creative energy of the revolution. A "repertoire of contention" (Tilly 1986), *dabke* gained political legitimacy as collective action, grounded in and by a historically specific cultural tradition, that enacted political claims in public space. Some observed in the early days of the revolution that "every village has come up with its own *dabke*" (Al-Zubaidi 2012). This phrasing suggested that *dabke* circles became a symbol of the revolution's translocal geography, especially in its early months, as activists organized weekly protests each Friday in towns and villages across Syria. The protesters' tactical occupation of public space through folk dance in Kafr Rouma was not a singular happening. Rather, their use of folk dance as political action can be situated within broader regional histories in which circle line dances have often embodied, and continue to embody, cultural resistance. From Palestinians resisting Israeli occupation (McDonald 2013; Rowe 2010) to Kurdish nationalists in Turkey (Bayraktar 2019), activists have historically appropriated social dances into and as embodied "choreopolitical" actions (Lepecki 2013) that claim political sovereignty and fight cultural erasure.[3]

Witnesses also celebrated the joyful role of dance in "wag[ing] an aesthetic revolution" (cooke 2016, 13).[4] At the 2012 Marrakech Biennial, a Morocco-based platform for the arts to address social issues and promote dialogue, film curator Rasha Salti remarked that "one of the most surprising features of the insurgency [was] the dancing. Invariably, in freezing cold and excruciating heat, at night and during the day, and even in some funeral processions, insurgents . . . perform a version of the *dabkeh* where dancers stand side by side, their arms stretched on the shoulders of one another, forming a chain of solidarity and moving in synchrony" (Salti 2012, 170). Political alliances surged through the "life-affirming language" of insurgent *dabke*, elaborated Salti. She further suggested that these embodied practices are indicative of "the revival of the body" in the "reclaiming of political agency, rearticulating of the civic self, and forging of a new body politic" (170). The insurgent body, in this address, mediated a phenomenological presence that Salti interpreted through the Arabic concept of *wujdān*, which translates into modes of affective, emotional, and existential being. At this early juncture of the Arab revolutions, *wujdān* promised the emergence of "a *sui generis* subjectivity" (171) in the Arab world.[5] In her desire to create affective alliances with the "Arab street," Salti mapped counterhegemonic tactics onto embodied movement and turned corporeal interactions into the political metaphor of a "chain of solidarity." She was not alone. Academic reckonings with the affective politics of performance, critiques Nomi Dave, tend to either associate affect (especially pleasure) with the "thrill of subversion and resistance" (2019, 3) or absolve affect as an irreducible phenomenon that remains "unsullied by politics" (4).

However, this approach to the pleasurable politics of cultural expression reinforces a general misperception about the politics of performance that I challenge in this chapter in several ways. First, I push back on the impulse to romanticize *dabke* (and popular culture in general) as a force of resistance to hegemonic forces (such as the regime) by demonstrating how *dabke* as dance and music appeals to and is co-opted by all sides of the conflict.[6] Second, like Dave, I problematize the phenomenological framing of the body that imbues the body with political value by naming it as an "unmediated" (Butler 2015) political force. Instead, I draw on dance studies (Foster 2003; Lepecki 2013)[7] to explain the political efficacy of gesture, movement, and other embodied acts of communication through an analysis that situates bodies in relation to specific social structures. Finally, I recognize how the digital and networked dimensions of the conflict demand that the eventness of embodied performances be "disentangl[ed] from their rootedness in physical and temporal copresence" (Fuentes 2019, 36–37). Instead, as Marcela Fuentes argues in her work on "performance constellations," the "synergetic relations between on- and offline environments" (41) extend and rearrange the temporality and spatiality of a given event, and the conflict as a whole, in ways that forge new political geographies, subjects, and narratives. In this chapter's study of the politics of performance, I aim to dismantle the myth that embodied performance is an "unmediated" act that collectively resists state and regime powers. Instead, I situate the doings of performance in the social relations and quotidian spaces of conflict as well as the material conditions of digital and networked media.

As I engage with conflict actors from across the political spectrum, I do not portend to be objective or to remove bias from my analyses of the conflict—I support the revolution and have done so throughout the conflict. As part of this commitment, I seek to make legible ordinary persons and banal spaces that engender conflict world making but that are generally not considered political, such as classrooms and military barracks. These sites, subjects, and spaces are not the dominant spectacle of the conflict in global media, which tends to train its lens on crowds of protesters, bombed-out buildings, and other sensational-ized features that feed narratives of hyperbolic violence. But this is precisely the point. Frances S. Hasso and Zakia Salime argue that "the dominance of this spectacle often concealed the quotidian, dispersed, embodied and less visible dimensions of especially sexual and gendered dynamics" (2016, 5). My focus on the social effects of *dabke* (both as popular music and as social dance) in the Syrian conflict reveals how *dabke* practice is politically fluid in the sense that it generates meanings and values that depend on the ideological framings and political persuasions of those practicing it, rather than on any kind of intrinsic political bias or field of political action that privileges one conflict actor over another. Moreover, by examining these social effects, I demonstrate how *dabke* practice strengthens alliances within political movements in ways that fuel politi-cal antagonisms and increasingly divide Syrians from one another.

Throughout this chapter I identify and trace the ways that *dabke* practice builds relationships of trust, solidarity, and political alliances in the context of the unfolding social tensions and political dynamics of the Syrian conflict. These relationships are built through both homosocial play and pleasure, including what I call relational masculinity and the production of social distinctions between listening publics.[8] This chapter builds on my earlier analyses of the role of pleasure and play in the social life of authoritarian states by demonstrating how performance culture shapes the lifeworlds of activists, regime supporters, active fighters, and others entangled in conflict world making. Here, I situate the proliferation of sociopolitical divisiveness in gendered modes of leisure, play, and distraction. Conflict and war, as I demonstrate through several distinct bodies of repertoire, are culturally constituted through intimate doings that powerfully link violence, combat, and resistance to casual forms of recreation. First, I examine how propaganda music videos shore up political solidarities on all sides of the conflict, especially in the first phase of the conflict. I then turn to the appearance of *dabke* circles in active zones of war, arguing that these generate storylines of male defenders against imagined enemy subjects in ways that not only whet the ideological edges of the conflict but specifically gender the conflict. Finally I look at the gains in women's political participation in Kurdish zones of governance in the later stages of the conflict in order to attest to how territorial and political boundaries are fought over and contested through performances of gender and ethnicity. Altogether, these sites of performance generate a more complex optics of the tensions and divisions in Syrian society than tends to be derived from dominant media narratives of the uprising and conflict. This chapter aims to deepen understandings not only about how Syrians relate to each other but also about how Syrians are perceived by those external to the conflict.

CLASHING ANTHEMS

There is arguably no song more impactful for the social movement against the regime than "Yalla Irhal Ya Bashar" (Come on Bashar, get out). (Listen to this chant at CLIP 5.2 on the companion website.) Originally performed in the *'arada* (a traditional song genre performed at wedding celebrations) style at a local protest in the city of Hama in the summer of 2011, "Yalla Irhal Ya Bashar" circulated across social media to become the anthem of the Syrian revolution. Anthems, writes Shana Redmond in the context of Black American life, are "devices that make the listening audience and the political public merge" (2013, 2). They may be detached from the national body that they purportedly represent, and in so doing, help to "sustain world-altering collective visions" (2) by "construct[ing] an alternative constellation of citizenship" (13). "Yalla Irhal Ya Bashar" was one among several key songs that emerged early in the Syrian uprising, defied the regime, and inspired revolution through anthem's alternative world-making possibilities.

In July 2011, Ibrahim Qashoush stood in front of a swelling mass of protesters in Assi Square in Hama and chanted insurgent poetry in a pounding rhythm: "Bashar you're a liar / To hell with you and your speech / Freedom is at the door / Come on, Bashar, leave . . . come on, Bashar, get out!" (Al-Jundi and Revolutionary Dabke 2014, 212–13). The song mocked the Syrian president by making fun of his lisp; called out the nepotism of the regime; and named the president a traitor, an "ass," a "nothing," and an "infiltrator." Qashoush quite literally "demanded freedom" and "our rights back," calling for "death over humiliation" (212–13). He subverted regime rhetoric, utilizing a tradition of satire and humor to critique authoritarianism that goes back decades.[9] The song's abrasive and emboldened lyrics not only subverted the culture of fear and obedience that has dominated performances of citizenship for decades, it did so through the festive register of the 'arada genre, a song form primarily performed by men and known for the "exuberance" of its lyrics, rhymes, and beats (Halasa, Omareen, and Mahfoud 2014, 210). In his 'arada performance, Qashoush decants lines in a declamatory singing style with a hard accent on each metric downbeat. The crowd responds, "Yalla Irhal Ya Bashar!" The jeering rhymes, chippy rhythms, and cheering crowd coalesced into a political happening, one that rendered exuberance and pleasure through masculinized performance in public space.

The infectious 'arada was captured by an anonymous protester, who recorded a blurry, lo-fi video with a wide-angle view of the protesters in Assi Square. The live, outdoors conditions are evident in the amateur video—Qashoush's voice is transduced over the loudspeaker, which adds a slightly shrill feedback, while the wind's noise blows into the audio recording input. The crowd hurrahs, roars, and whistles at intermittent moments in ways that convey the physical space of the protest. No instrumentals are audible, other than a persistent, driving rhythmic accompaniment played, most likely, on the darbukka. Shortly after the live event, an online group called Creative Memory reposted the video with significant postproduction edits. They laid synthesized dabke rhythms, specifically digital ayyub rhythms and handclapping, over Qashoush's upbeat rhymes.[10] The music producers transformed the live performance into the digital sonic aesthetic associated with dabkāt in ways that resonated so strongly with listening publics that it broke down "walls of fear," empowering listeners to connect with one another through *dabkāt* rather than remain isolated due to anxiety over the iron fist of the authoritarian regime.

The newly retitled video, "Syrian Revolutionary *Dabke*," went viral. Users shared its driving dance beats, loud and distorted audio effects, and sardonic, witty lyrics across networked platforms. Listeners (re)performed it live in public and private spaces. A group named Qashoushi Microphone—Freedom Speaker Campaign played recordings on loudspeakers at events.[11] Children as young as six chanted Qashoush's lyrics for audiences on the street, at home, and online (Issa 2018). In one YouTube recording, a young Syrian boy from Khalidiyya, a district of Homs in central Syria later decimated by regime bombing, precociously emulates Qashoush.[12] As viewers listened and watched fellow activists in other towns singing "Yalla Irhal Ya Bashar" over social media, the text's performance and circulation cemented translocal political geographies newly forged in the uprising. Eminent arts scholar Hassan Abbas observed, "Millions of Syrians chanting the same song, that is our public forum" (Al-Zubaidi 2012).

For many, the story of "Yalla Irhal Ya Bashar" replayed and remixed the theme of the anthem, a story in which this singular *dabke* track and its digital "onlife" (Della Ratta 2018) galvanized an incredibly courageous uprising against a ruthless dictator. "Syrian Revolutionary *Dabke*" expanded traditional repertoires of social mobilization, such as ʿarada and chanted slogans, into networked spaces. The protest event in Homs became an "extended event" (Fuentes 2019) through its life as a recorded and edited video that endured (and continues to at the time of this writing) in virtual domains. Its "replayability" contributed to the formation of "affective publics" (Papacharissi 2014), that is, publics formed through participatory internet culture who are shaped by the politics of emotion as much as, if not more than, ideology and discourse. The sonic aesthetic of "Syrian Revolutionary *Dabke*" was central to the building of a political movement against the regime, its nepotism, and widespread corruption, through the pleasures and joys of sonic excess. That which had been stigmatized as working-class, rural street music gained new currency in the creative insurgency that appealed to millions across social classes.

But this narrative omits a subsequent development in the life of the anthem. At the peak of acclaim for "Yalla Irhal Ya Bashar" in 2011, a popular singer co-opted the revolutionary anthem with a pro-regime, catchy pop music video, "Nahna Rijalik Ya Bashar" (We are your men, Ya Bashar; also known as God, Syria, and Bashar). Such intertextual co-optation was common in the cultural battlegrounds of the conflict. Anti-Assad protesters and pro-Assad supporters frequently subverted and appropriated each other's rhetoric, including memes, flyers, banners, and slogans, both in real-time spaces and networked spaces of the conflict.[13] Regime supporters, often referred to as "*minhubbak-ji*" (derived from the phrase "*minhubbak*," or "we love you," an expression of devotion to the president), reworked the chant "People want Bashar to go!" into "People want Bashar to stay!"[14] Another anti-Assad chant "God, Syria, and only Freedom" was rewritten into "God, Syria, and only Bashar"[15] at a protest in Suq al-Hamidiyya in Damascus on March 15, 2011.

Asking why regime supporters so often retooled the symbols and discourse of antiregime activists, Rana al-Abdlaki suggests that the power of antiregime rhetoric "scared the regime into releasing their own songs, copying Qashoush, to use them in their pro-government parades."[16] Songs were also used to intimidate and taunt. Purportedly the most popular song among regime supporters was "Ana Wiyak" (You and I). Among the countless versions remixed and uploaded onto social media was one sung by a child who threatened to eliminate specific towns and their inhabitants. Free Syrian Army fighters responded to this act of sectarian violence with "Ana Wiyak Jaysh Hurr" (You and I are the Free Army) by offering solidarity with those targeted in pro-regime sectarian versions (though a later version, also by FSA fighters, requited the sectarian violence).[17] The back-and-forth of remixed internet song culture suggests that songs were a means for individuals to insert their voices, at times original and at other times rehearsed rhetoric, into the struggle to articulate righteousness, enmity, unity, corruption, justice, and more, and to do so, argues Abu Hajar (2018), in ways that collectively complicated any singular narrative of the conflict's ideological contours.

As an affirmation of Assad's legitimacy of rule, "Nahna Rijalik Ya Bashar," performed by pop singer Rami Kzaour, contests the antiauthoritarian rhetoric of "Yalla Irhal Ya Bashar." Kzaour imitates the chanting four-beat cadence and rhyming structure of the ʿarada form in "Yalla Irhal Ya Bashar" but replaces the offensive lyrics against Assad with praise and adoration of the president. His lyrics employ rhetorical techniques that have been used to propagate the cult of Assad throughout the regime's tenure. Repeated throughout the song is the line, "Millions of Syrians want none other than Bashar," an aphorism that performatively enacts popular support for the Syrian president. The song's alternative title, "God, Syria, and Bashar," plays off what Beau Bothwell describes as the "constant metonymic presentation of Assad as Syria," as well as the construction of Assad as a "proxy for the divine" (2013, 173). In addition to maxims abundantly familiar to all Syrians who grew up recanting Assadist rhetoric in schools and state demonstrations, the song invokes the long-held regime tenet of anti-imperialism.[18] Cited in the lyrics are Yusuf al-Azma, Ibrahim Hananu, Sultan Pasha, and Shaykh Saleh — all military commanders who fought against the French occupation in the early Mandate period and long valorized as heroes in the patriotic discourse of anti-imperial Baʿthist nationalism. Their inclusion in this song connected the long-standing Baʿthist ideology of anti-imperialism to unfounded claims that the revolution was comprised of Islamic militants supported by American imperial interest in regime change. (View this song at CLIP 5.3 on the companion website.)

"Nahna Rijalik Ya Bashar" not only manipulated the lyrics and themes of "Yalla Irhal Ya Bashar" into Assadist rhetoric and ideology, it also embedded the authoritarian rhetoric within the musical style, arrangement, staging, and choreography of a professional music video in the *dabke* pop style. In stark contrast to the original's amateur quality of production, "Nahna Rijalik Ya Bashar" is a fully arranged and composed studio production that is unabashedly in the style of *dabke* pop. *Dabke* pop, as described in chapter 4, is a Westernized adaptation of traditional *dabke* that departs from the shrill instrumental timbres and driving duple rhythms of *dabkāt* (the latter of which characterizes "Yalla Irhal Ya Bashar") to offer a softer arrangement based on the verse-chorus form typical of global pop. These musical aesthetics appealed to many who desired the "good life" made accessible through neoliberal markets and streamed constantly on satellite TV and radio, especially those owned by transnational media and communication companies with vast influence over media content in Syria. There is generally a popular understanding that *dabke* stars such as Kzaour tended to be pro-regime (Abu Hajar 2018). In 2011, a "Syrian List of Shame" circulated online that named entertainers who supported the regime, many of whom were *dabke* pop vocalists, most famously including Ali El Dik.[19]

"Nahna Rijalik Ya Bashar" features a strophic arrangement that alternates verse and chorus with instrumental breaks interrupted by brief choral phrases.[20] Instrumental breaks consist of short riffs with heavy digital reverb on electro-*mijwiz*. A walking bass line emphasizes the tonic and fifth pitches, with an occasional harmonization on the fourth, all of which produce a *dabke* pop quality because it plays with, though does not completely land in, Western harmonic patterns. Western drumkit sonorities appear through the snare hits that land on each beat and build on the handclapping sounds that fill out the rhythm and bass section. A mixed-gender chorus sings responsorial phrases, including interjections of "*Suriya!*" (Syria!) and "*Halla Halla!*" (Now now!) that pepper the instrumental break. Featuring reverb, balance, and fullness, all vocal tracks are clearly recorded and edited in a professional-quality studio. From the use of drum tracks and electric bass harmonization to a bel canto singing style that is significantly softer than the *sha'bī* vocals of Qashoush, "Nahna Rijalik Ya Bashar" subverts the biting slurs of the original lyrics and vigorous *dabke* rhythms into a mellifluous aesthetic whose sweet pleasure belies the brutality that it supports.

The music videos clearly expressed their opposing political alliances through the distinct musical aesthetics of *dabkāt* and *dabke* pop, respectively. Kzaour's ability to imitate and co-opt the anthem of the antiauthoritarian movement harnesses the political affect of the anthem and emplaces it within regime propaganda. Copying and manipulating the revolution's anthem dislodges the style, lyrics, themes, and beats of "Syrian Revolutionary *Dabke*" from its relationship to the revolution, instead using the power of mimesis to forge new political alliances with the same aesthetic material. Yet the relationship between politics and aesthetics was not necessarily as clear-cut as these two songs suggest.

Part of the difference in aesthetics was driven not by what appealed to listeners across political publics but by an asymmetrical divide in terms of access to production studios, audio equipment, and related material resources. Hassan, a young male music producer who worked on numerous antiauthoritarian songs, noted that revolutionary songs tended to be produced "on a home computer in a small room in someone's house, using very basic microphones . . . then released the songs on YouTube by ourselves." Regime songs, he speculated, "are recorded on the most well-equipped studios, using the best sound equipment. [They are] accompanied by a video clip and are freely broadcast on . . . television and radio."[21] His comments endow the home studio and YouTube platform with a certain kind of authenticity grounded and constructed through a lack of industry resources and lack of access to conventional commercial media.

To be clear, Hassan was not necessarily conflating the asymmetrical access to audiovisual technology and studio resources with a definitive "economic geography of the revolution" (Wedeen 2013). When these music videos circulated in the first years of the conflict, political divisions crossed all existing social boundaries such that the ideological complexity of the conflict defied any simple characterizations. Some outside analysts attempted to portray the revolution as a story in which the rural underclass revolted against the status quo, supported by the privileged urban class in order to improve their lot in life; however, this portrayal failed to acknowledge the social complexities of the conflict.[22] Rather than casting revolutionaries as underresourced due to economic class or lack of technical skills, what Hassan referred to was in fact a more complex condition of political precarity that constrained cultural production.

Lebanese artist Rabih Mroué attributes differences between the cultural production of the regime and that of the antiregime resistance movement to what he calls a "tripod effect" (Mroué, Nawfal, and Martin 2012). The regime, he elaborates, produces videos that are taken with a tripod, a device that stabilizes and steadies the act of shooting video. This steadiness, according to Mroué, stands in contrast with the on-the-move, spontaneous, and at-home aesthetics of the protester's video. "The stability of the tripod," continues Carol Martin, writing on Mroué's work, "is the same as the intention of the state to stay in power" (Mroué, Nawfal, and Martin 2012, 20). The "tripod effect" is thus a correlation between political stability and spatial representation, wherein the recording process and editing quality of media is directly affected by the political conditions in which such processes take place. In the case of the two music videos under discussion here, the "tripod effect" becomes visible and audible in the ways that both construct the live demonstration as a key component of and for political action.

Political demonstrations were a set of spatialized tactics for public assembly used by antiregime activists to contest political and social orders, and by the regime to assert the continual perpetuity of these orders. The choreopolitics of embodied assembly and movement in public spaces were critical to claiming political power precisely because bodies were not permitted to assemble in public under the Assadist regime's "state of emergency." Antiregime protesters generally occupied public spaces only until security forces violently dispersed them.[23] They considered violence, such as imprisonment and torture, a likely end-horizon of their public assembly. Paradoxically, however, mass public demonstrations were staged throughout decades of authoritarian rule in Syria, in ways that, as Lisa Wedeen (1999) has cogently addressed, reproduced the cult of personality bound to President Assad.[24]

This is evident in "Nahna Rijalik Ya Bashar," which opens with a live political demonstration that is quite literally staged for spectators, online and in real time. Performing on a fully outfitted outside music platform, Kzaour chants the song's title phrase to the crowd, who reply in responsorial fashion. Behind Kzaour, an all-male group of charismatic dancers perform a choreography of staged *dabke*. The performers flaunt a wartime masculine chic by coordinating their attire with camouflage jackets and pro-Syrian scarves. The video shifts from close-ups of Kzaour to close-ups of male and female demonstrators chanting, dancing *dabke*, and generally enjoying themselves. Adorned with red, black, and white scarves, demonstrators wave Syrian flags and hold up Assad posters in a visually sharp display of regime support. Altogether, Kzaour, the professional dancers, and the demonstrators evince a spirited, carefree charisma. Throughout the music video, Kzaour croons directly into the camera's gaze with a sweet smile saturated with assurances, political and social, that all this is, quite literally, here to stay.[25] Such assurances are buoyed by the "tripod effect," in which the conditions for the public demonstration and its filming are viable because of the proverbial tripod, that is, the political security that ensures the continuation of regime power.

In contrast, the political efficacy of "Syrian Revolutionary *Dabke*" is arguably crafted through the on-the-move and spontaneous aesthetics of political precarity that, as Mroué suggests, occurred precisely because protestors' opportunity to assemble in public was constantly threatened by illegal detention, sniper fire, and more. The liveness of the protest event is constructed through the lo-fi acoustics and low-resolution images of the video, in which the details of the location are obscured by blurred pixelation and a smudgy audio quality. Shouts and rallying cries are staggered, stochastic, and entropic, while also rendering audible a collective sensibility that I have elsewhere described as "the grain of the crowd."[26] Vulnerability was sonified and visualized by the "tripod effect" of "Syrian Revolutionary *Dabke*," ultimately galvanizing the revolutionary alliances that were the groundswell for much political and affective public life. Thus, while both videos center political demonstrations as the key event that feeds political narratives, the time and space of each event is experienced quite differently. The contrast in political conditions between these events, with one as precarious as the other is stable, is therefore an indicator that what matters is not only that bodies assemble but the conditions of assembly. Which embodied acts of communication emerge during and as assembly reveals the conditions and "forms of power that people stand up to" (Abu-Lughod 1990, 65).

The power of these videos was not limited, of course, to spectacular political events and their media framings. The music videos circulated among millions participating in digital networked media platforms, generating affective publics at a historic moment in the conflict when social media was considered a force for change rather than a set of algorithms that reproduced sociopolitical biases or as an outlet for disinformation campaigns. In their online circulation, the music videos became tactics for both "networked authoritarianism" (MacKinnon 2011), which performs political power in the face of threats to that power, and networked disruptions of that power that used narrative and authorial voice to intervene in existing systems of power and authority and hold such systems accountable (Tufekci 2017).

The story of these videos is not that of haves and have-nots, nor of political actors using the same form of popular culture to antagonize one another. These interpretations would reinforce the notion that this was a "civil" war in which each faction bears some kind of symmetrical and shared worldview with the other. Rather, their interwoven dynamics reveal how power, capital, and performance aesthetics conjoined in the conflict to produce radical asymmetries. Though both drew on the same repertoire of the ʿarada song genre and *dabke* rhythms to slap at one another, their musical aesthetics organized distinct ideological and material worlds. Those who had access to public space and the right to assemble were also those behind well-resourced media productions. Those who assumed life-threatening political risks to show up in public spaces were also the subjects of shaky, blurred, and muffled mobile phone recordings. The videos aestheticized these asymmetrical conditions of power, providing a soundtrack for political precarity and political security, respectively. As two distinct affective registers of dance music, they generated divergent listening publics whose political, social, and aesthetic divisions widened exponentially as each video amassed a digital "onlife." The efficacy of these videos is arguably located in the events that they narrate, the aesthetics they perform, and the intermedial forms of power that they engender.

"AND IF WE DIE, WE DIE BY DANCING"

Set somewhat apart from political anthems and their galvanizing force on networked publics is a different body of recordings that document the role of performance traditions in everyday life on the front lines of the armed conflict. At barricaded street corners, in their barracks, and at military compounds, army soldiers, antiregime fighters, and others engaged in battle formed *dabke* circles and posted recordings of their casual dancing to popular social media platforms. Most but not all of these videos were of *dabke*—some featured other folk dances, while another popular video featured fighters dancing to a song by the American vocalist Usher.[27] These videos tell stories about wartime Syria, about how predominantly (though not exclusively) male fighters passed time, built up energy for battle, and cathartically relaxed after harrowing experiences. Emplaced in the ebb and flow of wartime Syria, *dabke* marks the liminal and peripheral moments of everyday life as a fighter. The performatics of *dabke* are linked to and constituent of world making during the conflict in ways that indicate how play and pleasure are embedded in and part of conflict making.

Moreover, the appearance of *dabke* circles situates the gendered dimensions of the conflict in embodied cultural expressions of masculinity. The conflict produced a crisis in masculinity across several domains. The war economy forced many to lose their primary source of income. This affected men in particular, as Syrian society attributes the social construct of "manhood" to the patriarchal role of family provider—the inability to fulfill this role due to financial struggles without future prospects negatively impacted perceptions of manhood. For young men in particular, the inability to secure jobs in any career sector upon graduation (a situation that predated the war) made normative masculine trajectories promoted by the discourse of paterfamilias (male head of household) unattainable (Monroe 2020).[28] War efforts also produced a disproportionate stress on men, who are mandated to serve in the Syrian military, and their families. Many young men left the country to avoid conscription, a process of related but distinct gendered precarities that I examine in the next chapter. The military service age range was expanded, and those conscripted were required to serve indefinitely rather than for a fixed set of months (this reverted back to a fixed period in May 2018). Low numbers of army personnel elicited public shaming by the regime, specifically Asma al-Assad (Szekely 2020), for the dereliction of male duty to the state that had been part of the patriarchal bargain between the state and its citizens. At the same time, boys and men were subjected to gender-based and sexual violence by multiple armed groups.[29]

Though the full extent of the crisis of masculinity fomented by the conflict is not yet fully comprehended, paramount to understanding this is the social significance of military service in modern Syria. Military service is foundational to the construction of citizenship in the Assadist regime. Similar to other authoritarian states, military duty is a fundamental rite of passage for manhood such that normative "masculine trajectories" (Ghannam 2013) enfold the "citizen-soldier" into the conventional path dictated by nationalist discourse.[30] This discourse, explains Rahaf Aldoughli, emboldens "men's readiness to die for the nation and a commitment to a masculinist conception of national membership based on militarism and chivalry."[31] Once male conscripts begin their period of duty, they often benefit from indirect effects of life in the barracks. They make meaningful contact with individuals from social groups not their own and engage in domestic labor (Monroe 2020). This is the first and often only time that men perform certain household tasks usually managed by women (due to long-standing gendered divisions in such labor; see Hill [1997]). The end of military service (in prewar Syria) was recognized as its own social transition back into civil society. Known as *tasrīḥ* (time of discharge), this re-entrance marked a readiness to find a secure means of employment and pursue marriage, both of which were considered key to consummating the roles of male provider and protector (Monroe 2020).

This trajectory has been fundamentally disrupted. The revolution severed the social contract that was the groundswell for the male "citizen-soldier." The president was no longer a benevolent father figure to serve, in large part because Assad had failed, in the years preceding the uprising and throughout the war, to provide the resources for a livable life for many Syrians. There was no longer the presumption that military service fulfilled a sense of collective duty. Conditions of male citizenship were further debilitated by government policies that fluctuated throughout the conflict, affecting service eligibility and exemptions, service period, conscription, and reserve duty, among other matters. Young men also endured recruitment and conscription from armed groups that opposed the regime, who viewed them as "potential combatants" (Monroe 2020, 273) in ways that increased vulnerability, fear, and risk for individuals and their families.

These destabilizing conditions are not explicitly addressed in the videos of *dabke* circles that fighters posted to social media. As Louise Meintjes notes in her analysis of South African cultural expressions of masculinity, "the process of converting performance into forms of power is diffuse and nonlinear" (2004, 175). But they do help to situate the desire to perform a practice connected to male competence and frivolity in the face of the increasing unattainability of the dividends of patriarchy. Those who fought in the war negotiated these marginalizing conditions by participating in "the institutions that organize and confer masculine authority upon men" (177), namely armed battalions of the regime and the many groups that opposed it. They assumed the hegemonic roles of male protector and defender for their political cause and the communal networks to whom that cause appealed. These roles were consummated not only through active warfare and the nationalist discourse of war propaganda but also through male camaraderie in the leisurely spaces of everyday life. Displays of masculinity in these spaces situate and attach fighters to the social fabric in ways that, I argue, reinforce their sense of self in an uncertain and hostile world. By dancing *dabke* on the front lines, male combatants insert kinship-based forms of sociality—from sons and brothers to cousins and uncles—into the social spaces of the conflict. In what follows, I examine a body of videos in which male fighters *dabke* in order to illustrate how dancing is a means to fortify the gendered imbalances instigated by the war.

In many of these videos, *dabke* sessions appear as recreational breaks from active duty or otherwise sit apart from active fighting. Consider, for instance, a casual *dabke* session recorded in military barracks, most likely that of the Syrian Army.[32] Two young men dressed in camouflage fatigues and athletic leisurewear *dabke* on the concrete of a courtyard in the barracks. The *awwal* spins his *misbaḥa* as they step forward and backward, performing to the sounds of an org playing repeated melodic motifs with a steady rhythmic groove. A man appears in the doorway to check out the activity, and another young man joins in with *dabke* towards the end of the brief clip. A casual flow emanates from their shared dance session in ways that produce male camaraderie among those in the barracks. (View this session at CLIP 5.4 on the companion website.)

The banality of the barracks is deceptive. Barracks do not usually appear in virtual cultural spaces that fetishize violence, especially in wartime societies. Evidence of domestic chores appears in the video, in which laundry dries in the sun on a clothing line behind the dancers. The significance of the wet clothes is evidence not only that men manage their own domestic labor (rather than depending on female kin) but also that living spaces are shared with persons from around the country from different ethnic and regional backgrounds. Joining in a *dabke* session, like drying laundry together, offers a moment to build friendships across social backgrounds during a male rite of passage. This video suggests the importance of recreational play in sustaining military life and building bonds grounded in forms of masculinity that reinforce normalcy.

Another video, posted on YouTube in 2012, features FSA fighters who *dabke* on a street corner that they actively guard. Behind their makeshift dance circle, a pile of sandbags indicates that their dance floor is also a combat zone. Dressed in an assortment of camouflage fatigues, jeans, a baseball cap, and other urban streetwear, they loosely coordinate their movements to recorded music played on a mobile phone. One fighter brandishes his firearm as a prop. Their *dabke* circle never quite attains flow, in the typical sense (described in chapter 3) of rhythmically precise movements that convey embodied communication between participants. But despite its casual and slightly off-tempo sensibility, the (presumably) spontaneous dance session is clearly a relaxed moment of frolic and camaraderie in the midst of actively defending a militarized front line. It serves to decompress the stress of active duty among those dancing and build solidarity among viewers (of similar political persuasion) who can relate to gendered forms of recreational play. (View this session at CLIP 5.5 on the companion website.)

Like the army soldiers dancing in their barracks, their playful movements seemingly distance them from the violence of war. But war is not as separate from communal life as this logic might suggest. Instead, I suggest that these *dabke* circles are less spaces of exception from active war and more a tactic for embodying male competence and participating in masculine rituals of play at a moment in which fighters are seeking to reinforce their male authority. Though seemingly innocuous, these videos of off-duty fighters dancing *dabke* are not separate from but rather reinforcing of the patriarchal forms of male domination that pervade everyday social spaces through play, pleasure, and performance. As I argue in chapter 3, young men enact the role of the proverbial *ibn al-balad* (literally: son of the village/country), itself a hegemonic form of masculinity in everyday social settings and kinship structures, through their participation in *dabke* circles.[33] Through dance, soldiers bring kinship-based forms of male sociality—from sons and brothers to cousins and uncles—to the front lines and barracks. As masculinized play in militarized spaces, *dabke* circles connect military life to family life in ways that constellate hegemonic relations of gender across multiple domains of the conflict.

In addition to expressing gender, these videos animate the ways in which *dabke* is politicized in the contested gender ideologies between various conflict actors. Embodied practices associated with pleasure and desire were highly contested during the conflict. Jihadists, including but not limited to the Islamic State, de-manded the exclusion of music and dance from everyday life. Many of the videos featuring *dabke* responded to this ban by asserting (in their written captions) that "dance" is a political liberty to be defended against jihadists who forbid so-cial dance. They rehearsed the perspective that militant jihadism is a threat to a certain way of life that the Syrian regime sought to protect. However, the precise positioning of the dancing subjects in relation to the external threat varies in ways that reveal the complex entanglements of the multifactioned conflict. The first video's caption, "Assad Soldiers Dance as Rebels Outlaw Music—Freedom VS Jihadi Islamist Slavery," identifies the dancing subjects as soldiers affiliated with the Syrian Army who are protecting Syrian culture and society from "rebels," who are assumed to be militant fundamentalist Islamists. The construction of antiregime factions as "terrorists" reinforces the regime narrative that all those opposing the Syrian state are motivated by jihad. This narrative reinforces the regime's claims that it supports secularism, tolerance, and religious minorities while also demonizing Islamists as external to the Syrian polity.

In contrast, the second video's caption, "Al-Qaʿida Don't Dance but Free Syria Army Does[:] Freedom Fighters Take a Break," slices through this monolithic (and distorted) categorization of who opposes the regime. By taking a stance against al-Qaʿida, the FSA "freedom fighters" who dance in this video distinguish themselves from the jihadist movement. The designation of "freedom fighters" in this caption carries a doubled set of meanings: the political liberty to practice an embodied form of pleasure and play and the antiauthoritarian campaign for freedom of expression and against illegitimate detention, torture, and other carceral tactics of the regime. In their protection and pursuit of "freedom," these FSA fighters embody the role of male defender, guarding the right to *dabke* that is threatened by al-Qaʿida's militant jihadism. Though they oppose the regime, they maintain the duty of the Syrian "citizen-soldier" by safeguarding a way of life through dance as a political act. The ideological contestations that frame these videos of masculine play in militarized spaces is indicative of how gendered pleasure is constitutive of, and not separate from, the social dynamics of the conflict.

Whereas these videos engender political commitments through jocular play, other videos construct *dabke* as an embodied expression of regime power in institutionalized spaces of violence. These scenarios are hardly surprising, given the regime's long-standing capacity to propagate emotional attachments to its paternalistic leader through ritualized gestures of loyalty and obedience that have included nationalist songs[34] and *dabke* (Khalifa 2016). But what the videos evince is how autocracy finds cultural expression in intimate and violent performances that play out between men who dance together. The embodied aesthetics of violence appear in a YouTube video posted in 2015, in which several army soldiers practice *dabke* in a vacant classroom.[35] (View this session at CLIP 5.6 on the companion website.) Like other *dabke* sessions, the soldiers appear to be on a break, during which they smoke, dance, and hang out. In this instance, they take their break in an empty school classroom, the exact location of which remains undisclosed. The clip starts with several soldiers improvising in a *dabke* circle in front of a lectern. Behind them is a classroom blackboard. One soldier bangs rhythms on the lectern while the others dance. The soldiers repeat a six-count stepping pattern of left, left, right, left, right, and *dabke*. They alternate between a resting mode, wherein steps are under their feet, with the foot kicking out casually on the half beat, and breakout modes that feature complicated footwork, including crossing over in a double-time tempo, stepping back while the foot arrives from underneath or bringing the knees up high in a military march. The dancer on the left takes a drag from a cigarette and eventually breaks off from the *dabke* circle. Two soldiers record the session with their phones as others watch from the doorway and generally lounge around.

There is a vivid contrast between the soldiers in their army fatigues and the classroom that they occupy. As dancing military subjects, the soldiers animate an institutionalized space of pedagogy. Their misfit appearance in this space calls attention to the absence of everyday subjects and activities—especially young children—in this learning environment. In their absence, the presence of the blackboard in the background and the lectern as a percussive object takes on a haunting quality. Perhaps the school had been vacant for months, or years, due to families and teachers seeking refuge elsewhere. Perhaps the children had left moments before the soldiers occupied the classroom with their insidious play. Irrespective of the conditions in which the school ceased to be a place of study, the *dabke* circle marks the shift in the function of this space, from a learning space for children to a building occupied by the Syrian army.

For some, this particular video has spurred debate about the subjectivity of the dancing soldiers. On the one hand, dancing serves as a reprieve. The soldiers are perceived as more humane, suggests Wedeen (2019, 131), because of their playful sociability on display in the video. Indeed, the dynamics between the dancing soldiers are blitheful, in part because these forms of leisure (smoking, lounging, dancing) are so recognizably masculine. Male bonding, as I have asserted, occurs in spaces of entertainment and leisure in ways that often reinforce hegemonic masculinities. On the other hand, there is a darker side to this play, which occurs in a site of military occupation and of children's education, disrupted and displaced by violence. This video, I argue, marks the intimate overlap between play, pleasure, and violence that occurs through male camaraderie.

Ossama Mohammed likewise situates this *dabke* circle in the darker structures of the war in his documentary film, *Ma' al-Fidda* (*Silvered Water, Syria Self-Portrait,* 2014) produced in collaboration with Wiam Simav Bedirxan.[36] This documentary generally assembles anonymous cell phone footage of the war into a collage of clips, excerpts, and flashpoints that reflect on life and death from the perspective of those experiencing the war directly. In the first half of the documentary, Mohammed juxtaposes this specific video clip of army soldiers dancing in a classroom with another of a torture victim. Immediately after the *dabke* circle (edited for length by Mohammed), the film presents a graphic loop of a deceased young male curled up in a fetal position, hanging in a closed doorway. The still body swings preternaturally back and forth, with enough arc to convey that the swinging is an effect of the sheer mass of the body rather than sentient movements of the body's vital systems. I read the transition between the two clips as intentionally continuous, in stark contrast to the film's general aesthetics of dissonance and arrhythmicity. Mohammed carries over the audio of the soldiers' footwork while the image cuts from the classroom to the swinging corpse. Live *dabke* footwork resonates over and across the bodily remains of torture in ways that, I argue, clearly spell out a masculinized perpetrator-victim relationship of violence.[37] By juxtaposing these videos with one another, Mohammed arguably implicates the jocular pleasures of dance with the perversions of torture.

The question raised by the original video, and by Mohammed's discriminating editing within his film, is about the role of *dabke* in propagating regime power during the conflict, specifically in military spaces. As I have discussed throughout this book, *dabke* as folkloric dance (chapters 1 and 2) and as pop music (chapter 4) is deeply entangled with statecraft. Similarly, *dabke* music is a form of propaganda, both regime and antiregime, as suggested in the earlier discussion of Qashoush and Kzaour's songs. But this video plunges deeper into the complicity of *dabke* with regime violence in ways that make it impossible to naively view *dabke* as a tactic for collective resistance or humanizing form of play. Indeed, this critique was anticipated by novelists who (as mentioned earlier) positioned *dabke* as a metaphor for carceral power by likening prison beatings to the rhythmic footwork of the dance (Silverstein 2021).[38]

The associations of *dabke* with carceral power are also evident in a 2013 video uploaded to LiveLeak, in which thirteen police officers form a *dabke* circle in a security compound. (View this session at CLIP 5.7 on the companion website.) Other officers watched or recorded with their mobile phones. Many of the traditional objects associated with *dabke* practice were replaced by security equipment. The lead dancer (*awwal*) rotated a police baton in his free hand rather than the typical rosary beads. The second dancer (*tānnī*) clutched a gun while grasping the grip of the lead dancer. All thirteen officers danced *dabke* around the compound in a counterclockwise direction. They were exceedingly coordinated as an ensemble, each stepping the same distance in a precise, rhythmic meter. Their upper bodies were rigid yet poised, and they coordinated shoulder raises and foot stomps as if this dance practice were the product of rigorous martial discipline. The video ended with a camera pan away to fellow officers watching and cheering in a military jeep parked nearby. A window decal bearing Assadist propaganda (ubiquitous on Syrian vehicles, especially security) appeared in the rear window of the jeep, a visual symbol of regime power.

Most striking about this video are the kinesthetics of the police officers' *dabke* circle. As discussed in chapter 1, one of the most appreciated qualities of a good *dabbik* is rhythmic precision. A *dabbik* who exhibits rhythmic precision maintains the core pulse of the rhythm while improvising around and through the beat with intricate footwork. The disciplined precision exhibited by the police officers, however, is somewhat distinct from the rhythmic precision aspired to in social *dabke*. The officers hold their backs erect, execute footsteps with a minimal level of effort, and maintain a symmetry of movement that suggests cadre or other forms of military training. While this video is similar to the others described earlier insofar as the *dabke* circle is clearly a moment of leisure in the everyday life of the officers, the kinesthetic precision is indicative of the links between bodily discipline, martial order, and pleasure that bind masculinized recreation to state violence and statecraft.

In another military video, the pleasure of dance is a prelude to the imminent horizon of violence. The video shows an army cadre before a major military operation known as Operation Damascus Steel, which took place from February to April 2018 and resulted in the Syrian army's defeat of opposition-held Eastern Ghouta. In "Syrian Army Soldiers Dancing before the Start of the Battle of Eastern Ghouta,"[39] at least twenty-five soldiers form a *dabke* circle in an empty field of a large military compound. A *dabke* song with the chorus "*Shina Shina*" fills the compound with low male vocals, heavy bass levels, a shrill electro-*mijwiz* melody, and catchy *dabke* beats with recorded *ṭabl*. The boosted bass and boosted beats of the instrumental break combine with the raised volume of the electro-*mijwiz* to construct that particular digital sonic aesthetic of *dabkāt* that rouses listeners. Soldiers milling around begin to walk towards the *dabke* circle and amass in the field. Several hold up their phones to record the moment. Some grab each other by the hand to form smaller *dabke* circles. Others lift their guns up and down in their right hands as they watch. Altogether, the spectacle is an impressive battle preparation that all participants, whether dancers or spectators, appear to enjoy. Comparable to other cultures and conflicts in which fighters listen to music to stimulate adrenaline before entering combat (Daughtry 2015; Pieslak 2009), *dabke* serves as a prelude to the battle. (View this session at CLIP 5.8 on the companion website.)

As an unequivocal display of power, the *dabke* circle is indicative of the role of embodied pleasure in conflict zones. The *dabke* circle transforms the military compound from an ordinary space for training into a sonic, visual, and kines-thetic spectacle that induces adrenaline and incites affective bonds between men before they head out to fight. The digital acoustics of the boosted and amped song construct a *sha'bī* aesthetic that induces pleasure among listeners. Yet pleasure is not the only affect present in this performance. A written description of the video provided by the YouTube user calls attention to the anticipation of death that comes with the horizon of war. It reads: "And if we die, we die by dancing[40] . . . the morale is very high before the start of the Battle of the liberation of the Ghouta . . . the fiercest battle in Syria Your prayers." Embedded in the horizon of death, inseparable from the experience of armed conflict, is a sense of sacrifice for Assad's Syria. This ethos is certainly attached to the regime's narrative that antiregime oppositionists are necessarily Islamist militants from whom Syrian territory must be liberated. But more interesting for my purposes here is how the ethos of sacrifice is attached to the act of dancing. The YouTube user suggests a role for dance that exceeds that of pleasure, adrenaline, and play. Ahead of Operation Damascus Steel, *dabke* becomes a call for higher purpose, a gendered expression of citizenly love for that which is Syrian and for which patriotic fight-ers, like generations of nationalists before them, fight.

From taking breaks while guarding territory to preparing for combat, the display of male camaraderie through *dabke* practice generates a sense of shared experience in conflict spaces and events. In some sessions, fighters consolidate their sense of purpose and commitment to the political cause that they defend through the accumulated power of group performance in a conflict zone. In oth-ers, the embodied pleasures of *dabke* are a vital force that accompanies, soothes, and prepares fighters for acts of violence. The synergy between innocuous forms of play and complicit participation in war is significant because it generates storylines by which people emplace themselves and each other in the political narratives that drive the conflict. Of the storylines generated in these videos, one that consistently emerges is the construction of an enemy subject, who looms beyond the *dabke* circle and out of the video's frame. The enemy is named in several of the videos: FSA fighters target Islamist militants, specifically al-Qa'ida, who threaten to ban embodied recreational practices; the regime's adversaries in the Battle of Eastern Ghouta are identified as the antiregime militant groups Jaysh al-Islam and Al-Rahman Corps, respectively.[41] In other videos, the enemy subject remains an unnamed specter that dwells beyond the choreography of the *dabke* circle and the performance space animated by the video, whether the front lines marked by sandbags in the FSA video or the deserted elementary school in the regime soldiers' video. The construction of an enemy subject through a *dabke* circle is arguably important to producing a sense of coherent group identity within factions of the conflict because it articulates boundaries between militia groups, the regime, and the FSA. Additionally, this subject reinforces the gendered dynamics of the conflict by creating the need for male guardians of freedom and nationhood (in some videos) and the assertion of male domination in occupied military zones (in other videos).

Recreational *dabke* practice in conflict spaces paradoxically moors sociality and generates political solidarity within groups through embodied performance while also hardening the ideological and territorial boundaries between conflict actors though the propagation of gendered subjects and narratives. These narratives shape and are shaped by the gendered construction of citizenship, patriotism, militarism, and jihadism in ways that feed back into the hegemonic forms of masculinity produced by wartime *dabke*, namely male defenders and protectors. Projecting these forms of masculinity through recreational moments in everyday military life, moments that "lodge" masculinity in the "socialized body" (Meintjes 2004, 195), arguably helps to secure a sense of male authority during social, political, and economic conditions that destabilize normative masculine trajectories.

KURDISH WOMEN'S PROTEST DANCE CIRCLES

While the focus of this discussion so far has been on the production and performance of Syrian masculinity in military zones, I now turn to a consideration of the role of Kurdish women's participation in political and military conflict through social dance traditions. Situated at the geopolitical edges of Syrian, Turkish, and Kurdish governance, these feminist performances are, I argue, political acts that destabilize the boundedness of Syrian dance traditions. In so doing, these dance circles return to the discussion of public assembly, protest, and structures of feeling that opened this chapter, in which I emphasized the role of festivity and celebration in the face of vulnerability and precarity. They also make visible the vital role of women's participation in political opposition movements (Stephan and Charrad 2020; Saleh 2020; Asha 2013), especially highlighting the impact of women's participation on the shift towards Kurdish political and cultural autonomy, which (as I discuss in chapter 2) was historically repressed by the Syrian regime. As the conflict progressed, the question of if and how women participated in public life, including protests, emerged as a key ideological contestation between conflict actors. These contestations became polarized in and after 2014, when Kurdish political movements and militias consolidated power and territory in the geopolitical entity of Rojava (literally: West, or Western Kurdistan) in and around Hasakah, and when the Islamic State became a dominant conflict actor with control of Raqqa, its self-declared capital city. Notwithstanding the reality of military contestations, ideological differences between these two conflict actors over the inclusion or exclusion of women in public life played an unusually powerful role in shaping the conflict (Szekely 2020). Kurdish political movements have supported and continue to strongly advocate for radical feminist and egalitarian forms of governance and society as concomitant with Kurdish sovereignty, grounding these platforms in the political philosophy of Abdullah Öcalan, one of the founders of the PKK. The Islamic State promotes an extremist agenda that endorses child brides, enslaves women, perpetuates sexual violence, and generally restricts female movement outside the home. The Syrian Army and the FSA, as well as Islamist militias fighting across the region, signaled their position on women's social status as a tactic to strategically situate themselves in relation to other conflict actors, similar to the politicization of male *dabke* circles in active conflict zones and in everyday military life.

Women's participation in political spaces emerged as a key symbol in these ideological contestations, particularly among Kurdish groups as they fought to gain and defend territory from a constellation of conflict actors (including the Islamic State, the Syrian regime, the Turkish state, and Islamist militant groups), all of whom constantly shifted political alliances and loyalties. As they had for decades against the Turkish state, Kurdish activists in Rojava embodied their political claims for "plurality, inclusivity, and perseverance" (Bayraktar 2019, 93) through cultural forms of resistance, namely dance circles. Several notable events, each with a distinct political function, help to demonstrate how women's dance circles enacted gendered claims for political autonomy and intervened in discourses of gender, ideology, and sovereignty in contested areas at the periphery of the Syrian conflict in 2018 and 2019.

In the "hundred-plus-degree heat of a Raqqa summer" in 2018, writes journalist Gayle Tzemach Lemmon (2021, 196), a group of mostly young women, with a few young men, formed a line, clasped hands together, and danced together in the middle of a town square (see figure 5.2). A *dabke* track blasted through the area. Their footwork and upper body movements modulated fluidly between styles that closely resembled Arabic *dabke* and Kurdish *halay*.[42] Some women

FIGURE 5.2 Participants in a dance circle at the Raqqa Women's Council opening celebration in Raqqa, Syria. August 2018. Still image from video by Gayle Tzemach Lemmon uploaded to Twitter.

were dressed in civilian clothes, ranging from abaya to jeans. Their sneakers were sharp, with bright whites, Converse, and other stylish footwear. Other women wore the signature military fatigues of the YPJ, which formed during the Syrian conflict alongside their male equivalent, the YPG. Their scarves, floral or black-and-white checkered, were tied around their heads with their hair flowing underneath in a look that signifies Kurdishness.

Lemmon, author of *The Daughters of Kobani* (2021), tweeted brief video clips of the opening celebration for the Raqqa Women's Council in mid-August 2018. After a three-year occupation by the Islamic State, Raqqa was taken back by the SDF, a loose coalition of primarily Kurdish and some Arab members that formed in 2015 to defeat the extremist movement. Influenced by the feminist political philosophy of Öcalan, the SDF established female participation in institutional politics as part of Raqqa's governance. The Women's Council was a significant part of these efforts because it advanced the possibility of women's self-representation in SDF-controlled Raqqa. The Raqqa's Women's Council was part of a larger constellation of women's councils that had already formed in nearby towns. Lemmon, who embedded with YPJ fighters for about a year, arrived at this celebratory occasion in Raqqa's town center with low expectations of how the Women's Council would be received and how its inaugural moment would be celebrated. She had previously attended many dry political events that favored public relations directed toward foreigners rather than actively engaging local needs and participation (Lemmon 2018). But she was surprised by this event. "Raqqa's resilience shone," she writes, "as the city's residents . . . came back to their town to begin rebuilding their homes and their lives" (Lemmon 2021, 197). Resilience was celebrated through the joy of dance and music for and by locals.

In her 2018 tweets, Lemmon framed the women's dance circle as an act of resilience that directly challenged the gendered violence of the Islamic State's occupation of Raqqa. Many of the women present at the opening celebration of the Raqqa's Women's Council had survived the Islamic State's bans on public appearances without a full black veil, holding hands with men, playing music, and dancing—all of which the Islamic State enforced by arrest and torture or capital punishment. This oppositional framing of SDF and YPJ members against the Islamic State echoed, to some degree, the contestations of gender ideology that fueled the conflict. But Lemmon's framing of the dance circle as itself a direct challenge to women's experiences under the Islamic State's regime also played into Western narratives about the redemptive role of Kurdish female combatants. Glamorized in the media and fast fashion through the aesthetics of military chic,[43] and elevated as heroines who escaped patriarchy and Islam through their embrace of secular modernity, Kurdish female combat fighters were idealized by Western journalists and pundits as the antidote to the misogynist and radicalized Islamic State terrorists with long beards and AK-47s who triggered global anxiety. Beyond the YPJ, female combatants also participated on the public relations front as well as in active conflict zones for the Syrian army, FSA, and United Arab Emirates (Szekely 2020).[44]

The role of female fighters exceeds that of serving as a symbol of state policies and gender ideologies. Female military participation in Kurdish political movements has been considered integral to these movements since they began in the 1960s with a few individual fighters and expanded to full brigades in the 1970s. Within the YPJ forces fighting in the Syrian conflict, many Kurdish women joined from Iran and Iraq to fight against the Islamic State, increasing the number of YPJ members from a few thousand to approximately twenty-four thousand. Despite the relative normalization of female combat in Kurdish society, female fighters often struggled within their communities for recognition and support of their efforts. Many female fighters came from low-income family backgrounds (particularly in Syria, where Syrian Kurdish households are generally lower income than Turkish or Iraqi Kurdish households) (Darden, Henshaw, and Szekely 2019). Female fighters were often stigmatized by their families and broader social networks. In military life, they also encountered negative perceptions of female capability in combat zones, and female commanders usually commanded all-female units rather than mixed units. The contradiction between the everyday challenges of confronting gendered norms and expectations that continued to limit women to traditional roles in the home and the fetishization of female combatants in the media complicated the myth that Kurdish female fighters are militarized heroines of the conflict, who defeated the Islamic State and ushered democracy into Raqqa. Instead of this Orientalist narrative, in which female combat against extremists produces the emancipation of women from Islam, the politics of the women's dance circle at the Raqqa Women's Council celebration was, I argue, only somewhat directed towards the Islamic State.[45] It explicitly responded to the Syrian regime's historic repression of Kurdish culture, politics, and communities.

In light of this long history of cultural erasure and political repression, the women's dance circle at the opening of the Raqqa Women's Council in a major city controlled by the SDF clearly reads as an act of Kurdish political sovereignty. The embodiment of Kurdish cultural expressions is exceptional not only because of the symbolic role of women's participation in the democratic process, but also because this public performance enacts Kurdish political autonomy in an area that was formerly part of the repressive Syrian Arab Republic. Also notable in this dance circle is that the legitimacy possessed and enacted by the participants can be ascribed to the political processes that empower them as individuals and as communities. As I detailed extensively in chapter 1's discussion of the fellaha in Syrian folk dance as a gendered symbol of Syrian nationalism, the figure of the female folk dancers has long served to authenticate nationhood in postcolonial expressions of modernity and support problematic policies of state feminism. The Kurdish dance circle that took place in Raqqa, however, did not tout dance as a hollow symbol for flawed statecraft. Rather, dance embodied the joy and enthusiasm associated with monumental political achievements.

In addition to the affective politics at play in Raqqa's public square during this moment, the dance circle blended Syrian Arabic and Kurdish popular performance cultures in ways that raised questions, for me, about what delimits each in relation to the other in this fluid political, social, and cultural space. (View this session at CLIP 5.9 on the companion website.) The *shaʿbī* music track that was broadcast across the square was punctuated with electro-*mijwiz* motifs, a driving duple meter, and Arabic vocals[46] that were more evocative of Syrian *dabke* than Kurdish *govend*. The dancers switched between different footwork sequences, depending on the particular clip that Lemmon uploaded to Twitter. One sequence appeared to be *dabke*, while another was more clearly identifiable as the popular *govend* style known as "three step," or "*se pe*" in Kurdish.[47] The latter is often performed at protests (Bayraktar 2019). In general, participants practiced the line spacing and arm positions associated with Kurdish *se pe*. This consists of holding hands tight at the sides, standing close together, and bouncing shoulders in sync with the rhythmic beat, often catching the double-time rhythms of the last rhythmic phrase.[48] Though the dance circle was legibly Kurdish in its stylistic choices, there remained a fluidity between the Arab *dabke* music and Kurdish *se pe* that collapsed any immutable constellation of culture, politics, and identity, perhaps even gesturing towards the realization of cultural pluralism.

Arguably more important than the specific aesthetic idioms at play was what Sevi Bayraktar calls "the novelty of acting together" (2019, 104). The dance circle was rather uncoordinated and decidedly not uniform in the timing and expression of movements. Some participants were not in sync with those around them. Two young women, second and third in the line at some point during the dance session, danced at an awkward distance from each other in comparison to the cozy spacing typical of *se pe*. The ad hoc and casual mode of participation attests to its spontaneous formation, a dance circle formed in a moment of high emotions rather than one programmed into the ceremony to serve a representational function. The "novelty of acting together" in democratic assemblies such as the Raqqa Women's Council was performatively enacted by the spontaneous emergence of an exuberant women's dance circle that engendered feminine homosociality and bonding. Also politically salient were the temporal and spatial conditions of this act of performance. Because Kurdish dance circles (in Turkey, Syria, and any state that perceives Kurdish alliances as a threat) more often than not proclaim political dissent through embodied forms of cultural expression, they often are characterized by "choreopolitical acts of dispersal" (Bayraktar 2019) in which protesters disperse from the site of public assembly upon the signaled arrival of security forces. In contrast to these survival tactics, this dance circle took place at leisure, without a security threat, due to the political privileges of stability and the right to assemble in SDF-controlled Raqqa.

Yet this political work, of the dance and of political movements and institutions, remains unstable. Though the SDF has remained in control of Raqqa (at the time of this writing), and women's participation is regarded as an important function of politics, challenges to political leadership emerged. Economic and political discontents against military conscription and unaffordable gas prices, as well as resentment about the perception of ethnic divisions that grant Kurds certain privileges and benefits and cast Arabs as second-class citizens,[49] destabilized politics. One of the more destabilizing moments in the broader region of SDF-controlled northern Syria was the 2019 Turkish military incursion into this territory. After a summer of negotiations, the US Trump administration turned its back on its SDF allies and gave the Turkish state the green light to begin air strikes and send ground troops into Rojava.

Tal Abyad is a divided city on the Turkish-Syrian border that sits in the Raqqa governate, or province. A contested town throughout the conflict, many of its inhabitants were initially displaced when the Islamic State defeated the YPG in 2014, forcibly expelled Kurds, and encouraged Turkmen and Arab households to flee from the active conflict zones and Islamic State rule. The YPG regained control of the town in June 2015 and eventually established SDF governance. A local council of Arab, Kurdish, Turkmen, and Armenian elected officials was led by two elected co-mayors of ethnic Arab and ethnic Kurdish descent, including the first female mayor, Layla Mohammed. Schools offering curriculum in either Arabic or Kurdish were established. In October 2019, however, during an offensive led by Turkey and supported by the Syrian National Army, the SDF lost control of Tal Abyad. Since late 2019 the city has been governed by Turkey.

Activists led a "sit-in" protest at the time of the Turkish incursion to condemn the military action as well as the withdrawal of US forces from the area. Documented by the Syrian Observatory for Human Rights (SOHR), activists formed a "Human Shield Tent" meters from the border with Turkey.[50] Similar protest actions took place in the nearby towns of Ayn al-Arab (Kobani), Ras al-Ayn (Sari Kani), and al-Malikiyya (Derik). Also present at the Tal Abyad sit-in was a women's dance circle consisting of approximately twenty young women dancing *shaykhānī*, a style of Kurdish *halay* practiced in the Hakkari region of southeastern Turkey, to a recorded track of what was possibly Sorani Kurdish music from Iraq.[51] (View this demonstration at CLIP 5.10 on the companion website.) The particular sequence is a complicated twelve-step pattern that moves forward and back, with a ninety-degree turn to the right that requires participants to flip their handgrip from a standard clasping at the sides to a rotated clasp at back and front, respectively. In the short video of the dance circle, the lead dancer carries an orange flag with a burst of sun rays at the center. Perhaps conspicuously absent from their attire are military fatigues or the YPJ/PKK colorful floral headwrap. Indeed, all dancers appear in civilian clothes, ranging from shirts and jeans to long tunics. Some wear *hijab*s, while most do not.

Their choreopolitics bears a historically specific politics of attachment in which, as I have mentioned, Kurdish folk dancing has long been politicized as a repertoire of contention among Kurdish activists in Turkey. At the same time, the political and cultural gestures of performance resonated beyond the specificities of Kurdish resistance in Turkey and with the broader Syrian conflict. Like the revolutionary activists of Kafr Rouma dancing in a public demonstration despite the ban on public assembly, their choreopolitics is locatable in the politics of embodied assembly. It is also legible in the ways that they adapted traditional accessories into political symbols. Instead of the prayer beads held by the leader of the dance circle, the circle leader held out the orange flag (similar to how dancers in Kafr Rouma costumed their *thawbs* into pre-Ba'thist symbols in acts of political sartorialism). Finally, they harnessed performance to insert pleasure into precarious political spaces. Smiles, merriment, and the energetic exchange of bodies jostling against each other in coordinated motion together resist the structures of feeling that military incursion, occupation, and even ethnic cleansing generally foster. Rather than fear, intimidation, isolation, repression, and unlivability, collective experiences of pleasure produce solidarity, especially in conditions of vulnerability and precarity (Butler 2006).[52] The women in this dance circle generate solidarity through their affective and symbolic mediations of political borders, military incursions, and cultural sovereignty.

Comparable to the role of captions in leveraging militarized *dabke* videos in the ideological battle between conflict actors, the caption of this video communicates the significance of this political action through gendered rhetoric. The dance circle is captioned on the SOHR website as "women's *dabke*" (a problematic mislabeling of Kurdish *shaykhānī* as [Arab] *dabke* that echoes the state's prior erasure of Kurdish cultural forms from the public sphere). This caption suggests that the dance circle is politically legible due to the visibility of women's participation.[53] In contrast, men's performance of *dabke* at political actions and in conflict zones remains unmarked in terms of gender, likely due to the assumption by the social media users who post the videos that dance circles are constituted through male participation. By categorizing the event and the dance through a gendered frame, the video becomes emblematic of the conflict's contestations in gender ideology, particularly those that link women's political participation to Kurdish political philosophy and governance.

These political narratives of women's participation in the conflict have shifted in relation to the rise and fall of conflict actors. At the time of the Tal Abyad sit-in in 2019, the Islamic State was no longer a dominant threat to the region. In the wake of its relative disappearance from the main stage of the conflict, dance circles no longer advanced the same polarized battle over women's exclusion or inclusion in public spaces. Rather, Kurdish dance circles, both in Raqqa and Tal Abyad, promoted the gender inclusion philosophy of the Kurdish national movements (known as *jineology*, or the science of women). The performance of Kurdish *shaykhānī* by female protesters inscribed political autonomy through women's movements.

By forming these dance circles, women actively embrace pluralistic, feminist, participatory, and collective modes of political action. They are a far cry from the historic figures of Syrian nationalism, namely the fellaha folk dancer who symbolized the Syrian homeland in mid-twentieth-century formations of post-colonial modern nationhood yet who was ultimately constrained by patriarchal structures. Fighting for their futures with joy and camaraderie, the women in these dance circles attest to the fluid ways in which womanhood remains a salient political symbol across shifting understandings and formations of cultural nationalism and political sovereignty.

———

This chapter has explored how people express their political solidarities and establish ideological boundaries with other conflict actors by conforming to or resisting the gendered norms embedded in *dabke* and related social dance and music practices. Importantly, I do not try to affix a particular political ideology onto a specific gender performance or dance practice, but rather demonstrate how the fluidity and mutability of techniques of the body open up emergent possibilities for multiple and contradictory moral interpretations. I dove into this nexus of gender, space, and cultural expression in order to better understand how gender and morality configure military and political spaces, and how these spaces are constituted through popular media, everyday life in armed combat, and political performances.

By tracing both the meaning-making and destabilizing effects of performance throughout the conflict, I illustrated how conflict actors establish and contest boundaries through the embodied storytelling of performance. Moreover, there is no singular political stance of dance, music, and performance. *Dabke* is not the province of the creative insurgency alone; rather it mediates the conflict as a dialogic force that reveals dynamics between political stability, political precarity, and material resources—what Mroué calls the "tripod effect." Neither is *dabke* exclusively the province of Syrian Arab nationalism, even as it shores up narratives of male heroes and defenders on the front lines of the conflict. Performances in and as conflict have blurred aesthetic and political boundaries between dance cultures, unraveling much of what historically defined and delimited Syrianness. After decades of cultural erasure and oppression by the Syrian Arab Republic, including the Arabicization of Syrian cultural heritage as discussed in chapter 2, Kurdish political and cultural sovereignty thrives in the autonomous region of Rojava. Kurdish and Syrian nationalist coalitions announce their political presence in contested political spaces where Syrian Arab and Kurdish social dance traditions overlap and articulate new political subjectivities.

The stories in this chapter are but a few of the many instances in which performance undoes that which appears to have social solidity. Accounts of conflict often neglect the significance of affect, instead focusing on international relations, military histories and strategies, and political ideology. Mainstream international media, conversely, often tell stories of conflict marked by spectacularly affective urgency, such as images of the White Helmets (a nonpartisan, civilian, volunteer emergency support coalition) rushing in to save victims from bombed buildings or plumes of smoke rising from balls of fire. As a result, outsiders cannot access the affective experiences of quotidian life that would generate a sense of solidarity and support among and for different conflict groups. This chapter intervenes in this media framing by focusing on play, recreation, and pleasure among ordinary Syrians, especially among Arab men, who are often demonized in mainstream media as prone to violence. I focus on violence and pleasure as intimate forms of sociality between men that invite new perspectives on the gendered dynamics of the conflict rather than neutralizing or romanticizing the spectacular(ized) violence of the conflict.

SIX

Translating Syrianness

On September 3, 2015, the image of a drowned toddler's body on the Turkish coastal border circulated across media platforms, upending the moral inertia projected onto Syrians, Kurds, and others forcibly displaced from Syria. The following day, thousands of migrants and refugees marched from Budapest to Vienna after Hungarian authorities prevented them from boarding trains out of Hungary, obstructing their pursuit of political asylum and livable lives. Though singular moments in the stories of the five million displaced persons leaving Syria, these two events catalyzed a global shift in the politics of forced displacement, claims for asylum, and border control. A social movement to "welcome refugees" gained steam across Europe. German chancellor Angela Merkel decisively shifted public policy by announcing that the Dublin system, a set of regulations established by the EU in 1990 that dictates that the country in which an asylum seeker first applies for asylum is responsible for processing the claim, was no longer the solution for the current problem. She opened Germany to asylum seekers.[1] However, other EU countries did not alter their border policies; instead, they increased detentions, processing times, and limbo. Meanwhile, a "European refugee crisis" was proclaimed by state actors and media outlets seeking to narrativize the deaths of thousands trying to cross the Mediterranean and the arrival of 1.3 million displaced persons in the EU.[2]

The unprecedented increase in the number of migrants seeking a livable life in Europe reinvigorated long-standing public debates on migration and the construction of ethnic and racial divisions. The construction of migrants as racialized threats to the imaginaries of a homogenous Europe (Fassin 2011) was not altogether new; rather, it was resituated in the events of 2015 by state actors and media accounts, from EU authorities and governing bodies to traditional mass media and social media (Holmes and Castañeda 2016; Triandafyllidou 2018). Their production of "crisis," or a sense of urgency and emergency at the borders of Europe, dramatized the complexities of forced displacement and migration into an event to be managed and controlled by state actors and institutions.[3] The "crisis" was therefore less about the sheer number of vulnerable asylum seekers and more about constructing, through the language of crisis, subjects that challenged the socio-moral balance between providing empathetic humanitarian solidarity and protecting against perceived threats to European unity (also under constant negotiation among EU member states) (Triandafyllidou 2018). The language of crisis perpetuated long-standing framings of migration into Europe as a problem external to the EU (therefore absolving the EU from accountability) at the same time that it falsely dramatized the events of 2015 as an exceptional and historic situation. What was arguably unprecedented about the migration of 2.5 million asylum seekers into Europe in 2015–16 was not only the numbers of people seeking refuge across a short period of time, nor the perception of urgency stemming from armed conflict and human rights violations, but that this exceptional period of migration marked a specific historic juncture in the increasing accessibility of Europe as a destination and the increasingly asymmetrical policies that determined asylum rights (Piguet 2021).

As EU officials, national political leaders, and media outlets perpetuated border concerns through their public rhetoric, xenophobia and nativism in Europe (and elsewhere) gained momentum.[4] Far-right political parties that espoused anti-immigrant rhetoric accrued significant support in mainstream politics across many European countries. At the heart of these politics is the figure of the Muslim Arab, perpetually alien and foreign to Europe due to the social entwinement of race and religion. Moreover, whereas migrants have always-already been racialized by nature of their movement across borders (Silverstein 2005), Muslim Europeans remain continuously Othered, regardless of whether they are second- or third-generation European citizens (El Tayeb 2011).[5] Often perceived as "strangers" (Ahmed 2000) who threaten public safety or who are "tolerated" through the management and regulation of aversion (Brown 2006), Muslims in Europe constantly seek to legitimate their presence as nonthreatening to liberal institutions and spaces.

The gendered politics of forced displacement from Syria further stressed these complex, long-standing formations of Islamophobia in Europe. The majority of Syrian asylum-seekers were young men fleeing persecution, military conscription, and coercion into combat groups, while also seeking economic opportunities to provide for extended families surviving war economies. As young, unaccompanied men, they faced barriers to migration from neighboring host countries (mainly Jordan, Lebanon, and Turkey) and were threatened by authorities in those countries (Turner 2019). Due to conflations of militarism, statecraft, and masculinity projected onto Muslim-majority countries, they were stereotyped as terrorists. They were also accused of cowardice based on perceptions that they had abandoned their military duty or familial duty. Additionally, young Syrian men were often emasculated in the process of becoming "refugees," a label that is commonly associated with women and children as "victims" of conflict who are more "vulnerable" to social and state violence and persecution than men (Allsopp 2017). These legal and social constructs frustrated many young Syrian men, who negotiated a matrix of vulnerabilities that exceeded the categories and capabilities of the international humanitarian sector.

Many individuals and organizations across Europe organized aid and relief efforts in order to mitigate the isolating effects of displacement, resettlement, and integration on asylum-seekers as well as to counter xenophobia, Islamophobia, and nativism. Known as the #WelcomeRefugees movement (*Willkommenskultur*, literally: welcoming culture, within Germany), these collective efforts encompassed a wide range of formal and informal social services, expansion of economic opportunities including in arts and culture sectors, and public dialogue on social issues such as the politics of integrating newcomers into host societies. What emerged out of this intense confluence of social organizing, funding, and other institutional resources was a period of historically unprecedented encounters between displaced Syrians and Europeans that destabilized perceptions of selfhood and collective identity while also prompting new inquiries into aesthetic forms and histories. This generation has fundamentally changed the scale and scope of Syrian arts production through their experimentations with aesthetic frameworks, reckoning with aesthetic genealogies, and collaborations with other artists. Making work in this historic moment presented an exceptional challenge, one that required translating Syrianness for an arts sector unfamiliar to them at the same time that artists strategically accommodated demands by European funders and audiences.

This chapter focuses on Syrian dance artists who presented new works for European audiences around or after 2015 that engaged with migration and resettlement. These projects include a choreography centered on *dabke* that disrupts dominant discourses on cultural heritage and community dance workshops led by emerging Syrian performers based in Europe, as well as by me, in which *dabke* pedagogy mediates spaces of encounter. I demonstrate how these projects are indicative of shifts in how Syrians related to one another and to non-Syrians during their experiences of forced migration. The first shift was to challenge the gendered stereotyping of refugees by Western media and governing institutions through the work of performance, while making space for antihegemonic expressions of masculinity and femininity foreclosed by Syrian society. The second shift was to craft markers of cultural authenticity and map difference on their own terms rather than remain beholden to the state-led discourses of cultural heritage. This shift is part of a broader transformation in the authorship of Syrian cultural production. No longer constrained by authoritarian censors bent on preserving political narratives and their ideological frameworks, individuals scripted their own stories and advocated for a plurality of expressions and perspectives of and on cultural memory, tradition, and heritage.

Yet even as Syrians forged new voices, platforms, and audiences as part of their response to displacement, their work remained deeply entangled with the gendered and racialized politics of migration specific to Europe in the mid-2010s. The social spaces that welcomed them were paradoxically linked, argues Sara Ahmed in *Strange Encounters* (2000), to spaces that discerned foreigners as risky and threatening. Ahmed contends that whereas the latter assumption considers the stranger to be the "origin of danger," the former considers the stranger to be the "origin of difference." These two subjects are linked by the logic that "welcoming the stranger keeps in place the fetishism on which discourses of stranger danger rely" (2000, 4). Thus even though welcoming acts enact an "ethics of alterity" that strives to correct for the hostility, suspicion, and xenophobia of stranger danger, they ultimately, according to Ahmed, perpetuate racialized and gendered constructions of difference historically specific to European society.[6]

In what follows, I attune to how displaced Syrian artists negotiate the phenomenon of "strange encounters" through artistic projects that center *dabke*. The insertion of Syrian *dabke* into European cultural spaces is in no small way attributable to the fact that its history as a national performance tradition and staged folk dance makes it legible for European audiences as a form of cultural difference. But these projects displace these histories of representation. In the projects that I discuss here, *dabke* is more than a folk dance and more than a form of intangible cultural heritage that promotes cultural citizenship and maps territory onto nationalized subjects (see chapters 1 and 2). Rather than adapting a fixed aesthetic and ideological framework for new audiences, these projects challenge the colonialist genealogy of folk culture they inherited as artists born and trained in Syria. Instead, they approach *dabke* as a strategical resource for navigating social life that sets "aesthetics in motion" (Hamera 2006, 3). They achieve this through their use of *dabke* as "technique," which Judith Hamera theorizes as a "synecdoche for the complex webs of relations that link performers to particular subjectivities, histories, practices, and to each other" (5). Technique is an embodied mode of communication that "organizes socialities" and "facilitates interpersonal and social relations as it shapes bodies" (5).

Reimagined for European audiences, the projects featured in this chapter unshackle *dabke* from the ethnonationalist project of *raqs sha'biyya*, conveying an irreverence for nationalism and dispensing of the need to reproduce Syrianness as an authentic, "whole" culture. With unique authorial voices, they wrangle these tensions into spaces of encounter in ways that shift the social relations in which *dabke*'s meanings are embedded. As I argue in this chapter, they unsettle hegemonic forms of masculinity often reproduced in the social spaces of family and friends where *dabke* is practiced while setting forth emergent strategies of masculinization that advocate for themselves as young male Syrians and as Syrian artists in European spaces that tend to render Syrian masculinity vulnerable. In my analysis of how such unsettling and rebalancing occurs, I detail how the artists reimagine *dabke* traditions through technique, including repertoire, rhythms, choreographic arrangements of bodies in performance, dynamics between music and dance, relationships between performers and audiences, and the political aesthetics of representation. I also position the ethics of my own pedagogical work as a non-Syrian, *hapa* woman teaching *dabke* in the United States in relation to the gender and racialized dynamics embedded in the negotiation of embodied pedagogical authority. Despite these major transformations that dislocate much of what Syrianness entails, I insist that these projects remain connected to the forms and meanings of sociality embedded in *dabke* practice. Pointing to the radical directions and risky movements that Syrianness assumes, this chapter suggests how displaced artists use *dabke* to negotiate strange encounters and in the process recalibrate the balance of how Syrians relate to each other, their cultural traditions, and European public life.

REIMAGINING *DABKE*

Prior to the conflict and forced displacement, most Syrian dancers completed their training at the dance conservatory within the Higher Institute for Dramatic

Arts in Damascus. As I mention at the end of chapter 2, the dance conservatory privileges classical ballet (specifically the Vaganova method that dominates Russian and East European ballet pedagogy) and also teaches contemporary global styles of dance, including modern, jazz, hip-hop, and tango, among others. Housed in a complex with other arts institutions, including the Higher Institute of Music, in central Damascus, the dance conservatory is the major vehicle for aspiring students to pursue their professional interests. It is, however, generally limited in its approach to dance as a set of physical techniques that formalize style rather than experimenting with movement as a domain for intellectual and conceptual exploration.[7] Some Syrian dancers pursued their training in European dance academies in Paris, Frankfurt, and other major European cities. Several dance companies participated in select European dance and other arts festivals, but these opportunities were not systematically supported in the 2000s.[8] Nevertheless, a contemporary Syrian dance scene emerged in this decade through efforts by Alaa Krimed (Sima Dance Company) and Mey Seifan (Damascus Contemporary Dance Platform), among others. After the onset of conflict, this scene dispersed worldwide. Some migrated to the Gulf, others to Lebanon and Turkey. In 2015 a critical mass of Syrian artists, including but not limited to dance artists, arrived in Europe to seek political and economic stability. This generation had generally spent their entire career in Syria (and Lebanon, for some). As they settled into European societies, they encountered aesthetic constructs and histories unfamiliar to them, often taking risks to learn and collaborate with European-based dance artists in workshops and projects.[9]

Among these works emerged a choreography that pivoted on *dabke*—conceptually, politically, and aesthetically. Created by Mithkal Alzghair, *Displacement* (2016) is historically unprecedented for its adaptation of *dabke* into and as contemporary dance. Through the repetition of weighted, rhythmic movements that pivot on and around the conventional six-step pattern of *dabke*, the work is a powerful statement about social resilience to invisible and subjugating forces of power. Alzghair conceived *Displacement* as an embodied revolt against authoritarianism and repression, state borders and statelessness, and the production of "crisis" in media worlds. The choreography addresses the effects of social and political structures on individuals, focusing on the role of isolation as a social experience and political force endemic to both authoritarianism (Arendt 1973) and migration (Allsopp 2017). It also, importantly, attests to the mitigating effects of collaborative and collective actions on isolation. A complex work that seeks to undo regimes of power by critiquing the social dynamics of such power,

Displacement makes a compelling statement about performance as a strategy for surviving the emasculating duress of autocracy and forced migration.

Displacement was borne out of Alzghair's sense of disconnection from Syrians and Europeans, respectively, as well as the paradoxical conditions of mobility and immobility that shape his political subjectivity. Comparable to the experience of many Syrians, Alzghair's career and mobility were disrupted by the conflict. When the uprising began in 2011, he was studying choreography at the Centre Chorégraphique National de Montpellier in France. He was unable to return to Syria because that would have obligated him to complete his compulsory military service, nine months of which he had served before starting his dance studies in Damascus.[10] Exiled in France, he, like many others, witnessed the rise and fall of revolutionary politics and dreams, as well as the daily impact of war on his family as they struggled to meet everyday needs for services such as electricity and gas. He felt immobilized, cut off from his home country. At the same time, he experienced alienation and Othering in his everyday encounters in Europe.[11]

As the rise of "welcoming culture" generated increased interest in Syrian culture, funders pressured Alzghair, who had already developed several works through his company, HEKMA, to develop a work that directly engaged with Syrian cultural heritage. *Displacement*, he shared with me in our interview, is his response to these demands. Alzghair targets the general public as the imagined audience for this work. He does not expect audiences, who he as-sumes are generally unfamiliar with Arab culture, to be able to identify what stage props, choreographic motifs, or instrumental timbres signify in a Syrian context. Rather, he leaves "room for multiple interpretations of the body's im-age"[12] and embraces the fluidity of meanings that emerge between artists and audiences. He privileges "empathetic" experiences of spectatorship (Foster 2011) over semiotic interpretations that focus on the symbolic production of meaning. Though he expressed appreciation for audience responses, which were generally "whole-hearted and positive," he did not fully concede to the European desire to stage Syrian difference as a nostalgic expression of cultural heritage or as an identitarian claim for recognition in multicultural spaces.[13] For him, *Displace-ment* is a space for embodied encounters between migrant artists and (mainly) European audiences that asks the general public to confront their expectations of what constitutes Syrianness.[14] Performance "choreographs empathy" (Foster 2011) by carefully "summoning other bodies into a specific way of feeling" (2) that is socially mediated and historically contingent with the particularities of contemporary Syrian migration to Europe.

Consider, for instance, the opening of the performance, which I attended in 2018 at the Contemporary Arts Center in Cincinnati, Ohio. The performance began with stage lights exposing a pair of black leather military boots placed on the stage floor. Alzghair entered from stage left, striding to center stage with a folded white fabric in his hands. He pulled on the boots, intended perhaps for travel or for military use, and stuffed his pants legs inside. Only then did he begin to shuffle his feet in a steady, rhythmic pattern. As I watched Alzghair dress himself in these opening moments of his performance, I felt an intimacy emerge between the artist and myself as a member of the audience. Whereas stage productions typically begin with the performer within the mise-en-scène, *Displacement* opened with a scene of what Constantin Stanislavski conceptualized as "public solitude," or acting as if one is in private despite being watched. This intimate act generates a kind of vulnerability that, I suggest, is different from the emasculation of the refugee-subject that occurs in the public sphere. It invites spectators such as myself into the banal and domestic routines that make the refugee-subject more relatable. In so doing, it subverts the normative gaze of audiences onto performers from that which is public-facing to that which is more private, which is itself an intervention in the political optics that so often position Syrian asylum-seekers in the glaring authority of the public eye in Europe.

To better understand the vulnerability at stake in this work, I offer an interpretive analysis of *Displacement* based on two modes of spectatorship: watching the performance live at the aforementioned staging and as a recorded video of a performance from the 2016 Tanz im August Festival in Berlin. While I incorporate some empathetic audience responses into my analysis that are based on a postperformance discussion in Cincinnati, I generally am not able to provide an ethnography of reception that accounts for how members of the general public (Alzghair's target audience) experienced the choreography. Based on my informed perspective as a scholar of Syria and student of *dabke*, what follows is a critical interpretation of the performance that extracts key aesthetic tropes and performance dynamics and weaves these into the theoretical interventions described by Alzghair in interviews as well as the issues of gender, migration, and representation that animate this chapter.

Repetition and Isolation in "Solo"

After putting on his boots, Alzghair stood and faced the audience. With his arms hanging down by his sides, he initiated small foot movements. He shifted right to left, side to side, alternately weighting and unweighting each foot for four rhythmic pulses. He tapped his left foot forward on the fifth beat, followed by a tap underneath his body on the sixth beat. This initial footwork offered a minimalist interpretation of *dabke al-shamāliyya* that displaces the grapevine crossover step with small, alternating marching steps while facing the audience. His efficiency of movement was evocative of the scale of motion among participants in a dance circle who dance for hours at weddings. However, the repetitive nature of his choreographic movements dulled the perception of spontaneity associated with everyday *dabke* practice in ways that differentiate the adaptation from its source.

A rhythmic cycle emerged from this footwork, a cycle that structured the entirety of the choreography through its repetitive and durational qualities. Alzghair consistently modified, built, and varied footwork within this rhythmic cycle as the choreographic means by which he crafted narrative. As discussed in chapter 3, footwork rhythm is a primary aesthetic of *dabke* practice that is felt differently among practitioners, who group steps into either three or six units, respectively. In this choreography, Alzghair established the rhythmic cycle as six steps that correlated with a repeating cycle of six rhythmic pulses.[15] This pulse grouping was significant not only because of its fidelity to *dabke al-shamāliyya* but also because the six-count phrasing did not abide by the eight-count phrasing typically used in productions of *raqṣ shaʿbiyya*, which generally utilize the eight-count units typical of concert dance. This eight-count phrasing was adopted by dance directors in the early 1960s seeking to modernize vernacular performance traditions by incorporating concert dance conventions. By aligning the pulse groupings of his choreography with those of vernacular practices, Alzghair challenged past Syrian interpretations of *dabke* rhythms that either rendered rhythms as immutable and generalizable (Ibn Dhurayl 1996) or modernized rhythms in ways that erased vernacularity (*raqṣ shaʿbiyya*).

From the introductory gestures of the first act to the final scene of the second act, the six-beat pulse grouping repeated throughout the choreography. Alzghair maintained a precise tempo as he stood, shuffled on his knees, and raised his arms high, kept them down by his side, or placed them behind his back. As an audience member who appreciated how rhythmic precision is valued as a skill and technique in social *dabke* practice, I admired how much this socioaesthetic component energized the choreography and constructed the male dancing subject. The insistent pounding of footwork also enacted live, embodied sound design. No matter how subdivided or aerobic, the unwavering consistency of this aesthetic element established the pulse grouping as a dominant temporal parameter. It was a time signature that itself acquired a structuring logic through its repetition, that is, the simultaneous expression of sameness and difference that is "repetition's mark" (Colbert, Jones, and Vogel2020).

According to Alzghair, repetition as an aesthetic construct of *Displacement* represents the unwavering strength of "systemic . . . forces that have shaped us [Syrians] — including military and religious forces."[16] Given the participatory group dynamics of social *dabke*, it is significant that repetition in this choreography is enacted in and as solo performance in the first act. The appearance of a solo dancer performing *dabke* in the absence of other dancers is, I suggest, foundational to this work's political critique. It marks the loss of relational masculinity, or more broadly the weakening of social bonds that, as Hannah Arendt (1973) argues, is one of the dominant effects of authoritarianism. The Syrian regime has for decades isolated both social groups and individuals from one another. Isolation, according to Arendt, is politically powerful because it inhibits the ability of people to interact with each other. Autocracy thrives because of the (often but not necessarily sectarian) divisiveness that it manufactures (Al-Haj Saleh 2017). By extracting the *dabke* dancer from the group, the solo performance of the first act is an allegory for the ways that authoritarian power extricates its subjects from the lifeworlds that provide social sustenance.

In addition to being an authoritarian tactic of governance, isolation is also a symptomatic condition of displacement that negatively impacts migrants. The solo male figure also indexes the main demographic for Syrian migrants: young, single men seeking a livable life outside of Syria while living apart from their families and other institutionalized support structures. In addition to being detached from vital social networks, these young men were vulnerable to the "stranger danger" aversion endemic to European public spaces. The multifaceted social alienation experienced by Alzghair and those in similar predicaments is captured by and as solo choreography. Though it may be initially counterintuitive to choreograph *dabke* as a solo performance, this choice is one of the main interventions of this work. Isolation is a social and political state constitutive of contemporary Syrian lived experience that finds composition in the aesthetics of repetition, rhythmic precision, and solo staging.

The first act is not solely about repetition and isolation as embodied metaphors for systemic oppression and its effects. While maintaining unfaltering footwork, Alzghair poses in theatrical shapes that craft a counternarrative to this constraint, perhaps similar to a revolutionary male citizen-subject who resists political and religious hegemonies. For instance, he rises up from the ground only to collapse

FIGURE 6.1 Mithkal Alzghair, "Solo," from *Displacement*. Courtesy of Mithkal Alzghair; © 2016 Tanz im August / Laura Giesdorf.

again in surrender, all while incessantly maintaining the steady tempo of *dabke*-inspired footwork. Rising and falling becomes a repetitive cycle that varies in terms of scale of motion—at times he raises his knees higher like a military march—or in terms of scale of effort, such as when he imbues selected movements with vigorous intensity and physical effort. These expressive phrasings culminate in a subjugated and fatigued prisoner figure who kneels on the ground, hands shackled behind his back, somehow maintaining the back-and-forth of *dabke* footwork in a display of sheer vulnerability (see figure 6.1). By sculpting composed figures through and against the force of repetition, Alzghair embodies both hegemonic and counterhegemonic relations in the same performative moments. Through this poetry of motion emerges the contradictory tensions of the male Syrian subject—one who is oppressed by and struggles against his own movements, one who resists succumbing to the stillness of oppression through exertion, stamina, and the steadfast will to keep moving. These tensions speak to and for the Syrian experience of autocracy and forced migration. Syrianness is constructed through the recognition that the coercive and repressive apparatus of the authoritarian state is an exceptionally Syrian mode of governance as well as the desire to resist authoritarianism and flee state violence.

Resilient Masculinities

Whereas the individual male dancer featured throughout "Solo" (the first act) portrays social and political isolation in the struggle to endure autocracy and migration, the appearance of three male dancers in "Trio" (the second act) arguably reframes how masculinity is socialized in performance. "Trio" features three male dancers who practice a relatively traditional interpretation of *dabke* in collective synchronicity. Their group bodywork is significant for how it produces a relational masculinity in which performers support each other using the codified techniques of social *dabke*. The expansion from a single dancer in "Solo" into the collaborative bodywork of "Trio" serves to deepen and strengthen male bonds and enable the transformation of male vulnerability into collective resilience for those who endure autocracy and forced migration.

As described in chapter 3, the floor choreography most specific (though not exceptional) to *dabke* practice is the *shakl dā'ira*, the open-ended line circle formed by participants who clasp hands or grab shoulders as they circle around the performance space. Whether on the dance floor at a wedding or in a living room during an informal gathering of friends and family, the dance circle is a highly participatory space without distinctions between artists and audiences. In "Trio," the *shakl dā'ira* is staged as a three-person group of male dancers who dance *en corps*, facing the audience. Their staging is neither the open-ended line circle common to social *dabke* nor the crisp lines of dancers standardized in folkloric *dabke*. Instead, they move in and out of contact with one another and move around the stage while facing forward in a proscenium fashion. They do not perfectly emulate the emergent modes of improvisation and the characteristic angles of the torso that occur in the dance circle. Nor do they embody the joy that is popularly associated with *dabke* circles. Faces neutral and bodies tense, they *dabke* in a state of perpetual distress. They remain rigid and upright in their torsos while perfectly synchronizing their choreographed footwork. Alzghair, along with Rami Farah and Samil Taskin, place their hands on each other's shoulders at times but generally remain detached from one another. Despite the adaptive staging and the inversion of emotions, however, the synchronicity and symmetry of their three bodies in motion reproduce the dynamics of the *shakl dā'ira*.

Several choreographic techniques enact the *shakl dā'ira* onstage. The dancers emphatically embellish their steps with double-time figures. They strike the floor with percussive effects that resonate on the bodies of the audience.[17] They raise their arms overhead at times, an ambivalent gesture that perhaps signifies an act of protest during demonstrations or a call for help during migration. They circle around each other onstage, creating a dynamic flow across the floor that belies the rigidity of their upper bodies. Between the choreographed floor work, intricate rhythmic footwork, dramatization of the upper body, and facial expressions, "Trio" evokes the corporeal play of bodies in the *dabke* circle.

These dynamics are not present in the first act, which features Alzghair dancing *dabke* solo and in the absence of a dance circle. The inclusion of two additional participatory bodies in the second act underscores the social effects of empathic kinesthetic perception and male bonding in the dance circle. The synchronization of the dancers' collective bodywork emerges from sensory awareness of each other in ways that affirm a social and embodied mode of performance. The steadfast momentum of their rhythmically precise, repetitive footwork is sustainable rather than virtuosic. They lean into one another for balance as they circle onstage together. Though their bodies appear beleaguered and weary, their copresent and collaborative movements create a dynamic flow across the floor that belies the rigidity of their upper bodies. Their support of one another is indicative of how balanced and coordinated movements are an everyday tactic of resilience in the face of struggle and conflict.

These intercorporeal dynamics became vitally apparent in the Cincinnati performance when one of the dancers, Samil Taskin, could not perform due to a visa denial by the US State Department. Alzghair and Rami adapted to the situation by extending their arms out as if to place them on Taskin's shoulder, in absentia, in the theatricalized *shakl dā'ira*. However, his absence profoundly affected Alzghair's experience onstage. "It felt different [with two dancers]," he noted, "especially in the line. With a group, it feels like a continuation." His assessment of the collaborative mode of bodywork in the *shakl dā'ira* corroborates the value of relational masculinity in mitigating the alienating effects of government restrictions on human mobility between borders.

One of the major choreographic events that occurs during "Trio" is a series of staggered and rhythmic handclapping patterns that evoke the interlocked and intercorporeal group dynamics of the *shakl dā'ira*. The event begins when Farah claps his hands four times, arms raised high overhead, followed by Alzghair and Taskin, who each clap their hands twice (see figure 6.2). They then transition into staggered rounds of handclapping, in which each dancer claps their hands four times, entering after two claps by the other performer. Though two dancers clap simultaneously, they rotate such that different dancers clap hands each time. The interlocked and staggered rounds of clapping displace the rhythmic footwork that

FIGURE 6.2 Mithkal Alzghair, Samil Taskin, Rami Farah, "Trio," from *Displacement*.
Courtesy of Mithkal Alzghair; © 2016 Tanz im August / Dajana Lothert.

dominates the choreography in two ways: first, the choreographic focus transfers from the lower body to the upper body as the primary choreographic domain; and second, the staggered rhythms disrupt the otherwise consistent downbeat of the six-part rhythm that is predominant throughout the performance. The effects of this rhythmic texture are to articulate the intercorporeal dependency of the three bodies on one another as they support each other through their sonic movements through space.

The closing event of *Displacement* similarly evokes the role of mutual support in coping with distressful conditions. The dancers slowly twist and fall in and out of a grotesque figure inspired by the *Memorial to the Deportees to Buchenwald-Dora Concentration Camp* sculpture by Louis Bancel.[18] The original sculpture features a cluster of three emaciated deportees, symbolizing suffering, solidarity, and dignity. Connecting the Syrian experience to European histories of collective trauma, Alzghair elaborates that this event is meant to "evoke death . . . a dying that is supported by each other. As one dancer falls, he is caught and another holds him up."[19] This closing event intertwines vulnerability and dignity with solidarity in the moment approaching, but not realizing, death.

Whether the resilience of *Displacement* leads to something beyond survival and towards something akin to hope is indeterminate. The stage, Alzghair insists, is at once a physical frame that limits Syrian mobility and freedom of expression and a platform that reveals the power relations between Syrians and Europeans. To expose audiences to these power hierarchies, Alzghair privileged staging techniques that amplified the liveness, realness, and imminence of bodies engaged in the labor of performance. For instance, performers directly faced the audience for nearly the entirety of *Displacement* while maintaining neutral facial expressions. The relentless repetition of their movements in the face of neutrality was intended, according to Alzghair, to make the spectators' experience uncomfortable such that the spectators became aware of their own embodied presence and their role as witnesses to the resilient struggle against autocracy staged through dance. At a curated discussion following the aforementioned show that I attended in 2018, one attendee admitted to Alzghair that she felt "exhausted. I'm so tired. What about you?" Her experience of fatigue as a spectator, as well as her desire to translate her fatigue into empathy for Alzghair, is indicative of the power of "fellow feeling" (Foster 2011, 187) in performance to complicate public perceptions of Syrianness.

Engagement with the physical labor of dance also occurs through sound design. The choreography is strikingly devoid of the popular music that typically accompanies social *dabke* practices, instead consisting of the live acoustic effects of bodywork (with one exception). These sounds produced by dancework include the vibrational thuds of boots hitting the floor and the deep exhales induced by physical exertion that punctuate movement. The effects of the in situ immersive sound world are, again, to suspend the conventions of performance that maintain the illusion of a fourth wall. Moreover, the materiality of sound produced through bodywork reinforces the "reality" of lived experience,[20] including that of staged performance. Alzghair insists that this reality is an important contradistinction from folkloric *dabke* that seeks to reproduce the authenticity of the social space that *dabke* refers to. He arrived at this directorial decision through feedback offered at workshops, such as when one participant remarked on the efficacy of the sound of boots hitting the floor. Alzghair then decided to eliminate the popular music he had programmed in earlier versions of *Displacement*, instead choosing to privilege the breathwork, footwork, and overall bodywork of the dancer as the sonic texture of the performance. The performative effects of such "realness," as Alzghair explained to me, are to integrate the liveness of bodywork, the labor of dance, and the transfer of affect between artists and audiences into the political work of performance.

Displacement is an artistically and historically significant work that positions *dabke* on new aesthetic terrain and emplaces Syrianness onto the European stage, all while accounting for the complicated histories of encounter that shape the formation of cultural difference. *Displacement* is not immune to reproducing some dominant social norms and cultural logics that persist in contemporary Syria, nor does it fully eschew the terms of cultural difference that ensure support from European cultural institutions. Nevertheless, it disrupts the long-standing aesthetic, political, and social conventions that have encumbered Syrian dance heritage. But *Displacement* is not only about presenting the Syrian experience. The work resonates with the politics of Syrianness in and around 2015 because of how Alzghair inserts the inherently destabilizing forces of conflict and displacement on societies into the meaning of the work itself. He and his fellow performers achieve a work in which intimacy and resilience are enacted through the relational masculinities embedded in *dabke* circles. They challenge the political and social vulnerabilities of isolation and displacement through techniques that privilege the corporeality of bodies in performance. In so doing, this work transforms the possibilities of what *dabke* signifies, represents, and connotes among both Syrian artists and European audiences. It also opens a space for artists and audiences to collectively engage with a fractious period that was overwhelming, frustrating, and sensationalized for many. Gaining proximity to the figure of the stranger through performance animates the politics of this work precisely because the origin of (Syrian) difference is embodied by the figure of the (Syrian) stranger. Through the convergence of performance theory and praxis, *Displacement* translates the embodied social aesthetics of Syrian *dabke* into a choreography that destabilizes complex relations of power and representation situated between Syria and Europe.

WILLKOMMENSKULTUR IN BERLIN

Around the time that *Displacement* was in gestation, numerous displaced Syrian artists across Europe were also adapting to precarious personal and political circumstances. Artists settled across European cities and towns, with many finding refuge in Berlin, an established and affordable haven for artists supported by Germany's robust state cultural funding. Berlin's history of political reconciliation, reunification, and rebuilding was inspiring for those fleeing the sociopolitical divisiveness and infrastructural damage of armed conflict in wartime Syria.[21] Its progressive, anarchic, and multicultural ethos appealed to Syrian artists, who came from across political and cultural spectrums yet found common ground in exile.[22] In Berlin, many pursued opportunities to present their talent, experience, and training in the city's arts spaces. They benefited from the perception that they could contribute creative capital to their host society in ways that made them "more deserving" (Kyriakides 2017) of asylum and related benefits and resources than other refugees with fewer (or different) resources.

In 2015 a generous flow of opportunities, resources, and networking was allocated by the German state for refugees. As mentioned earlier, the social movement to welcome refugees was a galvanizing force across Europe that practiced solidarity against nativist and xenophobic policies. The movement was particularly strong in Berlin, where it was known as *Willkommenskultur*, or "culture of welcome." *Willkommenskultur* encompassed a wide net of formal and informal cultural activities, many of which received funding from the German state. Those involved in it framed their efforts as a political intervention in the power of states to disregard refugees as "bare life" (Agamben 1998), or political subjects who dwell in a state of exception beyond the bounds of the juridical state. Also embedded in the ethos of *Willkommenskultur* was a commitment to migrants' economic and social integration into German society that addressed critiques of assimilationist approaches to migration. Cultural institutions converted arts spaces into "safe spaces" for "newcomers," a term that sought to redirect labeling of the refugee subject away from social stigmas and towards social integration. They also curated conversations on refugee issues; commissioned art that critically engaged the "refugee crisis"; and provided resources and opportunities for newcomers, who faced a daunting set of bureaucratic hurdles as part of state-controlled processes of social integration.

All this attention, however well-intentioned and beneficial, made some Syrian artists feel like their work was circumscribed as "refugee culture" and "refugee branding."[23] These terms referred to the ascription of added value to experiences, goods, and services that engaged or were provided by refugee subjects in ways that felt transactional and Orientalist and that devalued other components of the experience. Capturing this historic synergy was a 2016 independent arts magazine, *A Syrious Look: A Magazine about Cultural Displacement*, curated and edited by Syrian-Palestine poet and screenwriter Mohammad Abou Laban, Syrian theater director Ziad Adwan, and German publisher Mario Münster. *A Syrious Look* featured creative work by artists and writers as well as reflections on home, identity, and exile. The magazine featured numerous perspectives on making art in conditions of displacement and marked the specific historicity of this cultural moment. One of the major themes that emerged was how artists negotiated the ambivalent relationship between politics, art, and life. Some artists used their work to engage an anti-Islamophobic politics of resistance in which their work implicitly challenged stereotypes of Islam and terrorism, transforming vulnerability into advocacy. Some artists desired to be seen not as "Syrian refugee artists" but as artists immersed in historically specific lived experiences that shaped and structured the context for their work. Echoing Palestinians' cultural struggle for political autonomy (Kanaaneh, Thorsén, Bursheh, and McDonald 2013), they questioned whether their work is necessarily political because of external factors. Many expressed ambivalence, even resentment, that politics was "thrust" on them or "dealing with us" (Abou Laban, Adwan, and Münster 2016) because the value of their efforts was circumscribed by the discourses and politics of refugeehood (Cusenza 2019). Despite a certain degree of privilege conferred on them as artists, they were imbricated in the racialized logics of inclusion and exclusion that shaped migration, resettlement, and integration, including the friendly welcoming of their work because of its difference.

Numerous collaborative ventures were supported by *Willkomenkultur*. Syrian musicians joined existing fusion ensembles, such as the Babylon Orchestra, where they contributed to the multicultural landscape popular in Berlin (Silverstein and Sprengel 2021). Other musicians, especially lead vocalist Abdallah Rahhal, launched Musiqana, a *ṭarab* music ensemble that specialized in the song repertoire of Aleppo. The ensemble was managed by Rachel Clarke, a cultural impresario whom they met at her Storytelling Arena program, in which "newcomers" shared their stories at open mic events.[24] Similar collaborations sprang forth across the diverse arts landscape and cultural sectors of Berlin. Artists had different points of access to these sectors and arts networks, with some building on prior connections while others started out cold.

One Syrian dancer arrived in Berlin without contacts and without harboring any fantasy that he might be able to continue his profession. Medhat Aldaabal shared with me in a 2017 interview that he had danced with Enana Dance in Damascus for several years, following the completion of his formal dance studies at the Higher Institute in Damascus. Originally from Suwayda, he left Syria for Greece in order to avoid military combat. He stayed in Athens for a period of time, working to save funds to relocate elsewhere within the EU. After his arrival in Berlin, he found himself walking through the city center, feeling a bit despondent about his future prospects. He saw a public poster for Zuhören, a weekly dance workshop organized by Sasha Waltz & Guests (SWG), one of Germany's premiere contemporary dance companies, for unaccompanied Syrian minors, Syrian dancers, and SWG members. He attended the workshop and, not long afterward, SWG commissioned Aldaabal for a new choreography.

Aldaabal invited three of his colleagues (Mouafak Aldoabl, Fadi Waked, and Firas Almassre) to collaborate with him. They had arrived in Berlin from Damascus separately, each taking their own routes and risks. Together they developed a new language for what would become *Amal* (Hope, 2017, Berlin premiere).[25] *Amal* narrated their journeys during the armed conflict and through displacement. The dancers developed a movement vocabulary out of a series of workshops and rehearsals in which they experimented with the signifying capacity of gestures. They explored different ways to say "I" in a single gesture, as well as group work that conveyed their mutual support and interdependence on one another in spaces of trauma. Their technique, to return to Judith Hamera's framing, generated new aesthetics, subjects, and stories that had yet to be presented to audiences, making Syrian bodies "legible and intelligible" in ways that provided a "basis for interpretation and critique" for audiences who were themselves mostly non-Syrian and European. When I saw *Amal*'s premiere at Sophiensæle, an independent performance space, in 2017 during a research trip in Berlin, I was overwhelmed by the immediate presence of their bodywork. Having witnessed the conflict from afar, I was deeply affected by the liveness of the performance experience as well as the traumatic retelling of their lived experiences through gesture and movement.

Aldaabal and his colleagues toured *Amal* across Germany while also pursuing their own individual dance careers. Aldaabal and his cousin Mouafak Aldoabl collaborated with Israeli choreographer Nir de Volff on *Come as You Are* (2017), and Fadi Waked collaborated with Farah Saleh, a Palestinian choreographer-scholar, on an experimental digital dance work, "Gesturing Refugees" (F. Saleh 2020). Aldoabl and Waked joined folk dance ensembles, performing *raqṣ shaʿbiyya* at Syrian community events, including weddings and private parties. The dancers considered themselves students of their new host society and embraced opportunities to learn, explore, and create. Aldaabal shared with me that at one point in the making and touring of *Amal*, Sasha Waltz asked him if he had anything to teach her dancers.[26] His first reaction was shock and humility. He was there to learn "from" the company, to absorb new techniques and conceptual framings. These were the asymmetrical terms of encounter that he embraced, a hierarchy in which his vulnerability as a "newcomer" positioned him to learn from his host society. Enacting the "culture of welcome" in the best sense, Sasha

Waltz suggested that some of the best learning occurs through teaching, and that her dancers would benefit from his pedagogical contribution to German dance.

On reflection, he offered to organize workshops on *dabke* that approached it as a social dance tradition because he felt it best represented Syrian dance, despite an initial self-consciousness that it was too pedantic for SWG members. Aldaabal and Sasha Waltz successfully garnered funding from the German state for a series of community *dabke* workshops that introduced the dance tradition to Berliners. Ali Hasan, a percussionist who collaborated with Aldaabal for *Amal*, joined them out of a "sense of duty to give something back, to give some of our culture to Berlin."[27] The result is a series of workshops that began in 2017 and has continued since, notwithstanding a brief respite during the pandemic. The workshops attract anywhere from a smaller group to tens of dozens of participants, who range widely in experience, age, and background. Aldoabl, Almassre, and Waked often support and assist at the events.

The workshops have been transformative for Aldaabal and Hasan, particularly with regard to their perspective on *dabke* practices. They had previously taken this dance tradition for granted, distancing themselves from it because it was a social practice rather than an artistic discipline. But teaching *dabke* has helped them dismantle this high/low cultural hierarchy, instead facilitating a newfound respect for their cultural tradition.[28] The workshops have also become a space in which they advocate for and translate Syrianness. Generally, they have been frustrated with "stranger danger," sharing with me many stories of racism, xenophobia, and how speaking in Arabic in public spaces triggers associations of terrorism and violence among others passing through the same space. They view these workshops as an opportunity to challenge Islamophobia, resist gendered stereotypes, and reestablish dignity for refugees through compassionate and intercultural bodywork.

The series sponsored through SWG is not their only avenue for teaching. They teach frequently at festivals across Germany. This SWG-sponsored series is significant, however, because it launched their careers as teaching artists and because it has retained longevity. The workshops have continued well beyond the initial "culture of welcome" and "refugee crisis." The workshops are also significant because they denote a transformative moment in the cultural history of *dabke*, a moment in which the adaptation of *dabke* technique for pedagogical aims makes Syrian bodies legible and valuable, for both Syrians and Europeans. At the same time, the strange encounters that occur in these spaces can also be traced to the politics of difference that have historically shaped the presentation and performance of *dabke* since the twentieth century. I now turn to a closer discussion of what these workshops achieve in terms of technique, the translation of Syrianness, and navigating relations between and among Syrians and Europeans.

DABKE COMMUNITY WORKSHOPS

Medhat Aldaabal and Ali Hasan host several workshops each year at RadialSystem V, a spacious event venue in East Berlin. Awarded a funding grant by SWG, the workshops are open to the public and advertised as a family event. Children are encouraged to attend, and the events are held at family-friendly hours. At the workshop that I attended in November 2017, the attendance was approximately ninety persons of all genders, mostly non-Arab Europeans. It consisted of mostly first timers with a sizable number of repeat participants, including several professional SWG dancers (see figure 6.1). I attended with my spouse and child as well as my extended family, most of whom participated in the dance circle. Other workshops attract a similar demographic, with some Syrian participants attending now and again. Though most workshops are held at RadialSystem V, Aldaabal and Hassan also work with libraries, festivals, and other community spaces to reach different local communities.

Aldaabal and Hasan selected an event space that granted visibility and cultural authority to their workshop. The expansive theater space is used for a variety of programming, from stage productions and experimental arts workshops to panels and presentations. As a multifunctional performance space with auditorium seating, this room shapes and is shaped by the social forces (Lefebevre 1991) and aesthetic ideologies of Berlin's creative sector. It bears an "architectonic legacy" (Lepecki 2006) of an empty blank space that is intertwined with the masculine and solipsistic space of the writing chamber. Teaching *dabke* in this space connects the practice to past and future performances in the same space in ways that allow *dabke* to circulate in Berlin's aesthetic economies with a new kind of value and cultural authority. Additionally, Aldaabal and Hasan benefit from the institutional authority of this space insofar as it increases their sense of contribution to and purpose in German society, Syrian culture, and dance worlds. This effect is important as a "strategy of masculinization" (Suerbaum 2018) that combats the gendered vulnerabilities often concomitant with refugeehood.

The general aims of the workshops are to invite participants to experience the *dabke* circle as an embodied metaphor for multiculturalism and introduce several *dabke* styles. Some variations and embellishments are introduced, but

Aldaabal and Hasan assume that the average participant has no prior dance experience and are careful to limit the amount of technique and repertoire taught at a given event. Aldaabal generally leads the workshops, with frequent collaborators Mouafak Aldouabl, Firas Almassre, and Fadi Waked assisting when they are available. He cues in English, one of the primary languages of the global city of Berlin. Ali Hasan accompanies the participants on live percussion, usually handpan and *tar*.

At the November 2017 workshop that I attended, Aldaabal led participants through a series of warm-up exercises. Dressed in jeans, loose pants, sweaters, and athletic wear, participants stretched individual muscle groups—neck, shoulders, quads, and hamstrings. Recalling how *dabke* is known to strain knee joints, as older Syrian men joke (with sincerity), I appreciated the warm-up. Afterwards, Aldaabal introduced the basic six-step sequence of *dabke al-shamāliyya* (also known as *dabke al-daľūna*), the style that I discussed in chapter 3 as the backbone for embellishments, improvisations, and variations that is frequently taught in introductory workshops. Moving into the center of the room, with a lapel microphone hooked to him, Aldaabal isolated the pattern into distinct steps. He then sequenced these steps into patterns. He taught basic sequences, without embellishments, in order to align the skill level of the repertoire with the amateur capacity of participants. Aldaabal shared with me that students in the first set of workshops struggled to learn the common embellishment of "kick, ball, change," or *wāḥid-wa-nuṣ* (similar to my struggle to learn embellishments), and that he no longer teaches this embellishment in order not to overwhelm students. After teaching *dabke al-shamāliyya*, Aldaabal introduced three or four different styles that varied widely in their footwork and type of motion. He added embellishments to his demonstrations, such as adding a double-time step or varying the spacing between his steps, which some participants tried to emulate. After Aldaabal demonstrated each sequence, we practiced it in a large dance circle, hands interlinked, that moved counterclockwise around the room, accompanied by Ali Hasan on percussion (see figure 6.3). The workshop ended with a long *dabke* session in which we all performed the sequences learned in the past ninety minutes, with Hasan improvising on percussion.

Hasan played a variety of common duple meter dance rhythms, including *mālfūf*, *ayyub*, *choubi*, *hajjar*, and *katakafti* (which is similar to *nawari*). He accented the fifth and sixth steps to help us dancers anchor our movements. I appreciated being able to hear the rhythmic stress on those steps and connect my footwork to his playing. By providing these rhythmic accents on *tar*, Hasan

FIGURE 6.3 *Dabke* Community Dancing (with Medhat Aldaabal and Ali Hasan), developed in the context of "Zuhören: Third Space for Art & Politics," produced by Sasha Waltz & Guests. © 2019 Eva Radünzel-Kitamura.

enacted the percussive conventions of the *ṭabl* player at a *dabke* session, who, as I described in chapter 3, circulates around the *dabke* circle and adds a bass note to the rhythmic pattern to help dancing participants coordinate their footwork with the *dabke* beats. When Hasan sensed that we were more comfortable with the sequence, he improvised the rhythms in ways that created a sense of rhythmic displacement. Some participants filled in the missing beats with improvised embellishments. This participatory and emergent dynamic was an important part of the social experience of the workshop. It enabled Hasan and us dancers to make performance choices that amplified the dialogic relationship between movement and percussion. This would not have been possible (or would have worked differently) had recorded music, with its fixity, been provided. The dialogic relationship encouraged a sensory awareness of how embodied practice connects movement to rhythmic sound and generated a sense of empathy among participants.

Hasan's intentional choice to play instruments not typically used at *ḥafla*—the handpan and *tar* rather than the *ṭabl, darbukka*, or synthesizer track—produced a percussive texture that was strikingly different from typical *dabke* events. Instead of the heavily amplified duple beat grooves with a drive intensified by the sheer repetition of beats, Hasan played relatively soft acoustic patterns on a single percussive instrument. He layered these patterns in his solo performance, but importantly did not try to simulate the heterophonic texture of a *shaʿbī dabke* session. This is significant because it suggests that Hasan did not aim to simulate a *ḥafla*, that is, to recreate the ethnographic context for *dabke* practice in order to make the workshop more authentic. Relatedly, Hasan and Aldaabal did not provide an overview about the roles, social functions, or ritual spaces associated with social *dabke* practices. Instead, they focused on technique and bodywork in order to provide workshop participants with a fulfilling dance experience that was grounded in technique and expression rather than ethnographic fidelity to Syrian culture.

Aldaabal and Hasan framed *dabke* practice as a set of embodied techniques that were less about transmitting codified sequences of steps to cultural outsiders or imitating an ethnographic context for the sake of reproducing dance as cultural heritage and more about the experience of moving together in a collective circle. Their approach to *dabke* as bodywork, rather than as repertoire or ethnographic object, animated the "communal" work of technique (Hamera 2006) by emphasizing the ways that "lexical, descriptive endeavors" (5) are fundamentally about selfhood and sociality. Importantly, their technique adopted much of the language and techniques of contemporary dance worlds. These adoptions were a strategy for translating Syrianness into a meaningful experience for participants that exceeded the act of learning a few sequences of steps. The experience affected different participants in various ways—for some Syrians, it opened up ways to relate to *dabke* that destabilized the social norms and conventions they associated with *dabke* circles. For non-Syrians, it enabled an intimate connection to Syrian culture that was problematically linked to the fetishization of Syrian difference in both multicultural and *Willkommenskultur* spaces (which frequently overlapped). In this space of encounter, *dabke* technique was a strategy for mediating the racial and religious forms of difference constructed in *Willkomenkultur* and the broader discourse of refugee crisis while also empowering Syrians to reimagine their connection to cultural heritage.

Their first approach to technique was to situate bodywork within philosophies of "self-care." Aldaabal and Hasan continually reflected on and revised their workshops in order to build towards their ideal space of encounter. Hasan insisted that the workshops are a "platform to empower social life."[29] To this end, Aldaabal and Hasan encouraged participants to engage in "self-care" during the event, which for them referred to actively attending to spiritual and physical health on the individual level. They organized a set order of activities that included "self-care" exercises, such as setting intentions at the beginning of the workshop, a warm-up series, and closing with a meditation. The warm-up series identified and isolated specific muscles and areas of the body most impacted in *dabke* practice. Warm-up series are commonplace in dance, fitness, and other domains of physical culture but are not used in the casual and leisurely social spaces in which social *dabke* is practiced. Aldaabal's choice to insert a set of small movements that loosen the muscles, ligaments, and joints and generally increase body temperature at the outset of the workshop is indicative of both his training in physical culture industries (primarily dance) and his attentiveness to the corporeal demands of dance on bodies. His inclusion of mindfulness breathing and meditation at the end of the workshop as "acts of self-care" that facilitate a mind-body connection among participants is similarly indicative of recent shifts in physical culture industries that moralize the cultivation of the body.[30] Self-care is often imbued by practitioners with a political philosophy, stemming from Audre Lorde's declaration that "caring for myself . . . is an act of political warfare" (1988, 130), that approaches care as an embodied act of resistance to exploitative structures of the state, economy, and society. Given that the *dabke* community workshops emerged within *Willkomenkultur*, itself a movement to challenge the exercise of border controls and national security in the state apparatus, Aldaabal and Hasan's curatorial decision to prioritize self-care affirms the movement's ethos of counterhegemonic politics.

After the warm-ups, Aldaabal and Hasan shifted into group circlework. They did not fundamentally alter the social choreographies common to *dabke* practice. For example, they did not convert the *dabke* circle into the linear rows of participants executing floorwork that is traditionally directed in ballet and other dance classes. Neither did they ask participants to move across the floor in lines or small groups to execute sequences under the gaze of the pedagogue and other participants. Rather, Aldaabal positioned himself in the center of the stage while the participants formed a circle around him (see figure 6.4). This circular orientation disrupted the spatial norms of the studio, in which dancers perform for the pedagogue in linear formations, and of the stage, in which performers face the seated audience. It also established Aldaabal's authority

FIGURE 6.4 *Dabke* Community Dancing (with Medhat Aldaabal and Ali Hasan), developed in the context of "Zuhören: Third Space for Art & Politics," produced by Sasha Waltz & Guests. © 2019 Eva Radünzel-Kitamura.

because he led from the center, around which everyone flowed. Additionally, Aldaabal's pedagogical authority was constructed through the use of a lapel mic to project his voice throughout the venue. The mic dramatized Aldaabal's presence by amplifying his voice and broadcasting it to all corners of the expansive space. The lapel mic theatricalized Aldaabal's visual aesthetic and established him as an authority. Often associated with corporatized events and programs, such as the now-ubiquitous TED speaker series that promotes an individual as the bearer of specialized knowledge, or the fitness industry, in which instructors lead group classes suffused with theatrical lights and sound, the lapel mic has become a fixture of cultural authority. Between the social choreography of the event, the lapel mic, and the "architectonic legacy" of the event space itself, the material conditions of the RadialSystem V stage emplaced Aldaabal at the center of the spectacle.

Aldaabal's authoritative performance as a pedagogue was, of course, crucial to the workshop's dynamics. He did not base his authority to teach *dabke* on his village background, instead grounding his teaching in his professional dance training by privileging bodily discipline and standardized movements. Yet irrespective of his efforts to situate technique in contemporary dance idioms, his pedagogical authority was racialized by the "ontological linking" (Johnson 2003) of his lived experience with epistemological authority. This predicament is hardly singular to Aldaabal or his relationship to the pedagogical object. The scenario of "How to Teach the Other When the Other Is Self," to cite E. Patrick Johnson's reference to Mae Henderson's 1994 essay, is bound to the racialization of epistemological authority.[31] Referring to constructions and negotiations of Blackness in the university classroom, Johnson attests that "my body signifies in ways over which I do not necessarily have control, but for the performative reiteration of 'blackness' my body compels by its mere presence" (Johnson 2003, 246–47). While I fully acknowledge that the particular experiences and histories that structure Blackness as well as anti-Black racism in the United States may make comparisons to other racialized experiences and structures relatively facile, there is arguably a somewhat similar process at play in the *dabke* community workshops. Racialized as Muslim, Arab, and foreign in German public spaces, teaching *dabke* to a mainly cosmopolitan and creative social class based in Berlin both legitimated Aldaabal's presence and contribution to German society and retained his "strange" embodied presence within that society because of institutionalized exoticism and racism.[32]

Importantly, the racialization of foreigners intersects with gendered perceptions of refugees, especially Muslim refugees in the midst of the "European refugee crisis." As discussed earlier in the chapter, male refugee subjects often confronted stereotypes of militarized masculinity (conflated with terrorism for Muslim subjects), violent masculinity (conflated with sexual violence for Muslim and Arab subjects), and patriarchal domination (conflated with fatherhood and providing for the household), at the same time that refugees were often emasculated due to their political vulnerabilities. While Aldaabal and Hasan encountered these stereotypes in their everyday lives in Berlin, these workshops were generally a space of exception in which they constructed healthy, social masculinities based on pleasure (not fear), play (not violence), and friendship (not antagonism). The workshops thus resisted the emasculation of refugees that structures their lives and those of others in their networks. This benefited both Aldaabal and Hasan as workshop leaders who cultivated new forms of male authority and workshop participants. The open dynamics of these workshops encouraged participants to recognize their own gendered vulnerabilities and probe moments for empowerment. A middle-aged Syrian woman who joined one workshop afterwards told Hasan that she had not danced *dabke* before the workshop because, as a woman, she had been discouraged from dancing in public. Her experience, she elaborated, transformed her relationship to the tradition and her sense of femininity from shame and social stigmatization to self-worth and self-expression. Part of this impact can be attributed to the conditions of displacement that made this workshop possible because Syrians are distant from the social institution of the family, which shapes the gendered spaces of *dabke* circles in Syria. One of the major contributions of the workshops, then, is to facilitate new expressions of gender that challenge hegemonic constructions endemic to both Syrian society and the politics of difference in Europe.

Who presents movement as pedagogy is deeply embedded in complex economies of belonging, identity, and performance that themselves bear prior histories of colonial encounter. Pedagogical spaces, bodies, practices, and techniques shape and are shaped by the relations of difference in which they are embedded. Aldaabal's authority as a professional Syrian dancer, enacted through his bodily presence and his trained background, arguably enabled a more authentic experience in the workshop because it "enriched" the "text" (Johnson 2003) of the dance sequences that we learned. His teaching brought us participants, myself included, closer to the affective experience of difference that we desired. Indeed, one of the primary distinctions of learning spaces such as these is that participants enter with the multicultural liberal desire to "transform [their] perceptions of the world we live in and the people who share it with us."[33] This transformative work occurs through the production of "fellow-feeling," or empathy (Foster 2011), that emerges in kinesthetic pedagogy. *Dabke* workshops in particular facilitate utopic framings of kinesthetic experience insofar as the intercorporeal dynamics mediate "empathic kinesthetic perception," to invoke Deirdre Sklar's construct again, between participants.

Aldaabal and Hasan, however, redirect the interpersonal and intercultural work of their workshops away from the liberal desire to communicate intercultural empathy and more towards opportunities for self-care and confidence building. This is reflected in their activities, as described earlier, and their explicit aim to focus on participants' relationships to their own bodies. It is also reflected in their refusal to grant ethnographic proximity to Syrian culture. This refusal is achieved through their choices to provide acoustic percussion accompaniment rather than the digital *sha'bī* music that most often provides a musical setting for *dabke* circles and to not present information about how *dabke* is practiced in everyday Syrian life. Aldaabal and Hasan imbue the bodywork demanded in their *dabke* workshops as social, political, and even spiritual in the sense that it centers selfhood in the context of community. *Dabke* technique emerges through the labor of performance, specifically the iterative and emergent bodily acts that ascribe to, and navigate, the social space of the workshop through affective and social dynamics.

EMBODIED PEDAGOGY

As I mentioned earlier in this chapter, Europeans developed opportunities to welcome Syrians and learn about their cultural traditions as part of a sense of civic responsibility and empathy. *Dabke* gained popularity and relevance for those seeking out Syrianness because it mediated cross-cultural encounters and neutralized some of the more thorny tensions of race and religion through its ontological folkness. This was the case not only for the European cultural centers and nonprofits mapped out previously but also for American educators at universities and colleges responding to the Trump administration's "Muslim ban" in 2017.[34] Educators sought out Syrian cultural representatives for their programs as an opportunity to practice advocacy for US immigration, project the role of the US as a haven for refugees, and engage in American multiculturalism. These initiatives arguably echoed the "strange encounters" dynamic of the European response to mass migration in 2015 by fetishizing Syrian difference within the ethos of liberal advocacy.

In this political context, I received several opportunities to teach *dabke* to high school and college students. Ranging from an hour-long workshop for university dance students to a fifteen-minute workshop for high school students at a public high school, these opportunities raised the question of how all participants, including myself, negotiated the body politics of pedagogical authority, especially given the political context that structured these workshops. In recounting these workshops, I dwell on moments of doubt and skepticism in order to reflect on how participants construct the "origin of difference" when a non-Syrian American female is the principle cultural authority in these spaces.

"Excuse me," I said to a participant dancing next to me at Aldaabal and Hasan's Berlin workshop at Radialsystem V. "Your hips. Instead of facing them directly towards the person next to you in line, try turning them more towards the center of the circle. Like this." I quickly demonstrated my unsolicited tip and added: "You could also thrust your left hip forward a bit when you crossover with the left foot." I was speaking to a professional dancer with SWG. He earnestly danced alongside me with energetic steps that resembled wide and low lunges. Though we had not introduced ourselves to each other, his name tag clearly designated his role as a volunteer assisting with the event. I, however, remained unlabeled. I did not have a name tag, and my appearance did not project any cultural competence in Syrian *dabke*. The SWG dancer sized me up and pointedly deflected my suggestion. "I believe the hips do point this way," he replied. "I am following the *dabke* teacher." I replied with an added firmness intended to establish my authority: "Actually, the hips face the center. I studied *dabke* in Syria for two years and learned about this there." He listened to my remark and reoriented his hips.

It is rather predictable that my informal correction of a professional dancer was received with skepticism. Though Aldaabal had invited me to the workshop precisely because he knew about my research, other participants were not aware of my friendly relationship with the teachers or of my cultural competency with the material. Neither did I look the part as a nonwhite, cisgender woman whom others often perceive as racially ambiguous. Most Europeans at the workshop did not have any reason to situate me as a lead, teacher, or assistant in a space led by Syrians. But the banal obviousness of these perceptions is itself indicative of how pedagogical authority is socially constructed. As I described earlier, pedagogy was concentrated (through the theater of the event space) in the "master" figure (Aldaabal), who delegated some of that authority to his support instructors (Almassre, Waked, and Aldoabl), all of whom were young Syrian male dancers. Pedagogy was racialized and gendered in this space in ways that precluded the notion that a non-Arab, female participant might bear some kind of cultural authority.

The German dancer was not the only person who questioned my cultural authority to teach *dabke*. In 2018 I was invited to lead a lecture-workshop for high school students in Evanston, Illinois. The workshop was part of an outreach and diversity program that benefited students who identify with Asian and Middle Eastern society and culture. Approximately fifty students attended the workshop, including Asian, Middle Eastern, white, and Black students, plus several staff. After an introductory lecture, during which a video clip of an orchestra playing classical Arab music brought a female Syrian student to tears "because it reminded her so much of her country," I transitioned into a brief *dabke* workshop. We began in a big circle, which I led. I gave instructions for the crossover step, left foot over right foot. Across the room, a male Syrian student from Dar'a muttered "this isn't *dabke*" (in Arabic), just loud enough for me to hear. I caught his eye and called out "*bis da'iya*" (just a minute), while making a hand gesture (touching my index finger and thumb while shaking my hand up and down with a heavy, weighted feel) that communicates "patience, wait." I understood his skepticism. How would this female American teacher in her forties know anything about his communal tradition? Unlike salsa, tango, belly dance, and other global dance forms, *dabke* is not a mobile practice. It remains relatively insulated within communities, aside from its occasional appearance as an expression of Palestinian resistance staged for the international community. The crossover step did not inspire his confidence. My pedagogical rationale for leading with this step was that I assumed the students did not have any prior experience learning dance genres formally through an instructor. Most students in previous workshops that I had led were not proficient in the crossover step and needed to practice it in the line circle formation before acquiring new information. Finally, the crossover step is itself a cultural bridge because it is common to many popular dances and therefore a familiar point of departure for those learning a new set of embodied techniques.

Skepticism aside, I began to gain some respect from him when I led the *dabke* line through some variations, and especially when I added bounce and extended my coverage with each step. Towards the end, I invited him and his friends to form a smaller circle inside of the larger *shakl dā'ira* for leading and improvising (while also giving him space to decline respectfully). He accepted and tried to lead the circle with improvisation. But his sense of rhythm was off, and he was unable to transition into a flow state. He said to me, with some embarrassment, that he couldn't feel it. His embarrassment was likely related to a doubled vulnerability stemming from the desire to represent his culture and the gendered mandate from within that culture for young men to become *dabbikūn*.

As I explain in chapter 3's discussion of my experiences learning *dabke*, the lack of flow is more common than not in pedagogical spaces. Getting participants to feel proficient enough to improvise is a particular challenge for introductory level *dabke* workshops. Aldaabal, for instance, cut out a part for improvisation scheduled at the end of his *dabke* workshops that was intended for students to integrate what they learned with their own embodied knowledge, inclusive of amateur and professional levels of experience. He discontinued this section after learning, through trial and error, that most participants were not ready to take the risk of improvising, especially in front of others. For this high school student, the lack of a flow state could be attributed to any number of factors: the brevity of the session, the hybridity of a part instructional and part performance event, the disproportionate number of cultural outsiders to insiders that placed the pressure of representation onto his *dabke* movements, or social anxiety due to the risks of performing in front of his peers.

Though my pedagogical aims for workshops varied, they generally intended to introduce students to popular *dabke* styles as well as the fundamentals of posture, alignment, and directionality. I also introduced key terms and described key roles in the *shakl dāʾira*. I prepared footwork sequences (including embellishments and variations for those interested) based on video footage and field notes that I documented during fieldwork as well as the Berlin *dabke* workshop with Aldaabal. Musical accompaniment consisted of either a video CD of long-form *dabkāt* tracks that skewed more *shaʿbī* in style or a playlist of *dabke* pop songs available on Spotify, including the artists Melhem Zein, Wafeek Habib, Ayman Zbib, and Naim El Sheikh. Most workshops were scheduled for thirty minutes, with the exception of an hour-long master class targeted for dance students. With the exception of the latter master class, I found that (like Aldaabal) students with no prior experience in dance were able to learn basic footwork patterns, body alignment, and perhaps one embellishment or variation, which they practiced in an extended *dabke* circle at the end of the workshop. Rarely were they able to digest the material enough that they could synthesize the techniques into their own improvisation.

For most students across the various *dabke* workshops that I led, this program was sufficient. However, when I offered a *dabke* workshop to Northwestern University students at the end of a course on Syrian history and culture, they asked for an ethnographic context in which to emplace our movements. After weeks of analyzing literature, film, and performance, they understood that technique is not in and of itself constitutive of the practice, but is shaped by and embedded in social relations and performance conditions. I obliged, of course, with videos of weddings I had recorded during my fieldwork. Yet their request raised the question of when and whether such media can substitute for embodied and ethnographic forms of knowledge. In contrast, Medhat Aldaabal and Ali Hasan successfully detached their teaching from the desire or need to be authentic (e.g., to play a specific set of rhythms or teach only Syrian styles of *dabke*). What our different experiences and approaches suggest is that the construction of Syrianness depends on which subjects are authorized with the authority to authenticate Syrianness in a given social space (Johnson 2003, 238–39). These fluid processes are structured by everyday perceptions of race, gender, class, and nationality that are impossible to detach from the object of knowledge itself.

Though *dabke* has become more visible due to conflict and refugee politics, it is important to not limit the Syrian experience to conditions of precarity, survival, or disappointment. *Dabke* workshops often inspire joy, playfulness, and a burst of endorphins from energetic physical exertion. They also spur memories of past encounters with *dabke* and the worlds in which *dabke* is embedded. At the Northwestern course, one student insisted on learning *dabke* in order to build on her study abroad experience in Jordan and connect these two disparate education spaces through performance and tradition. A heritage student in a different course seized the opportunity to improvise and flaunt her skills to her peers at the end of the course. At Evanston Township High School, a student whom I perceived as South Asian came up to me after the workshop and shared his experience dancing with a *dabke* group in middle school. This workshop, he continued, prompted a pleasant nostalgia for his middle school exposure. At the College of Charleston, where I taught *dabke* to dance majors in a dance studio, a female undergraduate from the SWANA region stayed afterwards to teach me the local *khalījī* (Gulf) dance styles that her family practices.

What these spaces of performance and pedagogy enable are acts of cosmopolitan worldmaking. Bodywork enables fluid mobility between and among worlds that are often posed as whole, fixed, and immutable. Embodied expressions allow for diasporic and cosmopolitan subjects to tell their stories of in-betweenness and of experiences that do not fit tidily into any given cultural space. *Dabke*, for these students, was about past encounters rather than strange encounters. But these moments of mobility and interaction also generate "friction" (Tsing 2005) in which "heterogeneous and unequal encounters can lead to new arrangements of culture and power" (5). At the same time that some participants generate healthy connections across different parts of their lives, others are vulnerable to the tensions that stem from the phenomenon of "strange encounters." How individuals, including myself, navigate the relations of difference that structure these workshops is also about the racialized and gendered logics of embodied epistemology that shape pedagogical spaces.

———

This chapter has examined efforts by a displaced generation of dancers to present Syrian *dabke* for Western audiences through performance and pedagogy. Their projects stem from the hard realities of a war economy, military conscription, armed conflict, and forced migration. They were formulated in the heart of the tensions of "strange encounters," which fetishized Syrianness because of the perceived Otherness of Arab and Muslim subjects in European spaces, as well as the related exploitation of "refugee culture" during a heightened period of migration into Europe, the feminization of refugees, and the collective trauma of the ongoing war and mass migration. Out of these many challenges emerged choreographies and pedagogies that explored the imprint of lived experience on individual bodies in ways that attest to the singularity of Syrian history in the contemporary moment. The artists crafted new relationships to their cultural heritage, becoming researchers, teachers, and representatives of a practice that they had overlooked before their arrival in Europe. The artists negotiated their multifaceted predicament with perspectives that unsettled dominant social norms. Instead, what emerged were critical, compassionate, and counterhegemonic explorations of male Syrian bodies in motion.

One of the more impactful effects of these projects is their reflexive approach to masculinity during a period when hegemonic forms of masculinity dominated the narratives in mainstream media as well as social media. In *dabke* sessions on the front lines of the conflict, as discussed in chapter 5, men on active duty took to *dabke* as a tactic for situating themselves in the role of male defenders of traditional ways of life. Though many men were placed in vulnerable conditions due to military conscription, lack of employment, and a wartime economy, among other circumstances, they coped with these vulnerabilities through performances of masculinity including but not limited to *dabke* traditions. In contradistinction to this archive of hegemonic masculinity in everyday wartime life, Mithkal Alzghair, Medhat Aldaabal, Ali Hasan, and their collaborators focus on the fragility of male bodies in uncertain times, authoritarian regimes, and collective traumas. They resist the discourses that femininize male refugees, especially single, unaccompanied young men, because they are perceived to have abandoned war and their duty to bear arms and fight. Instead, their projects hold space for how Syrians can relate to their bodies and one another, especially men, through healthy, compassionate, and supportive relationships. Alzghair literally bares the flesh of his body as a corporeal mediation of power and gender. Aldaabal and Hasan approach movement technique as a modality of self-care for all bodies within the *dabke* circle. Together they empower masculinity as a resource for communal, creative, and empathetic bodywork that forges new social relationships in displacement.

While this chapter has focused on the brief but significant period immediately following mass migration into Europe in 2015, the challenges of this period will likely be relevant for years to come. Syrians will continue to face the predicament of "strange encounters" as they adapt to and are incorporated into host societies. Integration (itself a debated construct) is a nonlinear process of governance that, even well beyond the initial shock of arrival, impacts the ways that migrants experience and negotiate the power relations and inequities of where they dwell. What the projects discussed in this chapter offer to this predicament is that they utilize the value of embodiment to challenge stereo-types and intervene in structures of power. Rather than accommodating liberal perspectives that paradoxically reproduce the forms of difference they seek to bridge through cross-cultural advocacy, these projects foreground corporeality, liveness, technique, and performance as tactics to resist such accommodation. The translation of Syrianness through performance is about crafting technique anew, and in so doing, empowering both performers and audiences to critically evaluate the terms of their encounter.

CODA

Towards a New Balance

The 2017 Foster Beach World Refugee Day Picnic, held on July 8 on the north-side of Chicago, celebrated refugee communities from the Republic of Congo, Rohingya, Iraq, and Syria, among other countries. The annual event featured a human rights march; soccer tournament (won that year by the Afghan team); and the Culture Coach, an area for participatory and presentational performances. Intrigued by Arab pop music blasting out of the speaker system, my three-year-old and I passed by the Culture Coach, a van that opened to create a stage with an awning. There, a young man from Syria danced enthusiastically on his own in a grassy space in front of the ad hoc stage. When a *dabke* track came on, two men and a young woman joined the first young man in the green space, clasping hands to form a *shakl dāʾira*. The young man took the lead, and the four participants tried to sync their crossover steps with each other and lock into the duple meter groove. But they could not find their flow. After a minute or two the line broke up, and the young man began dancing solo again.

The young woman began to *dabke* with some female companions. My toddler and I joined in briefly but departed after he lost his shoe and began fussing. Meanwhile, the young women found their flow in the style of *dabke al-shamāliyya*. Seventeen participants of mixed gender, ethnic backgrounds, and religiosities gradually joined the dance circle. A Muslim couple danced in the *ḥalqa* while two young men circled around, taking a selfie video and clapping hands. The first young man took the *awwal* position again. He added embellishments, double-time steps to the fifth count of the six-pulse grouping, and increased his agility. He waved his right arm as if holding a *misbaḥa*, a set of rosary beads traditionally spun by the *awwal*. When another *dabke* track started, people divided into small groups rather than one big *shakl dāʾira*. The young girl who started the dance session shifted styles into *dabke al-ʿarab*. The music also shifted, into Egyptian *maḥraganāt* (a contemporary popular music genre) and a Maghribi groove. People generally danced on their own, enjoyed the sunshine and good weather, and watched others dance. My kid caught the spirit and danced freestyle. We then headed to the beach, as I had promised him.

Though softened by the spirit of inclusivity, volunteerism, and bright sunshine, the political stakes of the event were apparent. In the era of Trumpism, with nativists and nationalists occupying the White House and a "Muslim travel ban" scheduled for a hearing by the Supreme Court, participants from local communities and nonprofit organizations displayed banners with #RefugeesWelcome slogans. Their long-term commitments to mitigate against the effects of forced migration withstood Trumpist efforts to impede migration into the US. The citywide event engendered a civic spirit fostered by the display of vernacular cosmopolitanism among newly arrived and more established Chicago residents. *Dabke* was seemingly an apt performance practice for this atmosphere—the open participatory dynamics of the *shakl dāʾira* made it an inclusive practice that facilitated the easy flow of sociability at the event. But the actual dynamics of this particular *dabke* circle presented a more complicated portrait of the unstable experiences of refugee life. Though he was eager to dance, the young man did not initially find a flow state with the first set of participants trying to start up a *dabke* circle. He was not discouraged and continued to dance on his own. Eventually, with another set of mixed participants, everyone began to flow in the *dabke* circle. These dynamics embody the experiences of refugee life for unaccompanied, young men looking for a moment of lighthearted play to ease the gendered burdens of displacement yet needing to be flexible and adaptable in shifting social, political, and economic conditions until these stabilize and they gain their footing in their new lives. The mixed demographics of the *dabke* circles in front of the Culture Coach also speak to how migrant life has changed the ways that people of different genders, faith, and ethnicity interact with one another. The production of relational masculinity that occurs in displacement shapes and is shaped by the constant reshuffling of demographics and social norms. This book's discussion of the role of play and pleasure in generating hegemonic and counterhegemonic acts of masculinity will hopefully ground future research on how migrants negotiate the complex dynamics of citizenship, gender, religion, and family.

In displacement, *dabke* became an affective metonym for Syrianness. The performance in front of the Culture Coach mediated imaginaries of place, identity, and ethnicity and indexed where refugees hail from, that is, the "elsewhere" that structured the ontological conditions of their presence at World Refugee Day. Yet this *dabke* session was a cultural fragment that cannot bear the weight of its whole, similar to the struggle of the young man and other dancers to find their flow in the *shakl dā'ira*. Though the repertoire of *dabke* have remained more or less the same, dislocation and displacement have fundamentally unsettled the doings of performance and made life less assured and more uncertain. What constitutes "Syria" has become unstable and incoherent for many, a subject dissolved by the movement of millions across borders and into cities, towns, and refugee camps worldwide. What was the fraught balance of state and society in authoritarian Syria has collapsed. Whether and how a balance reemerges remains to be seen as antiregime opposition forces continue to resist Assadist offensives, nation-states begin to normalize their relations with Syria, and migrants pursue livable lives outside of Syria.

The war and forced migration have irreparably cleaved the balance of how Syrians relate to one another and to the world. And yet minoritarian and pluralist rhetoric within Syria has shifted to be more inclusive of non-Arab ethnic minorities, though some remain suspicious that such rhetoric fails to protect minorities from discrimination or marginalization.[1] Since at least 2018, cultural festivals that celebrate Syrian heritage have been regularly presented across Syria in towns such as Bloudan and at the National Opera House in Damascus, even as the regime continues to target antiregime forces in Idlib and Dar'a. These festivals have notably shifted their programming away from the Arab-centered vision of Syrian nationalism that had dominated the state-led production of cultural heritage since the 1960s. The vast majority of heritage festivals are now inclusive of Kurdish, Armenian, Circassian, and Syriac heritage through the presentation of folkloric songs, folkloric dances, and staged dramas distinct to each of these communities, their languages, and their histories. National rhetoric has expanded from the visual metaphor of the "mosaic" to that of the "rainbow," whose many colors and light are purportedly symbolic of the diversity within Syria. The inclusion of non-Arab ethnic minorities is not limited to cultural heritage festivals. Radio stations, newspapers, magazines, and websites that advocate for non-Arab minority expression and representation have burgeoned across Syria during the conflict, especially as political groups (including the regime) find it efficacious to curry favor with minority groups in the midst of conflicting political loyalties. Though the recognition of subnational difference within the Syrian polity has become inclusive, the terms of pluralism arguably continue to reproduce the logic that subnational difference is performed and authenticated within the frameworks determined by those holding or vying for state power (Povinelli 2002).

Even with these critical caveats, it is worth noting that these pluralist expressions and terms of discourse were not viable in the public sphere before the revolution. The reassembling balance of Syrian representation is about freedom of speech and freedom of expression (albeit to a limited extent within authoritarian Syria). It is also about the inclusion of new subjects within Syria's public forums, growth in the numbers of voices contributing to public life, and space for stories to be imagined differently from how they have been. The works of Alzghair, Aldaabal, Hasan, and their collaborators, for instance, reimagine the role of bodywork in enacting acts of solidarity that challenge stereotypes, resist hegemonic forces of power, and create new spaces for empathy and compassion. Participation in the Syrian public sphere is not only about crafting language and penning narratives. Some actively seek ways to balance the effects of collective trauma, and the persistent associations of Syrians with collective trauma in the public sphere, by finding ways to celebrate Syrianness with playful expressions of camaraderie, such as *dabke* circles. These politics of joy and pleasure have spurred dozens of festivals, workshops, club nights, and other events intent on creating spaces to empower Syrians and others who identify with or support those from the SWANA region.

The postconflict balance of how Syrians relate to each other and the world around them must account for the production of (Syrian) difference in Western societies. Though my research in this book has focused on the negotiation of difference in dance worlds, the politics of difference also affect the reception and circulation of *sha'bī* music outside of Syria. Electro-*dabke*, as it is sometimes called, is increasingly being played in nightclubs, not only as part of SWANA cultural nights such as Hishek Bishek in London but also as samples and tracks in electronic dance music. The crossover appeal of *dabkāt* arguably began when wedding singer Omar Souleyman released a record with the San Francisco–based record label Sublime Frequencies and became a darling of European rave festivals and US alternative music festivals (Silverstein 2016b). But it has rapidly been assimilated into nightclub culture since 2015 in ways that are no doubt part of the pattern of fetishizing that which is considered strange. *Sha'bī* music is not welcomed by everyone, though. The perceived loudness of *dabkāt* can be an indicator of the boundaries of assimilation, adaptation, and integration. At a picnic for Syrian refugee families in a Chicago public park, for instance, one Syrian woman asked another Syrian man to turn off the *dabke* track he was playing on his phone because she thought it was inappropriate for the public setting of the park and might disturb passersby.[2] Her desire to mute sonified difference as an adaptive strategy to avoid vulnerability in public spaces dwells in a paradoxical tension with the desire in electronic dance music scenes to amplify the same music as a strategy of recognizing difference in public spaces. This is the same "strange encounters" paradox addressed in chapter 6. In a postconflict world that has expanded the geography of Syrianness, this book offers a framework that foregrounds the role of embodiment in constructing Syrian difference and that situates such difference in the gendered, classed, and racialized logics in which it originates.

Despite the transformations over the past decade, this book offers a foundational set of explanations about social structures and performance processes that aims to help readers situate analyses of future events and phenomena in relation to the rich and complex lifeworlds documented in this work. I have focused on performance dynamics between men in order to position masculinity as that which is playful and pleasurable rather than reinforce stereotypes of Arab and Mediterranean masculinity as bound to violence or honor. I situated everyday performances as part of ritual events that celebrate kinship in order to illuminate how intimate sociabilities are grounded in embodied and gendered interactions. These rituals are important to archive—not only in this book but in general—because of present-day anxieties among some Syrians that such lifeworlds will be lost among a wartime generation growing up outside of Syria: Will young children raised in a pious community in displacement learn how to *dabke*? Will parents tell stories of going to school with those of a different background, or have these stories been erased by the war's sectarianization of society? Underlying these anxieties is a notion of Syria as a repertoire of movements and sounds that find form in ritual and everyday encounters. The disappearance of this repertoire is unsettling.

This book is in many ways an archive of a Syrian public culture animated by popular music and dance practices that circulated from the 1950s to the 2010s in Baʿthist Syria. I have traced the role of folkloric dance in nation-building efforts, noting where and how these pedagogical efforts failed to integrate the country's diverse social groups because they are ensconced in systems of privilege and discrimination. I have examined the effects of the circulation of popular music on social class during economic liberalization, and as a polarizing and fragmenting force during the conflict. My archival materials attest to the power of performance to instill a sense of cultural citizenship, solidify social groups, and aggravate social divisions. Yet this book is an incomplete archive, constrained by the political conditions in which it was assembled. There is an absence of Kurdish and Bedouin voices and histories due to their repression by the regime and surveillance methods that prevented me from accessing certain sites, spaces, and subjects during fieldwork. There is also an absence of Armenian, Circassian, Jewish, and other subnational minorities whose stories remain on the periphery of Syrian Arab nationalism. Similarly, my archive does not enter the contested territories of war or the unsettled spaces of internal displacement that weaken the state from within. In many ways, this book is symptomatic of the forces of political and cultural sovereignty that it attempts to critique.

While this book cannot abate anxieties about the future or curb the social forces that have disrupted Syrian society, I do hope that it has suggested ways to listen to and learn from Syrians as they negotiate rapidly changing worlds. It is vital to listen to Syrians in their own voices (an appeal that I recognize is in tension with the way knowledge is produced in North American universities). The tragic failure of the international community and world powers to support Syrians when they needed humanitarian aid and (arguably) intervention in the conflict, as well as the exploitation of "refugee culture" by media and culture industries, has irreversibly impacted how most Syrians approach knowledge production and cultural production. Issues of equity and representation can and should be addressed by expanding platforms for Syrian self-representation in media, cultural production, higher education, and policy institutes. This is particularly important in higher education, including the long-standing divide in language and arts curriculum in which brown and Black pedagogues tend to teach praxis (e.g., Arabic language courses or Arabic music and dance) while white and white-passing pedagogues teach theory (e.g., Middle East and North Africa [MENA] studies courses) (Johnson 2003). This divide has yet to be fully examined or accounted for in the pedagogical spaces of MENA studies, with the significant exception of Jessica Winegar and Lara Deeb's (2016) analysis of power hierarchies in academic research and public policy on the Middle East. In discussing how I negotiated embodied pedagogical authority as a *hapa*, female pedagogue leading *dabke* workshops, I hope to have started a conversation about the racialized and gendered logics of pedagogy in MENA studies and how to navigate the privileges of teaching and producing knowledge about the region.

Perhaps the lesson of how to navigate societal transformation and the body politics of representation can be learned from *dabke* itself. I suggest that *dabke* is not only an allegory for social (in)stability, but also embodies the wobbling balance of state and society. Balance is not about pursuing assurances of collectivism but about grounding oneself in the chaos of twenty-first-century life. Similar to the young *dabbik* at the Culture Coach, balance may not be achieved on the first attempt but may be fulfilled with sustained efforts. We need to lean on one another while attuning ourselves to the vibrational forces that enfold bodies into a balance, however fleeting. Throughout this book, I have traced how the social and political balance among Syrians wobbles across historical periods, from the inception of postcolonial modernity to authoritarianism, and then into the tumult of the conflict and forced migration. As the conflict simmers and as displaced persons forge their paths, what happens in the next decades remains to be seen. These future fluctuations can be understood through the groundwork established in this book, namely how performance is a multivalent force that may erode social cohesion precisely because of how it binds people together. Syria today is neither only a humanitarian disaster nor a destabilizing force with global impact; it is constituted through and deeply embedded in the spatial, temporal, and affective dynamics of body, performance, and culture.

NOTES

Introduction

1. The translation from Arabic into English is my own. Salabina Studio is a satirical Arab media platform that uses comedy to provide commentary on social issues. Syrian Salabina, "Syrian Dabke from Village of Sawran in the countryside of Hama . . . high 'fitness' (kicks?) and fabulous dance [*sic*]," Facebook, October 20, 2014, www.facebook.com/salabina/videos/729566920463562/.

2. Though this video of performance in Sawran went viral in 2014, the original live event likely occurred in 2008. This approximate date is suggested by the 4:3 screen ratio of the lo-fi video clip and the unit models of the mobile devices that appear within the recording. Thank you to Ameer al-Khodari for these observations regarding the consumption history of mobile technology.

3. Social media user comments convey the same lack of familiarity and fascination.

4. Suhail Shadoud, email message to the author, July 13, 2015. Sawran is an agricultural village with a prewar population of approximately 32,724 (as of the 2004 census) in the province of Hama in central Syria. It was hard hit by the war when it became contested territory between the Syrian army and rebels. The nearby town of Morek, fourteen kilometers to the north, was also won and lost by antiregime opposition when the army regained the town in October 2014, the month when this video was posted.

5. Ahmad Sadiddin, correspondence with the author, October 14, 2015.

6. Geographically, al-Sham is delimited as coastal, interior, and desert but excludes the far eastern regions of Syria that border Iraq, including Jazeera, Raqqa, and Hasakah. A shifting signifier that demarcates various localities, regions, and zones of intercultural contact, Bilad al-Sham is distinct from Syria in that it is a temporal imaginary that predates the formation of the postcolony.

7. SWANA refers to the region of South West Asia and North Africa. I choose to use this term as a tactic of decolonization that replaces other terms (e.g., Middle East) historically used to refer to this region that perpetuate Orientalism and colonialist bias.

8. According to the *Hans Wehr Dictionary of Modern Standard Arabic*, the trilateral root (دبك *dabaka*) is defined as the following: "to stamp the feet; to dance the *dabka* (syr.), [e.g.,] a group dance in which the dancers, lined up with locked arms or holding hands, stamp out the rhythm and sing" (Cowan 1990, 313). *Dabke* has also been translated into English as "stomping" (Racy 1994, 49) and the "stamping of the feet" (Cohen and Katz 2006), and into German as "Stampfrieden" (Dalman 1901).

9. Ibn Dhurayl (1996). Though absent from the classical Arabic lexicon, scholars agree that *dabke* has been part of colloquial Arabic dialects across the region since at least the mid-nineteenth century.

10. Bassel Kassem, interview with the author, Beirut, Lebanon, May 2006. It was unclear to me whether he was referring in particular to Palestine, Lebanon, or generally Bilad al-Sham (Greater Syria), a region that encompasses present-day Syria, Jordan, Palestine, and Lebanon, within which expressive practices such as *dabke* signify that which is pre-modern.

11. For example, see Bayt Al Fann, "Dabke is an Arabic folk dance which originated in the mountains of the Levantine region," Twitter, July 25, 2022, https://twitter.com /BaytAlFann/status/1551497258172125184.

12. See ʿAbbas (2018) for a study of traditional Syrian music. For details on related traditional song genres, see Hassan ʿAbbas, "Folk Music," Syrian Heritage Archive, accessed September 2, 2022, https://syrian-heritage.org/folk-music/.

13. Suhail Shadoud, interview with the author, Mount Holyoke, MA, August 19, 2011.

14. See Cowan (1990) for a comparative analysis of power in similar dance circles in northern Greece.

15. Pathbreaking scholarship by Ghannam (2013) and Inhorn (2012) situates the construction of masculinity as hierarchical, relational, and locatable in specific cultural contexts while works by Amar (2011), El Shakry (2007), and Al-Kassim (2013) raise critical questions about desire, embodiment, and normativity within studies of gender and sexuality in the Middle East. My focus on masculinity aims to contribute to renewed scholarship on masculinity in the Middle East that offers a critical response to, first, patriarchal formations of honor and shame as a discursive binary that perpetuates Orientalism in Arab, Mediterranean, and Middle East studies, and second, a scholarly focus on women's lived experience in feminist revisionist narratives that tended to occlude men.

16. Professor Nidaa Abou Mrad, interview with the author, Antonine University, Beirut, Lebanon, May 2006.

17. Professor Nidaa Abou Mrad, Antonine University, interview with the author, Beirut, Lebanon, May 2006.

18. The last census was taken in 2004. Pre- and wartime demographic figures in Syria remain a point of political contestation, as the census is rarely taken and is perceived

as a mechanism to control the recognition of populations by the state. See United Nations Office for the Coordination of Humanitarian Affairs, "2004 Census Data," https://data.humdata.org/dataset/syrian-arab-republic-other-0-0-0-0-0-0-0/resource/35d4e236-b0d2-41ee-be06-7b04e70e319a.

19. Note these percentages are approximate, as religious identity was last posed as a census question in 1960.

20. Druze communities consider the southwestern mountainous region of Jabal al-Druze (also Jabal al-Arab) to be their historic homeland, and 'Alawite communities historically lived in the coastal mountain regions of northern Syria before migrating farther to the coast of the Latakia region.

21. For excellent ethnographies of rural Syria, see Lange (2012) and Wessels (2019).

22. See Vazquez (2013) for an in-depth critique of genre studies and a demonstration of alternative approaches to musical details.

23. Relatedly, I was introduced as a close friend of the family and a musician from the United States who is Chinese, with the accompanying joke that objectified my identity while playing off stereotypes of global manufacturing: "Her parts are made in China and she is assembled in the United States."

24. See Deeb and Winegar (2016) and Lockman (2016) for critical accounts of area studies, especially MENA studies.

25. For instance, being profiled in an article by Samir Khaled, "From America, to Prepare a Doctoral Thesis on Folk Music!," E-Syria, July 25, 2008, www.esyria.sy/edamascus/index.php?p=stories&category=misc&filename=200807250150012.

INTERLUDE *Modern Syrian Society and State*

1. Al-Haj Saleh suggests the concept of "public caste" to refer to those who benefit or have a structural advantage; for example, 'Alawite are a "public political caste" and Sunnis are a "public religious caste." The notion of public caste articulates the "transformation of a pre-existing social category into a public caste that occupies a key [social or political position] within the state" (2017, 222).

2. The extensive archival holdings of the Institut Français du Proche-Orient did not offer any materials relevant to my research.

3. Some of these collections, such as televisual broadcastings of Omaya Ensemble productions in the 1960s, have begun to appear on YouTube since the media platform was legalized in 2011 and would benefit from future academic research.

ONE *Virtuous Figures*

1. Many of these ensembles emulated the historic Moiseyev Dance Company, established in 1937 by Igor Moiseyev as the State Academic Ensemble of Folk Dances of the Peoples of the USSR.

2. Around the same time, a number of European travelers produced travel narratives that described local cultural practices, including *dabke* (see Lane 1895; von Erlanger 1930). In her travelogue, *Marriage Conditions in a Palestinian Village*, Granqvist (1931) wrote that "dance was certainly the most visible social activity of the evening." According to Ahmed Wasfi Zakaria's 1955 book *Muhafazat Dimashq* (Provinces of Damascus), the French traveler Clement Ider visited the village of al-Nabak in 1878, approaching it from Saadnaya by way of the villages Maalula and Yabud. He observed *dabke* at various wedding ceremonies and dance performances in central Syria and noted that it was a "modest and non-flamboyant dance" (*Tara'if al-Ams, Ghara'ib al-Yawm*, 1936, 247, cf. Ibn Dhurayl 1996, 75).

3. Muhammad Kurd Ali founded the Arab Academy in Damascus in 1919 as part of his efforts to preserve Arabic and develop the language as a vehicle for disseminating literature and the sciences.

4. The emergence of new patronage structures has been linked to shifts in labor and household economies during this period as people migrated to the cities and emigrated from Greater Syria to Europe, West Africa, South America, and the United States (Khater 2001; Hourani 1991; Gualtieri 2009).

5. Al-Qabbani was the first arts director to choreograph *raqs al-samāḥ*, now considered a folk dance of Syria (Ibn Dhurayl 1996). He worked with Shaykh Saleh al-Jazba, M. Saleh Ben Said al-Bushi, al-Ghazi, and Muhammad Kurd Ali, all of whom constituted the earliest generation of Syrian folk dance directors (1858–1922).

6. These projects resumed in the 1970s with several essays published in the journals *Majallat al-Quran* and *Majallat al-'Omran* that examined popular traditions in Dar'a, Jabal al-Arab, Hawran, and Dayr al-Zur, respectively. See Abulhamid Sayasna, "Arts in Dar'a," *Majallat al-Quran*; Salman Baddish, "Folk Dance in Jabal al-Arab," *Majallat al-Quran*, 1970; Mahdi Saleh al-'Abid, "Dayr al-Zur Customs and Traditions," *Majallat al-'Omran*, 1971; and Abulhamid Sayasna, "Intellectual Life in the Province of Dar'a," *Majallat al-'Omran*.

7. Details of the study are published in 'Adnan ibn Dhurayl (1972, 25–26).

8. Khanashat ([1936] 1982).

9. Khanashat specifies that men's *dabke* styles include '*ashāriyya*, '*arjā*', *kurdiyya*, *sharqiyya*, *shamāliyya*, and *gharbiyya*.

10. Urban populations grew by 4 percent from 1950 to 1960 (359,000 to 530,000).

11. Nijat Qassab Hassan was born in Damascus to a middle-class family, the son of a

carpenter. He pursued education and completed his law degree at Damascus University in 1945, after which he practiced family law. He was committed to addressing social problems, which he found an avenue for in a radio program that ran for twenty-five years (1952–77). He also founded a satirical newspaper and journal, directed the Academy of Oriental Music in 1950, and served as director of arts in the Ministry of Culture and National Guidance in 1960. For more on Qassab Hassan, see Salamandra (2004). For an extensive account of Qassab Hassan's legacy in law and radio, see Martin (2015, ch. 2).

12. Born and raised in Aleppo, 'Umar al-Batsh was a musical master who is credited for his efforts to secularize the *muwashshahāt* of Aleppo, of which he composed many. He developed *raqṣ al-samāḥ* and is known for encouraging young women's participation in this dance form despite others' moral concerns. By request of Fakhri al-Barudi, he spent a brief period in Damascus to start a music institute before returning to Aleppo to continue his teaching, directing, and performing.

13. Ibn Dhurayl (1996) documented over fifty *dabkāt* that he transcribed and published in a 1996 anthology of folk dance (discussed extensively in the following chapter).

14. Al-Manini also discusses *raqṣ al-samāḥ* extensively in this method book. Though a full discussion of *raqṣ al-samāḥ* is beyond the scope of my research, it is worth noting that in contrast to *dabke's* rural and secular roots, al-Manini traces *raqṣ al-samāḥ's* origins to Sufi rituals, noting that the movements are distinct from but related to Sufi *mawlawiyya* practices across the eastern Mediterranean. Though others argue that *raqṣ al-samāḥ* emerged in the late nineteenth century as part of stage and theater culture (Ibn Dhurayl 1996) and cannot be attributed to ritual Sufi rituals, the juxtaposition of *dabke* as a secular tradition and *raqṣ al-samāḥ* as a sacred tradition is consistent with his colleagues' writings and with stage practice to today. As a folk dance, *raqṣ al-samāḥ* is characterized by circular movements, a syncopated accent on the front foot, arm extensions, and the asymmetrical placement of the right hand to the ear in a bent position, with the left arm extended low to the side. It is generally performed in a circle and accompanied by repetitive and cyclical rhythmic patterns performed on a *daf* (frame drum) (Ibn Dhurayl 1996).

15. Fakhri al-Barudi, interview in *Al-Jundi*, April 18, 1957. Republished as "From Syrian History: Al-Barudi Organizes a Competition to Unify Arab Dance," *Souriat*, April 16, 2016, https://souriat.com/2016/04/21419.html.

16. The eminent musicologist Majdi al-'Aqili also noted that "Syria has more than five kinds of *dabkāt* [which] differ in each region and province" (1976, 68–81). He indexed the following *dabkāt*: *ḥūrāniyya* (lit: from Ḥūrān), *kurdiyya* (lit: Kurdish), *ḥamawiyya* (lit: from Ḥama), *ḥalabiyya* (lit: from Aleppo), *idlibiyya* (lit: from Idlib), *druziyya* (lit: of the Druze), and *ashūriyya* (lit: from Ashur) (cf. Ibn Dhurayl 1996, 83–84).

17. A significant number of professional dancers and especially artistic directors are Palestinians. Palestinians reside in Syria under temporary "refugee" residency statuses, irrespective of how many generations have been born and raised in Syria since 1948.

Further research into this observed pattern in the dance sector has not yet been feasible but is worth exploration.

18. Joubin notes that the world of dance and drama overlapped, with many celebrities participating in television, theater, and Omaya, including Yasser al-'Azmeh of *Maraya*.

19. Abd al-Bittar, director of the National Artists Syndicate, interview with the author, Damascus, Syria. June 2008. Established in the 1960s under the Ba'th Party, this union continues to support the regime and suppress artists who speak out in opposition.

20. Salma Qassab Hassan, interview with the author, 2008.

21. Hanan Qassab Hassan, correspondence with author, January 3, 2019.

22. Salma Qassab Hassan, interview with the author, Damascus, Syria, October 24, 2008.

23. Ibn Dhurayl notes that Pataraya choreographed a program of *raqṣ al-samāḥ* that was received poorly because of the "flagrant use of ballet" (1996, 37–38).

24. The "virtuous citizen," argues Martin (2015), was promoted by Nijat Qassab Hassan in his radio program, on which he encouraged "virtuous behavior" in the daily life of Syrian citizens as a means to enact social stability and perform the ideals of justice and law.

25. By contrast, Rowe suggests that nationalist folklore discourse in the Palestinian Territories after 1967 reduced female participation and "rendered female dance heritage less active than in previous areas" (2010, 122).

TWO *Staging Difference*

1. In 2011, Idlib would later become the major center for antiregime opposition.

2. The mosaic has a longer history in culturalist representations of the Middle East. It first appeared in academic debates in Carleton Coon's 1951 book *Caravan: The Story of the Middle East*, in which Coon argued that one of the functions of the postcolonial state in the region was to hold together the "diverse social, ethnic, linguistic, occupational, and ecological groups" that comprise the mosaic. For a full critique of the mosaic in Middle Eastern studies, see Shami and Naguib (2013).

3. After a period of instability due to the armed conflict, folk troupes have resumed performing across Syria since at least 2018.

4. Promotional Campaign for DACC 2008, "Preliminary Draft Proposal," Instituto per il Mediterraneo and Lagos Communication Design, https://wikileaks.org/syria-files /docs/2103904_damascus-arab-capital-of-culture-2008.html.

5. This was likely part of shifting state policies that sought to strengthen, albeit modestly, the role of official religious institutions in order to accommodate and create outlets for increasing Sunni religiosity.

6. Comparatively, Stokes provides a nuanced analysis of how the mosaic is appropriated not only as orientalist representation in Turkey, but as local appropriations of orientalist

representation in localized political projects and contests. In a Turkish context, this often serves as a strategy to subvert state agendas that promote a "mono-ethnic nationalism" (2010, 130).

7. Hwaida Saad, "Now There is No One: The Lament of One of the Last Christians in a Syrian City," *New York Times*, January 23, 2022, www.nytimes.com/2022/01/23/world /middleeast/syria-christians-idlib.html.

8. Saad, "Now There is No One." See also "Silencing the Guns in Syria's Idlib," *International Crisis Report*, May 14, 2020, Report No. 213, https://www.crisisgroup.org /middle-east-north-africa/eastern-mediterranean/syria/213-silencing-guns-syrias-idlib.

9. For comparison, see Wedeen's discussion (1999, 20) of the 1987 Mediterranean Games in Latakia, which she critiques as a public spectacle at which participation was mandatory and regimented by the regime. Kastrinou (2016) also notes that audiences at the 2009 Idlib Folk Festival engaged meaningfully with the performances.

10. See, for instance, Shay's discussion (2002, 110) of a Lebanese "village dancer" who "readily discerned" the "conceptual distance" between the "spectacularized" version of *dabke* performed by a professional company and his village's *dabke* practices.

11. The use of prerecorded tracks is likely related to the fact that audiences in Syria, as well as Lebanon, generally do not attribute the same kind of value to live, embodied, acoustic performance as do Western audiences. I attended numerous concerts across the region that featured Arab pop stars across the region who used prerecorded vocals during their performances.

12. See also Dukhan: "Ask a townsman in Syria about the Bedouin and, as likely as not, the answer will be that there are no more Bedouin. In part this is because the Bedouin themselves are no longer particularly distinguishable from the settled people. In fact, many of the Bedouin in Syria today drive taxis and trucks or work as farmers, or soldiers or merchants. The past thirty years have seen a confusion of concepts which originated in the nation-state efforts to settle the Bedouin tribes" (2014, 63).

13. See also Sabry's critique that public discourses of unity maintained by political elite "mask difference and . . . produce a managed 'publicness'" (2010, 55) that render rhetorical categories such as *al-sha'b* "entirely unrealistic, if not meaningless." See also Al-Haj Saleh's analysis of the regime as a "Neo-Sultanic state," which he contends is fundamentally sectarian within inner circles of power. He elaborates that the concept of "public caste" refers to those who benefit or have a structural advantage, e.g., 'Alawite are a "public political caste" and Sunnis are a "public religious caste." The notion of public caste articulates the "transformation of a pre-existing social category into a public caste that occupies a key [social or political position] within the state" (2017, 222).

14. Ibn Dhurayl began his education at the Institute of the Marist Brothers, a French-based Roman Catholic association dedicated to public education. In 1950 he received his degree from the Department of Philosophy at Cairo University, after which he returned

to Syria. His work on Syrian music history, *al-Musiqa fi Suriya* (Music in Syria, 1969) is considered by many to be the definitive history of Syrian Arab music (Marcus 1989; Shannon 2006).

15. See Ibn Dhurayl (1996, ch. 3, n19) for a list of the extant studies assembled for his project.

16. The full breakdown of governates included in this catalog is as follows: unspecified (four), Aleppo (ten), Dar'a (two), Latakia (five), Tartous (eleven), Dayr al-Zur (three), Hama (four), Homs (three), Raqqa (five), Rif Dimashq (six), and Suwayda (five).

17. The Kurdish folk troupe from Ifrin, a village near Aleppo, received an award at the 2009 Idlib Folk Festival (Kastrinou 2016, 132).

18. According to Al-Saleh (2016), al-Attar led the Ministry of Culture from 1976 to 2000 and is widely praised for her charismatic and strong patronage of arts institutions and cultural expression.

19. See Shannon (2003) for an analysis of the neutralization of Sufism in cultural production and representation.

20. Ghazi al-Ammari (1952–2020, director of Omaya), interview with the author, Yarmouk, Syria, February 2008; and Muhammad Issa (director of Dance Arabia), interview with the author, Jisr al-Khamis, Syria, August 2008.

21. There are two state-run television channels administrated by the Ministry of Radio and Television. The "first" channel is dedicated to news, and the "second" channel, Syria Tanni, broadcasts a broad range of programs, including but not limited to miniseries, talk shows, cultural affairs, and educational programs. To the best of my knowledge, actors and production crews are employed through the Artists Syndicate.

22. Salma Qassab Hassan, interview with the author, Damascus, Syria, September 2008.

23. It was looted and damaged during the conflict (see Lawler 2014).

24. James Bennet, "The Enigma of Damascus," *New York Times*, July 10, 2005, www .nytimes.com/2005/07/10/magazine/the-enigma-of-damascus.html.

25. Several Syrian choreographers presented work at the Dancing on the Edge Festival (est. 2006, The Netherlands).

26. Medhat Aldaabal, interview with the author, Berlin, Germany, November 2017.

27. Hajo founded the first modern dance ensemble, Ramad Dance Troupe, in 2001. He was acclaimed by domestic and foreign audiences for his provocative and compelling critiques of Syrian society rendered through stunning and agile choreography. Hajo worked with an emerging generation of dancers who studied with a young modern dance teacher based at the Conservatoire in Damascus, Metaz Malatialy. In November 2009, however, Hajo was assassinated in his apartment in the Qudsiya neighborhood, and his apartment burned to the ground, just hours before the world premiere of "Effusion," a dance production that engaged with the complex relations between Islam and the body.

28. After training at the Czech Ballet Conservatory in the 1980s, Metaz Malatialy re-

turned to Syria to establish a dance department and launch a program in modern dance at the Higher Institute, which he directed for years.

29. The state aimed "to create an enduring festival for Damascus, like the annual Baalbeck Festival in Lebanon. Another aim was to highlight the different cultures, over a one-year period, that passed through Damascus. A third aim was to shed light on the historical and cultural evolution of the Syrian capital." See "Qassab Hassan: Celebrating Damascus as Capital of Arab Culture was the Brainchild of the Syrian First Lady," *Forward Magazine*, March 2008, www.fw-magazine.com/content/qassab-hassan-celebrating-damascus-capital-arab-culture-was-branchild-syrian-first-lady.

30. Hannan Qassab Hassan, interview with the author, Damascus, Syria, August 8, 2008.

31. The internationally recognized dance theater company Enana declined their request to develop choreography that aimed for an ethnographic representation of Syrian heritage, notwithstanding Enana director Jihad Mufleh's role as the main producer for DACC's spectacular opening gala.

32. Folk dance troupes such as Omaya and Firqa al-Hamami occasionally accompanied orchestras playing classical Andalusian and Sufi-based music as part of the DACC festival. For instance, Firqa al-Hamami performed *raqs al-samāḥ* to accompany an orchestra directed by ʿAdnan Abu al-Shammat, playing an extensive program of *muwashshaḥāt* in the summer of 2008 in Damascus. The association of folk dance with this musical repertoire arguably constructed a sense of urban cosmopolitanism through dance rather than the rural heritage symbolized by *dabke* traditions.

THREE *Floating Rhythms*

1. Tonality in Arab music is organized as a pitch-based system of musical modes that orient pitches according to the tonal space between pitches (Farraj and Abu Shumays 2019). Each *maqām* is identifiable through its particular yet open-ended patterns of pitch and development that generate its characteristic tonality. The setting of this *taqsīm* in the *maqām* known as *Rāst* is somewhat atypical, although not uncommon, as many traditional and popular songs in the Latakia region are set in a *maqām* known as *Bayātī*.

2. For a broader discussion of flow in ethnomusicology literature, see Berger, VanderHamm, and Riedel (2021), who notes that ethnomusicological discourse on flow has tended to depict the effects of flow on the construction of selfhood as a "loss of self" that often occurs "out-of-time." He critiques this direction, arguing instead that such analyses implicitly emphasize an interiority of self that romanticizes both the concept of flow and that of selfhood. Through ethnography, he posits, scholars might instead elaborate on how flow states emerge through and during social interaction in order to explore the intersubjective dynamics of selfhood. He also advocates for examining flow states that

occur in highly stimulating sensory environments in order to disquiet the assumption that flow states are dependent on the "quieting" of the mind for an introspective experience.

3. Music scholars, especially those committed to Black studies, have recently turned to the critical discourse of "choreography" in dance studies to theorize listening as an embodied set of cultural practices that negotiate social forms of life and the discourses that politicize racialized bodies. See in particular Crawley's (2017) concept of the "choreo-sonic" and Moten's *In the Break* (2003).

4. See Spiller (2010) for a similar study that emphasizes the tactility of dance and situates Sundanese dance and dance drumming as an embodied tradition that integrates aural and gestural actions into a singular domain of activity.

5. For a critique of Glennie's work, see Holmes (2017).

6. For example, Deeb and Harb (2013) offer an ethnographic analysis of how young modern and pious Shiʻi Lebanese navigate the moral politics of *dabke* at Shiʻi weddings in Lebanon, where women's participation in dance is increasingly disapproved.

7. Recent studies that also position the construction of Arab masculinities as (non) hegemonic and in relation to femininity and queerness include Jacob (2011), Naguib (2015), Inhorn (2012), Joubin (2013), Peteet (1994), and Ghoussoub and Sinclair-Webb (2000).

8. Omar Rajeh, communication with the author, Hamburg, Germany, June 11, 2017.

9. Folkloric *dabke* troupes have adopted some terminology that circulates in profes-sional and pedagogical spaces, and cultural entrepreneurs have recently begun to record and distribute tutorials online. See "ZoomTube33: Arab culture and Entertainment," accessed January 1, 2019, https://dabkemasters.com.

10. Stanley Dance, liner notes, *The Far East Suite*, "Party for Duke Ellington and Orchestra at Home of Mr. and Mrs. John Tobler," box 2, folder 3, series 2 (Performances and Programs, subseries 2A, International Tours), DEC, cited in Jackson (2013. 523).

11. Ellington is aware of the ethics of cultural appropriation and, when discussing his creative process, intentionally distances himself from "imitation" of what he has encoun-tered. Rather, he insists, he lets the full experience sit for awhile before "recalling" it in his own words (Jackson 2013, 518).

12. The modernist Syrian painter Adham Ismail (1922–1963) also rendered the "imag-ined rhythms" (Lenssen 2020, 134) of *dabke* into another modality of artistic expression. Ismail's *Dabke* (1950) is an oil painting that renders rhythmic movement through "looping linear traces . . . that appear to dance" (Lenssen 2020, 134).

13. Ibn Dhurayl (1996, 129).

14. Ibn Dhurayl (1996, 129).

15. In colloquial Syrian Arabic, ʻāl is a prepositional phrase that combines ʻala and al to translate as "in the way of."

16. It is also worth noting that there are significant distinctions in the social spaces in which *raqṣ sharqiyya* and *dabke* are typically performed in the SWANA region due to

the politics of gender, sexuality, class, and taste. *Raqṣ sharqiyya* is generally considered nightlife entertainment in which a single female performer dances for a crowd, whereas *dabke* is a social dance practiced in community spaces with no significant boundaries between participants and spectators.

17. A mid-twentieth-century study (published decades later) of Palestinian *dabke* suggested that *dabke* provides a "sense of certainty and directionality" that correlates with the upbeat rhythms of the practice (cited in Cohen and Katz 2006, 110).

18. Ibn Dhurayl (1996, 97).

19. Ibn Dhurayl summarizes these distinctions as follows: "*Shams dabke* from Jabal al-Arab occurs in quick two-pulse pairs; *Banet dabke* and *Tarbīʿ* from Idlib and Aleppo are performed in triple-pulse groupings; *Braziya dabke* in Hama and the traditional *Tartous dabke* are danced in five-pulse groupings; and, *Shawiya dabke* from Latakia and *Lawha dabke* from the outskirts of Latakia occur in seven-pulse groupings" (1996, 80–81).

20. The representation of meter and rhythm is a long-standing debate in ethnomusicology, particularly regarding Mediterranean musics. Singer (1974) and Stokes (1992) argue for how beats are negotiated and perceived in performance rather than striving to standardize metric perception as notated meters that empiricize an affective modality of performance. For studies of related folk dances and folk dance rhythms, see also And (1976) and Peter Pnuel BetBasoo "Thirty Assyrian Folk Dances," Assyrian International News Agency, 2003, www.aina.org/articles/tafd.pdf.

21. For more on entrainment, see Clayton, Sager, and Will (2004, 20).

22. *Dabke al-shamāliyya* consists of a cyclical pattern of six steps (*khaṭwāt*), with a "kick" on the fifth beat, that dancers repeat as they move counterclockwise in the *shakl dāʿira*. The first two steps of *dabke al-shamāliyya* are a grapevine-like figure in which dancers cross their left foot over the right then step out sideways with the right. This figure is repeated twice and followed by a *dabke* on the fifth beat in which the left foot taps the ground in front of the dancer. The sixth step is a retraction of the left foot leading to a foot tap in place before the cycle repeats.

23. He alternates a six-pulse metrical pattern (inspired by the dance) with a ten-bar melody of motifs and a four-bar tag derived from bars 7–10 of the melody (Jackson 2013).

24. "Close listening" is the sonic analog to the "close reading" method of literary theory that pays careful attention to structure and meaning in text.

25. See Monson (2008) for a discussion of "perceptual agency."

26. So You Think You Can Dabkeh Festival, Alwan for the Arts, New York, NY, June 2011.

27. I intentionally refrain from framing this rhythmic relationship as a hemiola. The hemiola is a concept of Western music theory that has been applied to African musical practices in order to analyze polyrhythms in relation to time. Koetting (1970) differentiates between "vertical" and "horizontal" hemiola, wherein the former refers to rhythmic

distinctions between parts and the latter refers to rhythmic distinctions over time, while noting ambiguities and centering West African perspectives on rhythm. While the additive nature of Middle Eastern dance rhythms (e.g., joining a series of rhythmic units over time) suggests a horizontal orientation to rhythm, the layering of the percussive rhythm with the danced rhythm suggests a vertical hemiola. Whether analyzed as a horizontal or vertical hemiola, or a playful blend of both, I am more keen to, following Stone (1986) and Monson (2008), recognize the perceptual tension between the duple and triple meter rhythms as that which entrains participatory performance rather than employ a Western concept.

28. Tamim and Silverstein (2021).

29. As a somatic phenomenon, *mīzān* challenges Eurocentric approaches to dance that privilege the visual spectacle of dance. In drawing attention to nonvisual modes of perception, I join scholars of movement and sound who seek to decenter the visual episteme that arguably continues to dominate music studies and dance studies (Power-Sotomayor 2020; Crawley 2017; Wells 2021) as well as scholars of embodiment and affect who seek to deprivilege the body as a given object of analysis and instead consider how the body materializes through corporeal interactions and boundaries (Ahmed and Stacey 2001).

30. *Mīzān* also translates as meter in Arab music practices.

31. For discussions of improvisation in social dance, see Shay (2019) and DeFrantz (2016).

32. Ibn Dhurayl (1996) uses the term *dābbak* interchangeably with *raqṣīn*, or dancers (despite his claim that there are ontological and semantic distinctions between *raqṣ* and *dabke*).

33. Wassim Muqdad, interview with the author, Berlin, Germany, June 19, 2017.

34. Cowan (1990) analyzes similar ritual performance spaces in her study of gender and the body politic in modern Greek society.

35. Ramzi El Idlibi, communication with the author, June 26, 2015.

36. One woman from Hama, based in Aleppo at the time of our introduction, was an excellent *dabbika* and started a Syrian folklore *dabke* troupe during her time studying in Cairo.

37. Ludic performance among boys has been widely regarded as a means by which they transition into adulthood, particularly in Mediterranean societies (Gilmore 1990).

38. Ahmad, interview with the author, Aleppo, Syria, July 2008.

39. Similar dance circle formations are commonly practiced across the region. See Cowan (1990) for Greek "dance-events" at weddings and Bayraktar (2019) for a detailed discussion of the participatory and political dynamics in the context of Kurdish spaces in Turkey.

40. For a thorough account of presentational and participatory modes of practice, see Turino (2008).

41. Inas Ḥouli, "Cry of a Rebel in an Oppressed Society" [*Sarkha Mutamarada fi Mujtamʿiyya Qamʿiyya*]. *Esyria*, July 31, 2010 (translation by author), URL no longer available.

42. Wassim Mukdad, interview with the author, June 19, 2017.

43. Questions about gender roles are often posed to me during presentations of my research. The question is usually asked from a womanist perspective: "Do women *dabke*?" "Do women take the lead, or improvise?" "Elsewhere [e.g., Lebanon, Palestine], I have seen women perform and participate. Is Syrian society different?" These questions tend to stem from feminist concerns that women are excluded from the *dabke* circle in ways that scholarship on *dabke* might redress. While I am sympathetic to these concerns, my present analysis of gender in *dabke* practice is not a project that aims to unveil women's participation nor explicitly attribute any unevenness or absence of participation as a consequence of patriarchy, Islam, colonialism, or other hegemonic social forces. Instead, I am primarily interested in understanding the social and embodied processes through which gender, especially masculinity, is constructed.

44. Thanks to Jiryis Ballan for pointing this out.

45. Solo male dancing in the SWANA region is a complex and understudied topic. For a postcolonial critique of *khawal* (young male dancers) in the libidinal economy of mid-nineteenth-century Egypt, framed by the broader discourse of gender, sexuality, and the Orientalist gaze, see Karayanni (2009).

46. I am unsure about how wedding guests perceived this young man's shimmies. I was unable to ask other guests their perspective because this was my first visit to the village and, given how homoerotics and homosexuality is generally a taboo topic, I did not have a deep enough rapport with wedding guests to start a conversation on this topic.

47. See Amar and El Shakry (2013); and Al-Kassim (2013). Queer theory presents a peculiar dilemma for ethnographers of non-Western societies. While writing about queer practices, desires, and categories makes more legible and comprehensible certain economies of desire, it is a process of translation that renders the local and particular visible through what Dipak Chakrabarty calls a "universal middle term." For a broader discussion of queer theory in non-Western contexts, see Gopinath (2005).

48. Chambers-Letson (2013) uses this phrase in conversation with Erving Goffman to facilitate the consideration of "a wide range of presentational and communicative behaviors as performance."

FOUR *Sonic Spectacularity*

1. Regarding his monikers, Saqer is attributed with the "King of ʿAtaba" pseudonym in several online videos. "Abu ʿAtef" ("father of ʿAtef") is a common nickname for fathers that accords prestige and honor on the basis of patriarchal family values that privilege

the first-born son of a given family, in this case, Saqer's son, 'Atef. According to Both-well (2013), the use of epithets (*kunya*) to refer to a given singer places the performer genealogically, among and within generations of musical artists. For instance, fans of George Wassouf often refer to him as Abu Wadi', because Wassouf named his son in recognition of Wadi' al-Safi, the legendary Lebanese singer a generation older than Wassouf (Bothwell 2013, 175).

2. Latakia is predominantly 'Alawite (an ethnoreligious Muslim minority who hold a disproportionate degree of regime power as the communal and regional base of the Assad family; see Seale 1988).

3. For a YouTube channel dedicated to Saqer's recordings, see www.youtube.com/channel/UC2lPQm1KSWJN9VwdFtQt7ng/featured. *'Ataba* is a nonmetric strophic love song repertoire that is organized into a codified rhyming structure.

4. For example, see "Ayman Zidane Challenges Ibrahim Saqer through Reproach, So Who Won? Watch the Video," King Recordings, December 7, 2016, YouTube video, www.youtube.com/watch?v=ztEEH1emLqk, featuring a *muḥāwara* with Ayman Zeidan in December 2016. For more on traditional song genres, see Abbas (2018).

5. *E'tazalt El Gharam* (Rotana, 2006). "Nashid El Zafaf" is an arrangement of Mendels-sohn's "Wedding March," with lyrics by Noha Najm.

6. Abu Hussayn, interview with the author, Beirut, Lebanon, June 29, 2006.

7. Both the bride's and groom's families identified as 'Alawite, a religious minority who are the dominant social group in Jable and the greater Latakia region. In contrast to Sunni mores, most 'Alawite social events permit alcohol, and 'Alawite women generally do not wear a religious headcovering.

8. Walser (1993) notes that the affective role of distortion in heavy metal listening experiences is linked to an excessive use of force that triggers a desire for "extreme power and intense expression." Note that there are several thriving heavy metal scenes across the SWANA region (Levine 2008).

9. See Shannon (2006), Racy (2003), and Farraj and Abu Shumays (2019). For recent extensions of this work into Arab rap and Arab-American cultural expression, see El Zein (2016) and Figueroa (2022).

10. As Racy relates, Sabah Fakhri stated in a 1990 interview that "it is the audience that plays the most significant role in bringing the performance to a higher plateau of creativity (*ibda*). . . . I like the light in the performance hall to remain on, so that I can see the listeners and interact with them. If they respond, I become inspired to give more. As such, we become reflections of one another. I consider the audience to be me and myself to be the audience" (quoted in Racy 2003, 130). Wadi' al-Safi also analogized *ṭarab* with a visual metaphor, suggesting in an interview in 1984 that "the audience and the performer are like two mirrors facing each other. The image, which stands for inspiration, appearing

in one mirror is reflected by the other mirror, and in turn the reflection is reflected again back and forth" (quoted in Racy 2003, 130–31).

11. Abu Husayn, interview with the author, Beirut, Lebanon, June 29, 2006.

12. It is worth noting that while some intellectual elites maintain strict boundaries between art and popular music, these boundaries are somewhat disingenuous in the context of a performance culture in which who performs *ṭarab* music and who performs *shaʿbī* music is often not a clearly articulated boundary at venues or across careers. Wadiʿ al-Safi, for instance, started out as a local *shāʿar* (poet-singer) before becoming one of the most eminent vocal artists and prolific recording artists of the twentieth century.

13. Kamal Feneish, interview with the author, Beirut, Lebanon, June 29, 2006.

14. I recognize that the value of embodiment in relation to liveness and presence is heavily contested within the field of performance studies (Auslander 1999; Phelan 1993; Fischer-Lichte 2008; Muñoz 1999; Nyongʼo 2022).

15. Bassel Kassem, interview with the author, Beirut, Lebanon, May 2006.

16. Usually played an octave higher than the vocal register of the *muṭrib,* the timbre of the *mijwiz* is produced by the stepped nature of air holes that create harmonic distortion and upper partials. It is also considered distinctive for upper and lower pedal tones, which, respectively, offer either a sporadic ornamental effect (upper) or "percussive ʻinterrup-tions' that punctuate the melody" (lower) (Racy 1994, 50).

17. *Nawari* has emerged as the dominant dance rhythm of *dabke* pop, included in songs by artists such as Fares Karam and Melhem Zein, such that it (along with *mijwiz*) is the primary indexical marker that classifies a song as *dabke.*

18. Musician and historian Samer Ali conjectures that these claims for genesis can likely be attributed to the fact that within this corridor (notably more in the countryside and less in the cities), *daʿūna* and adjacent song genres are mainly sung in a specific musical mode (*Bayātī*) and in a dialect that maintains some non-Arabic, pre-Islamic linguistic words, including *daʿūna* and *dabke.* Samer Ali, correspondence with the author, August 4, 2022.

19. Some intellectuals, including Ajjan, maintain that folk songs have historically transmitted musical modes from generation to generation; according to this theory, musical modes used in ancient Ugarit (third millennium BCE) can be distilled from contemporary Latakian folk song repertoire.

20. Latakia is a major port city in northern Syria that was originally established in ancient Phoenicia. It has grown exponentially during the twentieth century, from a popu-lation of 7,000 at the turn of the twentieth century to 650,000 as of the early twenty-first century due to significant investments in port development in 1950s and the growth of trade in the decade that followed (Commins and Lesch 2014, 215).

21. For a broader history of the synthesizer, see Pinch and Trocco (2004); for a history of the org in Arab America, see Rasmussen (1996).

22. This name is a pseudonym.

23. Khaled (pseudonym), interview with the author, Damascus, Syria, October 2008.

24. Walid Baghdadi, interview with the author, Beirut, Lebanon, June 13, 2006.

25. For instance, South African producers working in the *mbaqanga* music industry immediately after apartheid ended surrounded the *calabash* with seventeen microphones in an effort to simulate the acoustics of live performance and produce a "traditional" sound (Meintjes 2003).

26. For an essay on the (in)audibility of ululations in ethnomusicology, see Meintjes (2019).

27. Turkish music producers hire folk dancers to perform in the recording studio, specifically to capture the diegetic sounds of footstomps, which signify, in the final edited and mastered track, the live in situ event with which the music is associated (Bates 2016).

28. Some contend that the perceived authenticity of *dabke* is compromised by its rhythmic hybridity (*mizāj*, literally: mixed). Jamal al-Saqa, a renowned percussionist with the al-Kindi Orchestra and author of the first published study of Syrian rhythm, explained to me that *dabke* rhythms are "not understood . . . they are *mizāj* (mixed) according to the composer or song . . . This is the nature of popular music (*mūsīqā shaʿbiyya*)." Jamal al-Saqa, interview with the author, Higher Institute of Music, Damascus, Syria, August 3 2008. See also Al-Saqa (2005).

29. I refrain from using "groove" here, following Bates's critique of "groove" as a universal rhythmic phenomenon (2016, 280), in particular pointing out that the discussion of "groove" in Keil and Feld's seminal article (1994) mainly addresses timing and not much else.

30. This range of tempo reflects metronome readings taken from my video footage of live performance events in 2007–8. In historic and geographic contrast, Cohen and Katz (2006) suggest a tempo reading of 80–112 m.m. in their study, conducted in the 1960s, of Palestinian popular music. Some listeners have suggested to me that dance tempos have increased over the years.

31. Hiring practices for percussionists vary substantially depending on the location, financial resources, and preferences of a given event. When percussionists join, they typically play on *darbukka* (goblet drum), *ṭabl* (double-barreled drum), and *riq* (tambourine), depending on the occasion. For instance, weddings in Suwayda and Qunaytra typically did not feature a percussionist; rather, hosts hired an org player, and on occasion, a *muṭrib* and/or *mizmār* player. Meanwhile the same *ṭabl* drummer played at several weddings I attended in the northern districts of Latakia (including Saqer's event) and the central Syrian valley district of Dayr al-Atiya.

32. Porcello (2005) has demonstrated that Nashville-based producers of country music aim for a loss of liveness in their recordings in contrast to producers in Austin for whom liveness is a "hallmark" of the local.

33. I also have observed that at most weddings the bride and groom tend to recline for much of the evening. They sit on an elaborate rose-decorated white throne that frames their nuptial bodies as royalty, with the decor and fabric quality and scale depending on the resources of the hosts.

34. Fieldnotes, October 9, 2008.

35. This could be characterized as a Western-style arrangement of verse and chorus with a *dabke* rhythm (*nawari*, specifically) and *shaʿbī* instruments (*mijwiz*, mainly), along with other Arab dance rhythms and pop instruments.

36. Similarly, radio programs primarily broadcast *shabābī* pop music, though Bothwell (2013) notes that there was a gap between the radio industry and its consumers wherein call-in requests for music tended towards *shaʿbī* music rather than *shabābī*, which station managers favored for commercial purposes. Prewar radio stations targeted young, urban, middle- to upper-class listeners, most of whom were women.

37. When satellite distribution of *shabābī* pop music first began in the early 2000s, it was synced with telecommunications. Viewers could send text messages for display on screen while a music video streamed. Text messages (and ringtones) generated revenue for the telecommunications, television, and, less so, music industries, which benefited more from exposure through airtime (Sakr 2007). In Syria, the biggest beneficiary of *shabābī* music broadcasting was SyriaTel, the dominant telecommunications provider in Syria and target of anticorruption protests in 2011.

38. Khaled (pseudonym), interview with the author, Damascus, Syria, October 2008. "Bous al-Wawa" is a popular hit by Lebanese singer Haifa Wehbe.

39. Directed by Laith Hajo, *Spotlight* began in 2001 and aired its last season in the midst of armed conflict. Throughout its lifespan, the show received acclaim and recognition because it brought fresh perspectives on contemporary life in Syrian society in a moment of rapid transformation, challenging social norms as new ones emerged and critiquing the banality of state bureaucracy. For instance, it regularly scripted the Latakian dialect, a controversial move that played into the exclusionary politics of elite Damascene society.

40. Translated by Bothwell (2013, 129). Thanks to Bothwell for bringing this episode of *Spotlight* to my attention.

41. Their undermining of this moment may be related to broader shifts in listening publics. Men generally have had greater access to public spaces where listening is a collective public activity, such as at cafes, which have historically been a site for the formation of listening publics; in contradistinction, listening in private domains, such as at home or in cars, was more accessible for women, whose mobility in public spaces was (and remains) constrained (Bothwell 2013). These gendered distinctions between public and private spaces have shifted with the growth of neoliberal cafe culture insofar as these cafes, in comparison to more traditional cafes, are frequented by young women, who then listen to pop music in public spaces as part of their privatized cafe experience (Deeb and Harb 2013).

42. It is notable that no music is heard in the restaurant scene. Diegetic sounds of water flowing from the fountain can be heard in the background. The muting of *sha'bi* music in this restaurant space is possibly an intentional choice that positions this restaurant within a gentrified area of greater Damascus.

43. An important exception to this disciplinary gap is Wells (2021), which moves gracefully between the concept of "choreography" in dance studies and "listening" in musicology.

INTERLUDE *Conflict, War, and Displacement*

1. "Syria," FIDH (International Federation for Human Rights), 2012, www.fidh.org /IMG/pdf/femmesarabangbassdef.pdf.

FIVE *Conflicting Movements*

1. The flag was originally adopted when Syria gained its independence on April 17, 1946. Green symbolizes the Rashidun Caliphate, white represents the Umayyad Caliphate, and black symbolizes the Abbasid Caliphate. Originally, the three red stars represented the three districts of Syria: Aleppo, Damascus, and Day al-Zur. Free Syrian Army demonstrators commonly make use of this pre-Ba'thist or "Independence" flag through green, black, and white costumes and protest banners. For a detailed analysis of flags in the revolution, see "An Image, Two Flags, and a Banner" in Al-Haj Saleh (2017).

2. Kafr Rouma, a town in the Idlib Governate, has been contested between the FSA, Syrian regime, Jabhat al-Nusra and other Islamist militias, and ISIS throughout the conflict.

3. For Lepecki, the "choreopolitical" is a mode of "intersubjective action" that activates "the possibility . . . that some day we may know how to move politically [even if] . . . whatever moving accomplishes is provisional and incomplete" (2013, 20 and 26).

4. Similar exaltations of social dance (and popular music) as a liberatory practice have occurred within past and present political movements worldwide, from racial justice movements in the United States (Goldman 2010) to Argentina (Fortuna 2019) and Sri Lanka (Satkunaratnam 2020).

5. See also Kraidy (2016) for a full account of the role of the body in the creative insurgency of the Arab revolutions.

6. This approach is distinct from the "refusal" to be political first articulated by Muñoz (1999) insofar as I maintain a focus on embodied acts within and as fields of political action.

7. Also Anoush Kedhar, "'Hands Up! Don't Shoot!': Gesture, Choreography, and Protest in Ferguson," *Feminist Wire*, October 6, 2014, https://thefeministwire.com/2014/10 /protest-in-ferguson/.

8. Though I focus on male participation, female participation in political *dabke* circles occured, albeit not as commonly. Salti (2012) makes note of "video recordings of protests in cities known to be very socially conservative, such as Aleppo, [where] women visibly accompany their male counterparts" (170).

9. See Suleiman (2012). See also Silverstein (2012) for creative actions during the nonviolent phase of antiregime protests.

10. Mariam Abdullah (pseudonym), "A War of Songs Between Opposition and Regime Supports in Syria," Syria Stories, February 28, 2014, https://syriastories.net/en/a-war-of-songs-between-opposition-and-regime-supporters-insyria/.

11. Creative Memory added a rhythmic track to the *'arada* and named the remix "Syrian Revolutionary *Dabke*." In so doing, the remix track became a hybrid of two genres, not quite *'arada* (call-and-response without an associated dance genre) nor *dabke* (not typically performed to *'arada*). This is but one instance among many in which antiregime activists creatively reconfigured and reimagined traditions to performatively enact political claims.

12. Sarah Birke, "Twilight in Damascus," *New York Review of Books*, July 12, 2011, www.nybooks.com/daily/2011/12/07/twilight-damascus/. Birke writes that she heard kids chanting outside her window in Old Damascus, as they swung to and fro on a rusty metal swing.

13. Mohammad Abu Hajar, "Ana Wiyak: The War of Anthems," *Syria Untold*, December 19, 2018, https://syriauntold.com/2018/12/19/ana-wiyak-the-war-of-anthems/. See also "The People's 'Raised Hands,'" in Della Ratta (2018).

14. Wael Tamimi, "A History of Syria's Uprising through Protest Chants," Public Radio International, *The World*, March 20, 2013, https://theworld.org/stories/2013-03-20/history-syrias-uprising-through-protest-chants.

15. Tamimi, "A History of Syria's Uprising."

16. Mariam Abdullah, "A War of Songs between Opposition and Regime Supporters in Syria," *Syria Stories*, Institute for War and Peace Reporting, February 28, 2014, https://syriastories.net/en/a-war-of-songs-between-opposition-and-regime-supporters-in-syria/,

17. Abu Hajar, "Ana Wiyak."

18. Contemporary Syrian discourse on anti-imperialism refers antagonistically to the US-led invasion of Iraq in 2003 and generally claims resistance to the consolidation of political and economic power by Western nation-states. As Yassin al-Haj Saleh points out, however, the regime's anti-imperial stance remains hypocritical. He clarifies that "the Assadist state is not against imperialism in any way whatsoever . . . ironically the power elites protecting this neo-imperialism may well draw on classical anti-imperialist rhetoric in order to discredit local dissidence and suppress potential political schisms." See Yassin al-Haj Saleh, "The Syria Cause and Anti-Imperialism," translated by Yasser El Zayyar, May 5, 2017, www.yassinhs.com/2017/05/05/the-syrian-cause-and-anti-imperialism/.

19. Diana Al-Jassem, "Syrian Artists on 'Honor List' for Supporting Syrian Regime," *Arab News*, July 4, 2011, www.arabnews.com/node/382784.

20. The song arrangement aligns with the three-minute duration of most global pop charts, rather than the attenuated, extended additive form of traditional *dabkāt*, as discussed in the previous chapter.

21. Abdullah, "War of Songs between Opposition and Regime Supporters in Syria."

22. See Wedeen (2013) for a critique of claims that economic determinism was the dominant cause of the revolution.

23. See Bayraktar (2019) for a study of dispersal tactics through movement analysis in Kurdish political protests in Turkey.

24. See also Nihad Sirees's novel *The Silence and the Roar* (2013) for a literary critique of mass public demonstrations that preserve authoritarian power.

25. For more on Kzaour's style, see Elizabeth Arrott, "Syrian Singer Rallies Assad Forces," Voice of America News, January 27, 2012, www.voanews.com/a/syrian-singer -rallies-assad-forces-138256099/151264.html/.

26. See Silverstein (2020) for more on stochastic chants and the grain of the crowd.

27. "FSA Anti Bashar Dance Party Hard," June 14, 2013, YouTube video, 6:58, www. youtube.com/watch?v=NHPRN8dEIeU.

28. The unemployment crisis preceded the war and was a symptom of the neoliberal economic policy changes that began in the 2000s. The war economy further exacerbated these conditions.

29. Human Rights Watch, "They Treated Us in Monstrous Ways: Sexual Violence Against Men, Boys, and Transgender Women in the Syrian Conflict," Human Rights Watch, July 29, 2020, www.hrw.org/report/2020/07/29/they-treated-us-monstrous-ways /sexual-violence against-men-boys-and-transgender. Last accessed August 18, 2022.

30. Though normative, some individuals find ways to not participate in their military service, including paying fees to the government and studying abroad, among other evasive techniques.

31. Rahaf Aldoughli, "Belonging to a Militarized Syria as a Woman," Syria Untold, January 5, 2018, syriauntold.com/2018/01/05/belonging-to-a-militarized-syria-as-a-woman /; , cf. Monroe (2020, 278).

32. "Assad Soldiers Dance as Rebels Outlaw Music — Freedom VS Jihadi Islamist Slavery," May 23, 2015, YouTube video, 0:56, www.youtube.com/watch?v=3KSz87lchdk. The title perpetuates the regime-held narrative that Islamists are terrorists who threaten the secular society protected by the Assadist state.

33. See Hafiz (2012) for shifts in the subject-position of the *ibn al-balad* in twenty-first-century Egypt.

34. Aldoughli, "Belonging to a Militarized Syria as a Woman."

35. "Syria Soldiers Dance Dabke as FSA Opposition Outlaws Music & Dance," May 23, 2015, YouTube video, 3:48, www.youtube.com/watch?v=BbYfjQnw_MU.

36. See Silverstein (2021) for a full discussion of its inclusion in the documentary film.

37. See Silverstein (2021) for a discussion of the use of *dabke* as an allegory for masculinized regime power in Syrian cultural production.

38. The juxtaposition of *dabke* footwork's sonic rhythms with carceral abuse also appears in Mustafa Khalifa's novel *Al-Qawqaʿa* (*The Shell*, 2006).

39. "Syrian Army Soldiers Dancing before the Start of the Battle of Eastern Ghouta," February 25, 2018, YouTube video, 3:02, www.youtube.com/watch?v=N8JxyRs1NEg.

40. The full caption continues "the morale is very high before the start of the Battle of the liberation of the Ghouta . . . the fiercest battle in Syria Your prayers." See "Syrian Army Soldiers Dancing before the Start of the Battle of Eastern Ghouta," YouTube video.

41. "The Battle of Ghouta," Al Jazeera Centre for Studies, 2018, https://studies.aljazeera .net/en/positionpapers/2018/04/battle-ghouta-180409110904185.html. Last accessed August 15, 2022.

42. Thanks to Anoush Suni for her observations of this footwork and fashion signification.

43. Fashion retailer H&M received backlash in 2014 when it released a jumpsuit that allegedly imitated Kurdish combatant fatigues.

44. The regime's all-volunteer female force, known as Assad's Lionesses, primarily guarded checkpoints and staged military duties for regime propaganda uploaded to YouTube (Szekely 2020).

45. For an analysis of broader patterns of this phenomenon, see Abu-Lughod (2002).

46. Gayle Tzemach Lemmon, "ISIS bought and sold women on these streets. Now, a #womens council is opened in #Raqqa. Watch the joy shared," Twitter, August 16, 2018, 8:10 p.m., https://twitter.com/gaylelemmon/status/1030260502578880512?s=20.

47. Thanks to Anoush Suni. A common sequence in *govend* practice is left (passing), right, left (front) left (in place) right (front) right (in place)

48. Gayle Tzemach Lemmon, "#Raqqa: A city where ISIS bought and sold women. Now, the city's women come out to open the local #Women's Council. And share some joy," Twitter, August 18, 2018, 12:02 p.m., https://twitter.com/gaylelemmon/status/1030 862543625977856?s=20.

49. James Snell, "From Liberator to Occupier: SDF Rule in Syria after the Islamic State," *New Arab*, June 15 2021, https://english.alaraby.co.uk/analysis/liberator-occupier -sdf-rule-syria-after/.

50. "As the sit-in of residents continues in Tal Abyad and Ras al-Ayn near the border strip, demonstration in Malkiyyeh town condemns the Turkish threats to launch military operation against east Euphrates," The Syrian Observatory for Human Rights, October 9, 2019, www.syriahr.com/en/143205/.

51. Thanks to Anoush Suni for identifying these styles.

52. Butler's work on precarity as political rather than exclusively economic has been expanded on in performance studies (Nyong'o 2013) and dance studies (Pewny et al. 2019).

53. The mislabeling is problematic because it Arabicizes the dance circle at a moment when Kurdish political autonomy is precisely what is contested.

SIX *Translating Syrianness*

1. Germany has been the leading destination for asylum seekers since 2012. In 2015, 378,000 Syrians applied for asylum, the highest number of applicants of any single group of nationals; 1.3 million persons requested asylum in Europe in 2015, with declining numbers since then. "Number of Refugees to Europe Surges to Record 1.3 Million in 2015," Pew Research Center, August 2, 2016, www.pewresearch.org/global/2016/08/02/number-of-refugees-to-europe-surges-to-record-1-3-million-in-2015/.

2. "No End in Sight," UNHCR, June 2022, https://storymaps.arcgis.com/stories/0750 2a24ce0646bb9703ce96630b15fa.

3. Prem Kumar Rajaram, "Border Crisis: Rethinking the Population Movements at Europe's Border," *FocaalBlog*, October 19, 2015, www.focaalblog.com/2015/10/19/prem-kumar-rajaram-beyond-crisis/.

4. Richard Wike, Bruce Stokes, and Katie Simmons, "Europeans Fear Wave of Refugees Will Mean More Terrorism, Fewer Jobs," Pew Research Center, July 11, 2016, www.pewresearch.org/global/2016/07/11/europeans-fear-wave-of-refugees-will-mean-more-terrorism-fewer-jobs/.

5. El Tayeb (2011) notes that second- and third-generation Muslim Europeans are seen as *more* foreign and threatening than their foreparents.

6. Though displaced Syrians have generally been subjected to pernicious forms of racism in Turkey, Lebanon, and the Gulf, they have not experienced this phenomenon to the same extent as those affected by the hegemonic forces of multiculturalism, globalization, and postcolonialism that dominate in Europe and the United States.

7. The absence of intellectualism in the dance conservatory can be attributed to the restrictions on free speech and censorship of ideas in the Assad regime that impacted higher education and the arts, particularly literature and film. Adwan (2020) writes that the theater institute (adjacent to the dance conservatory) was conspicuously exempt from these restrictions and known as a space for the "freer circulation of critical and oppositional ideas."

8. These include Ramad Dance (directed by Lawand Hajo) in the Dancing on the Edge Festival and Leish Troupe (directed by Noura Murad) at the Julidans Dance Festival, both in Amsterdam.

9. Artistic themes and approaches among Syrian artists based in Europe took up a broad range of subjects that storified conflict and displacement (*Amal* 2017, dir. Medhat Aldaabal), diagnosed collective memory and trauma (*Siesta* 2017, dir. Mey Seifan),

disrupted public space through ritualized movement (*Sufi* 2017, dir. Jol Alholo), and portrayed violence and intimacy (*Trapeze* 2019, dir. Eyas al-Mokdad), among others.

10. Hailing from a family of painters in a village in Suwayda, Mithkal Alzghair began his formal dance studies at the Higher Institute of Dramatic Arts in Damascus with a specialization in ballet and Martha Graham technique. He moved to France after a brief period in Beirut, where he was inspired by his encounters with Europe-based choreographers at workshops and performances.

11. Mithkal Alzghair, interview with the author, Cincinnati, OH, January 2018.

12. Sara Elkamel, "Mithkal Alzghair: Dancing Displacement." *Guernica Magazine*, July 25, 2017. www.guernicamag.com/mithkal-alzghair-dancing-displacement/.

13. Alzghair, interview with the author.

14. Since its 2017 premiere, *Displacement* has primarily been staged for European audiences, with occasional performances in non-European countries including the United States, Korea, Tunisia, and Brazil.

15. He establishes a "pulse grouping" similar to Ibn Dhurayl, who uses pulse groupings as a category that distinguishes between local styles of *dabkāt* (see chapters 2 and 3). In contrast, however, to Ibn Dhurayl's assumption that pulse groupings are reproduced without variation or individualization in practice, Alzghair works with pulse groupings as a choreographic parameter whose continual rearrangement drives the narrative of the choreography.

16. Elkamel, "Mithkal Alzghair: Dancing Displacement." The representation of autocracy through *dabke* dance is itself not an original political claim. I have recently demonstrated (Silverstein 2021) how Syrian writers and film directors, from Sa'dallah Wannous to Khalid Khalifa, have repeatedly harnessed *dabke* as an embodied metaphor for masculinity and autocracy in plays, novels, and documentary film.

17. See Power-Sotomayor (2020) for a political elaboration on the materiality of vibrations in drumming and dance performance.

18. The sculpture was installed in 1964 in Division 97 of the Pére Lachaise Cemetery in Paris, an area dedicated to victims of World War II.

19. Alzghair, interview with the author.

20. Alzghair, interview with the author.

21. Wassim Muqdad, interview with the author, Berlin, Germany, June 19, 2017.

22. Ali Hasan, interview with the author, Berlin, Germany, June 24, 2019.

23. Doha Hassan, "Refyujee Brand," *Jadaliyya*, December 12, 2016, bidayyat.org/opinions_article.php?id=160#.ZBtx4ezMIdQ.

24. Rachel Clark, interview with the author, Berlin, Germany, June 2017. See also O'Toole (2017).

25. This production does not substantively feature *dabke* technique or repertoire,

with the exception of one moment in which the dancers-choreographers integrated *raqṣ shaʿbiyya* into their choreographic palette.

26. Medhat Aldaabal, interview with the author, Berlin, Germany, June 2017.

27. Jona Kallgren, "Syrian Migrants Bring Traditional Arab Dance to Berlin," AP News, April 24, 2018, www.apnews.com/45a4f56f032b41dca31aa8c2d819495e/.

28. Medhat Aldaabal, interview with the author, Berlin, Germany, November 2017.

29. Ali Hasan, interview with the author, June 24, 2019, Kreuzberg, Berlin, Germany.

30. Medhat Aldaabal, interview with the author, June 2019.

31. Henderson (1994), quoted in Johnson (2003, 245).

32. For a deeper analysis of these relations in Germany, specifically Berlin's multicultural music scene, see Silverstein and Sprengel (2021).

33. Harris (1998), quoted in Johnson (2003, 228).

34. On January 27, 2017, former president Donald Trump signed an executive order that banned foreign nationals from seven predominantly Muslim countries from visiting the United States for 90 days, suspended entry into the country of all Syrian refugees indefinitely, and prohibited any other refugees from coming into the country for 120 days. Despite numerous legal contestations, the ban effectively remained in place until January 20, 2021, when it was revoked by President Joe Biden.

CODA *Towards a New Balance*

1. Syrians for Truth and Justice, "How Can Folk Cultures Contribute to the Vision of a Pluralist Syria?," April 8, 2022, https://stj-sy.org/en/how-can-folk-cultures-contribute-towards-a-pluralistic-syria/.

2. Thanks to Ameer al-Khudari for sharing this anecdote with me in a meeting on June 2, 2016.

BIBLIOGRAPHY

ʿAbbas, Hassan. 2018. *Al-Musiqa al-Taqlidiyya fi Suriya* [Traditional music in Syria]. Beirut, Lebanon: UNESCO Office Beirut and Regional Bureau for Education in the Arab States.

Abboud, Samer. 2015. *Syria.* Hoboken, NJ: John Wiley & Sons.

Abdel Aziz, Moataz. 2010. "Arabic Music Videos and Their Implications for Arab Music and Media." In *Music and Media in the Arab World*, edited by Michael Frishkopf, 77–90. Cairo: American University of Cairo Press.

Abou Laban, Mohammad, Ziad Adwan, and Mario Münster. 2016. *A Syrious Look: A Magazine about Cultural Displacement.* Berlin: Independent Publishing.

Abu-Lughod, Lila. 1990. "The Romance of Resistance: Tracing Transformations of Power through Bedouin Women." *American Ethnologist* 17 (1): 41–55.

———. 2002. "Do Muslim Women Really Need Saving? Anthropological Reflections on Cultural Relativism and Its Others." *American Anthropologist* 104 (3): 783–90.

Adorno, Theodor W., and J. M. Bernstein. 2001. *The Culture Industry: Selected Essays on Mass Culture.* London: Psychology Press.

Adwan, Ziad. 2016. "The Opera House in Damascus and the 'State of Exception' in Syria." *New Theater Quarterly* 32 (3): 231–43.

Agamben, Giogio. 1998. *Homo Sacer: Sovereign Power and Bare Life.* Palo Alto, CA: Stanford University Press.

Ahmed, Sara. 2000. *Strange Encounters: Embodied Others in Post-Coloniality.* London: Routledge.

———. 2006. *Queer Phenomenology: Orientations, Objects, Others.* Durham, NC: Duke University Press.

Ahmed, Sara, and Jackie Stacey. 2001. *Thinking through the Skin.* London: Routledge.

Ajjan, Ziad. 2004. "'Ataba, Mijana, wa Zalghuta: Husasa li-l-Ams, Riqat al-Qalb" ['Ataba, Mijana, and Zalghuta: Sensitive to the touch, tender of heart]. *al-Wahida.* Document in author's possession.

———. 2008. "*Al-Lugha al-ʿArabiyya wa al-Musiqa*" [Arabic language and music]. *Binat al-Ajyal* 68 (3): 134–35.

Al-ʿAqili, Majdi. 1976. *al-Samaʿ ʿInd al-ʿArab* [The Arab art of listening]. Damascus: Manshurat Rabitat Kharriji al-Dirasat al-ʿUlya [The League of Higher Education Graduates].

Albright, Ann Cooper. 2013. *Engaging Bodies: The Politics and Poetics of Corporeality.* Middletown, CT: Wesleyan University Press.

Al-Dimashqi, Youmna. 2014. "War Sparks Virtual Romance: Online Marriages on the Rise."

Al-Ghazzi, Omar. 2013. "Nation as Neighborhood: How Bab Al-Hara Dramatized Syrian Identity." *Media, Culture and Society* 35 (5)): 586–601.

Al-Haj Saleh, Yassin. 2017. *The Impossible Revolution: Making Sense of the Syrian Tragedy.* Chicago: Haymarket Books.

Al-Husami, Ratib. 1954. "*Al-Ughniyya al-Rakhisa*" [The cheap songs]. *Majallat al-Idhaʿa al-Suriya* 21 (1).

Al-Jundi, Ghias, and Revolutionary Dabke. 2014. "Come On Bashar, Get Out!" In *Syria Speaks: Art and Culture from the Frontline*, edited by Malu Halasa, Zaher Omareen, and Nawara Mahfoud, 212–13. London: Saqi Books.

Al-Kassim, Dina. 2013. "Psychoanalysis and the Postcolonial Genealogy of Queer Theory." *International Journal of Middle East Studies* 45 (2): 343–46.

Allsopp, Harriet. 2014. *Kurds of Syria: Political Parties and Identity in the Middle East.* London: I. B. Tauris.

Allsopp, Jennifer. 2017. "Agent, Victim, Soldier, Son: Intersecting Masculinities in the European 'Refugee Crisis.'" In *A Gendered Approach to the Syrian Refugee Crisis*, edited by Jane Freedman, Zeynep Kıvılcım, and Nurcan Özgür, 155–74. Abingdon, Oxon: Routledge.

Al-Manini, ʿAdnan. 1961. *Qawaʿid Tadwin al-Raqs al-Shaʿbi* [Rules for notating folk dance]. Damascus: al-ʿAruba Press.

Al-Qayem, Ali. n.d. *Folklore Dance in Syria: Art of the Past.* Damascus: Ministry of Tourism Syria.

Al-Saleh, Asaad. 2016. "The Ministry of Culture in Syria: History, Production and Restriction of Official Culture." *Journal for Cultural Research* 20 (2): 137–56.

Al-Saqa, Jamal. 2005. *Al-Sahih fi al-Iqaʿ: Minhaj Mutakamal li-Dirasat Fan al-Iqaʿat* [The truth in the rhythm: Complete collection for the art of rhythms]. Vol. 1. Damascus: Dar Ekrema.

Al-Zubaidi, Layla. 2012. "In Syria." *London Review of Books* 34, no. 10, May 24.

Amar, Paul. 2011. "Middle East Masculinity Studies: Discourses of 'Men in Crisis,' Industries of Gender in Revolution." *Journal of Middle East Women's Studies* 7 (3): 36–70.

Amar, Paul, and Omnia El Shakry. 2013. "Introduction: Curiosities of Middle East Studies in Queer Times." *International Journal of Middle East Studies* 45 (2): 331–35.

Amine, Khalid, and Marvin A. Carlson. 2008. "*Al-Halqa* in Arabic Theatre: An Emerging Site of Hybridity." *Theatre Journal* 60 (1): 71–85.

Amit-Talai, Vered. 2000. *Constructing the Field: Ethnographic Fieldwork in the Contemporary World*. London: Routledge.

And, Metin. 1976. *Turkish Dancing: From Folk Dancing to Whirling Dervishes, Belly Dancing to Ballet*. Ankara: Dost Yayinlari.

Anderson, Benedict R. 1983. *Imagined Communities: Reflections on the Origin and Spread of Nationalism*. New York: Verso.

Anderson, Lisa, and Rashid Khalidi, eds. 1991. *The Origins of Arab Nationalism*. New York: Columbia University Press.

Anderson, Patrick, and Jisha Menon. 2011. *Violence Performed: Local Roots and Global Routes of Conflict*. Basingstoke, UK: Palgrave Macmillan.

Appadurai, Arjun. 1996. *Modernity at Large: Cultural Dimensions of Globalization*. Minneapolis: University of Minnesota Press.

Appert, Catherine M., and Sidra Lawrence. 2020. "Ethnomusicology Beyond #MeToo: Listening for the Violences of the Field." *Ethnomusicology* 64 (2): 225–53.

Arendt, Hannah. 1973. *The Origins of Totalitarianism*. New York: Harcourt, Brace, Jovanovich.

Armbrust, Walter. 2000. *Mass Mediations: New Approaches to Popular Culture in the Middle East and Beyond*. Berkeley: University of California Press.

Armbruster, Heidi, and Anna Laerke. 2010. *Taking Sides: Ethics, Politics, and Fieldwork in Anthropology*. New York: Berghahn Books.

Asha, Karel Layla. 2013. "Mothers at Home and Activists on the Street: The Role of Women in the Syrian Revolution of 2011–2012." *McGill International Review* 2 (3): 51–65.

Asmar, Sami W., and Kathleen Hood. 2001. "Modern Arab Music: Portraits of Enchantment from the Middle Generation." In *Colors of Enchantment: Theater, Dance, Music, and the Visual Arts of the Middle East*, edited by Sherifa Zuhur, 297–320. Cairo: American University in Cairo Press.

Auslander, Philip. 1999. *Liveness: Performance in a Mediatized Culture*. London: Routledge.

———. 2012. "Digital Liveness: A Historico-Philosophical Perspective." *PAJ: A Journal of Performance and Art* 34 (3): 3–11.

Austin, J. L. 1962. *How to Do Things with Words*. Cambridge, MA: Harvard University Press.

Banes, Sally. 1998. *Dancing Women: Female Bodies on Stage*. New York: Routledge.

Bar-Yosef, Amatzia. 1998. "Traditional Rural Style under a Process of Change: The Singing Style of the 'Hadday,' Palestinian Folk Poet-Singers." *Asian Music* 29, no. 2 (Spring–Summer): 57–82.

Barnard, Anne, and Hania Mourtada. 2013. "Lighthearted Videos Show Syrian Soldiers and Rebels Dancing." *New York Times*, February 8.

Baron, Beth. 2005. *Egypt as a Woman: Nationalism, Gender, and Politics*. Berkeley: University of California Press.

Bashkin, Orit. 2011. "Hybrid Nationalisms: Waṭanī and Qawmī Visions in Iraq under ʿAbd Al-Karim Qasim, 1958–61." *International Journal of Middle East Studies* 43 (2): 293–312.

Batatu, Hanna. 1999. *Syria's Peasantry, the Descendants of Its Lesser Rural Notables, and Their Politics*. Princeton, NJ: Princeton University Press.

Bates, Eliot. 2016. *Digital Tradition: Arrangement and Labor in Istanbul's Recording Studio Culture*. Oxford: Oxford University Press.

Bayat, Asaf. 2010. *Life as Politics: How Ordinary People Change the Middle East*. Palo Alto, CA: Stanford University Press.

Bayraktar, Sevi. 2019. "Choreographies of Dissent and the Politics of Public Space in State-Of-Emergency Turkey." *Performance Philosophy* 5 (1): 90–108.

Berger, Harris M., David VanderHamm, and Friedlind Riedel. 2021. "Phenomenological Approaches in the History of Ethnomusicology." In *The Oxford Handbook of the Phenomenology of Music Cultures*, edited by Harris M. Berger, Friedlind Riedel, and David VanderHamm. Oxford Academic (Online).

Berlant, Lauren. 2011. *Cruel Optimism*. Durham, NC: Duke University Press.

Bhabha, Homi K. 1994. "DissemiNation: Time, Narrative and the Margins of the Modern Nation." In *Nation and Narration*, edited by Homi Bhabha, 291–322. London: Routledge.

Billig, Michael. 1995. *Banal Nationalism*. Thousand Oaks, CA: Sage.

Bitar, Ahmad. 2010. "A Compelling and New Experience for Audiences in Aleppo." *Discover Syria* (volume number, page numbers, and specific date unavailable).

Boehmer, Elleke. 2013. *Stories of Women: Gender and Narrative in the Postcolonial Nation*. Manchester, UK: Manchester University Press.

Boëx, Cécile. 2011. "The End of the State Monopoly over Culture: Toward the Commodification of Cultural and Artistic Production." *Middle East Critique* 20 (2): 139–55.

Bohlman, Philip V. 2004. *The Music of European Nationalism: Cultural Identity and Modern History*. Santa Barbara, CA: ABC-CLIO.

Bordelon, Candace Anne. 2011. "Finding 'the Feeling' through Movement and Music: An Exploration of *Ṭarab* in Oriental Dance." PhD diss., Texas Women's University. ProQuest Dissertations Publishing.

Born, Georgina. 2013. *Music, Sound, and Space: Transformations of Public and Private Experience*. Cambridge: Cambridge University Press.

Bosse, Joanna. 2015. *Becoming Beautiful: Ballroom Dance in the American Heartland*. Urbana: University of Illinois Press.

Bothwell, Beau. 2013. "Song, State, Sawa Music and Political Radio between the US and Syria." PhD diss., Columbia University.

Bourdieu, Pierre. 1977. *Outline of a Theory of Practice*. Cambridge: Cambridge University Press.

Boym, Svetlana. 2001. *The Future of Nostalgia*. New York: Basic Books.

Brooks, Daphne, and Roshanak Kheshti. 2011. "The Social Space of Sound." *Theatre Survey* 52 (2): 329–34.

Brown, Wendy. 2006. *Regulating Aversion: Tolerance in the Age of Identity and Empire*. Princeton, NJ: Princeton University Press.

Bustani, Butrus ibn Bulus. (1870) 1977. *Muhit al-Muhit: Qamus Mutawwal li-l-Lugha al-ʿArabiyya* [Ocean of oceans: Comprehensive dictionary of the Arabic language]. Beirut: Maktabat Lubnan.

Butler, Judith. 1990. *Gender Trouble: Feminism and the Subversion of Identity*. New York: Routledge.

———. 2006. *Precarious Life: The Powers of Mourning and Violence*. London: Verso.

———. 2015. *Notes toward a Performative Theory of Assembly*. Cambridge, MA: Harvard University Press.

Butterfield, Matthew W., and Fernando Benadon. 2006. "The Power of Anacrusis: Engendered Feeling in Groove-Based Musics." *Music Theory* 12 (4).

Cachia, Pierre. 1973. "A 19th-Century Arab's Observations on European Music." *Ethnomusicology, USA* 17, no. 1 (January): 41–51.

Carlton, Donna. 1994. *Looking for Little Egypt*. Bloomington, IN: International Dance Discovery Press.

Caruth, Cathy. 1996. *Unclaimed Experience: Trauma, Narrative, and History*. Baltimore, MD: Johns Hopkins University Press.

Chaaban, Jad. 2009. "Youth and Development in the Arab Countries: The Need for a Different Approach." *Middle Eastern Studies* 45 (1): 33–55.

Chakrabarty, Dipesh. 2000. *Provincializing Europe: Postcolonial Thought and Historical Difference*. Princeton, NJ: Princeton University Press.

Chakravorty, Pallabi. 2008. *Bells of Change: Kathak Dance, Women and Modernity in India*. Calcutta, India: Seagull.

Chalcraft, John T. 2009. *The Invisible Cage: Syrian Migrant Workers in Lebanon*. Palo Alto, CA: Stanford University Press.

Chambers-Letson, Joshua Takano. 2013. *A Race So Different: Performance and Law in Asian America*. New York: New York University Press.

Chatterjee, Partha. 1993. *The Nation and Its Fragments: Colonial and Postcolonial Histories*. Princeton, NJ: Princeton University Press.

Chatty, Dawn. 2010. "The Bedouin in Contemporary Syria: The Persistence of Tribal Authority and Control." *Middle East Journal* 64 (1): 29–49.

———. 2017. *Syria: The Making and Unmaking of a Refuge State*. New York: Oxford University Press.

Chouliaraki, Lilie. 2013. *The Ironic Spectator: Solidarity in the Age of Post-Humanitarianism*. Cambridge, UK: Polity Press.

Chudnovskii, Mikhael A. 1959. *Folk Dance Company of the U.S.S.R.: Igor Moiseyev, Art Director*. Moscow: Foreign Languages Publishing House.

Chun, Wendy Hui Kyong. 2008. "The Enduring Ephemeral, or the Future Is a Memory." *Critical Inquiry* 35 (1): 148–71.

Clayton, Martin, Rebecca Sager, and Udo Will. 2004. "In Time with the Music: The Concept of Entrainment and Its Significance for Ethnomusicology." *ESEM Counterpoint* 1: 1–82.

Cohen, Dalia, and Ruth Katz. 1996. *Palestinian Arab Music: A Maqām Tradition in Practice*. Chicago: University of Chicago Press.

Colbert, Soyica Diggs, Douglas A. Jones, and Shane Vogel, eds. 2020. *Race and Performance after Repetition*. Durham, NC: Duke University Press.

Cole, Donald P. 2003. "Where Have the Bedouin Gone?" *Anthropological Quarterly* 76 (2): 235–67.

Commins, David, and David W. Lesch. 2014. *Historical Dictionary of Syria*. Lanham, MD: Scarecrow Press.

Connell, Raewyn, and James Messerschmidt. 2005. "Hegemonic Masculinity: Rethinking the Concept." *Gender and Society* 19 (6): 829–59.

Conquergood, Dwight. 2013. *Cultural Struggles: Performance, Ethnography, Praxis*, edited by E. Patrick Johnson. Ann Arbor: University of Michigan Press.

cooke, miriam. 2016. *Dancing in Damascus: Creativity, Resilience, and the Syrian Revolution*. London: Routledge.

Coon, Carleton S. 1951. *Caravan: The Story of the Middle East*. New York: Holt.

Couldry, Nick. 2004. "Liveness, 'Reality' and the Mediated Habitus from Television to the Mobile Phone." *Communications Review* 7 (4): 353–61.

Cowan, Jane K. 1990. *Dance and the Body Politic in Northern Greece*. Princeton, NJ: Princeton University Press.

Crawley, Ashon T. 2017. *Blackpentecostal Breath: the Aesthetics of Possibility*. New York: Fordham University Press.

Csikszentmihalyi, Mihaly. 1990. *Flow: The Psychology of Optimal Experience*. New York: Harper & Row.

Csordas, Thomas J. 1993. "Somatic Modes of Attention." *Cultural Anthropology* 8(2): 135–56.

Cusenza, Cristina. 2019. "Artists from Syria in the International Artworld: Mediators of a Universal Humanism." *Arts (Basel)* 8 (2): 45.

Dahi, Omar S., and Yasser Munif. 2012. "Revolts in Syria: Tracking the Convergence between Authoritarianism and Neoliberalism." *Journal of Asian and African Studies* 47 (4): 323–32.

Dajani, Omar M. 2015. "The Middle East's Majority Problems: Minoritarian Regimes and the Threat of Democracy." *Ethnic and Racial Studies* 38 (14): 2516–38.

Dalman, Gustaf. 1901. *Palestinischer Diwan: Als Beitrag Zur Volkskunde Palaestinas.* Leipzig: J. C. Hinrichs.

Dam, Nikolaos van. 1996. *The Struggle for Power in Syria: Politics and Society under Asad and the Ba'th Party.* London: I. B. Tauris.

Danielsen, Anne, and Ragnhild Brøvig-Hanssen. 2016. *Digital Signatures: The Impact of Digitization on Popular Music Sound.* Cambridge, MA: MIT Press.

Darden, Jessica Trisko, Alexis Henshaw, and Ora Szekely. 2019. "The Kurdish Regions: Fighting as Kurds, Fighting as Women." In *Insurgent Women: Female Combatants in Civil Wars*, edited by Jessica Trisko Darden, Alexis Henshaw, and Ora Szekely, 34–56. Washington, DC: Georgetown University Press.

Daughtry, Martin J. 2015. *Listening to War: Sound, Music, Trauma and Survival in Wartime Iraq.* New York: Oxford University Press.

Dave, Nomi. 2019. *The Revolution's Echoes: Music, Politics, and Pleasure in Guinea.* Chicago: University of Chicago Press.

De Certeau, Michel. (1980) 2002. *The Practice of Everyday Life.* Translated by S.F. Rendall. Berkeley: University of California Press.

Deeb, Lara, and Mona Harb. 2013. *Leisurely Islam: Negotiating Geography and Morality in Shi'ite South Beirut.* Princeton, NJ: Princeton University Press.

Deeb, Lara, and Jessica Winegar. 2016. "Anthropologies of Arab-Majority Societies." *Annual Review of Anthropology* 41 (1): 537–58.

DeFrantz, Thomas F. 2016. "Improvising Social Exchange: African American Social Dance." In *The Oxford Handbook of Critical Improvisation Studies*, edited by George Lewis and Benjamin Piekut, 330–38. New York: Oxford University Press.

Della Ratta, Donatella. 2018. *Shooting a Revolution: Visual Media and Warfare in Syria.* Cambridge, UK: Polity Press.

Denning, Michael. 2015. *Noise Uprising: The Audiopolitics of a World Musical Revolution.* London: Verso Press.

Denzin, Norman K. 2003. *Performance Ethnography: Critical Pedagogy and the Politics of Culture.* Thousand Oaks, CA: Sage.

Dils, Ann, and Albright Ann Cooper. 2001. *Moving History/Dancing Cultures: A Dance History Reader.* Middletown, CT: Wesleyan University Press.

Dixon, Steve. 2007. *Digital Performance: A History of New Media in Theater, Dance, Performance Art, and Installation.* Cambridge, MA: MIT Press.

Dolan, Jill. 2001. "Performance, Utopia, and the 'Utopian Performative.'" *Theatre Journal* 53 (3): 455–79.

Donati, Caroline. 2013. "The Economics of Authoritarian Upgrading in Syria: Liberalization and the Reconfiguration of Economic Networks." In *Middle East Authoritarianisms: Governance, Contestation, and Regime Resilience in Syria and Iran*, edited by Steven Heydemann and Reinoud Leenders, 35–60. Palo Alto, CA: Stanford University

Press.

Dukhan, Haian. 2014. "'They Talk to Us but Never Listen to Us': Development-Induced Displacement among Syria's Bedouin." *Nomadic Peoples* 18 (1): 61–79.

Eidsheim, Nina Sun. 2015. *Sensing Sound: Singing and Listening as Vibrational Practice.* Durham, NC: Duke University Press.

El Tayeb, Fatima. 2011. *European Others: Queering Ethnicity in Postnational Europe.* Minneapolis: University of Minnesota Press.

El Zein, Rayya S. 2016. "Performing El Rap El ʿArabi 2005–2015: Feeling Politics amid Neoliberal Incursions in Ramallah, Amman, and Beirut." PhD diss., City University of New York. ProQuest Dissertations Publishing.

Ellington, Edward Kennedy. 1973. *Music Is My Mistress.* Garden City, NY: Doubleday.

El-Shakry, Omnia. 2007. *The Great Social Laboratory: Subjects of Knowledge in Colonial and Postcolonial Egypt.* Palo Alto, CA: Stanford University Press.

Elyachar, Julia. 2011. "The Political Economy of Movement and Gesture in Cairo." *Journal of the Royal Anthropological Institute* 17 (1): 82–99.

Fabian, Johannes. 1998. *Moments of Freedom: Anthropology and Popular Culture.* Charlottesville: University of Virginia Press.

Faksh, Mahmud A. 1984. "The Alawi Community of Syria: A New Dominant Political Force." *Middle Eastern Studies* 20 (2): 133–53.

Farnell, Brenda. 2012. *Dynamic Embodiment for Social Theory: "I Move Therefore I Am".* New York: Routledge.

Farraj, Johnny, and Sami Abu Shumays. 2019. *Inside Arabic Music: Arabic Maqam Performance and Theory in the 20th Century.* New York: Oxford University Press.

Fassin, Didier. 2011. "Policing Borders, Producing Boundaries. The Governmentality of Immigration in Dark Times." *Annual Review of Anthropology* 40(1): 213–26.

Fast, Susan, and Kip Pegley. 2012. *Music, Politics, and Violence.* Middletown, CT: Wesleyan University Press.

Figueroa, Michael A. 2022. "Post-Tarab: Music and Affective Politics in the US SWANA Diaspora." *Ethnomusicology* 66 (2): 236–63.

Firro, Kais. 1992. *A History of the Druze.* New York: Brill.

Fischer-Lichte. Erika. 2008. *The Transformative Power of Performance: A New Aesthetics.* London: Routledge.

Fisher, Jennifer, and Anthony Shay, eds. 2009. *When Men Dance: Choreographing Masculinities Across Borders.* New York: Oxford University Press.

Fortuna, Victoria. 2019. *Moving Otherwise: Dance, Violence, and Memory in Buenos Aires.* New York: Oxford University Press.

Foster, Susan Leigh. 1998. "Choreographies of Gender." *Signs* 24 (1): 1–33.

———. 2003. "Choreographies of Protest." *Theatre Journal* 55 (3): 395–412.

———. 2011. *Choreographing Empathy: Kinesthesia in Performance.* London: Routledge.

Friedner, Michele, and Stefan Helmreich. 2012. "Sound Studies Meets Deaf Studies." *Senses and Society* 7 (1): 72–86.

Frishkopf, Michael. 2010. "Introduction: Music and Media in the Arab World." In *Music and Media in the Arab World*, edited by Michael Frishkopf, 1–64. Cairo: American University in Cairo Press.

Fuentes, Marcela A. 2019. *Performance Constellations: Networks of Protest and Activism in Latin America*. Ann Arbor: University of Michigan Press.

Fujii, Lee Ann. 2017. *Interviewing in Social Science Research: A Relational Approach*. London: Routledge.

Gandhi, Leela. 1998. *Postcolonial Theory: A Critical Introduction*. New York: Columbia University Press.

García, Cindy. 2013. *Salsa Crossings: Dancing Latinidad in Los Angeles*. Durham, NC: Duke University Press.

Garcia, Luis-Manuel. 2015. "Beats, Flesh and Grain: Sonic Tactility and Affect in Electronic Dance Music," *Sound Studies* 1 (1): 59–76.

———. 2020. "Feeling the Vibe: Sound, Vibration, and Affective Attunement in Electronic Dance Music Scenes." *Ethnomusicology Forum* 29 (2): 1–19.

George, Alan. 2003. *Syria: Neither Bread nor Freedom*. London: Zed Books.

Geros, Panagiotis. 2010. "Doing Fieldwork within Fear and Silences." In *Taking Sides: Ethics, Politics, and Fieldwork in Anthropology*, edited by Heidi Armbruster and Anna Laerke, 89–115. New York: Berghahn Books.

Geurts, Kathryn Linn. 2002. *Culture and the Senses: Bodily Ways of Knowing in an African Community*. Berkeley: University of California Press.

Ghannam, Farha. 2013. *Live and Die Like a Man: Gender Dynamics in Urban Egypt*. Palo Alto, CA: Stanford University Press.

Ghoussoub, Mai, and Emma Sinclair-Webb. 2000. *Imagined Masculinities: Male Identity and Culture in the Modern Middle East*. London: Saqi Books.

Gilman, Daniel J. 2014. *Cairo Pop: Youth Music in Contemporary Egypt*. Minneapolis: University of Minnesota Press.

Gilmore, David D. 1990. *Manhood in the Making: Cultural Concepts of Masculinity*. New Haven, CT: Yale University Press.

Gilsenan, Michael. 1996. *Lords of the Lebanese Marches: Violence and Narrative in Arab Society*. London: I. B. Tauris.

Goffman, Erving. 1973. *The Presentation of Self in Everyday Life*. Woodstock, NY: Overlook Press.

Goldman, Danielle. 2010. *I Want to Be Ready: Improvised Dance as a Practice of Freedom*. Ann Arbor: University of Michigan Press.

Goodman, Steven. 2010. *Sonic Warfare: Sound, Affect, and the Ecology of Fear*. Cambridge, MA: MIT Press.

Gopinath, Gayatri. 2005. *Impossible Desires: Queer Diasporas and South Asian Public Cultures*. Durham, NC: Duke University Press.

Gracyk, Theodore. 1996. *Rhythm and Noise: An Aesthetics of Rock*. Durham, NC: Duke University Press.

Granqvist, Hilda Natalia. 1931. *Marriage Conditions in a Palestinian Village*. Helsingfors: Akademische buchhandlung.

Gray, Hill. 1891. *With the Beduins: A Narrative of Journeys and Adventures in Unfrequented Parts of Syria*. London: TFUnwin.

Gray, Matthew. 1997. "The Political Economy of Tourism in Syria: State, Society, and Economic Liberalization." *Arab Studies Quarterly* 19, no. 2 (Spring): 57.

Grippo, James. 2010. "What's Not on Egyptian Television and Radio! Locating the 'Popular' in Egyptian *Sha'bi*." In *Music and Mass Media in the Arab World*, edited by Michael Frishkopf, 137–62. Cairo: The American University in Cairo Press.

Gualtieri, Sarah M. A. 2009. *Between Arab and White: Race and Ethnicity in the Early Syrian American Diaspora*. Berkeley: University of California Press.

Gupta, Akhil, and James Ferguson, eds. 1997. *Culture, Power, Place: Explorations in Critical Anthropology*. Durham, NC: Duke University Press.

Gutkin, Irina. 1999. *The Cultural Origins of the Socialist Realist Aesthetic, 1890-1934*. Evanston, IL: Northwestern University Press.

Haddad, Bassam. 2011. *Business Networks in Syria: The Political Economy of Authoritarian Resilience*. Palo Alto, CA: Stanford University Press.

Hafiz, Sherine. 2012. "No Longer a Bargain: Women, Masculinity, and the Egyptian Uprising." *American Ethnologist* 39 (1): 37–42.

Hage, Ghassan. 2015. *Alter-Politic: Critical Anthropology and the Radical Imagination*. Carlton, Victoria: Melbourne University Press.

Hahn, Tomie. 2007. *Sensational Knowledge: Embodying Culture through Japanese Dance*. Middletown, CT: Wesleyan University Press.

Hamera, Judith. 2006. "Performance, Performativity, and Cultural Poiesis in Practices of Everyday Life." In *The SAGE Handbook of Performance Studies*, edited by D. Soyini Madison and Judith Hamera, 46–64. Thousand Oaks, CA: Sage.

———. 2007. *Dancing Communities: Performance, Difference, and Connection in the Global City*. Basingstoke, UK: Palgrave Macmillan.

Harris, Trudier. 1998. "Lying through Our Teeth? The Quagmire of Cultural Diversity." In *Teaching African American Literature*, edited by Maryemma Graham, Sharon Pineault-Burke, and Marianna White Davis, 210–22. New York: Routledge.

Hasso, Frances S., and Zakia Salime, eds. 2016. *Freedom without Permission: Bodies and Space in the Arab Revolutions*. Durham, NC: Duke University Press.

Henderson, Mae. 1994. "What It Means to Teach the Other When the Other Is the Self." *Callaloo* 17 (2): 432–38.

Henni-Chebra, Djamila, and Christian Poche. 1996. *Les Danses Dans Le Monde Arabe Ou L'heritage Des Almees* [Dances in the Arab World, or, the Heritage of the Dancing Women]. Paris: L'Harmattan.

Henriques, Julian. 2011. *Sonic Bodies: Reggae Sound Systems, Performance Techniques, and Ways of Knowing*. London: Bloomsbury.

Herzfeld, Michael. 1997. *Cultural Intimacy: Social Poetics in the Nation-State*. New York: Routledge.

Hesmondalgh, David. 2009. "The Digitalisation of Music." In *Creativity, Innovation and the Cultural Economy*, edited by Andy C. Pratt and Paul Jeffcutt, 57–73. London: Routledge.

Heydemann, Steven. 1999. *Authoritarianism in Syria: Institutions and Social Conflict, 1946–1970*. Ithaca, NY: Cornell University Press.

Heydemann, Steven, and Reinoud Leenders, eds. 2013. *Middle East Authoritarianisms: Governance, Contestation, and Regime Resilience in Syria and Iran*. Palo Alto, CA: Stanford University Press.

Hill, Fiona. 1997. "The Gender of Tradition: Syrian Women and the Feminist Agenda." In *Remaking the Middle East*, edited by Paul J. White and William S. Logan, 129–52. Oxford: Berg.

Hinnebusch, Raymond A. 2001. *Syria: Revolution from Above*. London: Routledge.

Hirschkind, Charles. 2006. *The Ethical Soundscape: Cassette Sermons and Islamic Counterpublics*. New York: Columbia University Press.

Hobsbawm, E. J., and T. O. Ranger. 1983. *The Invention of Tradition*. New York: Cambridge University Press.

Holmes, Jessica A. 2017. "Expert Listening beyond the Limits of Hearing: Music and Deafness." *Journal of the American Musicological Society* 70 (1): 171–220.

Holmes, Seth M., and Heide Castañeda. 2016. "Representing the 'European Refugee Crisis' in Germany and Beyond: Deservingness and Difference, Life and Death." *American Ethnologist* 43 (1): 12–24.

Hood, Kathleen. 2007. *Music in Druze Life: Ritual, Values and Performance Practice*. London: Druze Heritage Foundation.

Hourani, Albert Habib. 1991. *A History of the Arab Peoples*. Cambridge, MA: Harvard University Press.

Human Rights Watch. 1991. *Syria Unmasked: The Suppression of Human Rights by the Asad Regime*. New Haven, CT: Yale University Press.

Humphrey, Caroline. 2008. "Reassembling Individual Subjects: Events and Decisions in Troubled Times." *Anthropological Theory* 8 (4): 357–80.

Ibn Dhurayl, ʿAdnan. 1969. *Al-Musiqa fi Suriya: al-Bahth al-Musiqi wa-l-Funun al-Musiqiyya Mundhu Miʾat ʿAm ila al-Yawm* [Music in Syria: Musical research and the musical arts from centuries ago to today]. Damascus: n.p.

———. 1972. *Turath al-Dabke fi al-Musiqa al-Shaʿbiyya fi Suriya* [Dabke heritage in popular music in Syria]. Damascus: n.p.

———. 1996. *Raqs al-Samah wa-l-Dabke: Tarikh wa Tadwin* [*Raqs al-Samah* and *Dabke*: History and collection]. Damascus: al-Tabʿa Press.

Ibn Khaldun and Franz Rosenthal. 1967. *The Muqaddimah: An Introduction to History.* Princeton, NJ: Princeton University Press.

Ingold, Tim. 2000. *The Perception of the Environment: Essays on Livelihood, Dwelling and Skill.* London: Routledge.

Inhorn, Marcia C. 2012. *The New Arab Man: Emergent Masculinities, Technologies, and Islam in the Middle East.* Princeton, NJ: Princeton University Press.

International Crisis Group. 2011. *Popular Protest in North Africa and the Middle East (VI): The Syrian People's Slow Motion Revolution.* Report.

Ismail, Salwa. 2011. "The Syrian Uprising: Imagining and Performing the Nation." *Studies in Ethnicity and Nationalism* 11 (3): 538–49.

Issa, Sadam. 2018. "Ibrahim Qashoush's Revolutionary Popular Songs: Resistance Music in the 2011 Syrian Revolution." *Popular Music and Society* 41 (3): 283–301.

Jackson, Travis. 2013. "Tourist Point of View? Musics of the World and Ellington's Suites." *Musical Quarterly* 96 (3–4): 523.

Jacob, Wilson Chacko. 2011. *Working Out Egypt: Effendi Masculinity and Subject Formation in Colonial Modernity, 1870–1940.* Durham, NC: Duke University Press.

Janenova, Saltanat. 2019. "The Boundaries of Research in an Authoritarian State." *International Journal of Qualitative Methods* 18: 1–8.

Johnson, E. Patrick. 2003. *Appropriating Blackness: Performance and the Politics of Authenticity.* Durham, NC: Duke University Press.

Johnson, E. Patrick, and Ramón H. Rivera-Servera, eds. 2016. *Blacktino Queer Performance.* Durham, NC: Duke University Press.

Joseph, Suad. 1999. *Intimate Selving in Arab Families: Gender, Self, and Identity.* 1st ed. Syracuse, NY: Syracuse University Press.

———. 2005. "The Kin Contract and Citizenship in the Middle East." In *Women and Citizenship,* edited by Marilyn Friedman. Oxford Scholarship Online.

Joubin, Rebecca. 2013. *The Politics of Love: Sexuality, Gender, and Marriage in Syrian Television Drama.* Lanham, MD: Lexington Books.

Kanaaneh, Moslih, Stig-Magnus Thorsén, Heather Bursheh, and David A. McDonald, eds. 2013. *Palestinian Music and Song: Expression and Resistance since 1900.* Bloomington: Indiana University Press.

Kandiyoti, Deniz. 1988. "Bargaining with Patriarchy." *Gender and Society* 2 (3): 274–90.

Kapchan, Deborah. 2017. *Theorizing Sound Writing.* Middletown, CT: Wesleyan University Press.

Karayanni, Stavros Stavrou. 2004. *Dancing Fear and Desire: Race, Sexuality, and Imperial Politics in Middle Eastern Dance*. Waterloo, ON: Wilfrid Laurier University Press.

Kaschl, Elke. 2003. *Dance and Authenticity in Israel and Palestine: Performing the Nation*. Leiden: Brill.

Kastrinou, Maria A. 2016. *Power, Sect and State in Syria: The Politics of Marriage and Identity amongst the Druze*. London: I. B. Tauris.

Keil, Charles, and Steven Feld. 1994. *Music Grooves: Essays and Dialogues*. Chicago: University of Chicago Press.

Kelly, Jem. 2007. "Pop Music, Multimedia, and Live Performance." In *Music, Sound, and Multimedia*, edited by Jamie Sexton, 105–20. Edinburgh: Edinburgh University Press.

Kerr, Michael, and Craig Larkin. 2015. *The Alawis of Syria: War, Faith and Politics in the Levant*. Oxford: Oxford University Press.

Kessler, Martha Neff. 1987. *Syria: Fragile Mosaic of Power*. Washington, DC: National Defense University Press.

Khalifa, Khaled. 2012. *In Praise of Hatred*. Translated by Leri Price. London: Doubleday.

Khalifa, Mustafa. 2016. *The Shell: Memoirs of a Hidden Observer*. Northampton, MA: Interlink Publishing Group.

Khalili, Laleh. 2005. "Places of Memory and Mourning: Palestinian Commemoration in the Refugee Camps of Lebanon." *Comparative Studies of South Asia, Africa, and the Middle East* 25(1): 30–45.

Khanashat, Yusuf Musa. (1936) 1982. *Taraʿif al-Ams, Gharaʿib al-Yawm* [Yesterday's odds, today's strangeness or Images from *al-Nabak* and *al-Qalamun* mountains in the mid-ninth century]. Beirut: Dar al-Raed. Reissued in 1982, Beirut: Syrian Ministry of Education.

Khater, Akram Fouad. 2001. *Inventing Home: Emigration, Gender, and the Middle Class in Lebanon, 1870–1920*. Berkeley: University of California Press.

Kheshti, Roshanak. 2015. *Modernity's Ear: Listening to Race and Gender in World Music*. New York: New York University Press.

Kim, Suk-Young. 2017. "Liveness: Performance of Ideology and Technology in the Changing Media Environment." In *Oxford Research Encyclopedia of Literature*. New York: Oxford University Press.

Kirshenblatt-Gimblett, Barbara. 1998. *Destination Culture: Tourism, Museums, and Heritage*. Berkeley: University of California Press.

Koch, Natalie. 2013. "Introduction—Field Methods in 'Closed Contexts': Undertaking Research in Authoritarian States and Places." *Area* 45 (4): 390–95.

Koetting, James. 1970. "Analysis and Notation of West African Drum Ensemble Music." *Selected Reports in Ethnomusicology* 1 (3): 115–46.

Kraidy, Marwan M. 2016. *The Naked Blogger of Cairo*. Cambridge, MA: Harvard University Press.

Kurd Ali, Muhammad. 1926. *Kitab Khutat al-Sham*. Damascus: n.p.

Kyriakides, Christopher. 2017. "Words Don't Come Easy: Al Jazeera's Migrant–Refugee Distinction and the European Culture of (Mis)Trust." *Current Sociology* 65 (7): 933–52.

Lane, Edward William. 1895. *An Account of the Manners and Customs of the Modern Egyptians Written in Egypt during the Years 1833-1835.* London: East- West Publications.

Lange, Katharina. 2012. "'There Used to Be Terrible Disbelief': Mourning and Social Change in Northern Syria." In *Ethnographies of Islam: Ritual Performances and Everyday Practices*, edited by Dupret Baudouin, Pierret Thomas, Pinto Paulo G., and Spellman-Poots Kathryn, 31–39. Edinburgh: Edinburgh University Press.

———. 2015. "'Bedouin' and 'Shawaya': The Performative Constitution of Tribal Identities in Syria during the French Mandate and Today." *Journal of the Economic and Social History of the Orient* 58: 200–235.

Larkin, Brian. 2014. "Techniques of Inattention: The Mediality of Loudspeakers in Nigeria." *Anthropological Quarterly* 87 (4): 989–1015.

Lawler, Andrew. 2014. "Satellites Track Heritage Loss Across Syria and Iraq." *Science* 346 (6214): 1162–63.

Lefebvre, Henri. 1991. *The Production of Space*. Oxford, UK: Blackwell.

Lemmon, Gayle Tzemach. 2018. "Women Rise as Raqqa Rebuilds Without the World's Help." *Defense One*, August 29.

———. 2021. *The Daughters of Kobani: A Story of Rebellion, Courage, and Justice*. New York: Penguin Press.

Lenssen, Anneka. 2020. *Beautiful Agitation: Modern Painting and Politics in Syria*. Berkeley: University of California Press.

Lepecki, André. 2006. *Exhausting Dance: Performance and the Politics of Movement*. New York: Routledge.

———. 2013. "Choreopolice and Choreopolitics: Or, the Task of the Dancer." *TDR: The Drama Review* 57 (4): 13–27.

Levine, Mark. 2008. *Heavy Metal Islam: Rock, Resistance, and the Struggle for the Soul of Islam*. New York: Three Rivers Press.

Lockman, Zachary. 2016. *Field Notes: The Making of Middle East Studies in the United States*. Palo Alto, CA: Stanford University Press.

Lorde, Audre. 1988. *A Burst of Light, Essays*. London: Sheba Feminist Publishers.

MacKinnon, Rebecca. 2011. "China's 'Networked Authoritarianism.'" *Journal of Democracy* 22 (2): 32–46.

Madison, D. Soyini. 2006. "The Dialogic Performative in Critical Ethnography." *Text and Performance Quarterly* 26 (4): 320–24.

———. 2011. *Critical Ethnography: Method, Ethics, and Performance*. Thousand Oaks, CA: Sage.

Mahadeen, Ebtihal. 2016. "Arabizing 'Masculinity.'" *Journal of Middle East Women's Studies* 12 (3): 450–52.

Mahmood, Saba. 2005. *Politics of Piety: The Islamic Revival and the Feminist Subject.* Princeton, NJ: Princeton University Press.

Maners, Lynn D. 2006. "Utopia, Eutopia, and E.U.-topia: Performance and Memory in Former Yugoslavia." In *Dancing from Past to Present: Nation, Culture, Identities,* edited by Theresa Jill Buckland, 75–96. Madison: University of Wisconsin Press.

Manuel, Peter. 1993. *Cassette Culture: Popular Music and Technology in North India.* Chicago: University of Chicago Press.

Marcus, Scott L. 1989. "Arab Music Theory in the Modern Period." PhD diss., University of California Los Angeles. ProQuest Dissertations Publishing.

Martin, Kevin W. 2015. *Syria's Democratic Years: Citizens, Experts, and Media in the 1950s.* Bloomington: Indiana University Press.

Martin, Rose. 2019. "Syria, Dance, and Community: Dance Education in Exile." *Journal of Dance Education* 19 (3): 127–34.

Massad, Joseph Andoni. 2007. *Desiring Arabs.* Chicago: University of Chicago Press.

Massey, Doreen. 1994. *Space, Place, and Gender.* Minneapolis: University of Minnesota Press.

McDonald, David A. 2013. *My Voice Is My Weapon: Music, Nationalism, and the Poetics of Palestinian Resistance.* Durham, NC: Duke University Press.

McNeill, William Hardy. 1995. *Keeping Together in Time: Dance and Drill in Human History.* Cambridge, MA: Harvard University Press.

Meftahi, Ida. 2017. *Gender and Dance in Modern Iran: Biopolitics on Stage.* New York: Routledge.

Meintjes, Louise. 2003. *Sound of Africa! Making Music Zulu in a South African Studio.* Durham, NC: Duke University Press.

———. 2004. "Shoot the Sergeant, Shatter the Mountain: The Production of Masculinity in Zulu Ngoma Song and Dance in Post-Apartheid South Africa." *Ethnomusicology Forum* 13 (2): 173–201.

———. 2019. "Ululation." In *Remapping Sound Studies,* edited by Gavin Steingo and Jim Sykes, 61–76. Durham, NC: Duke University Press.

Mitchell, Timothy. 1991. *Colonising Egypt.* Berkeley: University of California Press.

Mitchell, W. J. T. 2012. "Report from Morocco." *Critical Inquiry* 38, no. 4 (Summer): 892–901.

Mittermaier, Amira. 2015. "Death and Martyrdom in the Arab Uprisings: An Introduction." *Ethnos* 80 (5): 583–604.

Monroe, Kristin. 2020. "Masculinity, Migration, and Forced Conscription in the Syrian War." *Cultural Anthropology* 35 (2): 264–89.

Monson, Ingrid. 2008. "Hearing, Seeing, and Perceptual Agency." *Critical Inquiry* 34, no. 2 (Winter): 36–58.

Moten, Fred. 2003. *In the Break: The Aesthetics of the Black Radical Tradition.* Minneapolis: University of Minnesota Press.

Moubayed, Sami. 2008. "Ambassador to the Stars." *Gulf News*, February 15.

Mroué, Rabih, Ziad Nawfal, and Carol Martin. 2012. "The Pixelated Revolution." *TDR: The Drama Review* 56 (3): 18–35.

Mulvey, Laura. 1975. "Visual Pleasure and Narrative Cinema." *Screen (London)* 16 (3): 6–18.

Munif, Yassir. 2020. *The Syrian Revolution: Between the Politics of Life and the Geopolitics of Death.* London: Pluto Press.

Muñoz, José Esteban. 1999. *Disidentifications: Queers of Color and the Performance of Politics.* Minneapolis: University of Minnesota Press.

Mürer, George. 2020. *Her Biji Granî* [Long live Granî]. Ethnographic documentary from Turkey.

Naguib, Nefissa. 2015. *Nurturing Masculinities: Men, Food, and Family in Contemporary Egypt.* Austin: University of Texas Press.

Najmabadi, Afsaneh. 2005. *Women with Mustaches and Men without Beards: Gender and Sexual Anxieties of Iranian Modernity.* Berkeley: University of California Press.

Nyong'o, Tavia. 2013. "Situating Precarity Between the Body and the Commons." *Women & Performance* 23 (2): 157–61.

———. 2022. "Unburdening Liveness." *TDR: The Drama Review* 66 (4): 28–36.

O'Toole, Michael. 2017. "Our Music: Syrian *Tarab* and the Politics of Refugee Representation in Germany." Presented at Society for Ethnomusicology, Denver, CO, October 28.

Ozturkmen, Arzu. 2002. "'I Dance Folklore.'" In *Fragments of Culture: The Everyday of Modern Turkey*, edited by Ayşe Saktanber and Deniz Kandiyoti, 128–46. New Brunswick, NJ: Rutgers University Press.

Papacharissi, Zizi. 2014. *Affective Publics: Sentiment, Technology, and Politics.* New York: Oxford University Press.

Peristiany, John G. 1966. *Honour and Shame: The Values of Mediterranean Society.* Chicago: University of Chicago Press.

Peteet, Julie. 1994. "Male Gender and Rituals of Resistance in the Palestinian 'Intifada': A Cultural Politics of Violence." *American Ethnologist* 21 (1): 31–49.

Pettan, Svanibor. 1998. *Music, Politics, and War: Views from Croatia.* Zagreb: Institute of Ethnology and Folklore Research.

Peutz, Nathalie. 2011. "Bedouin 'Abjection': World Heritage, Worldliness, and Worthiness at the Margins of Arabia." *American Ethnologist* 38 (2): 338–60.

Pewny, Katharina, Annelies Van Assche, Simon Leenknegt, and Rebekah J. Kowal. 2019. "Editors' Note." *Dance Research Journal* 51 (1): 1–6.

Phelan, Peggy. 1993. "The Ontology of Performance: Representation without Reproduction." In *Unmarked: The Politics of Performance*, 146–66. London: Routledge.

Pieslak, Jonathan. 2009. *Sound Targets: American Soldiers and Music in the Iraq War*. Bloomington: Indiana University Press.

Piguet, Etienne. 2021. "The 'Refugee Crisis' in Europe: Shortening Distances, Containment and Asymmetry of Rights—a Tentative Interpretation of the 2015–16 Events." *Journal of Refugee Studies* 34 (2): 1577–94.

Pinch, Trevor, and Frank Trocco. 2004. *Analog Days: The Invention and Impact of the Moog Synthesizer*. Cambridge, MA: Harvard University Press.

Pink, Sarah. 2016. *Digital Ethnography: Principles and Practice*. Los Angeles: Sage.

Pinto, Paulo G. 2011. "'Oh Syria, God Protects You': Islam as Cultural Idiom Under Bashar Al-Asad." *Middle East Critique* 20 (2): 189–205.

Porcello, Thomas. 2005. *Wired for Sound: Engineering and Technologies in Sonic Cultures*. Middletown, CT: Wesleyan University Press.

Potuoğlu-Cook, Öykü. 2006. "Beyond the Glitter: Belly Dance and Neoliberal Gentrification in Istanbul." *Cultural Anthropology* 21 (4): 633–60.

Povinelli, Elizabeth A. 2002. *The Cunning of Recognition: Indigenous Alterities and the Making of Australian Multiculturalism*. Durham, NC: Duke University Press.

Power-Sotomayor, Jade. 2020. "Corporeal Sounding: Listening to Bomba Dance, Listening to Puertorriqueñxs." *Performance Matters* 6 (2): 43–59.

Prager, Laila. 2014. "Introduction—Reshaping Tribal Identities in the Contemporary Arab World: Politics, (Self-)Representation, and the Construction of Bedouin History." *Nomadic Peoples* 18 (2): 10–15.

Purkayastha, Prarthana. 2014. *Indian Modern Dance, Feminism and Transnationalism*. London: Palgrave Macmillan.

Qassab Hassan, Nijat. 1994. *Al-Hanna wa-l-Sanabal: Muhadarat* [The compassion and the harvest: Lectures]. Damascus: Al-Ahali.

Rabo, Annika. 1996. "Gender, State and Civil Society in Jordan and Syria." In *Civil Society: Challenging Western Models*, edited by C. M. Hann and Elizabeth Dunn, 153–74. London: Psychology Press.

———. 2008. "Doing Family: Two Cases in Contemporary Syria." *Hawwa* 6 (2): 129–53.

Racy, Ali Jihad. 1981. "Legacy of a Star." In *Fayrouz: Legend and Legacy*, edited by Kamal Boullata and Sargon Boulus, 36–41. Washington, DC: Forum for International Art and Culture.

———. 1994. "A Dialectical Perspective on Musical Instruments: The East-Mediterranean *Mijwiz*." *Ethnomusicology* 38, no. 1 (Winter): 37–57.

———. 1996. "Heroes, Lovers, and Poet-Singers: The Bedouin Ethos in the Music of the Arab Near-East." *Journal of American Folklore* 109, no. 434 (Autumn): 404–24.

————. 2003. *Making Music in the Arab World: The Culture and Artistry of Ṭarab*. Cambridge: Cambridge University Press.

Rasmussen, Anne K. 1996. "Theory and Practice at the 'Arabic Org': Digital Technology in Contemporary Arab Music Performance." *Popular Music* 15 (3): 345–65.

Redmond, Shana L. 2013. *Anthem: Social Movements and the Sound of Solidarity in the African Diaspora*. New York: NYU Press.

Reed, Susan A. 1998. "The Politics and Poetics of Dance." *Annual Review of Anthropology* 27: 503–22.

Reyes, Ian. 2010. "To Know Beyond Listening: Monitoring Digital Music." *Senses and Society* 6 (2): 322–38.

Rivera-Servera, Ramón H. 2012. *Performing Queer Latinidad: Dance, Sexuality, Politics*. Ann Arbor: University of Michigan Press.

Rowe, Nicholas. 2010. *Raising Dust: A Cultural History of Dance in Palestine*. London: I. B. Tauris.

Sabbagh, H. 2010. "Qassab Hasan: Dar Al-Assad to Produce Artistic Projects to Spread Culture and Arts." *Sana* (volume number or date unknown).

Sabry, Tarik. 2010. *Cultural Encounters in the Arab World: On Media, the Modern and the Everyday*. London: I. B. Tauris.

Said, Edward W. 1978. *Orientalism*. New York: Pantheon Books.

Sakr, Naomi. 2007. *Arab Television Today*. London: I. B. Tauris.

Salamandra, Christa. 2004. *A New Old Damascus: Authenticity and Distinction in Urban Syria*. Bloomington: Indiana University Press.

Saleh, Farah. 2020. "Defying Distance." *IMG Journal* 3: 366–79.

Saleh, Layla. 2020. "'The Factory of the Revolution': Women's Activism in the Syrian Uprisings." In *Women Rising in and beyond the Arab Spring*, edited by Rita Stephan and Mounira Charrad, 354–62. New York: NYU Press.

Salti, Rasha. 2012. "Shall We Dance?" *Cinema Journal* 52, no. 1 (Fall): 166–71.

Samudra, Jaida Kim. 2008. "Memory in Our Body: Thick Participation and the Translation of Kinesthetic Experience." *American Ethnologist* 35 (4): 665–81.

Satkunaratnam, Ahalya. 2020. *Moving Bodies, Navigating Conflict: Practicing Bharata Natyam in Colombo, Sri Lanka*. Middletown, CT: Wesleyan University Press.

Sawa, George. 2009. *Rhythmic Theories and Practices in Arabic Writings: Annotated Translations and Commentaries*. Ottawa: Institute of Medieval Music.

Sbait, Dirgham H. 1986. "Poetic and Musical Structures in the Improvised-Sung Colloquial Qasida of the Palestinian Poet-Singers." *al-'Arabiyya* 19: 75.

Scarry, Elaine. 1985. *The Body in Pain: The Making and Unmaking of the World*. New York: Oxford University Press.

Schade-Poulsen, Marc. 1999. *Men and Popular Music in Algeria: The Social Significance of Raï*. Austin: University of Texas Press.

Schechner, Richard. 2003. *Performance Theory*. New York: Routledge.

———. 2006. *Performance Studies: An Introduction*. New York: Routledge.

Schulze, Kirsten E., Martin Stokes, and Colm Campbell, eds. 1996. *Nationalism, Minorities and Diasporas: Identities and Rights in the Middle East*. London: I. B. Tauris.

Schutzman, Mady. 2006. "Ambulant Pedagogy." In *The Sage Handbook of Performance Studies*, edited by D. Soyini Madison and Judith Hamera, 278–95. Thousand Oaks, CA: Sage.

Seale, Patrick. 1986. *The Struggle for Syria: A Study of Post-War Arab Politics, 1945–1958*. New Haven, CT: Yale University Press.

———. 1988. *Asad of Syria: The Struggle for the Middle East*. Berkeley: University of California Press.

Sedgwick, Eve Kosofsky. 1985. *Between Men: English Literature and Male Homosocial Desire*. New York: Columbia University Press.

Sedgwick, Eve Kosofsky, Michèle Aina Barale, and Jonathan Goldberg. 2003. *Touching Feeling: Affect, Pedagogy, Performativity*. Durham, NC: Duke University Press.

Segal, Lynne. 1990. *Slow Motion: Changing Masculinities, Changing Men*. New Brunswick, NJ: Rutgers University Press.

Shami, Setenay, and Nefissa Naguib. 2013. "Occluding Difference: Ethnic Identity and the Shifting Zones of Theory on the Middle East and North Africa." In *Anthropology of the Middle East and North Africa: Into the New Millenium*, edited by Sherine Hafiz and Susan Slyomovics, 23–46. Bloomington: Indiana University Press.

Shannon, Jonathan Holt. 2003. "Sultans of Spin: Syrian Sacred Music on the World Stage." *American Anthropologist* 105 (2): 266–77.

———. 2006. *Among the Jasmine Trees: Music and Modernity in Contemporary Syria*. Middletown, CT: Wesleyan University Press.

Shay, Anthony. 1999. *Choreophobia: Solo Improvised Dance in the Iranian World*. Costa Mesa, CA: Mazda Publishers, 1999.

———. 2002. *Choreographic Politics: State Folk Dance Companies, Representation, and Power*. Middletown, CT: Wesleyan University Press, 2002.

———. 2019. "In the Moment: Improvisation in Traditional Dance." In *The Oxford Handbook of Improvisation in Dance*, edited by Vida L. Midgelow, 705–18. New York: Oxford University Press.

Sheehi, Stephen. 2004. *Foundations of Modern Arab Identity*. Gainesville: University Press of Florida.

Siham, Alatassi. 2022. "The Role of the Syrian Business Elite in the Syrian Conflict: A Class Narrative." *British Journal of Middle Eastern Studies* 49 (3): 433–45.

Silverstein, Paul A. 2005. "Immigrant Racialization and the New Savage Slot: Race, Migration, and Immigration in the New Europe." *Annual Review of Anthropology* 34 (1): 363–84.

Silverstein, Shayna M. 2012. "Syria's Radical Dabke." *Middle East Report* 263: 33–37.

———. 2013. "New Wave Dabke: The Stars of *Musiqa Shaʿbiyya* in the Levant." In *Out of the Absurdity of Life*, edited by Theresa Beyer and Thomas Burkhalter, 62–67. Solothurn, Switzerland: Traversion Press.

———. 2015. "Cultural Liberalization or Marginalization? The Cultural Politics of Syrian Folk Dance during Social Market Reform." In *Syria from Reform to Revolt: Culture, Society and Religion*, edited by Leif Stenberg and Christa Salamandra, 77–91. Syracuse, NY: Syracuse University Press.

———. 2016a. "Public Pleasures: Negotiating Gender and Morality through Syrian Popular Dance." In *Islam and Popular Culture*, 278–96. Austin: University of Texas Press.

———. 2016b. "The Punk Arab: Demystifying Omar Souleyman's Techno-Dabke." In *Punk Ethnography: Artists and Scholars Listen to Sublime Frequencies*, edited by Michael Veal and E. Tammy Kim, 265–87. Middletown, CT: Wesleyan University Press.

———. 2019. "Disorienting Sounds: A Sensory Ethnography of Syrian Dance Music." In *Remapping Sound Studies*, 241–60. Durham, NC: Duke University Press.

———. 2020. "Mourning the Nightingale's Song: The Audibility of Networked Performances in Protests and Funerals of the Arab Revolutions." *Performance Matters* 6 (2): 94–111.

———. 2021. "The 'Barbaric' *Dabke*: Masculinity, Dance, and Autocracy in Contemporary Syrian Cultural Production." *Journal of Middle Eastern Women's Studies* 17 (2): 197–219.

Silverstein, Shayna M., and Darci Sprengel. 2021. "An (Un)Marked Foreigner: Race-Making in Egyptian, Syrian, and German Popular Cultures." *Lateral: Journal of the Cultural Studies Association* 10 (1).

Simon, Andrew. 2022. *Media of the Masses: Cassette Culture in Modern Egypt*. Palo Alto, CA: Stanford University Press.

Singer, Alice. 1974. "The Metrical Structure of Macedonian Dance." *Ethnomusicology* 18 (3): 379–404.

Singerman, Diane. 2013. "Youth, Gender, and Dignity in the Egyptian Uprising." *Journal of Middle East Women's Studies* 9 (3): 1–27.

Singerman, Diane, and Paul Amar. 2006. *Cairo Cosmopolitan: Politics, Culture, and Urban Space in the Globalized Middle East*. Cairo: The American University in Cairo Press, 2006.

Sklar, Deidre. 1991. "On Dance Ethnography." *Dance Research Journal* 23 (1): 6–10.

———. 2001. "On Dance Ethnography." In *Moving Bodies/Dancing Cultures: A Dance History Reader*, edited by Ann Dils and Ann Cooper Albright, 30–32. Middletown, CT: Wesleyan University Press.

Slyomovics, Susan. 1998. *The Object of Memory: Arab and Jew Narrate the Palestinian Village*. Philadelphia: University of Pennsylvania Press.

Small, Christopher. 1998. *Musicking: The Meanings of Performing and Listening.* Hanover, NH: University Press of New England.

Sontag, Susan. 2002. *Regarding the Pain of Others.* New York: Farrar, Straus and Giroux.

Spiller, Henry. 2010. *Erotic Triangles: Sundanese Dance and Masculinity in West Java.* Chicago: University of Chicago Press.

Stephan, Rita, and Mounira Charrad. 2020. *Women Rising: In and Beyond the Arab Spring.* New York: New York University Press.

Sterne, Jonathan. 2003. *The Audible Past: Cultural Origins of Sound Reproduction.* Durham: Duke University Press.

Stokes, Martin. 1992. *The Arabesk Debate: Music and Musicians in Modern Turkey.* Oxford: Clarendon Press.

———. 1994. *Ethnicity, Identity and Music: The Musical Construction of Place.* Oxford: Berg.

———. 2010. *The Republic of Love: Cultural Intimacy in Turkish Popular Music.* Chicago: University of Chicago Press.

Stone, Christopher Reed. 2008. *Popular Culture and Nationalism in Lebanon: The Fairouz and Rahbani Nation.* London: Routledge.

Stone, Ruth M. 1986. "Commentary: The Value of Local Ideas in Understanding West African Rhythm." *Ethnomusicology* 30 (1): 54–57.

Suerbaum, Magdalena. 2018. "Becoming and 'Unbecoming' Refugees: Making Sense of Masculinity and Refugeness among Syrian Refugee Men in Egypt." *Men and Masculinities* 21 (3): 363–82.

Sugarman, Jane C. 1997. *Engendering Song: Singing and Subjectivity at Prespa Albanian Weddings.* Chicago: University of Chicago Press.

Suleiman, Arjwan. 2012. "Syrians Create Protest Songs from Their Traditional Heritage [Arabic]." *Elaph,* January 11.

Szekely, Ora. 2020. "Fighting about Women: Ideologies of Gender in the Syrian Civil War." *Journal of Global Security Studies* 5 (3): 408–26.

Tambar, Kabir. 2010. "The Aesthetics of Public Visibility: Alevi Semah and the Paradoxes of Pluralism in Turkey." *Comparative Studies in Society and History* 52 (3): 652–79.

Tamim, Muhammad, and Shayna Silverstein. 2021. "Conversations at the CCD: Dance, Ritual, and Resistance." Cologne University, June 15.

Taussig, Michael T. 1993. *Mimesis and Alterity: A Particular History of the Senses.* New York: Routledge.

Taylor, Diana. 2003. *The Archive and the Repertoire: Performing Cultural Memory in the Americas.* Durham, NC: Duke University Press.

Tejel, Jordi. 2008. *Syria's Kurds: History, Politics and Society.* London: Routledge.

Terc, Amanda. 2011. "Syria's New Neoliberal Elite: English Usage, Linguistic Practices and Group Boundaries." PhD diss., University of Michigan.

Théberge, Paul. 2015. "Digitalization." In *The Routledge Reader on the Sociology of Music*, edited by John Shepherd and Kyle Devine, 329–38. New York: Routledge.

Thompson, Elizabeth. 2000. *Colonial Citizens: Republican Rights, Paternal Privilege, and Gender in French Syria and Lebanon*. New York: Columbia University Press.

Tilly, Charles. 1986. *The Contentious French*. Cambridge, MA: Harvard University Press.

Totah, Faedah M. 2014. *Preserving the Old City of Damascus*. Syracuse, NY: Syracuse University Press.

Traboulsi, Fawwaz. 1996. "La *Dabké*: Sexe, Folklore et Fantaisie" [*Dabke*: Sex, folklore, and fantasy]. *L'Orient-Express*, no. 10: 44–49.

Triandafyllidou, Anna. 2018. "A 'Refugee Crisis' Unfolding: 'Real' Events and Their Interpretation in Media and Political Debates." *Journal of Immigrant & Refugee Studies* 16 (1–2): 198–216.

Tsing, Anna Lowenhaupt. 2005. *Friction: An Ethnography of Global Connection*. Princeton, NJ: Princeton University Press.

Tufekci, Zeynep. 2017. *Twitter and Tear Gas: The Power and Fragility of Networked Protest*. New Haven, CT: Yale University Press.

Turino, Thomas. 2008. *Music as Social Life*. Chicago: University of Chicago Press.

Turner, Lewis. 2019. "Syrian Refugee Men as Objects of Humanitarian Care." *International Feminist Journal of Politics* 21 (4): 595–616.

Turner, Victor. 1977. *The Ritual Process: Structure and Anti-Structure*. Ithaca, NY: Cornell University Press, 1977.

Van Aken, Mauro. 2006. "Dancing Belonging: Contesting *Dabkeh* in the Jordan Valley, Jordan." *Journal of Ethnic & Migration Studies* 32 (2): 203–22.

van Eijk, Esther. 2016. *Family Law in Syria: Patriarchy, Pluralism and Personal Status Codes*. London: I. B. Tauris.

van Nieuwkerk, Karin. 1995. *A Trade Like Any Other: Female Singers and Dancers in Egypt*. Austin: University of Texas Press.

van Nieuwkerk, Karin, Mark LeVine, and Martin Stokes. 2016. *Islam and Popular Culture*. Austin: University of Texas Press.

Vazquez, Alexandra. 2013. *Listening in Detail: Performances of Cuban Music*. Durham, NC: Duke University Press.

Vermeyden, Anne. 2017. "The Reda Folkloric Dance Troupe and Egyptian State Support during the Nasser Period." *Dance Research Journal* 49 (3): 24–37.

Vinson, Pauline Homsi, and Nawar al-Hassan Golle. 2012. "Challenges and Opportunities: The Women's Movement in Syria." In *Mapping Arab Women's Movements: A Century of Transformations from Within*, edited by Nawar Al-Hassan Golley and Pernille Arenfeldt, 65–92. Cairo: The American University in Cairo Press.

von Erlanger, Rodolphe. 1930. *La musique arabe*. Paris: P. Geuthner

Walser, Robert. 1993. *Running with the Devil: Power, Gender, and Madness in Heavy Metal Music*. Hannover, NH: University Press of New England.

Wannous, Sa'dallah, Robert Myers, and Nada Saab. 2019. *Sentence to Hope: A Sa'dallah Wannous Reader*. New Haven, CT: Yale University Press.

Ward, Heather D. 2018. *Egyptian Belly Dance in Transition: The Raqs Sharqi Revolution, 1890–1930*. Jefferson, NC: McFarland.

Warner, Timothy. 2003. *Pop Music — Technology and Creativity: Trevor Horn and the Digital Revolution*. Aldershot: Ashgate.

Watenpaugh, Keith David. 2006. *Being Modern in the Middle East*. Princeton, NJ: Princeton University Press.

Wedeen, Lisa. 1999. *Ambiguities of Domination: Politics, Rhetoric, and Symbols in Contemporary Syria*. Chicago: University of Chicago Press.

———. 2013. "Ideology and Humor in Dark Times: Notes from Syria." *Critical Inquiry* 39 (4): 841–73.

———. 2019. *Authoritarian Apprehensions: Ideology, Judgement, and Mourning in Syria*. Chicago: University of Chicago Press.

Wehr, Hans. 1976. *A Dictionary of Modern Written Arabic*. 3rd ed. Edited by J. Milton Cowan. Ithaca, NY: Spoken Language Services.

Weiss, Gail. 1999. *Body Images: Embodiment as Intercorporeality*. London: Routledge.

Weiss, Max. 2013. "Who Laughs Last: Literary Transformations of Syrian Authoritarianism." In *Middle East Authoritarianisms: Governance, Contestation, and Regime Resilience in Syria and Iran*, edited by Steven Heydemann and Reinoud Leenders, 143–68. Palo Alto, CA: Stanford University Press.

Wells, Christi Jay. 2021. *Between Beats: The Jazz Tradition and Black Vernacular Dance*. New York: Oxford University Press.

Wessels, Joshka. 2019. *Documenting Syria: Filmmaking, Video Activism, and Revolution*. London: Bloomsbury Press.

Western, Tom. 2020. "Listening with Displacement: Sound, Citizenship, and Disruptive Representations of Migration." *Migration and Society* 3 (1): 294–309.

White, Benjamin Thomas. 2011. *The Emergence of Minorities in the Middle East: The Politics of Community in French Mandate Syria*. Edinburgh: Edinburgh University Press.

Wilcox, Emily. 2018. "Dynamic Inheritance: Representative Works and the Authoring of Tradition in Chinese Dance." *Journal of Folklore Research* 55 (1): 77–111.

Williams, Raymond. 1976. *Marxism and Literature*. Oxford: Oxford University Press.

Winegar, Jessica, and Lara Deeb. 2016. *Anthropology's Politics: Disciplining the Middle East*. Palo Alto, CA: Stanford University Press.

Yassin-Kassab, Robin, and Leila Al-Shami. 2016. *Burning Country: Syrians in Revolution and War*. London: Pluto Press.

Yessayan, Maral Tatios. 2015. "Lingering in Girlhood: Dancing with Patriarchy in Jordan." *Journal of Middle East Women's Studies* 11 (1): 63–79.

Yuval-Davis, Nira. 1997. *Gender and Nation*. Thousand Oaks, CA: Sage.

Zak, Albin. 2001. *The Poetics of Rock: Cutting Tracks, Making Records*. Berkeley: University of California Press.

Ziter, Edward. 2013. "The Image of the Martyr in Syrian Performance and Web Activism." *TDR: The Drama Review* 57 (1): 116–36.

INDEX

citizenship (cultural), 19–20, 37–38, 40, 47–51, 58, 67, 77, 91, 244
Clarke, Rachel, 221
classical Arab music, 5–6, 233
classicization, 43, 55, 86, 162
College of Charleston, 236
Cologne University, 116
colonialism, 18, 22, 28, 42, 44, 46–47, 65, 91, 107, 208, 231. *See also* French Mandate period
Come as You Are (dance performance), 222
communitas, 21, 137
conflict (Syrian, 2011–): *dabke* during, 3, 9, 21, 175–76, 184–94, 202–3, 236–37; ethnography during, 14, 22, 170–71; and forced displacement, 4, 8, 142, 204–8, 219, 222; and Kurdish women, 194–202; overview of, 12–13, 165–70. *See also* revolution (Syrian, 2011)
Coon, Carleton, 252n1
corporeality, 20, 103, 127, 219, 238, 258n29
coup (1963, Syria), 29, 31
coup (1970, Syria), 11, 39
Covid-19 pandemic, 13–14, 17
Cowan, Jane, 104
Creative Memory, 177, 265n11
Csikszentmihalyi, Mihaly, 102, 124
cultural citizenship. *See* citizenship (cultural)
cultural diversity (Syrian), 9, 20, 28, 68–71, 89, 241, 252n2
cultural geography, 77–83

dabkāt (popular *dabke* music): definition of, 2, 132; digital sonic aesthetic of, 21, 136–45, 161, 177, 192; and liveness, 145, 148–51; popularity of, 6, 154–60, 162, 242; recordings of, 7, 154, 235; rhythms of, 102, 108, 111; and the Syrian conflict, 177–78, 180–81
dabke (styles of), 43–44, 49, 78–80, 84–86, 111, 250n9, 251n13, 251n16. *See also individual styles*
dabke al-shamāliyya, 108–9, 112–15, 122, 128–29, 212, 225, 239, 257n22
dabke al-sha'arāwiyya, 128–30
dabke circles (*shakl dā'ira*), 45, 79, 101, 145, 157,

215–16, 224–28, 231–35, 239–42, 257n22, 265n8; balance within, 7, 117; gender in, 4, 8, 55–58, 103–4, 115, 118–22, 124–28, 130–32, 237, 259n43; and masculinity, 8, 21, 104–6, 116, 118, 120–21, 124–32, 159–60, 162, 219, 259n43; and rhythm, 109, 112–14, 129, 149; and *tabl*, 1, 85, 124, 130, 132, 134–35, 140–41, 144, 262n31; and war, 173–74, 176, 184–94. *See also awwal* (first in *dabke* circle); *tānnī* (second in *dabke* circle)
Damascus, Syria: arts and culture in, 68–70, 84, 88, 100, 209–10, 221, 255n29; class in, 156–58, 160, 263n39; *dabke* from, 80, 85, 90; demographics of, 11, 28, 47, 69; folkloric dance in, 49–50, 52–54; gentrification in, 21, 66; history of, 10, 29; protests in, 179; research in, 1, 14–15; tourism in, 66, 87, 89, 96; weddings in, 133, 149
Damascus Arab Capital of Culture (2008), 68–70, 87–90, 255n29, 255nn31–32
Damascus Contemporary Dance Platform, 88–89, 209
Damascus-Homs corridor, 44
Damascus International Fair Theater, 52
Damascus Spring, 97, 99
dance. *See individual styles*
dance studies, 6, 20, 103, 115, 175, 210, 221, 236, 256n3, 258n29, 264n43, 267n52
dance theater (*raqs masrah*), 5, 87
Dar'a, Syria, 13–14, 165, 233, 241, 250n6, 254n16
Dave, Nomi, 174
Dayr al-Zur, Syria, 80, 85–86
Deeb, Lara, 244
de Volff, Nir, 222
digital sonic aesthetics, 19, 21, 138, 143–51, 161, 177, 192. *See also* audio technology
displacement. *See* migration; refugees
Dixon, Steve, 153
Donati, Caroline, 89
Druze peoples, 10, 12, 28–29, 32, 44, 249n20

economic liberalization, 68, 88–90, 95–99, 243
Egypt, 12, 29, 42, 51, 69, 74, 154–55, 169, 240
El Dik, Ali, 155, 157, 180
electro-*dabke*, 242

El-Funoun Palestinian Popular Dance Troupe, 51
El Idlibi, Ramzi, 119
Ellington, Duke, 107–9, 113, 256n11
embodied pedagogy, 16, 208, 232–36, 244
embodied performance, 8, 78, 87, 103–4, 108, 161, 175, 194
empathic kinesthetic perception, 103, 105, 116, 122–23, 213, 216, 231
Enana (dance company), 115, 221, 255n31
ethnography: in authoritarian states, 33–35; on *dabke*, 42, 78–79, 83–84, 91, 131, 227, 231, 235; digital, 4, 14, 17, 20, 170–71; ethics, 22; and folkloric dance, 73–75, 78; of performance, 6, 14, 103, 106–7; in Syria, 14–15, 22, 170–171
Europe: *dabke* in, 21, 114, 208–11, 224–36; Syrian dance in, 217–19, 268n9, 269n14; Syrian refugees in, 13, 17, 90, 169, 171, 204–8, 219–20, 237, 268n1. *See also individual countries and cities*
European Union, 13, 170, 204–5, 221
Evanston, Illinois, 233, 236

Facebook, 1–2, 17, 166, 170
Fairouz, 154
Fakhri, Sabah, 260n10
Farah, Rami, 215–17
fellaha (peasant woman), 20, 37, 39–40, 58–63, 65, 198, 202
fellahin (rural subjects), 37, 42, 44, 49, 54–55, 72
femininity, 40, 61, 121, 131, 158, 207, 231. *See also* women
feminism, 20, 45, 60, 127, 166, 169, 194–98, 202, 238n15, 259n43
Firqa al-Hamami, 65, 255n32
Firqa al-'Asi, 66–67, 72
flow states: and balance, 7, 115–16, 122–24, 138, 216; definition of, 7, 20–21, 102–3, 131–32, 255n2; failure of, 234, 240–41; and rhythmic precision, 111–12, 114, 234, 240; and sensory disorientation, 106, 234, 240–41
folkloric dance (*raqs sha'biyya*), 83–85, 88, 90, 157, 208, 212, 222, 269n25; adaptation of *dabke* into, 5, 8, 20, 37, 41–47; and the

fellaha, 58–63, 198, 202; invention of, 20, 27, 39–40, 51–58, 64–65; and nation-building, 19–20, 38, 47–51, 75, 77, 162, 243; state-sponsored festivals of, 66–71, 76, 91, 148. *See also* fellaha (peasant woman); fellahin (rural subjects); *individual dance styles*
Foster, Susan, 124
Foster Beach World Refugee Day Picnic, 239–41, 245
Free Syrian Army, 166–69, 179, 187, 189, 193–95, 197, 264n1
French Mandate period, 28–30, 32, 38, 40, 42, 44–48, 51, 180
Friedner, Michele, 137

Garcia, Luis-Manuel, 145
gender: in *dabke* circles, 4, 8, 103–4, 115, 118–22, 124–27, 130–32, 259n43; and ethnography, 18; and folkloric dance, 19–21, 40, 45–47, 56, 58, 61, 63, 65; and the Islamic State, 197; and music, 138; and pedagogy, 223, 236, 244; in *Spotlight*, 158, 160, 162; and Syrian conflict, 166, 169, 175–76, 184–88, 194–95, 201–3; and Syrian refugees, 205, 207–8, 223–24, 231, 240. *See also* femininity; masculinity; participation; play; relational masculinity; spectatorship; women
Germany, 19, 169–70, 204, 219–20, 222–23, 230, 268n1. *See also* Berlin, Germany
Geros, Panagiotis, 31
Ghouta, Syria, 13, 192–93, 266n40
Glennie, Evelyn, 103
Goodman, Steven, 151
govend (Kurdish dance), 9, 81, 195, 198–200, 266n47

Habib, Wafeek, 158, 235
Haddad, Marwan, 51
Haddad, Wadia Jarrar, 51
Hafiz, Abdel Halim, 110
ḥaflāt (party), 116, 118, 120, 125, 132–33, 144, 146, 148, 150–51, 161. *See also* weddings
Hajar, Abu, 179
Hajo, Laith, 263n39
Hajo, Lawand, 88, 254n27

television: dance on, 33, 52, 78, 83–87; music on, 139, 154–55, 180; rosettes and mosaics on, 20, 69; Syrian, 96, 254n21. *See also* *Al-Ughaniyya al-Sha'biyya wa-l-Raqsat al-Sha'biyya*; *Spotlight* (TV show)

thawb (robe), 1, 58–59, 63, 74, 201

Theater al-Hamra, 52

Théberge, Paul, 143

travel narratives (about *dabke*), 250n2

tripod effect, 182–83, 202

Trump, Donald, 200, 232, 240, 270n34

Turkey: and Kurdish peoples, 9, 168–69, 174, 194–95, 199–200–201; and the mosaic, 252–53n6; music in, 149, 262n27; Syrian border with, 80, 98–99, 168, 200; and Syrian conflict, 165; Syrian refugees in, 13, 169, 204, 206, 209, 268n6

Twitter, 17, 199

'ūd (Arab lute), 15, *70*, 144, 147

Umm Kulthum, 110

United Arab Emirates, 197

United Arab Republic, 30, 47, 51

United Nations: Security Council, 168; UNESCO, 68, 86

United States: author from, 16–18, 23, 121, 234; Black people in, 176, 230; *dabke* in, 16, 114, 208, 232–36, 239–40; foreign policies of, 12, 98–99, 168, 180, 200, 265n18; refugees in, 171, 232, 240, 270n34; *sha'bī* music in, 242

University of Chicago: Middle East Music Ensemble, 14

urbanization (of Syria), 38, 40, 47, 52–54, 74–75, 98, 142. *See also* neoliberalism

Vazquez, Alexandra, 107

vibration, 7, 21, 103, 136–37, 145–46, 151–52, 218, 245

videos: of *dabke*, 1–3, 247n2; of *dabke* during Syrian conflict, 21, 173, 176–84, 186–94, 196, 200–201; at *dabke* workshops, 233, 235; music, 154–55, 264n37; of weddings, 15, 120, 136, 152–53, 235. *See also* Facebook; YouTube

Waked, Fadi, 222–23, 225, 233

Waltz, Sasha, 222–23. *See also* Sasha Waltz & Guests (SWG)

Wannous, Sa'dallah, 64

weddings: bride and groom at, 262n33; *dabkāt* during, 21, 133–36, 138–41, 144, 148, 151–53, 242, 262n31; *dabke* during, 2, 5, 43, 52, 78, 85, 101–2, 112–13, 118–20, 250n2; and masculinity, 8, 105, 125–31; reenactments of, 66, 71–76; videos of, 15, 120, 136, 152–53, 235; women's chants at, 116–18, 149. *See also* *'arada* (song genre); *ḥaflāt* (party); *muṭrib* (wedding singer)

wedding singer. *See* *muṭrib* (wedding singer)

Wedeen, Lisa, 97, 160, 182, 190

White Helmets, 203

Willkommenskultur, 206, 219–24, 227–28

Winegar, Jessica, 244

women: and belly dancing, 110; and folkloric dance, 36–37, 39–40, 55–63, 73, 86, 162, 252n25; Kurdish, 21, 169, 176, 194–202; participation in *dabke*, 8, 43, 46–47, 79, 120, 131, 239, 251n12, 256n6, 259n43, 265n8; as refugees, 206; spectatorship of, 118–19, 124, 126; in Syria, 29, 45, 65, 127, 186, 263n41; and the Syrian conflict, 166–67, 182, 267n44; wedding chants of, 116–18, 149. *See also* fellaha; femininity; feminism; participation; spectatorship

workshops (of *dabke*), 16, 21, 112, 114, 116, 221–36, 244. *See also* teachers (of *dabke*)

World Refugee Day. *See* Foster Beach World Refugee Day Picnic

xenophobia, 13, 205–7, 220, 223

"Yalla Irhal Ya Bashar" (song), 176–80, 183, 265n11

Yazidis, 11, 28

YouTube, 17, 170, 172, 178, 181, 187, 189, 193, 249n3. *See also* videos

Yugoslavia, 53–54

Zaydal, Syria, 43

Zein, Melhem, 154, 159, 235, 261n17

Harris M. Berger
Stance: Ideas about Emotion, Style,
and Meaning for the Study
of Expressive Culture

Harris M. Berger and
Giovanna P. Del Negro
Identity and Everyday Life:
Essays in the Study of Folklore,
Music, and Popular Culture

Franya J. Berkman
Monument Eternal: The Music
of Alice Coltrane

Dick Blau, Angeliki Vellou Keil,
and Charles Keil
Bright Balkan Morning: Romani Lives and
the Power of Music in Greek Macedonia

Susan Boynton and Roe-Min Kok, editors
Musical Childhoods and the Cultures
of Youth

James Buhler, Caryl Flinn,
and David Neumeyer, editors
Music and Cinema

Patrick Burkart
Music and Cyberliberties

Thomas Burkhalter, Kay Dickinson,
and Benjamin J. Harbert, editors
The Arab Avant-Garde: Music,
Politics, Modernity

Julia Byl
Antiphonal Histories: Resonant Pasts
in the Toba Batak Musical Present

Corinna Campbell
The Cultural Work:
Maroon Performance in
Paramaribo, Suriname

Alexander Cannon
Seeding the Tradition: Musical Creativity
in Southern Vietnam

Daniel Cavicchi
Listening and Longing: Music Lovers
in the Age of Barnum

Susan D. Crafts, Daniel Cavicchi,
Charles Keil, and the
Music in Daily Life Project
My Music: Explorations
of Music in Daily Life

Jim Cullen
Born in the USA: Bruce Springsteen
and the American Tradition

Anne Danielsen
Presence and Pleasure: The Funk Grooves
of James Brown and Parliament

Peter Doyle
Echo and Reverb: Fabricating Space
in Popular Music Recording,
1900–1960

Andrew Eisenberg
Sounds of Other Shores:
The Musical Poetics of Identity
on Kenya's Swahili Coast

Ron Emoff
Recollecting from the Past:
Musical Practice and Spirit Possession
on the East Coast of Madagascar

Yayoi Uno Everett and
Frederick Lau, editors
Locating East Asia
in Western Art Music

Susan Fast and Kip Pegley, editors
Music, Politics, and Violence

Heidi Feldman
Black Rhythms of Peru: Reviving African Musical Heritage in the Black Pacific

Kai Fikentscher
"You Better Work!" Underground Dance Music in New York City

Ruth Finnegan
The Hidden Musicians: Music-Making in an English Town

Daniel Fischlin and Ajay Heble, editors
The Other Side of Nowhere: Jazz, Improvisation, and Communities in Dialogue

Wendy Fonarow
Empire of Dirt: The Aesthetics and Rituals of British "Indie" Music

Murray Forman
The 'Hood Comes First: Race, Space, and Place in Rap and Hip-Hop

Lisa Gilman
My Music, My War: The Listening Habits of U.S. Troops in Iraq and Afghanistan

Paul D. Greene and Thomas Porcello, editors
Wired for Sound: Engineering and Technologies in Sonic Cultures

Tomie Hahn
Sensational Knowledge: Embodying Culture through Japanese Dance

Edward Herbst
Voices in Bali: Energies and Perceptions in Vocal Music and Dance Theater

Deborah Kapchan
Traveling Spirit Masters: Moroccan Gnawa Trance and Music in the Global Marketplace

Deborah Kapchan, editor
Theorizing Sound Writing

Max Katz
Lineage of Loss: Counternarratives of North Indian Music

Raymond Knapp
Symphonic Metamorphoses: Subjectivity and Alienation in Mahler's Re-Cycled Songs

Victoria Lindsay Levine and Dylan Robinson, editors
Music and Modernity among First Peoples of North America

Noel Lobley
Sound Fragments: From Field Recording to African Electronic Stories

Laura Lohman
Umm Kulthūm: Artistic Agency and the Shaping of an Arab Legend, 1967–2007

Preston Love
A Thousand Honey Creeks Later: My Life in Music from Basie to Motown—and Beyond

René T. A. Lysloff and Leslie C. Gay Jr., editors
Music and Technoculture

Ian MacMillen
Playing It Dangerously: Tambura Bands, Race, and Affective Block in Croatia and Its Intimates

Allan Marett
Songs, Dreamings, and Ghosts: The Wangga of North Australia

Ian Maxwell
Phat Beats, Dope Rhymes: Hip Hop Down Under Comin' Upper

Jonathan Holt Shannon
Among the Jasmine Trees: Music and Modernity in Contemporary Syria

Daniel B. Sharp
Between Nostalgia and Apocalypse: Popular Music and the Staging of Brazil

Shayna M. Silverstein
Fraught Balance: The Embodied Politics of Dabke *Music in Syria*

Helena Simonett
Banda: Mexican Musical Life across Borders

Mark Slobin
Subcultural Sounds: Micromusics of the West

Mark Slobin, editor
Global Soundtracks: Worlds of Film Music

Tes Slominski
Trad Nation: Gender, Sexuality, and Race in Irish Traditional Music

Christopher Small
The Christopher Small Reader

Christopher Small
Music of the Common Tongue: Survival and Celebration in African American Music

Christopher Small
Music, Society, Education

Christopher Small
Musicking: The Meanings of Performing and Listening

Andrew Snyder
Critical Brass: Street Carnival and Musical Activism in Olympic Rio de Janeiro

Maria Sonevytsky
Wild Music: Sound and Sovereignty in Ukraine

Tore Størvold
Dissonant Landscapes: Music, Nature, and the Performance of Iceland

Regina M. Sweeney
Singing Our Way to Victory: French Cultural Politics and Music during the Great War

Colin Symes
Setting the Record Straight: A Material History of Classical Recording

Kelley Tatro
Love and Rage: Autonomy in Mexico City's Punk Scene

Steven Taylor
False Prophet: Field Notes from the Punk Underground

Paul Théberge
Any Sound You Can Imagine: Making Music/Consuming Technology

Sarah Thornton
Club Cultures: Music, Media, and Subcultural Capital

Michael E. Veal
Dub: Soundscapes and Shattered Songs in Jamaican Reggae

Michael E. Veal
Living Space: John Coltrane, Miles Davis, and Free Jazz, from Analog to Digital

Michael E. Veal and
E. Tammy Kim, editors
Punk Ethnography: Artists and Scholars Listen to Sublime Frequencies

Robert Walser
Running with the Devil: Power, Gender,
and Madness in Heavy Metal Music

Dennis Waring
Manufacturing the Muse: Estey
Organs and Consumer Culture
in Victorian America

Lise A. Waxer
The City of Musical Memory:
Salsa, Record Grooves, and Popular
Culture in Cali, Colombia

Mina Yang
Planet Beethoven: Classical Music
at the Turn of the Millennium

ABOUT THE AUTHOR

Shayna M. Silverstein is an assistant professor in performance studies at Northwestern University. Her teaching and scholarship broadly examine the politics and aesthetics of sound, movement, and performance in contemporary Middle Eastern cultural production. Silverstein's research has been funded by the Institute for Citizens & Scholars and the Fulbright Program, as well as the Alice Kaplan Institute for the Humanities and Buffett Institute for Global Affairs at Northwestern University. Her scholarly work includes an award-winning essay in the *Journal of Middle East Women's Studies* as well as articles in *Performance Matters, Remapping Sound Studies, Middle East Journal of Culture and Communication*, and *Lateral: Journal of the Cultural Studies Association*, as well as an audiography in *[in]Transition: Journal of Videographic Film & Moving Image*. She received her PhD in ethnomusicology from the University of Chicago and her BA in history from Yale University.